CONVAIR

B-36 PEACEMAKER

COLD WAR NUCLEAR BOMBER
AND LARGEST MASS-PRODUCED
PISTON-ENGINED AIRCRAFT EVER BUILT

GRAHAM M SIMONS

AIR WORLD

AIR WORLD

Convair
B-36 Peacemaker

First published in Great Britain in 2024 by Air World Books,
an imprint of Pen & Sword Books Ltd,
Yorkshire - Philadelphia

ISBN: 9781526787316

Typeset in 10pt Times by GMS Enterprises
Printed and bound by Replika Press Pvt Ltd.

Pen & Sword Books Ltd incorporates the imprints of Air World Books, Pen & Sword Archaeology, Atlas, Aviation, Battleground, Discovery, Family History, History, Maritime, Military, Naval, Politics, Social History, Transport, True Crime, Claymore Press, Frontline Books, Praetorian Press, Seaforth Publishing and White Owl.

For a complete list of Pen & Sword titles please contact:

PEN & SWORD BOOKS LTD
47 Church Street, Barnsley, South Yorkshire, S70 2AS, UK.
E-mail: enquiries@pen-and-sword.co.uk
Website: www.pen-and-sword.co.uk

Or

PEN AND SWORD BOOKS,
1950 Lawrence Road, Havertown, PA 19083, USA
E-mail: Uspen-and-sword@casematepublishers.com
Website: www.penandswordbooks.com

FSC www.fsc.org
MIX
Paper | Supporting responsible forestry
FSC™ C016779

Contents

Acknowledgements

A book of this nature would not have been possible without the help of many people and organisations too numerous to individually mention. I am indebted to many for providing photographs and information - first-hand and anecdotal - for this story, but in some cases it has not been possible to identify the original photographer or information source and so credits are given in the appropriate places to the immediate supplier. If any of the pictures have not been correctly credited, please accept my apologies.

I would however, like to offer my special thanks to a small group of people - many of whom work in the global aviation industry as flight or ground crew or indeed 'on the spanners' - for freely letting me have access to their collections of images and information, including John Hamlin, Ian Frimston, Peter Clegg, David Lee, Simon Peters, Roger Deere and Jeff Duford, National Museum of the US Air Force and Dr Harry Friedman.

Introduction

'Its ten engines develop as much horsepower as nine locomotives; its wing tanks hold enough fuel to drive an automobile around the world sixteen times; the volume of the B-36 bomber approximates the volume of three average five-room houses.

'Wingspan of the B-36 - 230 feet- was greater than the first flight made by the Wright Brothers...

'The B-36 could haul a heavier load of bombs a greater distance than any aeroplane in existence.'

Superlatives about the Convair B-36 intercontinental bomber come easy - it was hailed as 'the most effective and versatile aerial weapon in history' and 'the world's biggest and best bombing plane.' One pilot's view was: 'We don't think of it as an airplane - we think of it as a flying battleship.'

Over the years, I have been lucky to be allowed to write about aircraft that have intrigued me. I remember hearing the 'Aluminium' or was it 'Magnesium Overcast' droning over East Anglia on their way to Burtonwood on temporary duty here in the UK in the 1950s.

One of those I heard may well have been flown by Wing Commander Kenneth Horatio Wallis DSO MBE CEng FRAeS RAF (b. 26 April 1916, d.1 September 2013) - he of James Bond's 'Little Nellie' autogyro fame - for he had been an exchange pilot from 1956 to 1958 on secondment from the Royal Air Force to United States Strategic Air Command, where he flew the mighty B-36H.

However, it was not until 1980 that I got 'up close and personal with the preserved example in the National Museum of the United States Air Force and, through the kind permission of Tom Brewer there, that I got inside it. Frankly, it may have been slow and never saw actual combat, but that aircraft has charisma by the bucket-load! As I sat in the Aircraft Commander's seat, it was clear that flying it truly must have been like one pilot is supposed to have said, '...like standing in the bay window and flying your house.'

The B-36 was certainly big, and was a remarkable engineering accomplishment for its era. Although laughably slow by today's standards, it was probably an effective weapon until very late in its career.

It should be remembered that early ground-based radars were not effective at long ranges, even against targets as large as the B-36. The problem was separating the signal from the noise - there was no 'computer power' to assist, so it was done in hardware or by the operator. By the time the operators were sure they had a target, it was likely too be too late to scramble fighters which needed half an hour to climb to the altitudes the B-36s flew. If one made it to altitude by chance, the B-36 could outmanoeuvre it, thanks to a huge wing area and turbo-supercharged engines that did not lose their effectiveness like the early jet engines.

The high aspect ratio laminar-flow wing was seven-and-a-half feet thick at the root, permitting access to the six twenty-eight-cylinder piston engines in flight. The 162-foot long circular-section fuselage had pressurised crew compartments fore and aft of the four-section bomb bay.

Opening up that hatch at the rear of the flight deck and peering into the inky blackness of the eighty-five-foot intercommunication tunnel, was somewhat daunting. It was through this - passing along the left side of the bomb-bay - that a member of the five-man relief crew, going forward to the flight deck, had to traverse on his back on a four-wheeled truck running on rails,pulling himself along by grasping an overhead cable.

That tunnel must have been claustrophobic when the aircraft was powered up, but now, with the aircraft inert, it was frankly terrifying! I knew that this was my one chance to see the entire aircraft, so it was time to 'suck it up, buttercup', and I made that journey, first having made certain that the hatch was very firmly locked 'open'!

The bomb-bay itself was capable of housing either two 42,000 pound bombs or an undisclosed number of H-bombs. The gross weight of the B-36J was 410,000 pounds - that's 183 tons! Not surprisingly, landing gear design posed many problems. The two prototypes, the XB-36 and YB-36 and their sister design the XC-99, had single mainwheels shod with nine-foot two in by three-foot ten-inch Goodyear tyres, the largest aircraft tyres ever built.

The design became mired in politics and massive internecine battles that saw inter-service rivalry between the US Navy and fledgling United States Air Force. There was no clear winner and deep, lasting divisions were created.

The Convair B-36 represented the climax of more

'...like standing in the bay window and flying your house.'

than thirty years of piston-engined bomber development by the major powers. In December 1948 a B-36 flew more than 9,600 miles non-stop, from Fort Worth, Texas, to Hawaii, dropping a then thousand pound bomb-load on the return leg. In July 1949, another B-36 flew more than ten thousand miles non-stop with a similar load.

Unfortunately - or perhaps fortunately? - the B-36 was never given a chance to prove its effectiveness under actual combat conditions. The Korean War, from June 1950 to July 1953, came and went, but no attempt was made to deploy the giant bomber in the conflict. The later B-52 operations in Vietnam would suggest that the B-36 could profitably have been used for saturation bombing attacks with conventional bombs in Korea.

However, even if the B-36 was never used in anger, it did perform an incalculable service during the 1950s as the mainstay of the US nuclear deterrent.

Writing this book has proved to be challenging - reading it may be the same. As usual with much of my work, the use of American quotations brought forth difficulties that spring from treating them as sacrosanct. I am English, so I write in that language; however, as a sign of respect to the nation that built the B-36 and it's derivatives, if I am quoting an American, I use their spelling and phrasing. This directly clashes with the differences of the so-called 'common language' British and Americans share. Color becomes colour, program becomes programme, and of course, American phrasing is often different from English. Then there is the dreaded use of plane instead of aircraft; I don't care what anyone says, a plane is a cutting tool used to smooth wood!

This brings me neatly to the conundrum of whether to use Imperial or metric units of measurement. Invariably there are times when I must use both, but by and large, my writing rules are simple: if the aircraft was designed using Imperial units, so I use Imperial measurements.

For an aircraft design that never fulfilled its primary purpose of dropping bombs in anger, it certainly did a lot - often in the area of testing and development. It also lived up to its unofficial name during the first ten years or so of the Cold War before being superseded by the B-52 and the Intercontinental Ballistic Missiles. This then is the story of the B-36 'Peacemaker'.

Graham M Simons
Peterborough, UK
September 2022

Chapter One

Origins

The genesis of the gigantic Convair B-36 can be traced back to early 1941 - before the United States of America entered World War Two. At the time, the threat existed that the United Kingdom could still possibly fall to the German 'Blitzkrieg', making a strategic bombing effort by the United States Army Air Corps (USAAC) against Germany impossible with the aircraft designs available at that time. The Boeing B-17 Flying Fortress and Consolidated B-24 Liberator had nowhere near the range, and nor had the then-proposed Boeing B-29 Superfortress.

The USA realised that it would need a completely new class of bomber capable of reaching Europe and returning unrefuelled to bases in North America, necessitating a combat range of at least 5,700 miles, the length of a Gander, Newfoundland to Berlin round trip. Therefore, the USAAC sought a bomber of truly intercontinental range, similar to the German Reichsluftfahrtministerium's (RLM) ultralong-range Amerikabomber programme, the subject of a thirty three-page proposal submitted to Reichsmarschall Hermann Goering on 12 May 1942.

The origins of this design - and the thoughts behind it - are shrouded in claim and counterclaim and none of it appears to have been that secret. According to Albert Speer's book, Spandau: The Secret Diaries, Führer und Reichskanzler Adolf Hitler was fascinated with the thought of New York City in flames. In 1937, Willy Messerschmitt hoped to win a lucrative contract by showing Hitler designs for what would become the Messerschmitt Me 264 designed to reach North America from Europe.

On 8 July 1938, just two years after the death of Germany's main strategic bombing advocate, Generalleutnant Walter Wever, and eight months after the Reich Air Ministry awarded the contract for the design of the Heinkel He 177. Luftwaffe's commander-in-chief Hermann Göring gave a speech, complaining that the Luftwaffe lacked bombers capable of round-trip flights to New York with a 4,500-kilogramme bomb load: 'I would be extremely happy to possess such a bomber, which would at last stuff the mouth of arrogance across the sea.'

Walther Wever was born on 11 November 1887 in Wilhelmsort in the county of Bromberg. He was the son of Arnold Wever, the one-time director of a Berlin bank and the grandson of the Prussian Prosecutor-General Dr Carl George Wever. After his final secondary examinations, he settled in Schweidnitz, where he trained as an officer. Wever

Left: Wilhelm Emil 'Willy' Messerschmitt (b. 26 June 1898, d. 15 September 1978), a leading German aircraft designer and manufacturer. Messerschmitt was appointed Honorary Professor by the Munich Technical College in 1930, and the Vice-President of the Deutsche Akademie für Luftfahrtforschung (German Academy of Aeronautical Research). The German government also awarded him the title of Wehrwirtschaftsführer (defense industry leader). In 1938, Adolf Hitler bestowed upon Messerschmitt the German National Prize for Art and Science.

Right: Generalleutnant Walther Wever, (b. 11 November 1887, d. 3 June 1937) Chief of the Luftwaffe General Staff.

The second He 177 A-0 'Grief', or Griffon, production prototype (A-02) with broad-bladed propellers, bearing the radio code 'DL+AQ.'

saw action in World War One and served as a staff officer for the OHL (Oberste Heeresleitung, Army High Command).

He was a proponent of the theory of strategic bombing as a means to wage war while opposing the theories of Italian General Giulio Douhet. In his book Douhet argued that air power was revolutionary because it operated in the third dimension. Aircraft could fly over surface forces, relegating them to secondary importance. The vastness of the sky made defence almost impossible, so the essence of air power was the offensive. The only defence was a good offence. The air force that could command the air by bombing the enemy air arm into extinction would doom its enemy to perpetual bombardment. Command of the air meant victory.

Douhet believed in the moral effects of bombing. Airpower could break a people's will by destroying a country's vital centres. Armies became superfluous because aircraft could overfly them and attack these government, military, and industrial centres with impunity, a principle later called 'The bomber will always get through.' Targeting was central to this strategy, and he believed that air commanders would prove themselves by their choice of targets. These would vary from situation to situation, but Douhet identified five basic target types: industry, transport infrastructure, communications, government, and 'the will of the people.' The last category was fundamental to Douhet, who believed in the principle of total war.

The chief strategy laid out in his writings, the Douhet model, is pivotal in debates regarding the use of airpower and bombing campaigns. The Douhet model rests on the belief that in a conflict, the infliction of high costs from aerial bombing can shatter civilian morale. This would unravel the social basis of resistance and pressure citizens into asking their governments to surrender. The logic of this model is that exposing large portions of civilian populations to the terror of destruction or the shortage of consumer goods would damage civilian morale into submission. By smothering the enemy's civilian centres with bombs, Douhet argued the war would become so terrible that the ordinary people would rise against their government, overthrow it with revolution, then sue for peace.

This emphasis on the strategic offensive would blind Douhet to the possibilities of air defence or tactical support of armies. In his second edition of The Command of the Air, he maintained such aviation was useless, superfluous and harmful. He proposed an independent air force composed primarily of long-range load-carrying bombers. He believed interception of these bombers was unlikely but allowed for a force of escort aircraft to ward off interceptors. Attacks would not require great accuracy. On a tactical level, he advocated using three types of bombs in quick succession; explosives to destroy the target, incendiaries to ignite the damaged structures, and poison gas to keep firefighters and rescue crews away.

The entire population was in the front line of air war, and they could be terrorised with urban bombing. In his book The War of 19-- he described a fictional war between Germany and a Franco-Belgian alliance in which the Germans launched massive terror bombing raids on the populace, reducing their cities to ashes before their armies could mobilise. Because bombing would be so terrible, Douhet believed that wars would be short. As soon as one side lost command of the air, it would capitulate rather than face the terrors of air attack. In other words, the enemy air force was the primary target. A decisive victory would hasten the wars end.

However, subsequent conflicts would largely discredit Douhet's theory. Air Marshal Arthur 'Bomber' Harris set out in 1942 to prove Douhet's theories valid during World War Two. Through four years under his command, RAF Bomber Command attempted to destroy the main German cities. By 1944–1945, in partial concert with the USAAF, they had largely achieved this aim; but no revolution toppled the Third Reich. The heavy bombers involved in the Combined Bomber Offensive did not win the war alone, as Harris had argued they would. Douhet's theories about forcing the population to start a revolution, when subjected to practical application, were shown to be ineffective. In fact, there is considerable evidence to show the bombings did nothing but antagonise the German people, galvanising them to work harder for their country, and the final defeat of Germany was not achieved until virtually the entire country had been occupied by Allied land forces.

Wever became the Commander of the Reichsluftfahrtministerium on 1 September 1933. On 1 March 1935, he became Chief of Staff of the Luftwaffe shortly after its creation on 26 February 1935, a post he held until his death. Wever was a supporter of the strategic bomber and recognised its importance as early as 1934. He supported the aviation companies, such as Junkers and Dornier, in their respective projects to produce the Ju 89 and Dornier Do 19 competitors for the Ural Bomber production contract competition. Wever outlined five key points to air strategy:

1. To destroy the enemy air force by bombing its bases and aircraft factories and defeating enemy air forces attacking German targets.
2. To prevent the movement of large enemy ground forces to the decisive areas by destroying railways and roads, particularly bridges and tunnels, which are indispensable for the movement and supply of forces.
3. To support the operations of the army formations, independent of railways, i.e., armoured forces and motorised forces, by impeding the enemy advance and participating directly in ground operations.
4. To support naval operations by attacking naval bases, protecting Germany's naval bases and participating directly in naval battles.
5. To paralyse the enemy armed forces by stopping production in the armaments factories.

After Wever's death, other strategists, like Ernst Udet and Hans Jeschonnek, favoured smaller aircraft as they did not expend as much material and manpower. They were proponents of the dive-bomber (Junkers Ju 87) and the doctrine of close support and destruction of the opposing air forces on the battleground rather than through attacking enemy industry. As a result, high-speed medium-bombers such as the Heinkel He 111, Dornier Do 17, and Junkers Ju 88 were developed with much initial success. While some large strategic bomber programmes were initiated, most notably the Ural Bomber project, which morphed into the He 117 programme, without a proponent of strategic bombing in the upper echelons of the Luftwaffe, the programmes saw little progress. It would ultimately be developed too late into the war to have any meaningful effect.

On 3 June 1936 Wever flew from Berlin to Dresden, to give a lecture at the Luftkriegsschule

Left: Marshal of the Royal Air Force Sir Arthur Travers Harris, 1st Baronet GCB OBE AFC (b.13 April 1892, d.5 April 1984), commonly known as 'Bomber' Harris by the press and often within the RAF.

Right: General Giulio Douhet (b. 30 May 1869, d. 15 February 1930) was an Italian general and air power theorist. He was a key proponent of strategic bombing in aerial warfare. He was a contemporary of the 1920s air warfare advocates Walther Wever, Billy Mitchell and Hugh Trenchard.

Klotzsche to a gathering of Luftwaffe cadets. When he received the news of the death of World War One German hero Karl Litzmann, he immediately set off for Berlin. On his return journey, the Heinkel He 70 Blitz that he was flying had not been properly examined during preflight checks, and the aileron gust locks were not removed. The aircraft was airborne when the wing dipped, and the Heinkel stalled and went into a horizontal cartwheel. It crashed and exploded in flames, killing Wever and his flight engineer.

After Wever's death, a Luftwaffe bomber wing, Kampfgeschwader 4 General Wever was named after him, which fittingly enough in the later war years, would be equipped with and use in combat the one aircraft created for the design competition that started on the day of General Wever's death, the Heinkel He 177A. His son, also named Walther Wever, was a fighter pilot who was killed in action in April 1945.

The origin of the Me 264 design came from Messerschmitt's long-range reconnaissance aircraft project, the P.1061 of the late 1930s. A variant on the P.1061 was the P.1062 of which three prototypes were built, with only two 'engines' to the P.1061's four. They were, in fact, the more powerful Daimler-Benz DB 606 'power systems', each comprising a pair of DB 601 inverted V-12 engines conjoined together. These were also successfully used in the long-range Messerschmitt Me 261, itself originating as the Messerschmitt P.1064 design of 1937. The DB 606's later use in the Heinkel He 177A's airframe design resulted in derision by Reichsmarschall Hermann Göring as 'welded-together engines' in August 1942 due to what was perceived as badly designed engine installations.

The Me 264 was an all-metal, high-wing, four-engine heavy bomber of classic construction. The fuselage was round in cross-section and had a cabin in a glazed nose, comprising a 'stepless cockpit' with no separate windscreen section for the pilots, which was common for most later German bomber designs. The wing had a slightly swept leading edge and a straight trailing edge. The empennage had double tail fins. The undercarriage was a retractable tricycle gear with large-diameter wheels on the wing-mounted main gear.

The planned armament consisted of guns in remotely operated turrets and in positions on the sides of the fuselage. Overall, it carried very little armour and few guns as a means of increasing fuel capacity and range. The Me 264's first prototype was originally fitted with four Junkers Jumo 211 inverted V12 engines using the then-new Kraftei, or 'power egg' unitised powerplant installation as standardised for the earlier Ju 88A Schnellbomber, but inadequate power from the Jumo 211 engines led to their replacement on the Me 264 V1 first prototype with four similarly unitised BMW 801G engines. In order

The Messerschmitt Me 264 was a long-range strategic bomber developed during World War Two for the Luftwaffe as a strategic bomber. The design was selected as Messerschmitt's competitor in the the German Air Ministry Amerikabomber programme, for a strategic bomber capable of attacking New York City from bases in France or the Azores.

Three prototypes were built but production was abandoned to allow Messerschmitt to concentrate on fighter production and the Junkers Ju 390 was selected in its place.

to provide comfort on the proposed long-range missions, the Me 264 featured bunk beds and a small galley complete with hot plates.

Historians have claimed that the plan started due to discussions by Hitler in November 1940 and May 1941 when he stated his need to deploy long-range bombers against American cities from the Azores. Due to their location, he thought the Portuguese Azores islands were Germany's 'only possibility of carrying out aerial attacks from a land base against the United States.' At the time, Portuguese Prime Minister António de Oliveira Salazar had allowed German U-boats and navy ships to refuel there, but from 1943 onwards, he leased bases in the Azores to the British, allowing the Allies to provide aerial coverage in the middle of the Atlantic.

Requests for designs, at various stages during the war, were made to the major German aircraft manufacturers; Messerschmitt, Junkers, Focke-Wulf and the Horten Brothers. Heinkel's bid for the project had occurred sometime shortly after February 1943, by which time the RLM had issued the Heinkel firm the airframe type number 8-277, for what essentially became its entry.

The Amerikabomber project plan was completed on 27 April 1942 and submitted to Reichsmarschall Hermann Göring on 12 May. The 33-page plan was discovered in Potsdam by Olaf Groehler, a German historian. It appears that ten copies of the plan were made, with six going to different Luftwaffe offices and four held in reserve. The plan specifically mentioned using the Azores as a transit airfield to reach the USA. If utilised, the Heinkel He 277, Junkers Ju 390, and the Messerschmitt Me 264 would have reached American targets with a 3,000 kilogramme, 5,000 kilogramme, and 6,500-kilogramme payload, respectively. Although it is apparent that the plan itself dealt only with an attack on American soil, it is possible the Nazis saw other interrelated strategic purposes for the Amerikabomber project. According to some historians, Hitler saw in the Azores the possibility for carrying out aerial attacks from a land base against the United States which in turn would force it to build up a large anti-aircraft defence. The anticipated result would have been to force the United States to use more of its anti-aircraft capabilities - guns and fighter aircraft - for its own defence rather than for Great Britain, thereby allowing the Luftwaffe to attack the latter country with less resistance.

In May 1942, Generalfeldmarschall Erhard Milch requested the views of Generalmajor Eccard Freiherr von Gablenz on the new proposal, with regard to the aircraft available to fill the needs of an Amerikabomber, which had then included the Me 264, Fw 300 and the Ju 290. von Gablenz gave his opinion on the Me 264, as it was in the second half of 1942, before von Gablenz's commitments in the Battle of Stalingrad occurred: the Me 264 could not be usefully equipped for a true trans-Atlantic bomber mission from Europe, but it would be helpful in a number of very long-range maritime patrol duties in co-operation with the Kriegsmarine's U-boats off the US East Coast.

The most promising proposals were based on conventional principles of aircraft design and would have yielded aircraft very similar in configuration and capability to the Allied heavy bombers of the day. These would have needed ultra-long range capability similar to the Messerschmitt Me 261 maritime reconnaissance design, the longest-ranged intended design flown during the Third Reich's existence. Many of the developed designs, themselves first

Left: Eccard Freiherr von Gablenz (b.26 January 1891, d.17 December 1978) was a German general in the Wehrmacht during World War Two who commanded several divisions. He was consulted over the Amerikabomber project.

Right: Generalfeldmarshall Erhard Milch (b. 30 March 1892, d. 25 January 1972) was a German Field Marshal who oversaw the development of the Luftwaffe as part of the re-armament of Nazi Germany following World War One. During World War Two, he was in charge of aircraft production.

submitted during 1943, suggested tricycle landing gear for their undercarriage, a relatively new feature for large German military aircraft designs of that era. These included the Messerschmitt Me264, the Focke-Wulf Ta 400, the Junkers Ju 390 (based on the Ju 290, the second and last built and flown, with the Ju 290 itself submitted in May 1942), and the Heinkel He 277 as it underwent engineering development through 1943, itself first specified by its RLM airframe number by February 1943.

Three prototypes of the Me 264 were built, but it was the Ju 390 that was selected for production. A verified pair of the Ju 390 design were constructed before the programme was abandoned. After World War Two, several authors claimed that the second Ju 390 actually made a transatlantic flight, coming within twelve miles of the northeast US coast in early 1944, but this claim has since been discredited as Ju 390 V2 never flew. As both the Me 264 and He 277 were intended to be four-engined bombers from their origins, the troubling situation of being unable to develop combat-reliable piston engines of around two thousand horsepower and above led to both designs being considered for six-engined upgrades, with Messerschmitt's paper project for a 47.5 metre wingspan Me 264B airframe upgrade to use six BMW 801E radials, and the Heinkel firm's 23 July, 1943-dated request from the RLM to propose a 45-metre wingspan, six-engined variant of the still-unfinalised He 277 airframe design that could alternatively accommodate four of the troublesome, over-two thousand horsepower output apiece Junkers Jumo 222 twenty-four-cylinder six-bank liquid-cooled engines, or two additional BMW 801E radials beyond the original quartet of them that it was originally meant to use.

Another idea similar to Mistel-Gespann was to have a Heinkel He 177 bomber carry a Dornier Do 217, powered with an additional Lorin-Staustrahltriebwerk (Lorin-ramjet), as far as possible over the Atlantic before releasing it. For the Do 217, it would have been a one-way trip. The aircraft would be ditched off the east coast, and its crew would be picked up by a waiting U-boat. When plans had advanced far enough, the lack of fuel and the loss of the base at Bordeaux prevented a test. The project was abandoned after the forced move to Istres increased the distance too much.

The Huckepack Projekt was brought up again at multiple joint conferences between the Luftwaffe and Kriegsmarine. After a few weeks the plan was abandoned on 21 August 1942. Air Staff General

The Focke-Wulf Ta 400 was a large six-engined heavy bomber design developed in Germany in 1943 by Focke-Wulf as a serious contender for the Amerika Bomber project. One of the first aircraft to be developed from components from multiple countries, it was also one of the most advanced Focke-Wulf designs of World War Two, though it never progressed beyond a wind tunnel model.

Designed as a bomber and long-range reconnaissance plane by Kurt Tank, the Ta 400 had a shoulder-mounted wing with a four-degree dihedral. One of the most striking features was the six BMW 801D radial engines, to which two Jumo 004 jet engines were later added.

Kreipe wrote in his diary that the Kriegsmarine could not supply a U-boat off the USA to pick up the aircrew. The plan failed since the Kriegsmarine would not cooperate with the Luftwaffe.

Other proposals were far more exotic jet- and rocket-powered designs, e.g. a flying wing. The Horten brothers designed the Horten Ho XVIII, a flying wing powered by six turbojets based on experiences with their existing Ho X design. The Arado company also suggested a six-jet flying wing design, the Arado E.555.

Other designs were rockets with wings. Perhaps the best-known of these was Eugen Sänger's pre-war Silbervogel ('Silverbird") sub-orbital bomber. While the A4b rocket, winged version of the V-2 rocket and probably its successor A9 rocket were tested several times in late 1944/early 1945, the A9/A10 Amerika-Rakete, planned as a full two-stage ICBM, remained a project.

Included in the plan was a list of twenty-one targets of military importance in North America. Many of these would not have been viable targets for conventional bombers of World War Two, operating from bases in Europe. Of these targets, primarily but not exclusively located in the eastern United States, nineteen were located in the United States; one in Vancouver, British Columbia, Canada (a possibly achievable target for a similar Japanese project) and one in Greenland. Nearly all were companies that manufactured parts for aircraft, so the goal was likely to cripple US aircraft production.

Allis-Chalmers in La Porte, IN.
Allison Division of GM in Indianapolis, IN.
Aluminum Corp. of America in Alcoa, TN.
Massena, NY; Badin, NC; and Vancouver, British Columbia.
American Car & Foundry in Berwick, PA.
Bausch & Lomb in Rochester, NY.
Chrysler Corp. in Detroit, MI.
Colt Manufacturing in Hartford, CT.
Corning Glass Works in Corning, NY.
Cryolite Refinery in Pittsburgh, PA, and Cryolite Mine in Arsuk, Greenland.
Curtiss Wright Corp. in Beaver, PA; Buffalo, NY; and Caldwell, NJ.
Hamilton Standard Corp. in East Hartford, and Pawcatuck, CT.
Pratt & Whitney Aircraft in East Hartford, CT.
Sperry Gyroscope in Brooklyn, NY.
Fellows Gear Shaper, Springfield, VT.

Were New York City to be bombed, the required combat radius was 7,256 miles, as the bomber would have needed to make a return trip without refuelling. The only German aircraft already built and flown that had a range close to this was the Messerschmitt Me 261 Adolfine, with a maximum range of 6,850 miles.

Had sufficient time and resources been devoted to the project at a point in time early enough, an Amerikabomber may have become operational before the war's end. However, Nazi Germany had no central authority for the development and construction of advanced weaponry, including new aircraft concepts and designs, as well as critical problems in developing high-powered aviation engines - that is, with output of over 2,000 horsepower each, which could operate reliably in combat conditions - that would have been required.

Hitler was often persuaded to waste time, money and resources on new 'miracle weapons' and other projects that were unlikely to be successful. The Amerikabomber project was not one of the projects so favoured. In addition, Allied bombing became so intense during the middle of the war that it disrupted critical German supply chains, particularly fuel; in addition, ever-greater proportions of resources were reserved for home defence purposes. German scientists were forced more and more to compete for ever scarcer resources. Together, all of the above political and strategic constraints made production of such an aircraft increasingly less likely.

It was unlikely that any damage caused to targets in North America, by the relatively small conventional bomb loads that could be delivered by such an ultra long range bomber, would be significant enough to justify the loss of such a bomber. Nazi Germany's nuclear programme was years behind the Allies, and did not include weapons in the form of aerial bombs, so it was unlikely that the Amerikabomber could have made a major difference to the outcome of the war.

Ultimately, all of the aircraft designs under consideration were deemed too expensive and/or ambitious and were abandoned. Post-war, however, they continued to be of interest to aerospace engineers: the British Air Ministry considered development of the Horten H.XVIII as an airliner, and the theoretical groundwork done on the Sänger Silbervogel would prove seminal to lifting body designs in the space age – one of the designs for the Amerikabomber would use a concept similar to a space shuttle.

It is not surprising that the British also got involved. As early as 1937, the Bristol Aeroplane Company had already conducted studies into future very large bomber designs, one of which received the internal company designation of Type 159 and another undesignated design that broadly resembled the eventual configuration of the Brabazon. Additionally, Bristol's design team had already been considering the requirements of a prospective aircraft capable of conducting routine transatlantic flights, which had resulted in projections of the necessary size, weight, and range of such an airliner. Amongst these, it was determined that a minimum payload of 100 passengers should be carried by the type in order to be profitable.

In 1942, the Air Ministry issued a draft operational requirement from the Air Staff, which sought a heavy bomber design capable of carrying a payload of at least fifteen tons of bombs. In response, Bristol dusted off their original work and updated it to account for their newer and substantially more powerful Bristol Centaurus engines. The Bristol design team, led by Leslie G Frise and Archibald Russell, worked with several key performance parameters; these included a range of 5,000 miles, 225 foot wingspan, eight engines buried in the wings and coupled to drive four pusher propeller installations, and enough fuel for transatlantic range. In early concepts, the aircraft featured top, bottom, and tail turrets, each with four 20-millimetre cannon and an internal bomb bay; defensive armament was later dropped, altitude being used for defence.

In addition to Bristol, many of the leading British manufacturers had provided several preliminary studies in response to the Air Ministry's operational

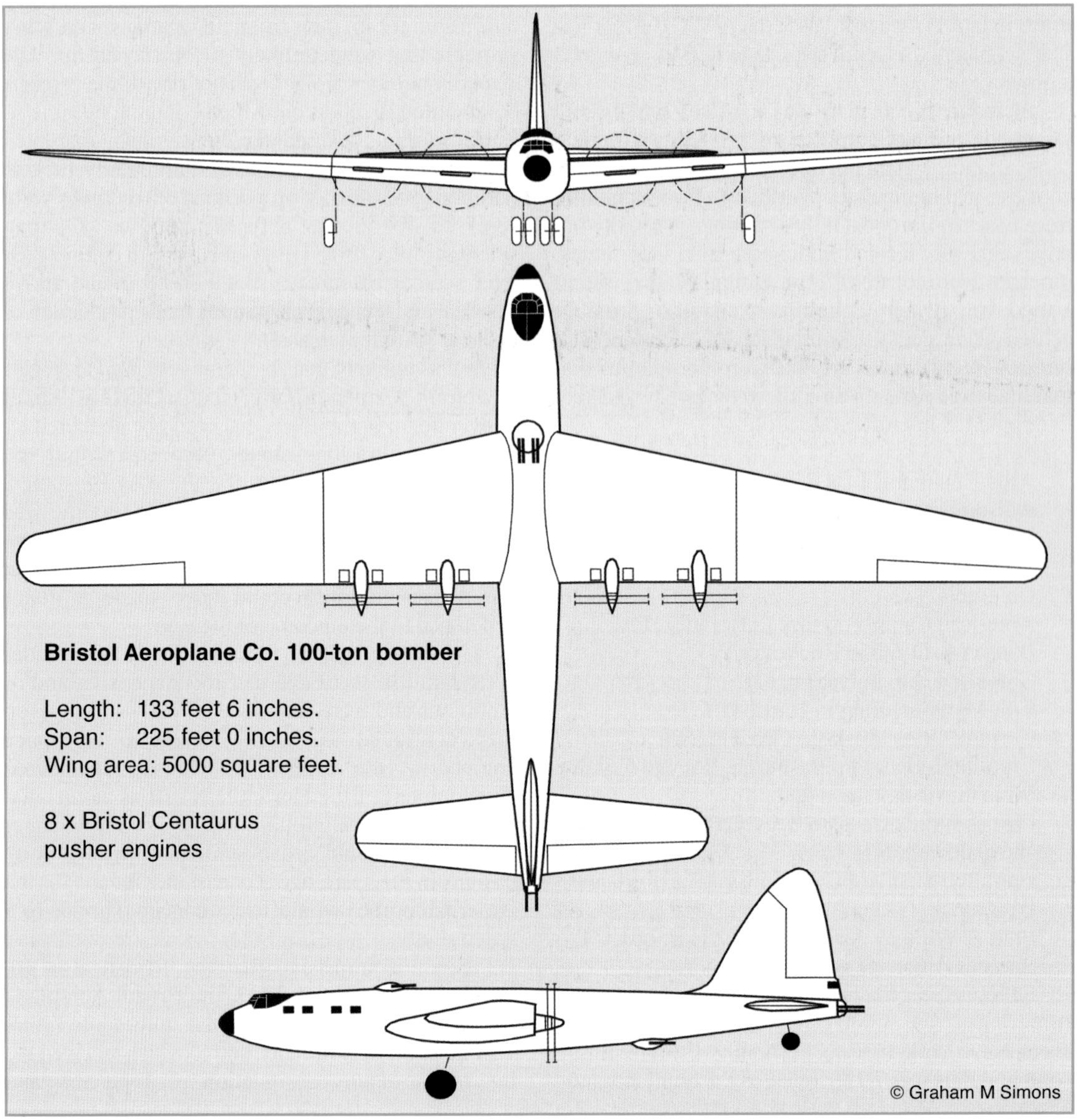

The Boeing Model 294, known by the Army as the XB-15. It was a colossal aircraft in its day, and first flew on 15 October 1937.

requirement; however, in expectation of long development times and the difficulties associated with balancing the aircraft's range, load and defensive armament, the Ministry never proceeded to take up any of the British manufacturers designs. Instead, it was decided to continue the development of the existing Avro Lancaster, which led to the production of the improved Avro Lincoln.

The 100-ton bomber never appeared but metamorphosed into the Bristol Type 167 Brabazon airliner of the immediate post-war years, of which two were ordered and one completed and flown. (See Bristol Brabazon, the History Press 2013 by the same author). Somewhat curiously, there is a direct connection between the Brabazon and the B-36, for in April 1949, Bristol Chief Test Pilot Arthur John 'Bill' Pegg visited Convair at Forth Worth and was allowed to fly a B-36 ahead of the first flight of the Brabazon a few months later. This is even more curious given the then-secret nature of much of the B-36 that a foreigner was allowed even near, let alone fly the huge machine. One suspects that there may well have been discreet co-operation going on between the two companies.

But that is getting ahead of the story somewhat.

Across the Atlantic, the USAAC sent out the initial request on 11 April 1941, asking for a machine that had a 450 mph top speed, a 275 mph cruising speed, a service ceiling of 45,000 feet, beyond the range of ground-based anti-aircraft fire, and a maximum range of 12,000 miles at 25,000 feet. These requirements proved too demanding for any short-term design - far exceeding the technology of the day - so on 19 August 1941, they were reduced to a maximum range of 10,000 miles, an effective combat radius of 4,000 miles with a 10,000 pound bombload, a cruising speed between 240 and 300 mph, and a service ceiling of 40,000 feet, above the maximum effective altitude of Nazi Germany's standard anti-aircraft guns.

Germany was not the only country developing long-range aircraft - the Japanese had Project Z, also called the 'Z Bombers Project', which was similar to the Nazi Amerikabomber project, to come up with a design for an intercontinental bomber capable of reaching the west coast of the USA and Canada.

The aircraft was to have six 5,000 horsepower engines, with the Nakajima Aircraft Company quickly developing engines, proposing twinned Nakajima Ha-44 powerplants, the most powerful aircraft engine available in Japan at the time. Designs were presented to the Imperial Japanese Army, including the Nakajima G10N, Kawasaki Ki-91, and Nakajima G5N. None, save for the G5N, developed beyond prototypes or wind tunnel models. Late in the war, Project Z and other heavy bomber projects were cancelled.

The Soviets and the British did not have any reason to go for longer range than they already had, simply because the front line with the enemy was so much closer!

From the American Perspective.

In several respects, the second phase of American strategic bombing strategy began with the Combined Bomber Offensive in the second half of 1942, when the United States joined Britain against Hitler. That would greatly encourage planners to equip the US Army Air Forces with aircraft capable of intercontinental offensives.

The development of US strategic bombing began when it declared war on Germany in April 1917 and studied the evolution of aerial warfare in Europe over the preceding two years to fix plans for its own use of airpower. In plans drawn up for the Expeditionary Force, advocates of strategic bombing such as William 'Billy' Mitchell and Benjamin D Foulois opposed the tactical use of airpower as favoured by Gen William Pershing.

Under post-war restructuring, the development of military aviation for varied tasks such as bombing, attack, defence and reconnaissance proceeded on a more or less equal footing.

By the early 1930s, several different all-metal monoplane bombers were competing with each other, and the subsidy of trans-continental mail-carrying aircraft, together with the development of trans-Pacific flying boats, sponsored the technology for

The roll-out of the Model 299 at Boeing Field/King County Airport, Seattle on 16 July 1935. The aircraft carries the experimental civil registration of X13372. Boeing employees are about to push the new bomber back into the hangar after its photocall.

A view of the XB-24 during a a test flight high over California.

fast, long-range bombers, typified by the Boeing Model 299 - the famous B-17. This aircraft was designed to a concept of self defence in the belief that single-engine fighters could never be expected to escort long-range bombers all the way to the target and back. Bristling with machine guns, the B-17 was appropriately named Flying Fortress, and the Army Air Corps flew it on flights across Central and South America to demonstrate its performance and boast its capability. (see Boeing B-17 The Fifteen Ton Flying Fortress, by the same author and Dr Harry Friedman, Pen & Sword).

Carrying a crew of eight, the XB-17 had four defensive machine gun positions with a bomb-carrying capacity of up to 4,800 pounds and four Pratt & Whitney Hornet engines with a top speed of 236mph and a range of 3,100 miles. It was the B-17E that would enter the fray from US Eighth Air Force bases in the UK during the second half of 1942. With four Wright R-1820-65 engines, it had a maximum speed of 317 mph, a cruising speed of 224 mph and a range of 2,000 miles with a 4,000 pound bomb load.

The B-17E carried nine machine guns and the addition of a ball turret in the under-fuselage position but the B-17G was the definitive development, 8,670 being manufactured by Boeing, Vega and Douglas. Incorporating a new nose turret tested on the B-17F, the G had up to thirteen machine guns and a maximum bomb load of 9,600 pounds. Of course the maximum bomb load compromised range and the assumption that the B-17 would be capable of defending itself proved flawed, driving a pause on the strategic bomber offensive for a redefinition of tactics more akin to that followed by the RAF.

The need for escort fighters pushed the development of long-range versions of the Republic P-47 and the North American P-51 but Luftwaffe pilots found the hail of fire from the bomber formations a formidable obstacle, pushing for a high-risk attack in nose-on-nose engagements. With closing speeds of up to 540 mph, a sharp pull-up to fly the length of the bomber's fuselage from nose to tail and away was a tactic performed only by the brave, especially when, in peeling off, the fighter would come under fire from other B-17s in the formation.

Opposition to the Combined Bomber Offensive came from a distinct difference of opinion on the way to employ the bombers: the British wanted large scale bombing of cities to destroy the factories and the homes of industrial workers while the Americans sought to pursue pinpoint bombing of critical targets, factories and unique facilities. The debate harked back to a study of strategic bombardment at the Air Corps Tactical School in 1930, from which textbooks called for the development of specialised bomb-aiming equipment. That resulted in the much-hyped Norden and superior Sperry bombsights, and the development of those items preceded the arrival of the B-17 so that when operations began from England in 1942, the US Army Air Corps had distinctly superior bomb-aiming equipment.

The established view that it was morally indefensible to target civilians in war would be a source of robust debate between the Army Air Forces and the Royal Air Force throughout the European war but that dissipated when the US deliberately targeted urban residential areas close to industrial facilities in the war against Japan. The shift in thinking had begun shortly after Pearl Harbor, 7 December 1941, when the Japanese Imperial Navy attacked the US base in a pre-emptive strike before a declaration of war.

Long before this day, in May 1940 after Germany took Norway, attacking France and the Low Countries, recognising that at some point the US would have to become involved, President Roosevelt made unrealistic demands of the aviation industry. He asked Congress to approve a force of 50,000 aircraft. At that date the entire industry had produced only 40,000 aircraft since the Wright Brothers first flew in 1903. In 1940 the US aviation industry could produce only 2,000 aircraft.

The emergency forced politically by the escalating war in Europe and the threat of England falling under the Nazi hammer blows spurred on procurement of the Consolidated B-24 Liberator, the Martin B-26 Marauder, and an entirely new type of bomber, the Boeing B-29. Eventually known as the Superfortress, the B-29 and its contemporaries ran to a new mantra - transitional acquisition practices were torn up and replaced by a new flow rate for aircraft design, development, manufacture and introduction to service deployment.

The US mobilised its technical resources, quickly supplemented by an escalating capacity in the RAF to drop large quantities of bombs on targets deep in the Ruhr and across the towns and cities of Nazi-occupied Europe. Contested by the Americans, who preferred pinpoint bombing of selected industrial targets, the British demonstrated the capacity of massed bomber formations to burn out cities, creating firestorms and widespread panic in the workforce striving to replenish German forces on the battlefield. Either way, both major allies signed up to the concept of strategic warfare.

Historically, the Army had bought its aircraft through research, design development and engineering, followed by production. This was an orderly, systematic and predictable cycle to which the US aviation industry had worked for several decades. Due to the limitations of the US aviation industry in fast-track development and manufacture, the Army compressed this conventional acquisition cycle into what became known as concurrency.

The Consolidated B-24 Liberator, the Martin B-26 Marauder and Boeing B-29 Superfortress were the first project types to adopt this flow path, which entered production much earlier in the development stage. This led to detailed design lacking in certain areas, which could have catastrophic results. (see

The Douglas XB-19 offered a 37,100 pound bomb load with a range of 7,700 miles - and all at a speed of 135 mph!

Consolidated B-24 Liberator Pen & Sword, by the same author). For instance, the B-26 entered production with a wing too small to prevent five of the first six aircraft from crashing due to a high stall speed. While the type was entering service, only 'concurrent' modifications and redesign were partially solved, resulting in what was always a tricky aircraft to fly. But the Army wanted aircraft, fast, and

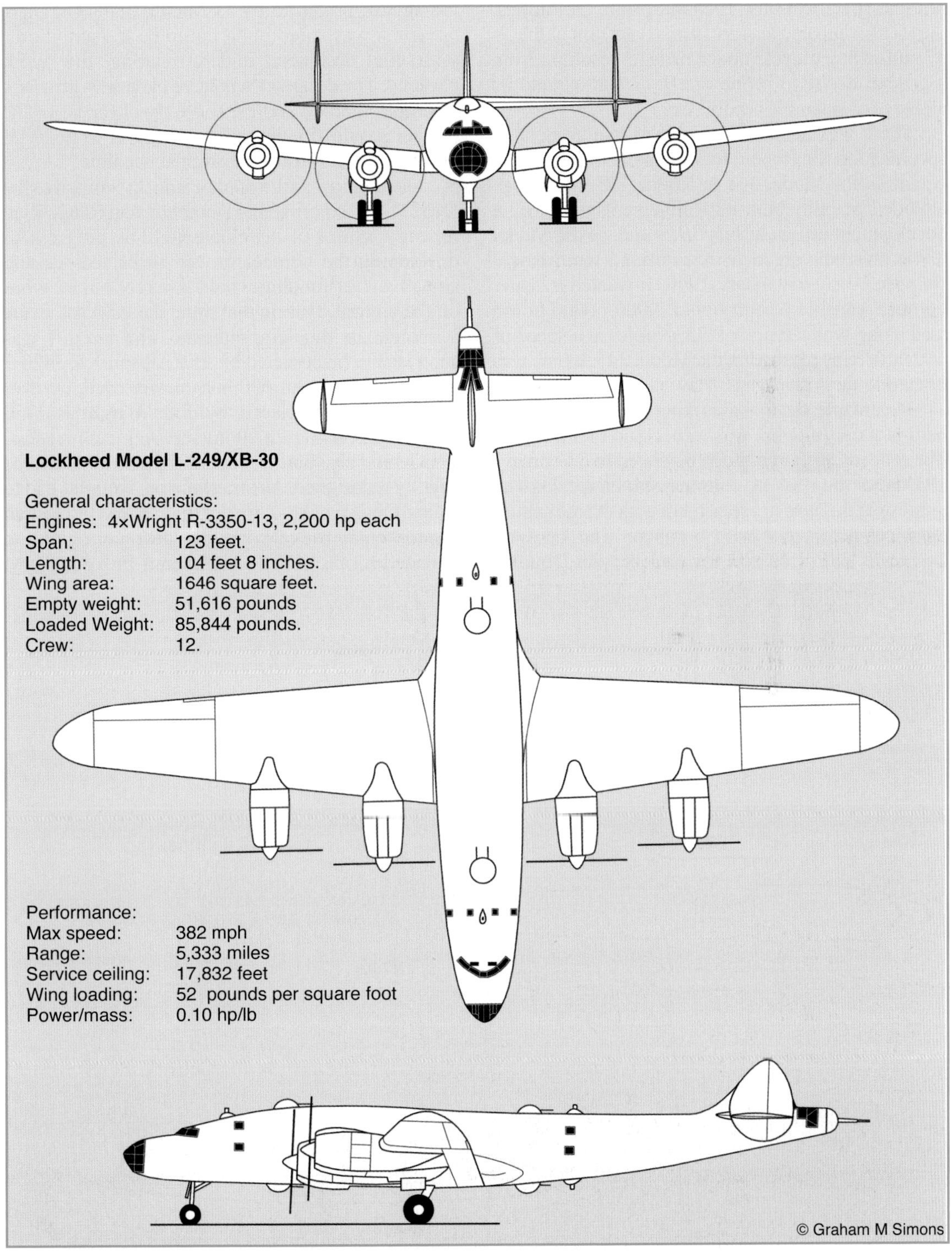

some degree of risk was accepted, the price for concurrency.

Risks adopted by concurrency with relatively conventional aircraft did not bode well for sophisticated requirements, advanced design and unusual specifications. Technologically ambitious, the B-29 originated as a pressurised version of the B-17 and with a tricycle undercarriage, resulting from a general desire to refine the B-17 and expand its already considerable capabilities.

There was no particular Army requirement or specification for Boeing to work to and design had begun on the Model 334 in March 1938 with high altitude capability built-in. Refinements produced a development design in July 1939 and, as the Model 334B, this converged with a defined requirement from the Army in January 1940. It wanted a 'super bomber' capable of carrying a 2,000-pound bomb load along with a range of 5,333 miles at a speed of 400 mph. This resulted in the Model 345, which was briefed to the Army on 11 May 1940.

Meanwhile, the Douglas Aircraft Company were hard at work on what was to become their XB-19. The roots of this aircraft can be traced to 5 February 1935 when the USAAC commenced 'Project D.' The purpose of this was to experiment with the maximum distances achievable with bombers. The USAAC contacted and discussed the project with Douglas Aircraft Company and Sikorsky. Douglas representatives agreed to the terms of the design, and plans were made during a conference on 5 June 1935. The initial plan was to begin the basic design on 31 July, detailed designs on 31 January 1936, and have the aircraft produced by 31 March 1938. The plan, however, was soon found out to be too ambitious, with the designers underestimating the work required. The designers would be plagued with a lack of proper funding and the enormity of the task. The project would finally be completed in May 1941, nearly four years after the original deadline.

The huge aircraft would be initially known as the 'XBLR-2' (Experimental Bomber Long Range 2) in its early stages of development. The progress of developing the bomber proved to be tedious and slow. Lack of funding would severely hinder work on the aircraft. During that time, the USAAC made a change to the requirements. The aircraft was supposed to be powered by four Allison XV-3420-1 engines producing 1,600 horsepower each, but was ordered to be replaced by four Wright R-3350 engines producing 2,000 horsepower each instead. This would also hinder work as the aircraft had to be slightly redesigned. As time went on, Douglas had to loan a Douglas OA-4A from the USAAC to test an experimental tricycle landing gear configuration intended for the XBLR-2. The tests proved to be a

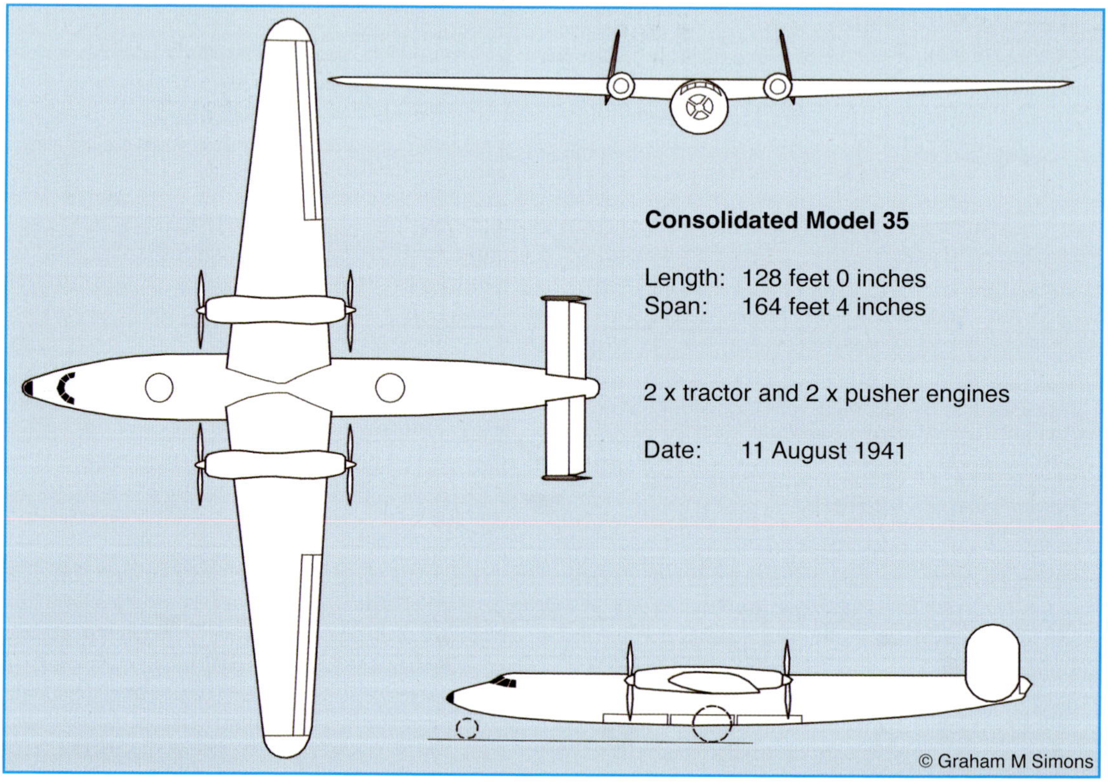

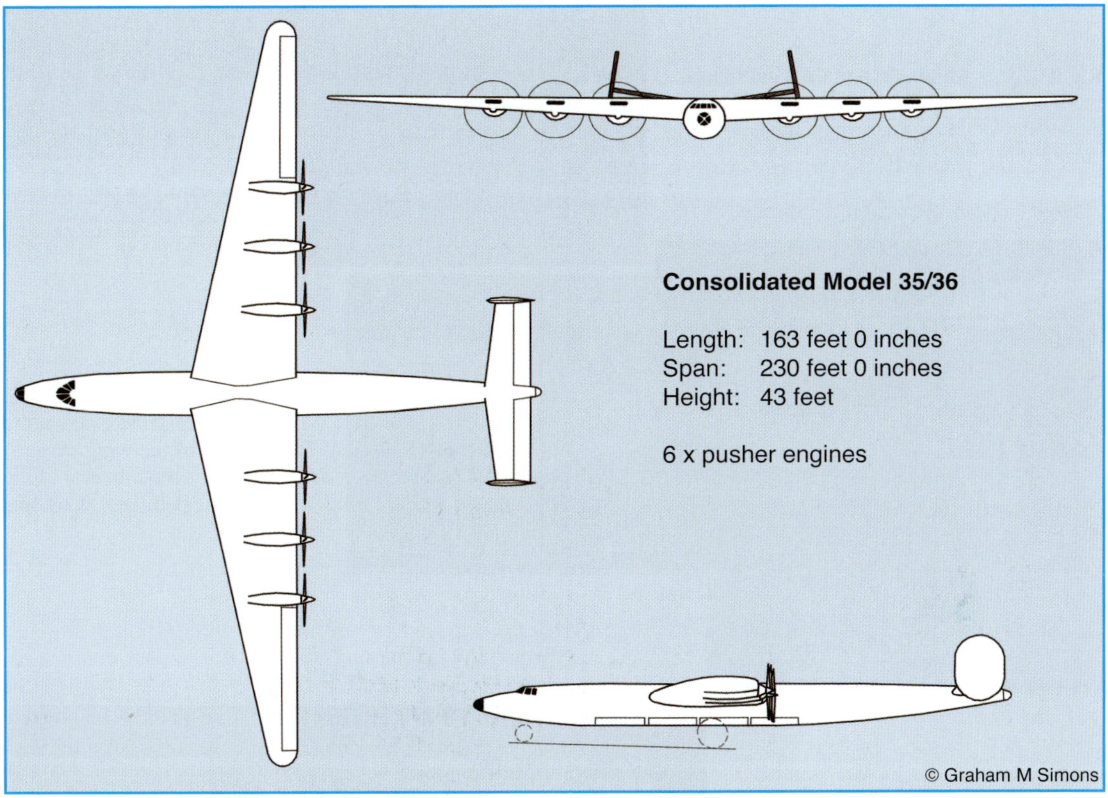

success. Later, the XBLR-2 would be redesignated as 'XB-19' (Experimental Bomber 19). Douglas eventually managed to scrape together enough funds to produce a prototype.

The Douglas XB-19 was the largest bomber aircraft built for the United States Army Air Forces until 1946. Despite advances in technology that made the XB-19 obsolete before it was completed, the Army Air Corps believed the prototype would be useful for testing despite Douglas Aircraft wanting to cancel the expensive project. Its construction took so long that competition for the contracts to make the XB-35 and XB-36 occurred two months before its first flight.

The aircraft first flew on 27 June 1941, more than three years after the construction contract was awarded. In 1943 the Wright R-3350 engines were replaced with Allison V-3420-11 V engines. After completion of testing, the XB-19 was earmarked for conversion into a cargo aircraft, but modifications were not completed, and the aircraft flew for the last time on 17 August 1946. It was eventually scrapped at Tucson in June 1949.

The B-29 is important in the story of the B-36 for several reasons, the former introducing new features which would be standard on the latter. These included the pressurised cabin, remote-control gun turrets, new engines and propellers and a requirement for high altitude flight in addition to the installation of precision bomb-aiming equipment. Again, it was fast-tracked through the concurrency approach introduced to get hardware on the ramp as quickly as possible, even if that meant accepting design flaws and a potential increase in risk for the crew. The technical challenges with this aircraft, heavier than anything built before, were greater than with any previous type, the wing loading being beyond anything previously flown. But against opposition from the Air Corps, Boeing stuck to its design and introduced Fowler flaps to assist during take-off and landing, increasing wing area by twenty per cent when extended.

The almost parallel development of the B-29 and the B-36 was remarkable and symbolic when several specifications were written in rapid succession for aircraft relatively close in sequential growth but each significantly enhanced in performance.

Although Boeing had a head start with the successor to the B-17, the requirement in the Air Corps originated years earlier via a special investigative committee set up by General Henry H Arnold, head of the Air Corps, and chaired by Brig Gen W G Kilner. The committee was tasked with determining the Air Corps requirements over the next

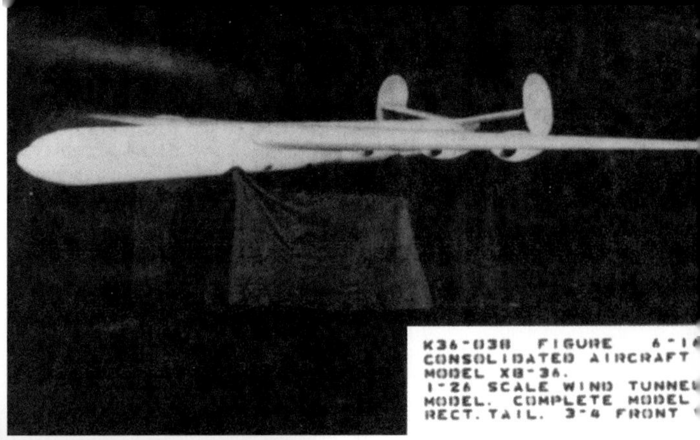

Right: a one-twenty-sixth scale wind tunnel model of the XB-36. This, and the image below shows the intake arrangement as it was during mid-1942. (Convair)

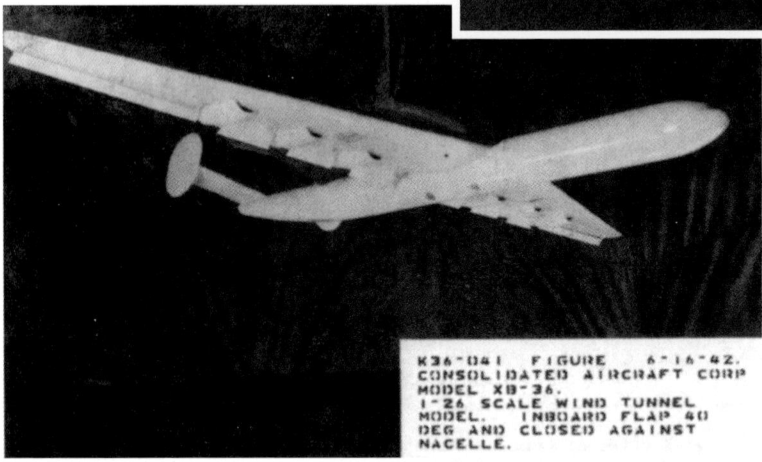

Left; The intakes stopped at the mid-chord of the wing. Also of interest is the dihedral of the horizontal stabiliser (Convair)

Right: This model - thought to be for display only - was sent up to Wright Field. (Convair)

several years. It was also influenced by Charles Lindbergh following his tour of the Third Reich and German aircraft factories at the invitation of the Deutsches Reich.

Throughout the late 1930s, Charles Lindbergh, accompanied by his wife Anne, travelled the globe as an ambassador without portfolio. After a six-month stay in Britain, the Lindberghs travelled to Germany in October 1938, where they were treated as honoured guests of the Third Reich, and Hermann Göring decorated him with the Service Cross of the German Eagle. Lindbergh visited centres of military aviation, where he assessed the pace of Germany's rearmament, while Anne was fêted in Berlin. Lindbergh praised the Luftwaffe's fighter and bomber designs, and he asserted that 'Europe, and the entire world, is fortunate that a Nazi Germany lies, at present, between Communistic Russia and a demoralised France.' Lindbergh viewed the Soviet Union as the major threat to Western civilisation. His

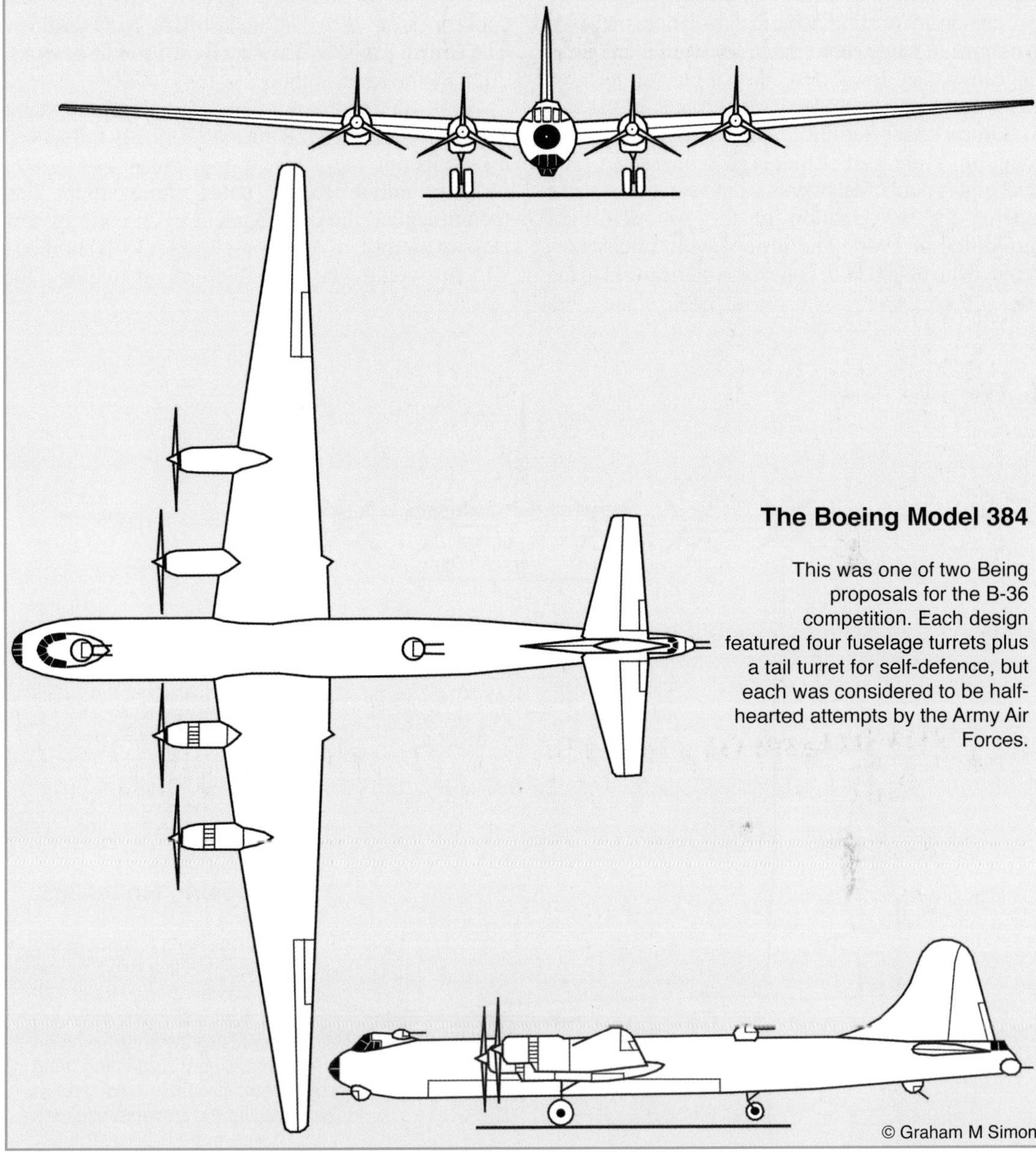

The Boeing Model 384

This was one of two Being proposals for the B-36 competition. Each design featured four fuselage turrets plus a tail turret for self-defence, but each was considered to be half-hearted attempts by the Army Air Forces.

belief in the supremacy of air power led him to conclude that Britain and France were effectively prostrate before the growing might of the Luftwaffe.

While this led to considerable criticism, Lindbergh remained enormously popular with the American public. The Lindberghs were preparing to purchase a house in the Berlin suburb of Wannsee when the Nazis carried out the pogroms that came to be known as Kristallnacht on the night of November 9–10, 1938. Lindbergh and his family instead moved to Paris before relocating to the United States just months before the outbreak of World War Two.

Upon his return, Lindbergh became a vocal advocate for American neutrality. He viewed the European conflict as a fraternal squabble between an ascendant Germany and those countries that sought to deny it a place of power and prestige; Germany alone, Lindbergh argued, could 'dam the Asiatic hordes' and prevent the overrunning of Europe. In an essay for Reader's Digest in November 1939, Lindbergh cautioned against 'a war within our own family of nations, a war which will reduce the strength and destroy the treasures of the white race,' and he further pleaded, 'let us not commit racial suicide by internal conflict.' Lindbergh was not the only person advocating American isolationism based on notions of white supremacy, nor was he unique in suggesting that Jews were the single group most interested in involving the United States in the war in Europe. Anti-Semitic radio preacher Charles Coughlin embraced Lindbergh's message, and Lindbergh's public statements would serve as a prime impetus for the creation of the America First Committee in 1940. The group, which boasted a membership of 800,000, opposed American aid to the Allies and counted Lindbergh as its most prominent spokesperson. (see The Secret Plan To Overthrow The British Empire: War Plan Red, Frontline Books, 2020 by the same author)

It is on record that the special investigative committee chaired by Kilner were greatly influenced by Lindbergh.

The initial report dated June 1939 had recommended the development of an entirely new class of aircraft, a Very Long Range (VLR) bomber, which would be capable of matching the

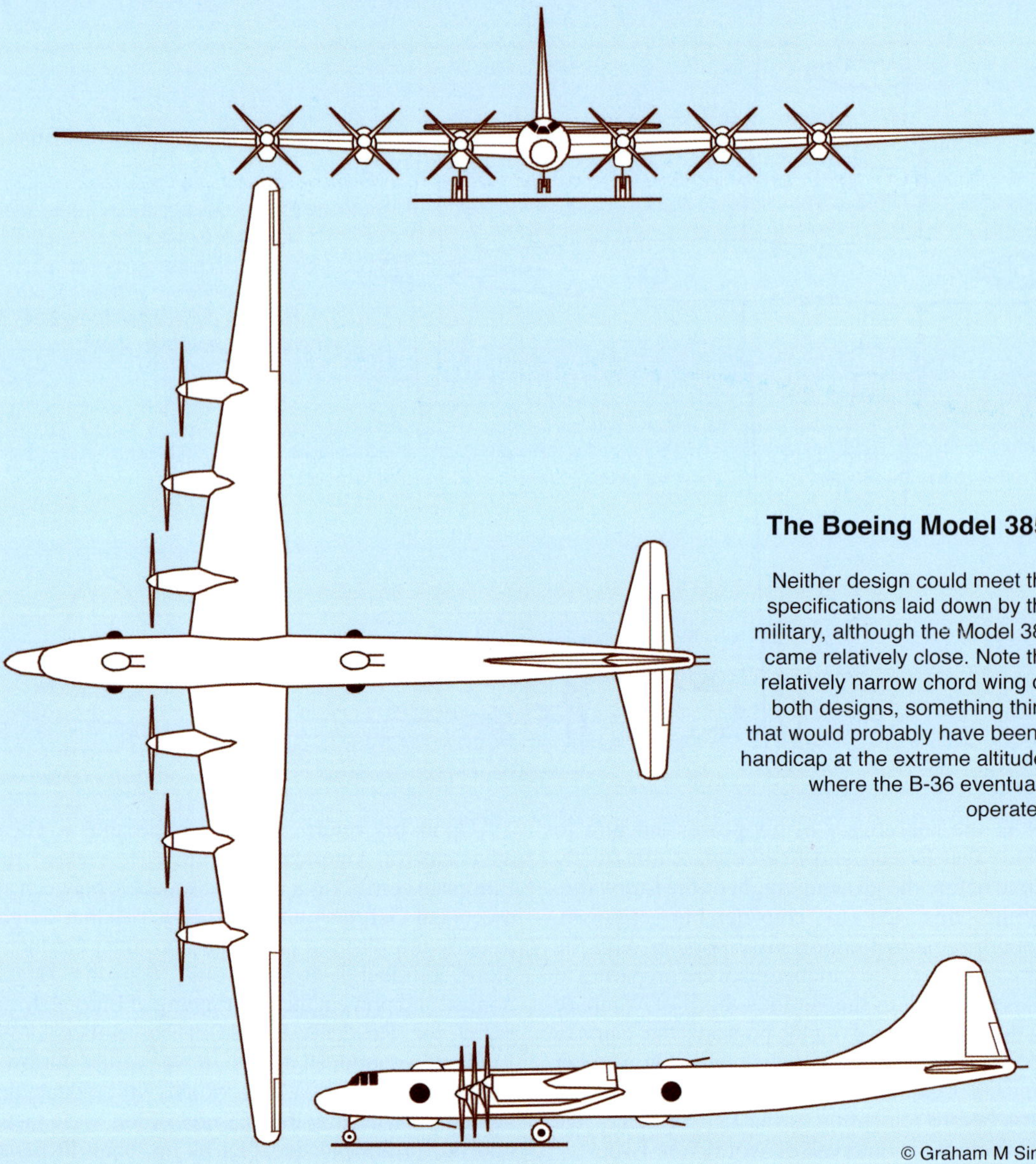

The Boeing Model 385.

Neither design could meet the specifications laid down by the military, although the Model 385 came relatively close. Note the relatively narrow chord wing on both designs, something thing that would probably have been a handicap at the extreme altitudes where the B-36 eventually operated.

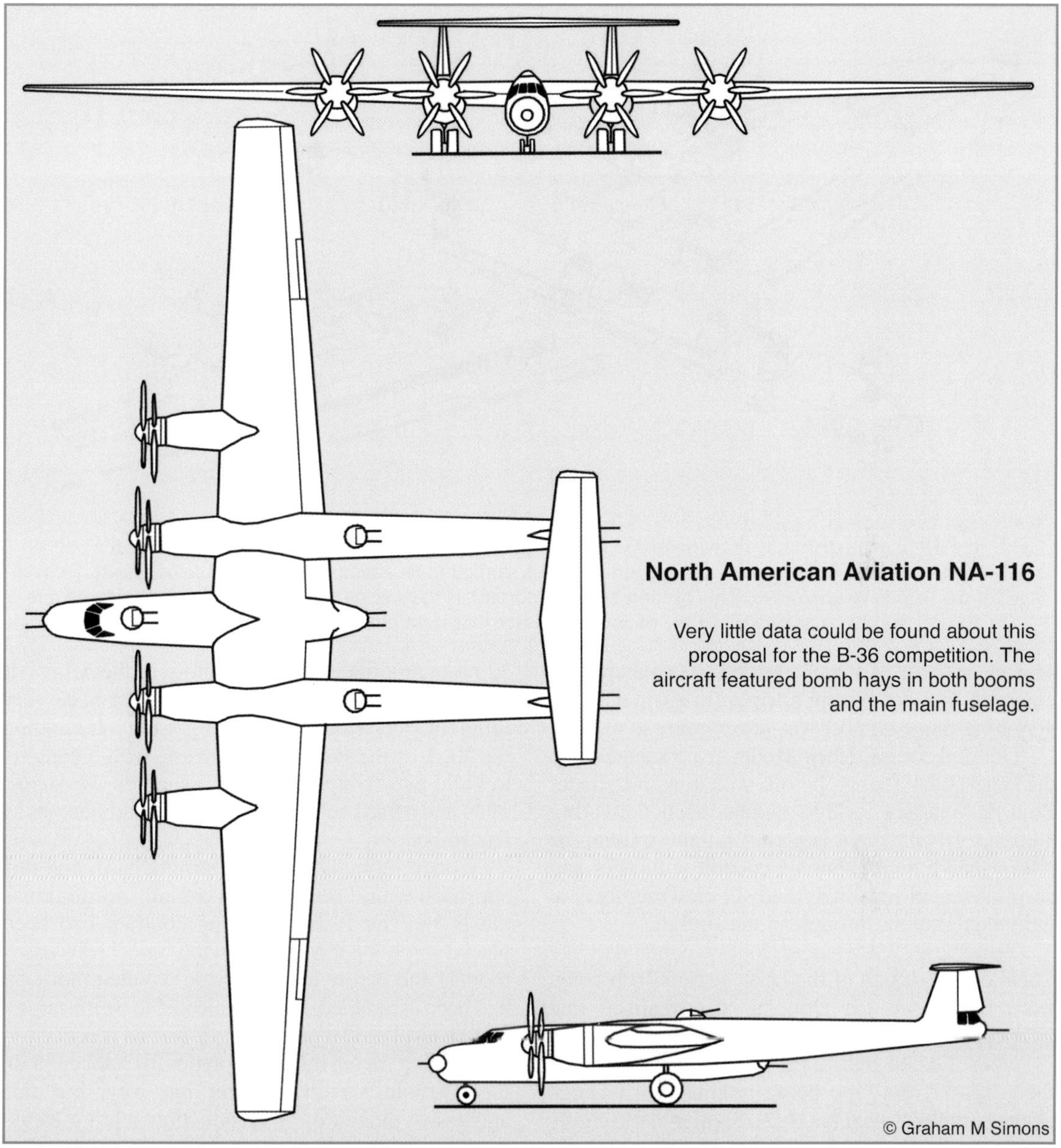

North American Aviation NA-116

Very little data could be found about this proposal for the B-36 competition. The aircraft featured bomb hays in both booms and the main fuselage.

specification to which Boeing had originally pegged the Model 334. That specification was upgraded in January 1940 in light of the German attack on Poland and it was to this requirement that the Boeing design goal was paired. But it was required to go through competitive tender.

Incorporating improved protective armour, self-sealing fuel tanks, greatly increased defensive armament and several refinements to the original specification, a Request for Data B-40B and Specification XC218 was issued by the War Department on 29 January 1940. In addition to Boeing, it was also sent to Consolidated, Douglas and Lockheed, and on 27 June 1940, around the time France was finally falling to German forces, the Air Corps issued contracts for engineering data with Boeing's bid designated the XB-29, Lockheed the XB-30, Douglas the XB-31 and Consolidated the XB-32.

Lockheed opted for a twelve-man aircraft powered by 2,200hp Wright R-3350-13 air-cooled radial engines in a pressurised compartment but in starting late, it conceded a technical disadvantage to Boeing and withdrew. Much of its initial work on the XB-30, however, went into the L-049 Constellation for a design that originated prior to the bomber

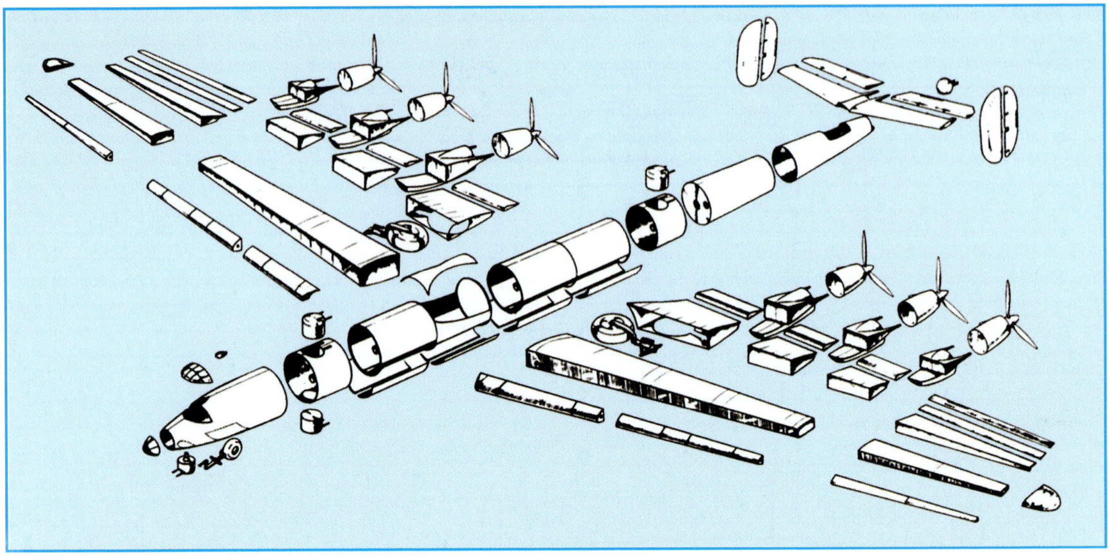

This mid-1942 exploded view drawing of the XB-36 shows a chin turret, one under-fuselage turrent a pair of upper turrets and a tail turret, one of many configurations studied in an attempt to provide full-hemisphericcoverage for the defensive armament. This became more important as the war progressed. The drawing also demonstrates all of the major assemblies that went into the aircraft.

project and out of which the XB-30 concept had emerged. But converting a triple-fin airliner into a very long-range bomber was never going to work.

Douglas designed their Model 423 contender into the largest of all four proposals, with four 28-cylinder Pratt & Whitney R-4360 radials, each delivering 3,000hp. Displaying a large tail fin and rudder, the XB-31 had a double-bubble cockpit with pilot and co-pilot seated separately and six crewmembers at individual stations throughout the aircraft.

There never was a single Douglas contender; like Lockheed, so much of the heritage had been taken from the DC-4 and Douglas also realised that airliners do not make good bombers!

Consolidated had marginally better luck with their XB-32, the type being retained as a hedge against problems with the B-29. Similar to the highly successful B-24, initially, the XB-32 had a twin-fin tail unit, but that was replaced by a large dorsal fin and rudder. The aircraft was beset with technical problems and design flaws which prevented it being deployed in the role for which it was designed. This failure was due largely to those delays and the fact that the B-29 proved such a success. Only fifteen entered service as the Convair B-32 Dominator in 1945, but it had a limited role.

The company changed its name to Convair when it merged with Vultee Aircraft in March 1943, more formally known as Consolidated Vultee. In that regard, the story of the B-32 blends into that of the B-36. Had the B-29 been less successful and the B-32 more prominent in the inventory of the Army Air Forces, the story of the B-36 may have been very different. Nevertheless, Boeing got the job building the VLA as the B-29 Superfortress, with a contract to build two flying prototypes issued on 24 August 1940 and a third being added in an amendment on 14 December.

Concurrency hit the programme hard, and this approach would set in and eventually compromise the B-36. The B-29 prototype contract had been placed solely on the basis of wind tunnel tests using models and before any full-scale wooden mock-up had been assembled. It was projected to be the largest and fastest bomber yet ordered, and so it proved to be. Pushing for ten more prototypes in October 1940, Gen Arnold would not get his way, but this aggressive pursuit of pre-production activity would set the scene for fast-track procurement which would compromise so many projects of the war years and their immediate aftermath.

To understand this is to gain insight to the tortuous path taken by the B-36. Somewhat surprisingly, the wooden mock-up was completed by November 1940 and was the sole example of the B-29 until late spring 1941 when, on 4 May, the engineering plans had been completed, and manufacturing began in Plant No 1 at Boeing's Seattle, Washington, facility. In that month, President Roosevelt moved the VLR bomber to the forefront of government war strategy, ordering a production lot of 500 a month as the target for the B-29.

Convinced that America would have to fight Nazi Germany from US soil, he saw in this aircraft the opportunity to strike enemy-occupied Europe when the need arose.

In May 1941, the Army sent Boeing a letter of intent for the initial production run of 250 aircraft, all to be built at a massive new, government-owned facility at Wichita, Kansas. On 20 June, President Roosevelt authorised the establishment of the US Army Air Forces, merging the Air Corps with the General Headquarters under the War Powers Act. Two days later, Hitler launched the biggest land assault in the history of warfare when the Wehrmacht attacked the Soviet Union. In January 1942, the B-29 contract was increased to 500 aircraft.

The full story of the B-29 is told elsewhere - see B-29 Superfortress Giant Bomber of World War Two and Korea, Pen & Sword 2012 by the same author.

As flawed as the B-29 was, it transformed the concept of strategic bombing, and the possibilities were made large through the carrying capacity of an aircraft that could deliver a 16,000-pound bomb load on a target more than 1,500 miles distant and return home. The transformative capacity of the B-29 was fully realised with the dropping of the atomic bomb on Hiroshima on 6 August 1945, followed by a second bomb on Nagasaki three days later.

These two raids brought an end to Japanese hostilities. They demonstrated the transition into an acceptance of total war conducted from the air in a manner that could not be duplicated by land or sea forces. This fed directly into the world's first truly intercontinental bomber and the first strategic bomber deployed with an airborne nuclear deterrent. Within that environment, the B-36 emerged on a scale far beyond anything that had been anticipated before.

The first response to the 11 April 1941 requirement was submitted by Consolidated Aircraft on 3 May 1941 for its Model 35 with four engines but with twin fins and rudders, retaining the manufacturer's preference for the configuration adopted for the B-24. The Model 35 had a fuselage length of 128 feet, a wingspan of 164 feet 4 inches with four engines in a paired pusher-tractor configuration on each inner wing extending twenty-five feet six inches between the forward and aft propeller bosses. The twin fins spanned forty-nine feet nine inches. The aircraft would have had a conventional cockpit layout with a tricycle undercarriage, three bomb bays, and unspecified defensive armament. But the reality existed that an aircraft with this range would have to fly without an escort because no single-seat aircraft could equal that. Aerial refuelling was not an accepted practice, and aircraft of intercontinental range would have required long-range tankers of at least half that capability.

Consolidated had been working on the large bomber concept for several months, its own money now supplemented by a fee of $435,523 divided between Consolidated and Boeing, the winner getting just over $300,000 and the loser being compensated with the balance. The Model 35 was impressive, larger than the B-29, the first prototype of which was then being assembled, but it was unimpressive and unable to meet the stipulated requirement, a problem experienced by the other contenders.

Submitted on 3 May, Boeing's Model 384, and its later 385, failed to impress as they each appeared to be a lacklustre attempt at meeting a compromise position on range. The Model 384 had four engines with tractor propeller arrangements and looked somewhat like a stretched B-29; the Model 385 had six tractor engines. Each design featured defensive armament in two dorsal, two ventral, and single tail turrets. Characteristically, the 385 had a high-aspect-ratio wing very similar to the B-29.

Within several weeks of the initial request for concept designs, Northrop and Douglas got involved, with Consolidated, Boeing and Douglas submitting design data for their individual concepts. Northrop had been keen to push its flying wing concept, and on 27 May, the Air Materiel Command requested further details, but while it could satisfy the 10,000-pound bomb load, the range was a poor 6,000 miles, far short of that required. Northrop's flying wing was a radical concept to minimise drag and improve aerodynamic efficiency by eliminating the need for tailplanes, a conventional fuselage incorporating crew and bomb-carrying equipment within a blended wing centre-section.

The Northrop flying wing would eventually pose the biggest challenge and threat to the B-36 and become embroiled in vicious behind-the-scenes politics with veiled mutterings of sabotage.

Other manufacturers, including North American Aviation, proposed a twin-boom layout, a single boom extending back from each inner pair of its four engines and a truncated fuselage emerging from the wing centre-section. Bomb bays were fitted to each tail boom assembly. Designated NA-116, this proposal had very little traction and disappeared from the list of contenders. Nor was the initial proposal from Douglas acceptable, their Model 423 design featuring the same range limitation as the Northrop flying wing. All four major studies got bogged down in the complexity of producing a workable design to meet the demanding specification.

Responding, officials from the newly renamed

Before Consolidated Aircraft's merger with Vultee to form Convair, Consolidated built a full-scale wooden XB-36 mock-up at its San Diego plant. The mock-up is seen here in 29 July 1942. Only one wing was present on the mock-up as was one of the pair of verticals. (Convair)

Army Air Force (AAF) and Air Staff leaders met on 19 August for a conference to discuss the study results. They issued an amended requirement, retaining the full range and bomb load but downgrading the speed requirement while setting a service ceiling of 40,000 feet. Defensive armament was to comprise six 37 mm cannon and eight 50-calibre machine guns to match the need to defend against attack from three fighters simultaneously. This added to the weight of the aircraft and threatened a solution to the range problem.

Urging an accelerated approach, the AAF leadership anticipated that a prototype could not be ready before early 1944 and consideration of the design requirement further emphasised a mission radius of 4,000 miles. A flaw lay in the lack of synergy between the availability of design data and the final decision on requirements. The 19 August meeting took place before Boeing received formal approval for its studies, while Consolidated had still to complete its final investigation. Nevertheless, the four contractors were pressed to submit their proposals immediately, and all were in the hands of the AAF by mid-September, at which point Douglas and Boeing dropped out, the former believing the specification asked the physically impossible.

Perhaps through preoccupation with existing and pending contracts as the aviation and munitions industry went into war-fever, none of the four contenders had provided proper studies to the satisfaction of the customer, the AAF report declaring that 'in no case was sufficient aerodynamic data submitted to permit a complete check' of the performance', and 'only one of the design studies contained data giving the amount of fuel carried, and only one study was accompanied by a general arrangement drawing'.

It was difficult to remove the politics of the situation: with a new level of authority within the Army structure, should war come the AAF was proudly expecting to offer great expectations; the White House wanted to push fast with war-winning weapons (aware of how the US had been unable to produce a single home-grown aircraft of any meaningful contribution for the First World War); and industry saw lucrative, lower-hanging fruit with which to expand its contract base. Suddenly, in six months after Air Materiel Division had requested studies into the 'aeronautical art' of the future, there was a pressing urgency for a new intercontinental bomber, without wind tunnel tests or any detailed proposal.

But the final determination was that the Northrop and Consolidated concepts were 'within current boundaries' of the possible and within two months had determined, without any further data, that the Northrop flying wing had tremendous potential and that Consolidated's more conventional proposal was worthy of further analysis.

The detailed proposal from Consolidated was sent to the AAF on 6 October 1941 along with a costing analysis and a request for $800,000 to assemble two prototypes.

The company was aware of difficulties defined earlier under the fast-track, concurrency management concept and specifically asked that it be kept free of interference and continuous changes and revisions to the requirement. In fact, the B-36 would prove to be one of the most troubled, dysfunctional programmes of the period and continuously in a state of flux, demonstrably exhibited by its evolution long after production orders had been received. But it was not the proposal from Consolidated that had first excited the AAF.

Chapter Two

Genesis of a Giant

In October 1941, Brigadier General George C Kenney, then head of the USAAF Experimental Division at Wright Field, presented the Consolidated proposal and engineering drawings - along with his recommendations - to General Henry H 'Hap' Arnold, recently designated chief of the Army Air Forces. As evaluated by the Air Materiel Division, Kenney felt that the Consolidated proposal had the best potential to meet the 11 April requirement. As the first commander of the postwar Strategic Air Command, Kenney would later become one of the biggest opponents of B-36 deployment within the postwar USAAF.

General Arnold agreed with Kenney's 1941 comments and directed that arrangements were completed to purchase two experimental aircraft from Consolidated under the designation XB-36.

Consolidated Aircraft Corporation was, by that time, one of the leading aircraft makers in the USA. Major Reuben Fleet had organised it in 1923 in East Greenwich, Rhode Island. The company moved to Buffalo, New York, in 1925, and to San Diego in 1933 with a staff of 900. By 1939 it had grown to 6,000 employees. As the expansion of the American aircraft industry took place, it grew to around 40,000 employees by the middle of 1940.

During World War Two, Consolidated operated thirteen divisions throughout the country. There were manufacturing plants at Downey and San Diego in California and Fort Worth, Nashville, Louisville, Allentown, New Orleans, Miami, and Wayne, Michigan. Modification plants were to be located in Tucson, and Elizabeth City, New Jersey. A research division was at Dearborn, and Consolidated also operated a transpacific airline called Consairway for the USAAF Air Transport Command. The plants at Downey and Nashville were included due to a merger with Vultee Aircraft Corporation in March 1943, when the company became the Consolidated Vultee Aircraft Corporation, soon - and eventually universally - known as Convair. Further mergers would result in Convair becoming a division of General Dynamics.

The XB-36 contract, designated W535-AC-2232, was awarded on 15 November 1941, less than one month before the Japanese attack on Pearl Harbor. Consolidated would receive a fixed fee of $800,000. The total cost of the design competition had come to $435,623, of which $135,455 was paid to Consolidated, who won the contest. The balance, $300,168, went to Boeing as the loser.

A month later, the notion of fighting a world war against Germany and Japan was no longer a theoretical possibility for the United States. Theoretical future needs faded before the immediate requirement for weapons. The XB-36 was seen as a

The Convair plant in San Diego, California in 1950. This is where the B-36 was developed before work transferred to Fort Worth, Texas. (GMS Collection)

key strategic weapon in a national battle for survival. With this in mind, the most extensive research programme ever associated with an American war aircraft was initiated.

The two XB-36 machines were intended to be built in San Diego, the first to be delivered by May 1944, and the second months later.

Consolidated was faced with design problems never before encountered. Most of these stemmed from the very large size of the aircraft because at the time, there was little experience with the structure/gross weight ratios dictated by the machine's huge dimensions.

The basic design for the XB-36 prototype was, of course, to be based on Consolidated's Model 35, which was a circular-fuselage, high-wing, twin-tail bomber intended to be powered with four pusher engines. However, the XB-36 would not be identical, and the company designation for the XB-36 would be Model 36, conveniently the same number as that assigned by the USAAF.

While the Model 35 was larger than the B-29, with a wingspan of 164 feet, a length of 128 feet and a wing area of 2,700 square feet, the Model 36 was still larger. It had a wingspan of 230 feet, a length of 163 feet and a wing area of 6,772 square feet. Aside from this, most of the main characteristics of Model 35, including the twin tail, were retained in the Model 36/X1336 design, at least for a while.

The Consolidated engineering team began work on the XB-36 almost immediately after the award of the contract. It was no easy task. So as to fly a 10,000-mile mission of nearly two days' duration, the aircraft had to have low aerodynamic drag, low fuel consumption, and high engine durability. The fundamental factor influencing the selection of the pusher-type design was the need for smooth air flow over the wing, and the location of the nacelles in the rear portion of the wing minimised external drag. Directional stability was also improved. Consolidated would have to pay particular attention to aerodynamic smoothness and weight, and an enormous amount of new development work would have to be undertaken.

The development of manufacturing processes to produce smooth-skin, bonded structures began since unnecessary protuberances and joints between skins would affect the speed and range and absorb horsepower. Everyone on the project exercised severe weight control, as the design of details, assemblies and equipment had to be kept strictly within the weight allotments for each part of the structure. For each pound of weight over the allowance, two pounds of fuel would have to be added to achieve the maximum range of 10,000 miles. New system equipment was required, much of which was beyond the then-current state of the art. For example, a 5,000 pounds per square inch hydraulic system was deemed necessary. New pumps, valves, and actuating mechanisms had to be developed from scratch.

The resulting weight of the system equipment was considerably less than that of the standard 1,500 psi systems then in use. Around the same time, the USAAF's developmental laboratories at Wright Field were considering a new 400 cycle, 208 volt, three-phase alternating current system. This would permit the use of new, lightweight actuating motors. A sixteen horsepower geared motor of 3,500 rpm would weigh only twenty-three pounds in a typical application compared to one hundred pounds for a similar motor of the direct current system. Greater reliability with higher rotation speeds could be obtained and since no commutator or brushes were required, the troublesome problem of arcing at high altitudes was also overcome.

The engine for the Model 36/XB-36 was to be the 28-cylinder Pratt & Whitney 'X' engine, which delivered 3,000 horsepower. In 1941, this engine existed only on paper. However, Pratt & Whitney proceeded with its design, working closely with the powerplant laboratory at Wright Field and Consolidated's Powerplant Group. This engine, consisting of a pair of 14-cylinder R-1830 Twin Wasp engines combined, had to put out 3,000 hp at 2,700 rpm for the XB-36's take-off conditions and to develop the stamina for a 10,000-mile mission. The 3,500 hp R-4360 Wasp Major, as it came to be designated, was a tremendous achievement by itself. In addition to powering the B-36, it was also used to power the Boeing Stratocruisers and KC-97s in the postwar period.

At the head of the chain of command at Consolidated was Isaac Machlin 'Mac' Laddon, the executive vice president and the man who effectively ran Consolidated. He was an engineer and had been chief engineer for several years on projects that included the great Catalina flying boat. Laddon had brought the project through its preliminary design and proposal stages, and he was confident in Consolidated's ability to produce the aircraft. As events later turned out, Mac Laddon had to direct the programme through some difficult periods and, in the postwar period, he personally defended the B-36 from severe critics.

Under Laddon, the key members of the Model 36/XB-36 team were Harry A Sutton, head of the Engineering Department; Ted P Hall, head of the Preliminary Design group; Ralph L Bayless, head of

Left: General George Churchill Kenney (b: 6 August 1889, d: 9 August 1977). Kenney became the first commander of the newly formed Strategic Air Command. He was encouraged by Secretary of the Air Force Stuart Symington to join him in the political battle surrounding the establishment of an independent United States Air Force.

Right: Isaac Machlin 'Mac' Laddon (b: 25 December 1894, d 14 January 1976) was Executive Vice-President and Chief Engineer, who effectively ran Consolidated and oversaw theXB-36 project.

the Aerodynamics Group; Ken Ward, who was in charge of finalising the external shape; and Robert H Widmer, who began preparations for the long wind tunnel programme.

On the engine side, Consolidated's Powerplant Group was directed by O W 'Bud' Woerschel, with Bob Goodyear as his assistant. The senior powerplant design engineer, Dalton B Suggs, who had been on the PBY Catalina and B-24 Liberator engine programmes, was assigned to the XB-36 in early 1942. With Paul Lynch and a small cadre of engineers, Suggs made the initial engine layout and general arrangement studies.

By the spring of 1942, a wooden 1/26th scale wind tunnel model had been constructed. Bob Widmer conducted and evaluated the tests in wind tunnels at both the Massachusetts Institute of Technology and the California Institute of Technology. He attempted to achieve the highest possible aerodynamic efficiency, so great effort was put into laminar flow wing design.

The June 1942 wind tunnel tests showed that the first airfoil selected, the National Advisory Committee on Aeronautics NACA 65, had unsatisfactory drag characteristics. A new wind tunnel model was constructed, but it was delayed for almost a year as competing aircraft programmes had higher priorities. They got into the wind tunnel ahead of the intercontinental bomber! Ultimately, wind tunnel tests were scheduled into the large tunnels at Langley Field and Ames laboratory at Moffett Field.

The wind tunnel tests conducted during 1945 determined that the NACA 63 series of airfoils were superior to the NACA 65. Further analysis led to the decision to sweep back both wings three degrees without redesigning the wings themselves. It was not thought worthwhile at this stage to redesign the engine nacelles, which, due to the sweepback, were now also three degrees off-axis. This would remain a distinctive feature of the B-36. Widmer's engineers made tests of flap and aileron effectiveness and surface control deflections, in addition to the usual tests to derive primary data on lift, drag, pitch, and roll and yaw movements as well as side forces. With the wind tunnel programme underway, and preliminary drawings of outline and equipment spacing beginning to come from the drafting boards, a full-scale mock-up had been built in the spring of 1942. Constructed of wood and assembled in a long building adjacent to the engineering department at Consolidated's San Diego plant, it represented the complete fuselage, half the wing, and the twin tail.

The full-scale mock-up, which was finally approved by the USAAF Air Materiel Command in September 1942 was moderately detailed. The landing gear and armament turrets were included, but both of these aircraft sections were to undergo considerable change in the months ahead. The size and vulnerability of the single-wheel landing gear caused much concern, and so did the placement of the defensive gun turrets because of their relationship to the bomb bays. Meanwhile, the number and types of guns to be used would not be finally determined until almost the end of the design process.

Meanwhile, a methyl bromide fire extinguisher system was developed to replace the usual carbon dioxide system for the engines. Methyl-bromide, having a much lower boiling point than carbon dioxide, allowed it to be stored as a liquid at lower pressure, thus permitting lighter weight storage tanks and conducting lines. This was not used on the first XB-36, but it was installed on the second machine, which became the YB-36, and on the subsequent production aircraft.

From San Diego to Forth Worth

By mid-1942, Consolidated's San Diego plant had become saturated with work on the PBY and B-24 programmes, so the XB-36 project was moved to a factory built by the government at Fort Worth, Texas.

The War Department had selected Forth Worth for heavy bomber production as early as January

1941. The huge factory, designated as Government Plant Number 4, was built across the field from Fort Worth Army Air Field. It was to be operated by Consolidated, primarily to assemble sections of the B-24s built at the Ford Motor Company's Willow Run Plant near Detroit, Michigan. The first B-24 was delivered from Government Plant Number 4 in April 1942, only a month after ground was broken.

In August 1942, with the wooden Model 36/XB-36 mock-up secured to a railroad flatcar, the nearly 200 engineers and other personnel assigned to the project boarded a Santa Fe passenger train bound for Fort Worth. When they arrived, the engineers were placed in an area of the government factory paint shop. At the same time, new facilities were being prepared, and a huge mock-up was installed in the experimental department. However, it soon became apparent that this area would not be large enough, and funds were requested for an addition to the building. Not finally completed until the spring of 1944, the new facility was constructed with a 90,000 square foot bay and an open work height of sixty feet.

The XB-36 project was now under the umbrella of two Consolidated divisions. Responsibilities for these were set up by Laddon and directed through Harry Sutton, who headed engineering at both. Under the plan, San Diego would be responsible for basic design and wind tunnel testing. Stress analysis, weight control, fabrication and construction of the two prototypes, as well as the eventual flight test programme, were to be implemented by Fort Worth.

R C Sebold became chief of engineering, and Herbert W Hinkley became the XB-36 project engineer. Jack W. Larson became assistant chief engineer at Fort Worth, and Henry K Growald came in as Hinkley's assistant. Sebold and Growald were chosen for their experience in areas important to the XB-36. Hinkley had been a stress analyst at Consolidated from 1933, and had worked on the B-24. Growald was a specialist in armament. Stress analysis and structures were in the hands of Les Moffett, who moved into the position of assistant project engineer on the structural design.

In September 1942, General Arnold had ordered the highest priority to both the Northrop XB-35 and Consolidated XB-36. The USA was taking heavy losses in the Pacific at the Japanese hands, and an Allied counterstrike against the Germans in Europe or North Africa was still a pipe dream. By the end of the year, things began to change.

Winning the war was not on the horizon in the last days of 1942, but on the other hand, American and other Allied planners could look at the unprecedented and almost unbelievable industrial mobilisation that had taken place, and they could see that the war would not be lost.

By the end of 1942, not long after the arrival of the XB-36 programme in Fort Worth, the project was downgraded in importance. Delays were experienced in the development programme as wind tunnel tests were downgraded in priority. Additional months were lost in the wing trailing edge redesign, and even the move contributed a loss of three to four months.

During 1943, as the fall of China seemed imminent, the priority of the XB-36 programme was moved to the fore again because if China fell to the advancing Japanese, the USAAF could not base long-range B-29s there, as they planned to do in 1944. They would need either an aircraft with the intended range of the XB-36 or they'd need other long-range bases for the B-29s. Eventually, the island-hopping campaign in the Pacific brought bases

Above: the B-36 nose mockup in June 1945. The dummy 20mm frontal gun installation included barbette gun turrets mounted either side of the nose, below the raised cockpit canopy.

Below: the mock-up of the raised bubble canopy that covered the two pilots and flight engineer. (both GMS Collection)

Above: A technican stands below one of the XB-36 wind-tunnel models. In this version, each engine has two intakes, one in the leading edge of the wing, and one well aft of it. This version also has the single vertical tail. (GMS Collection)

Right: One of the air intakes in the wind-tunnel model, with pressure instrumentation installed. Airflow through and around the powerplant was a major part in engine nacelle development. In this test, the lower intake does not extend to the wing leading edge. The image does show the different ducting inside the intake: In the top section, from left to right is the intercooler air, engine cooling fan, and another intercooler air duct. In the lower section as turbocharger air ducts either side of the oil cooler duct. (Convair/General Dynamics)

Much work was done inside the forty by eighty foot NACA wind tunnel at the Ames Research Laboratory in Palo Alto, CA. By 24 October 1945, when the image on the lower right was taken, the intake was almost in its final position at the wing leading edge. Glenn Parva Collection)

within B-29 strike distance, but the re-conquest of Guam and the Marianas could not be foretold with certainty in mid-1943.

The most difficult obstacle to the project's progress became the shortage of manpower as the war grew in intensity. The lack of experienced and qualified engineering personnel was noticable on a project as large and complex as the XB-36. In 1943, the average aeronautical engineer had only fifteen months of experience. By mid-1943, the accelerated B-24 programme was siphoning off personnel, and selective service attrition took its toll.

Another factor that delayed the XB-36 also impacted other programmes. This was the difficulty

Above: The XB-36 main landing gear clearly marked 'Not For Flight' on the wheel rim seen on 13 May 1946. The brake assembly is on the right.

Below, above right and right: functional tests were conducted on the main gear test specimens using test rigs and mock-ups made from plywood.

that all manufacturers were having in getting urgently needed parts to complete existing orders. However, the big problem with the XB-36 was that the USAAF had only committed to just two XB-36s. Consolidated Vultee's new president, Thomas P Girdler, complained to Robert A Patterson in the War Department that it was difficult to get subcontractors to work on an order for only two machines. He suggested that suppliers would be more interested in the XB-36 if the programme held some promise for large-scale production.

In July 1943, after discussing this with General Arnold, Patterson directed General Oliver P Echols, the USAAF's head of procurement, to issue the letter of intent to build one hundred B-36 bombers at Fort Worth. This commitment, plus the increased priority prompted by the decline in the mainland China campaign, gave new impetus to the lagging XB-36 programme, but again, as the situation in the Pacific improved, the project slipped into competition for scarce resources. It would be over a year before the letter of intent was replaced with a firm contract.

In August 1944, the USAAF finally ordered one hundred B-36 production-model machines. By this time, the war against Germany was imagined to be almost over, and though planners envisioned the war against Japan dragging on until 1947, no priority was assigned to the production of the B-36s. The estimated cost of the production B-36s was around $1,250,000 each, with government-furnished equipment estimated at $500,000. One hundred aircraft costing approximately $1,750,000 each - just slightly more than two days' cost during the war. In the latter days of the war, in the interest of achieving increased progress, it was decided that as much as two years could be cut from the developmental time of the B-36 by beginning production even before the two experimental models were rolled out.

Following the capture of Guam and the Marianas in October 1944, B-29s - as well as the small number of Consolidated B-32s - could bomb the Japanese homeland without needing bases in China. With this in mind, Consolidated Vultee was ordered to step up the B-32 programme, and once again, the XB-36 stood down for a readily available aircraft.

As early as July 1944, a letter to Harry Woodhead from General B E Meyers, of the USAAF Air Materiel Command, directed 'positive and vigorous action to place the B-32 on a Number One priority from an engineering, tooling and production standpoint, without reference to the effect this action may have on the XB-36 and B-36 programs.'

By the end of 1944, the XB-36 Experimental Shop was eighteen months behind schedule, and this blow further complicated the materiel delays, armament revisions and minor redesigns of system equipment.

Designing the beast

In the two years from the time the XB-36 project moved to Fort Worth and the summer of 1944, when it was pushed behind the B-32 in importance, the intercontinental bomber had evolved in a series of fits and starts. One of the refinements in the original Model 36 design came in the fall of 1943. Air Materiel Command was doing the static tests of the twin-tail configuration. After research and conferences with Convair, it was decided to abandon them, favouring a single fin and rudder. Static tests showed that the twin-tail, with its large vertical fins and rudders and associated control brackets, could shear off in a hard landing or severe flight conditions.

The engine test stand, located outside the Experimental Building at Convair Fort Worth on which hundreds of test hours were run. (Convair/General Dynamics)

In another part of the aircraft, a single-wheel landing gear was incorporated - there was no experience to design multi-wheel gear with adequate braking capacity that could be accommodated in the wing trailing edge as retracted. On the other hand, the USAAF was concerned about the single-wheel safety factor. The possibility of a blowout on takeoff or landing was real, as it would make the entire machine vulnerable. A parallel issue was the footprint of the big aircraft or the amount of weight put on a single spot through a single tyre. Special runways would have to be constructed with concrete at least twenty-two inches thick. When the B-36 did make its initial flight, there were still only three airfields capable of accepting it on landing: its home field at Fort Worth, Eglin Field in Florida, and Fairfield-Suisun Army Air Field in California.

Research into single, dual, triple and quadruple-wheel designs progressed during 1944 and continued into 1945, existing brake design would require a sixty-five-inch tyre width in a four-wheel arrangement, which could not be housed in the wing. Consequently, Convair continued to work within the parameters of a single-wheel design, with the Goodyear Tire & Rubber Company as subcontractor. The resulting 110-inch diameter, forty-six-inch wide tyre was the largest aircraft tire ever developed. Each tyre weighed 1,475 pounds. Eventually, a fifty-six-inch diameter, sixteen-inch wide, high-pressure tyre in a four-wheel gear became possible because of the development of an improved braking system. The new gear would not be used until the development of the B-36A several years after the XB-56 was first flown, and both the XB-36 and the YB-36 would be flown with single-wheel landing gear arrangements.

The first Pratt & Whitney R-4560-SP Wasp Major test engine was hand made and delivered to Fort Worth in May 1943. Design improvements delayed it until October, but by December, the full-scale wind tunnel tests were begun in Wright Field's twenty-foot wind tunnel. Convair's Dalton Suggs directed this series of tests in close association with the Air Materiel Command Powerplant Laboratory and Pratt & Whitney engineers.

Air inlet configuration and the intricate interior air duct system were influential in the external configuration of the aircraft. Because of this, tests on these features were conducted first, along with the engine cooling fan and diffuser system, which affected engine performance. An extensive fan redesign was necessary, along with cooling correlation tests. The lower forward portion of the nacelle was redesigned for aerodynamic and engine intake efficiency.

As it had been delivered from Pratt and Whitney, the R-4360-SP engine was equipped with a type 11-

Lindbergh Field, San Diego, the Convair plant housing the drawing offices for the B-36. This room alone houses over 800 employees. (Convair/General Dynamics)

This picture was taken in August 1945, when the XB-36 was temporarily rolled outside the Experimental Building. The wings and tailplane were little more than the main spars. (Convair/General Dynamics)

11A cooling fan, designed to be in operation continuously while the engine was running. The carburettor was nearly twenty-two inches wide - and this partially restricted a straight-through flow of air over the top engine cylinders. The actual shape and direction of the intake vanes had to be determined by powered wind tunnel testing. The results, plus revised cylinder head baffling, helped correct the flow of cooling air over the engine.

Engine cooling tests were run through 1944 and into 1945 when seven different fan designs were tested. The 11-11A type was replaced with a thirty-four-blade fan, and the air diffuser tunnel belled out to increase its cross-sectional area within the nacelle. This slowed down the air and greatly improved the cooling. Air Materiel Command Powerplant Laboratory was also developing a fan that improved the engine's cooling during ground operations.

In August 1945, under the direction of Dalton Suggs, the engine tests were moved to the full-scale 40 x 80-foot wind tunnel at the Ames Laboratory at the Moffett Field Naval Air Station in California. The first engine test using the R-4360-SP failed in September, so a replacement was brought over from Fort Worth.

Testing to determine the aerodynamic characteristics of the wing-flap trailing edge, in combination with the propeller, was resumed in October 1945 with a Curtiss Electric 19-foot diameter test prop. The propellers were to be automatically and synchronously controlled to maintain selected rpm speeds within a few revolutions of each other from engine to engine on the aircraft.

The propeller hub incorporated an intricate motor mechanism utilising hydraulic and electric combinations to change the blade angle. In normal flight operation, the propeller was able to change pitch 4.5 degrees per second at 1,000 rpm. For feathering or reversing, the change was to be 45 degrees per second. The same propeller hub was used as had been used in the tests at Wright Field, but with an integral oil pump and high-speed clutch installed. During the tests, difficulties were experienced with oil leaks and excessively high temperatures within the propeller control unit. These were later remedied by engineers at the Curtiss company.

Another view of the XB-36 taken in August 1945. This head-on shot does not initially show the true scale of the machine, until one realises the sizes of the men near and under it! (Convair/General Dynamics)

The left wing and trailing edge of the XB-36. The number 3 engine on the right has a four-blade propeller fitted for test purposes, something that was never adopted for the B-36. (Convair/General Dynamics)

The evaluation of the test results indicated that the high resonance points were in two ranges: 1,150 to 1,350 rpm, and 1,950 to 2,175 rpm. The passage of the propeller blades through the wake of the wing caused a high degree of stress in the low-pressure area directly behind the moving airfoil. This could be overcome by operating the engines at speed, altitude and rpm ranges that would minimise the effects of buffeting of the propeller blades on the adjacent flap structure. As a result, the recommendation was that continuous operation at certain speeds should be avoided. For twenty degrees of flap, speeds should not exceed 170 mph, and for forty degrees of flap, speeds should not exceed 110 mph.

While there had been a good deal of technical progress on the XB-36 from 1942 and 1945, the USAAF's ambiguity toward the once-vital project caused it to languish with no clear sense of when a real aircraft would ever be built and flown. In the same facility where a B-24 had been completed, rolled out and flown away every few hours for years, the single XB-36 prototype still sat, unfinished, on the shop floor.

In reviewing the progress of the war, USAAF planners were sobered by the tremendous price paid in lives and materiel during the campaign for bases in Guam, the Marianas, and especially for Iwo Jima. In August 1945, the advent of atomic weapons provided yet another argument in favour of the development of the intercontinental bomber. In a future atomic war, retaliation would have to be immediate, and could not wait for the conquest of overseas bases. In early August 1945, an Air Staff Group conference recommended that four groups of B-36s be included in the mobile task force of the proposed seventy-group postwar Air Force.

Although the XB-36 was now back in favour with the USAAF, the programme did not resume with ease. Four years of fits and starts, as well as the lack of official interest, had taken a toll. When Sebold and Herbert Hinkley became involved in an investigation of the workmanship on the XB-36 structure as its fabrication passed into their control, they became aware that quality control had gotten out of hand during the war years. It appeared that there were many parts of the structure not given proper heat treatment or that were fabricated from improper materials.

For example, the integral fuel tanks required excessive rework to stop leaks. Wing contours were not according to design, although this was not considered detrimental to the XB-36 performance.

In July 1945, when Wright Field heard that the XB-36 programme was suffering from disorganisation, an inspection team of Air Materiel Command officials visited the Experimental Shop. The team consisted of Major W M. Cade of the Air Technical Services Command Engineering Division, Lieutenant J A Boykin Jr, of the XB-36 Project Office, L J Marts of Inspection, and Lieutenant

Colonel R E. Ludick, the USAAF Plant Representative. An inspection of the detail parts, assemblies, tools, and manufacturing techniques and an examination of structural repairs was made. In a letter to Convair's President Woodhead on 29 August 1945, Brig. General L C Craigie, commander of the Air Materiel Command Engineering Division at Wright Field, expressed concerns about the poor workmanship.

Craigie asked Convair to take corrective action, and Convair responded with a metallurgical survey of the types of material - and heat treatments of all primary structures of the XB-36. Of the more than 15,000 samples tested, some twenty per cent were of different materials than specified by drawings, and up to ten per cent were under strength. Extensive repairs were undertaken, but the essential structural components of the XB-36 were considered satisfactory, and the programme proceeded. The USAAF also put additional inspectors to work, along with those of Convair, to tighten up the quality control system.

The end of the war and assignment of new administrative personnel to the Convair Fort Worth Division gave a new feeling of enthusiasm for the XB-36 programme. Retired Navy Commander Roland G Mayer succeeded George Newman as plant manager. Ray Ryan had been brought from the Downey (formerly Vultee) Division in January 1945 by Sparky Sebold as assistant manager of the Experimental Shop, a month after the shop had been placed under engineering control instead of the division manager. Ryan was made Experimental Shop manager in April, succeeding R C Maving.

Reorganisation and closer supervision by Ray Ryan brought new efficiency and a new mood. In August, Ryan was moved up to assistant division manager, and Wesley 'Wes' Magnuson came from the Downey Division as the third Experimental Shop manager. Hinkley became assistant chief engineer for production design, and Henry Growald, a very competent engineer, took his place as project engineer. This and other changes helped to re-establish confidence in Convair's development of the aircraft.

In September 1945, just three weeks after VJ Day, the XB-36 was rolled out of the Experimental Shop on its own gear. After several design changes and many refinements, the XB-36 was a reality at last. The biggest obvious design change, the huge single tail, now rose nearly 47 feet above the ground.

Now that there was a giant airframe to be seen, there was a constant stream of visitors to the Fort Worth plant. Though they were not always enthusiastic about the aircraft and the entire programme, they could not help being impressed by

The XB-36 nears completion in the Experimental Shop in April 1946. (Convair)

the size of the XB-36. Convair's engineering staff, and that of the USAAF plant representative's office, extended themselves to show off the new giant, but serious delays by materiel suppliers in furnishing needed components and strikes by the American Federation of Labor unions would affect both engineering and production.

Although the completed XB-36 was parked on the tarmac at Fort Worth during the last week of September 1945, there was still work to be done before it would lift into the air. There were still problems facing the design team before the machine could be finished, including the ever-present weight of the final configuration. Redesign of the tail and the engine nacelles, minor revisions, and the failure of some of the Government Furnished Equipment manufacturers to meet their weight restrictions gradually added a few thousand pounds to the total.

The required crew was increased to fourteen, and in early 1945 the USAAF had requested armament changes which added nearly five tons. The original call for eight .50 calibre machine guns and six 37 mm cannons had been stepped up to ten .50 calibre and five .37 mm guns, but the USAAF had changed its mind again. The Air Materiel Command decided to use eight General Electric powered, remotely controlled turrets housing two 20 mm cannons each. All turrets were to be completely retractable except those at nose and tail. This final arrangement was to be used on the production B-36Bs, but was never installed on the XB-36.

As the final year of the XB-36 development programme began in January 1946, Maj. Stephen P Dillon came to the Fort Worth plant as assistant USAAF plant representative under Colonel Fred Henry. Maj. Dillon had flown B-17s in North Africa, and because of his combat experience, he later assisted Wright Field in developing improved firepower, performance and combat serviceability for the B-17 and P-38. Prior to his assignment at Convair he was at Bell Aircraft's Marietta plant conducting flight-acceptance testing of B-29s. The B-36 was a logical progression from the B-17s and B-29s he had flown, and he began a close liaison with Convair engineers, learning and understanding every facet of the new bomber.

Men on the multi-level workstand put the finishing touches to the almost forty-seven feet high tail of the XB-36. The serial 42-13570 has been applied. No tail turret was fitted to the prototype. (Convair)

Other refinements involved the most complex component aboard the big bomber - the engines. It was originally proposed that the propeller drive in the Wasp Major engine incorporate a two-speed, shiftable gear with .29 and .50 ratios. When Pratt & Whitney encountered difficulty in design, the two-speed gear was changed to a single ratio gear of .381. This would result in a loss of 300 miles from the intended range and 21 mph from the proposed top speed. An additional loss of 270 miles from the range would be due to higher fuel consumption. However, the decision to use ground powered starters instead of engine self-starters obviated a further weight gain.

The XB-36 runs up its engines in preparation for the first flight. As with a number of images here, I am suspicious that this picture has been 'colorized.' (Convair/General Dynamics)

The completed XB-36 basks in the hot Texas sun outside the Experimental Shop. A portable air conditioning unit is cooling the front crew compartment. (Convair)

Meanwhile, the integral fuel tank system was determined to be necessary because of the weight of conventional rubber cells. So as to retain some self-sealing resistance to combat punctures, rubber panels were fitted externally to the bottom and sides of the tanks. The covering was not applied to the inboard tanks as the fuel in these would be used first, and they would be empty over the target area.

Convair had taken extensive steps to keep the weight of this very large structure and its components to a minimum, and indeed, this had become a general design philosophy.

New materials and processes were studied as the design progressed and technology increased. The new 758 aluminium alloy, of greater strength than the 24S alloy then in common use, was investigated, and though it came into limited application in the XB-36, the postwar production B-36s were able to derive a significant weight advantage from this material. Though comparatively little used before World War Two in aircraft structures, magnesium was incorporated in every possible place, as technicians from Dow Chemical Company and American Magnesium Corporation worked closely with Convair in the design stages.

Still, the weight increased. As the final phase of XB-36 development began in the autumn of 1945, the XB-36 gross weight had increased from 265,000 pounds in the 1941 proposal to 278,000 pounds. The top speed had changed from 369 mph to 323 mph at 30,000 feet. The service ceiling was reduced from 40,000 feet to 38,200 feet. The estimated takeoff roll of 5,000 feet had been stretched out to 6,100 feet, and the maximum range had slipped from the originally-specified 10,000 miles to 9,360 miles. A 24 April 1947 report done after the B-36 had flown indicated further decreases in top speed for the XB-36. The original contract called for the XB-36 to have a guaranteed high speed of 369 mph at 30,000 ft with 250,000 lbs gross weight. Additional wind tunnel testing, revising drag resulted in a sixteen mph decrease in estimated top speed to 353 mph. Mechanical changes and an increase to 270,000 pounds design gross weight caused further speed reductions to 523 mph. Flight tests twelve and thirteen of the XB-36 resulted in speeds averaging

Beryl A Erikson, left, in the pilot's seat and Gus Green, co-pilots were the Convair test pilots responsible for taking the XB-36 into the air for the first time. The size of the cockpit is particularly noticable with access to the bombardier position being made by ducking under the instrument panel. (Convair)

The XB-36 seen from above following it's roll-out in September 1945. The streamlined airliner-style canopy and nose are clearly visible, as is the deliniated walkways on top of the wings, fuselage and engines. (Convair)

sixteen mph less than predicted, causing a further reduction to 303 mph - slower than a B-29. However, twelve mph was recovered due to the aircraft not being as aerodynamically clean as it should have been during those test flights, plus the main landing gear doors not being installed. As a result, the XB-36 was rated with a top speed of 315 mph.

The first of the production-type R-4360-25 engine was delivered in August 1945, to be used for the ground engine tests. Dalton Suggs began testing almost immediately and continued in the nacelle test stand outside the Convair Experimental Building through the next year, performing service life and functional checks on practically every part of the engine. The flight engines for the XB-36 arrived one at a time through November 1945, each arrival being the cause for a minor celebration.

Henry Growald, the project engineer, was so anxious for the delivery of the propellers that he asked Curtiss to consign them to him personally. He assumed that they would come to the plant and be immediately directed to his attention. He was much surprised in the middle of one night when the propellers, each requiring four crates for various components, were unloaded in front of his house!

Through the first postwar winter, the refinements to the still-unflown XB-36 continued. Quality control problems were smoothed out, but two AFL union strikes in October 1945 and February 1946 affected both engineering and production. The XB-36 programme, if not the XB-36 prototype itself, moved forward. The USAAF was eager to get the XB-36 into the air at the earliest possible date and had met with Convair to determine ways of expediting the initial flight. A Convair internal memo, dated 6 February 1946, from Isaac Laddon to R G Mayer, expressed frustration over the XB-36: 'The Douglas company started the B-19 airplane in 1933, designed,

The airliner-type nose of the XB-36 with an instrument probe mounted high above so that it was not affected by fusealage airflow. (Convair)

redesigned and finally constructed an airplane that flew in late 1939. Obviously, it was underpowered and obsolete at the time it flew. I feel that way about our XB-36 performance. While it may have been better than Douglas', it's a hell of a long way from being as good as it should have been. While we can share the blame for the various delays with the Government, I still feel that under better conditions, this airplane could have been designed, built and flown in three years. By 15 April, four years and four months will have passed since the project was started. That is plenty of time to do the job.'

The engines were tested and eventually hung, but when Convair began run-up tests on 12 June, the wing flaps literally disintegrated. The magnesium alloy fabric-covered flaps could not withstand the tremendous punishment caused by propeller turbulence. The structure experienced rib-cracking and fabric rupture up to the torque box, and it was necessary to delay further testing for six weeks while stronger aluminium alloy flaps were fabricated.

A '689 Safety Board' of Air Materiel Command officials, so nicknamed for the numeric designation of the report they issued, arrived to inspect the huge aircraft in July. Among decisions reached was that the 689 Board would make an informal inspection from the safety standpoint only. This meant that only the Number 1 and Number 4 bomb bays needed to be operative. Because the USAAF was extremely anxious not to hold up the XB-36 any longer than necessary, the 689 Board conceded that vibration testing of the complete aircraft with empty fuel tanks could be deferred, along with cabin pressurisation testing.

The board finished its work as Convair engineers huddled and re-worked the design of the wing. Finally, by the first week of August 1946, the XB-36 was ready to take to the air.

The man chosen to take the big machine on its initial flight was Beryl A Erickson. He had been working on the project for nearly two years. Born in Santa Monica, California, he had attended Venice High School with Stephen Dillon, now the assistant USAAF plant representative for the XB-36, and had learned to fly in his teens. He and Dillon graduated in 1934. Twelve years later, Beryl Erickson was about to make another memorable flight. Erickson had become an American Airlines pilot and flew DC-3s in the late thirties. He joined Consolidated in early 1941 and did much of the developmental flying for both the B-24 and B-32 bombers. He was one of the few pilots checked out in the Douglas XB-19, which was the largest landplane in the world until the XB-36. Meanwhile, Dillon had served in the USAAF

The size of the XB-36 is very noticable when parked next to this Boeing B-29. (Convair)

It flies! The XB-36 takes to clear Texas skies for the first time on 8 August 1946 The main gear doors had not yet been fitted. I suspect this image has been 'colorized' at some point. (Convair/General Dynamics)

during World War Two and returned from combat in the North Africa theatre for a brief stint at Wright Field before being sent to Wichita with three other USAAF pilots for development flight testing on the B-29 programme.

Erickson had begun with taxi tests on 21 July to check out and confirm that all flight systems were airworthy. The flight control system of spring servo-tabs was unconventional, and there were some qualms over whether it might be overbalanced, so Erickson and his co-pilot, G S 'Gus' Green, put the XB-36 through a series of fairly sophisticated tests, including simulated high-speed take-off runs with safely decelerated stops. The highest speed test was at 97 mph, just below take-off speed.

Gus Green, who had actually been the flrst pilot assigned to the XB-36 programme, grew up in the small Texas town of Cleburne, thirty miles south of Fort Worth, and had gone to school with Dalton Suggs. He joined Convair during the war, flight testing production B-24s and B-32s.

Officially, Erickson was chief test pilot, while Green was his superior as chief of flight, and Easley was chief flight engineer. Joining them was James McEachern, a flight engineer, and A S 'Doc' Witchell, a test pilot. These men would form the nucleus of the new Flight Department.

As the delivery system evolved, Convair crews made several shakedown flights in each B-36 as it came off the production line, checking out the systems and the individual aircraft's performance. Then it was turned over to an Air Force crew, who made one of several acceptance flights before it was officially turned over to its new owner. But that is slightly ahead of the story.

Taxi tests continued through 7 August. Erickson thought he might take the XB-36 up that afternoon, but as the day wore on and early evening approached, it grew too dark.

In the warm morning hours of 8 August, Erickson made two preliminary takeoff runs while over 7,000 Convair employees lined the fence along the runway. The entire factory had turned out to watch the event. It was going to be another hot Texas summer day, with the temperature near 100 degrees Fahrenheit. It seemed that everyone realized the importance of this initial flight, the culmination of the most expensive project in military aviation history.

As the XB-36 was such a costly piece of machinery, it was handled with extreme care. The aircraft was designed to be a robust machine, to perform like no other machine before it. Convair engineers did not wish to subject it to any difficulties such as high winds. However, one day in early summer 1946, that is just what did happen. The XB-36 had been parked outside the hangar in the yard north of the Experimental Building when darkening clouds were seen forming to the north. It was a Texas Norther, a fast-moving cold front marked by a rapid drop in temperature, strong winds, and dark blue or 'black' skies. The Texas windstorm blew across the plant area and the nearby Fort Worth Army Air Field. Though not quite a tornado, the storm blew men, ground equipment, and debris all over the north yard. Personnel grabbed ropes and whatever they could to steady the XB-36, while one man deliberately ran his ground vehicle into a rolling work stand to stop it from smashing into the aircraft.

Finally, on 8 August 1946, Black scanned the sky as well as his weather maps and gave Erickson the thumbs up. A B-25 photographic aircraft from Wright Field rose to observe and record the historic flight. .

The eight-man crew aboard the XB-36 were all Convair employees. Gus Green was the co-pilot, William Easley and James McEachern were the flight engineers, and Robert E Hewes was the flight test engineer. W H Vobbe and A W Gedeman were the flight test analysts, and there were two observers, W L Daniel, Jr. and J M Hefley. The machine's gross weight stood at 200,000 pounds, including 8,000 gallons of fuel and 600 gallons of oil.

At 10:10 am, the XB-36 slowly began to roll. Finally, the huge machine rose from the runway and steadily gained altitude. Aboard the XB-36, the engineers and technicians monitored the aircraft's performance as Erickson levelled off at 3,500 feet with an airspeed of 140 to 155 mph. They flew across the outlying sections of Fort Worth and then briefly over the downtown area, with the distinctive drone of the six Wasp Majors causing thousands of citizens to turn their eyes skyward.

The maiden flight was judged to be a good one. The only minor mishap was a wing-flap malfunction, in which the Number 2 flap would not retract. The XB-36 had been in the air for thirty-seven minutes. The second flight took place a week later on 14 August, with the same crew were on board for this two hour, forty-three-minute flight. With them was Maj. Stephen P Dillon, the USAAF's XB-36 flight acceptance officer.

The sixth test flight was made to demonstrate the XB-36 to General Carl A 'Tooey' Spaatz, Commanding General of the USAAF, and his party. Erickson brought the XB-36 over the runway on a very low-level, high-speed pass. It was an impressive sight for General Spaatz, a wartime strategic air commander and a proponent of the intercontinental bomber, who would later play an essential part in keeping the B-36 programme alive.

The flight test programme continued through the autumn of 1946, beset with difficulties. Undoubtedly, the XB-36 prototype was advancing state of the art for its era, and the many problems inherent in the experimental aircraft's developmental process were magnified. Two of the main issues were the lack of proper engine cooling and propeller vibration stress, although both of these problems had been extensively investigated in the wind tunnel test programmes.

Engine cooling became a problem that would result in the inability of the XB-36 to maintain high altitude operations for extended periods of time above 30,000 feet. A two-speed cooling fan was later developed to keep engine temperatures within safe operating limits, along with refinements to the carburettor and the ignition system.

Propeller vibration, which received negative publicity resulting from incidents brought into public view, was of great concern. Although the Moffett Field wind tunnel tests had been passed satisfactorily and had given some sense of the vibration stress that was to be expected, the pusher configuration and the attendant punishment imposed on the wing flap structure, engines and propellers were more significant than anticipated.

During a series of flight tests devoted to solving this difficulty, it was discovered that the wing flaps and the propeller shaft and the propeller hub and shank were all under strength. Furthermore, under clean-wing conditions and within a fairly wide speed range, propeller vibration stress was acceptable. Still, additional stress occurred with flaps down or under high power settings, such as experienced in a climb or a field go-round.

No aerodynamic means of eliminating the reactions caused by the passage of the propeller blade through the wing wake could be found, so the affected structures were strengthened, and new rpm, speed, and altitude combinations were specified for flight operations. Due to the flap structure damage on the first flight, the new aluminium-alloy flaps had been installed. They were six times heavier than the original magnesium alloy fabric-covered design - a

Five turning, one stopped! The XB-36 - now with main gear doors fitted - overflies the Texas countryside with the starboard inner propeller feathered and stopped. (Convair/General Dynamics)

Taken some time after the first flight, this picture shows the more streamlined 'airliner' nose on the XB-36, which was much sleeker than the production unit. (Convair/General Dynamics)

considerable weight gain.

Due to the weight being added to strengthen the prototype, using a single-speed engine cooling fan and the General Electric BM-2 Turbosupercharger instead of the improved General Electric BH-2, the highest official altitude the XB-36 reached was 37,000 feet, obtained on 14 August 1947.

During one of the early flights, a propeller broke loose, taking a piece of the wing flap with it and fell 10,000 feet, landing in a farmer's field. An unforeseen fault in the design of the shaft was remedied by the simple addition of a curved notch to avoid fatigue and breaking off at that point.

Meanwhile, wind tunnel tests at the NACA Langley Laboratory in Virginia had predicted poor stalling characteristics for the swept wings. To help with this, adjustable slots were incorporated into the outboard wings. Still, during the flight test programme, it was shown that the stalling characteristics were satisfactory without them, so they were permanently closed on the XB-36 and eliminated altogether from later models.

There were numerous failures of the electrical system because of the poor fatigue characteristics of aluminium wiring. The electrical design group tried aluminium conductor instead of the proven but heavier copper to keep within budgetary weight. Vibration stress upon the electrical and other supporting systems caused all three engines of one wing to quit on one flight. On another, stress caused the inboard wing flaps to come off. On another flight, an electrical fire in the bomb bay broke out, which was not extinguished until after the XB-36 landed. Spark plugs were redesigned to address the increased wear due to the high lead content of the fuel used.

In the early afternoon of 30 September, another incident occurred which brought disparaging headlines. While calibrating an airspeed indicator suspended from the XB-36 by a seventy-five-foot cable attached to a winch in the bomb bay, the cable snapped, and the fifty-pound instrument fell to the ground, smashing through a skylight in a Fort Worth elementary school boys' restroom. Seven children were injured, although none seriously, with cuts and abrasions from the shattered pieces of the indicator and the concrete floor. The instrument gouged a seven-inch hole in the concrete, throwing fragments all over the room. One of these broke the nearby commode, putting it out of commission. There were jokes about a million-dollar aircraft bombing a toilet! It was a relatively unsophisticated first target for the world's most extensive and most expensive bomber. Damages to the school and insurance claims on behalf of the children were settled quickly.

The XB-36 is prepared for another flight. (Convair/General Dynamics)

Left: The aftermath of the XB-36 landing with a semi-collapsed landing gear leg.

Below: Beryl Erikson, pilot on the 16th test flight when the landing gear nearly collapsed receives a commendation from Convair President Harry Woodhead. Erikson and the rest of the crew were recognised at a testimonial dinner in the Blackstone Hotel in downtown Forth Worth. (Both Convair/General Dynamics)

There was a near catastrophe during the 16th test flight of the XB-36, scheduled for Wednesday, 26 March 1947. The planned tests included stress surveys of the Number 4 and Number 5 propeller hubs at 10,000 feet.

After the pre-flight check, Beryl Erickson and his co-pilot Gus Green taxied the XB-36 down to the north end of the Fort Worth runway and requested takeoff clearance. The gross weight for the flight was 254,000 pounds, including 11,050 gallons of fuel. Aboard were twelve crew members, including Maj. Dillon, two Curtiss-Wright representatives, Arthur D Nordhem and Lewis Clark, and two Air Materiel Command technicians, Master Sergeant Dillon W Mathews and Lieutenant Wister G Williams.

At 12:20 pm the XB-36 sped down the runway into a 20 mph headwind. Having reached an airspeed of 130 mph, they were airborne, and the crew began to retract the landing gear. Suddenly, with the gear near its fully retracted position, a sharp, violent jolt shook the aircraft. The right-hand main landing gear hydraulic retraction cylinder had burst, causing the side brace strut to break loose from its fltting in the rear wing spar. As Erickson and Green worked to maintain stability, the huge, nine-foot diameter wheel swung heavily past its normal 'down' position. It continued outward, smashing into the lower portion of the adjacent right inboard engine nacelle and crushing fuel, oil and hydraulic lines. An observer scanner in the aft compartment announced over the intercom that heavy smoke and flames were coming from the Number 4 engine and a failure of the right-hand landing gear.

Erickson cut the power and ordered the engine feathered as the broken landing gear dangled from the wing at an unorthodox angle. What was to have been another routine test flight had now become an emergency. He continued his climb upward and levelled off at 10,000 feet. Believing that only the drag strut had failed, Dillon went aft to inspect the damage, but realized that it was much more severe. He returned to the cockpit to tell the pilot and co-pilot what he'd seen, and Erickson went back to view the situation for himself while Dillon took the controls.

Flight engineers Jim McEachern and William Easley climbed out over the wheel well and attempted to clear some of the damaged hydraulic lines, but little could be done to repair the broken landing gear.

Erickson, Green and Dillon conferred and decided to try and bring the crippled machine in on its broken landing gear after the rest of the crew members had parachuted to safety. It would be an extremely dangerous operation, with the possibility of a disastrous explosion and fire if it crashed on landing. They decided to have Dillon bailout first and set up two-way radio contact with Erickson to help 'talk him down' in the damaged bomber.

For three hours, the XB-36 circled the field,

Three views of the Goodyear tracked landing gear experimentally fitted to the XB-36. The main gear, right, seems to have sunk into the soft ground, while the nose gear, below, was photographed for whatever reason with a towing bar attached while the aircraft was sitting on jacks! (Convair/General Dynamics)

According to a contemporary Goodyear Aviation Products advertisement, the purpose was that 'This tracked gear gives the B-36 a footprint three times larger than conventional gear - makes it light enough on its feet to use many additional runways.'

Below: The XB-36 gets airborne for the one and only flight with the tracked undercarriage attached. After a circuit of Forth Worth, a landing was made during which a trail of parts was left on the runway as the gear slowly self-destructed. Poor quality colour movie footage of this one and only flight does survive.

The 'BM-570' on the fuselage is known as a buzz-number, a post-war method of identifying US aircraft, particularly those guilty of buzzing cities. BM stood for the B-36 type and 570 was the 'last three' of the serial number. (Convair)

Right: One of the few known photographs of the tracked landing gear in colour. The event was the Open House at Carswell AFB on 20 May 1950. (GMS Collection)

burning up fuel while the pilots talked calmly to the tower, making arrangements for the crew to jump and for their possible rescue in the event there should be a fire during their crash landing. A radio-telephone network was set up between two ambulances, the field tower and the Convair plant, ready to spot where the downed men hit the ground. A BT-13 training aircraft was also sent up to circle the field to assist in spotting the men.

At 3:45 pm, Erickson reported over the radio that the first two men were away at 6,000 feet. As the men parachuted, two by two, from the lower right aft scanning blister on six different passes over the field, the pilots would radio the tower, which in turn called the ambulances. Nine received serious injuries.

Maj. Dillon had jumped first and suffered a sprained ankle on impact, but despite his painful injury, Dillon insisted that the ambulance attendants take him back to the field so that he could communicate with Erickson and Green as planned.

The following two hours were sweated out in circling continuously, consuming fuel and lessening the load by dumping all the water ballast. Since there was no provision for fuel dumping, the consumption of 7,015 gallons took five hours.

Ironically, while the XB-36 drama was being played out in the Texas skies, the Consolidated-Vultee Aircraft Corporation Board of Directors was meeting in New York. A telephone call alerted them to the situation, and they were patched into the communications between the tower and the stricken aircraft. The board members clustered around, listening to the dramatic incident as it unfolded.

Everyone was asking themselves whether Erickson and Green could bring the XB-36 in safely. By late afternoon, radio reports of the incident had brought thousands of people to the area, crowding the highways near the airfield, waiting to see what would happen to the giant bomber. Curious civilians and Convair personnel gathered, as did hundreds of soldiers from Fort Worth Army Air Field.

Finally, at 6:15 pm, Erickson made his final turn over Lake Worth. The approach was slow, from the north into a twenty-five mph headwind, and with full flaps. Number 4 engine was silent and feathered. The large crowd of spectators watched, pressing protesting Army guards forward to obtain a better view of the moment.

Erickson flared out just barely above the ground, the engines fully throttled before contact with the runway. Erickson put the big aircraft down gently on both wheels, expecting the right gear to collapse, sending the right wing crashing onto the runway. Immediately after ground contact, he reversed the huge propellers for braking action.

Meanwhile, Dillon monitored the angle of the landing gear strut. Erickson steered off the pavement to the left of the runway as Dillon directed. Suddenly, the XB-36 disappeared from Dillon's view in a depression in the runway. He told Erickson to guide the aircraft, continuing to the left until he could see it again. There was no need to keep moving. The XB-36 had come to a stop with the broken landing gear wedged against the damaged nacelle, having rolled some 5,500 feet down the 8,200-foot runway. Damage to the engine nacelle was minor.

Over the loudspeaker system throughout the Convair plant was announced 'The XB-36 has landed safely.' Many paused for the announcement and then continued to work. Later, to the press, Division Manager Roland G Mayer, head of the Fort Worth plant, described it as 'a most difficult landing satisfactorily accomplished.'

The aircraft was quickly repaired and back in the air. Eventually, the aircraft was turned over to the Air Force in mid-1948, but as was expected, the XB-36

The XB-36 flight engineers station (left) was considerably different from the production models. The picture shows most of the engine instrumentation, throttles and mixture controls. The pilot's station (right) also differed considerably from the production cockpit. (both Convair/General Dynamics)

An image that has suffered the ravages of time with severe colour fading is this one of the XB-36 climbing above Lake Worth, the Convair factory, and Carswell Air Force Base complex at Fort Worth, Texas. To the lower right is the runway complex that served the factory and the air base, and to the top of the right side of the runways are some of the buildings of Carswell. (Convair)

had limited operational value and was used primarily for ground training and to evaluate various proposed changes to the interior configuration.

The XB-36 did participate in one further flight test series. In early 1950 an experimental track-type landing gear was installed, similar to ones also tested on a B-50 and C-82 around the same time. The specially-designed Goodyear system of V-belts applied only fifty-seven pounds per square inch to the runway, compared to 156 pounds per square inch for the production four-wheel bogie-type undercarriage. This would, in theory, allow very large aircraft to use unprepared landing strips instead of specially-built runways. Each of the two belts on the main landing gear was sixteen inches wide, 276 inches in circumference, and had a thickness of one inch except for an additional one inch in a 'V' in the centre that fitted into a slot on the bogie wheel to keep the track centered. Each belt was made of rubber reinforced with brass-plated steel cables and had a pull strength of 150,000 pounds. The bogie wheels were made from a magnesium alloy that contained zirconium. Friction was reduced through the use of 185 tapered roller bearings weighing around 500 pounds. The track-style gear added approximately 5,000 pounds to the normal 16,000-pound landing gear. Nevertheless, this was only two-thirds of the expected increase when the project began.

A series of low and medium speed taxi tests were conducted during early March 1950 using the runways at Fort Worth. The new landing gear's first flight came on 29 March 1950, and the resulting 'screeching' sound was frightening to those aboard the aircraft. There seems to be some disagreement about when the only flight occurred, especially as it was claimed that it at least partially disintegrated on landing and yet it was photographed at the Carswell open house the next month. There was never any intention of using the track-type gear on production B-36s, and the XB-36 was used as a testbed simply because it was a very heavy aircraft that was readily available. Several organisations - including the Air University - did propose equipping production B-36s with track-style landing gear, but nothing came of the suggestions.

The aircraft was put out to grass at Carswell, with engines and other useful parts removed. It eventually was put on the fire dump and burnt.

Chapter Three

Early Production

The initial XB-36 contract - which was designated as W535-AC-2232 and dated 15 November 1941 - called for two machines to be built in San Diego, with the first to be delivered by May 1944, and the second to be delivered in November 1945. In fact, no XB-36s were delivered in 1945, and only one would be built. The second aircraft would be built, but much later than the first, and it would be delivered under the designation YB-36. While the 'X' prefix meant 'experimental', the 'Y' prefix identified the second B-36 as a 'service test' aircraft, officially earmarked as the flight test aircraft for the joint use of Convair and Air Force personnel.

When Japan was defeated, the USAAF rapidly decelerated most development programmes, but the contrary was true with the B-36 programme. Fabrication of basic components for the second prototype was pushed ahead faster. By the spring of 1946, design and engineering changes that had come about during the development of the first prototype were incorporated into the second, and it became the YB-36 before it was built.

As it took shape during the winter of 1946-1947, the YB-36 began to differ from the XB-36 in many ways, principally by its redesigned flight deck. The XB-36's limited visibility had been noted by Beryl Erickson and Gus Green, but engineering studies had already begun on an improved layout. Actually, a full-scale mock-up of a revised flight deck had existed as early as June 1945.

Another factor in the redesign was the desire by the USAAF to put a nose turret on the B-36 because experience during the war had shown bombers to be vulnerable to head-on attacks by fighters. The XB-36 would never have a nose turret, but the YB-36 and its successors would have a much different flight deck that allowed a twin-cannon turret.

The new and improved forward cabin design visibility was much improved by the bubble-type canopy covering the pilot, co-pilot and flight engineer. In addition, there was improved efficiency in this layout because the flight engineer was now facing aft and could scan the engines in flight.

The XB-36 flight engineer station had been laid out by designers who were not flight personnel. Some controls had been placed unnecessarily close to the flight engineer, and others were scattered all over the station in inconvenient locations - it was an ergonomic nightmare! Chief Flight Engineer William Easley lent his expertise and was responsible for designing the new flight engineer's station. Easley, who was left-handed, endeared himself to future flight engineers by laying out the station for most straightforward operation by a left-handed person. Later, when the USAF decided that flight engineers should be commissioned officers - due to the greater educational background required - Easley was called on to help write the flight engineer's manual at the Pratt & Whitney plant in Hartford. Unfortunately, the new title of 'Aircraft Performance Engineer' was

42-13571, the sole YB-36. It was fitted with the same single-mainwheel landing gear, but had the 'bubble-top' cockput glazing that became the production standard. (Convair/General Dynamics)

coined for the new officers by bureaucrats with apparent disregard because the acronym was 'APE.' The term 'Fight Engineer' was substituted.

The YB-36 flew for the first time on 4 December 1947. However, as rolled out, the YB-36 still had the original single-wheel undercarriage and lacked armament and most production equipment. Convair was expected to retain the YB-36 for six to twelve months for test and evaluation purposes and also to use the aircraft to identify future production line changes.

The first flight of the YB-36 was sixteen months after the first flight of its sister ship. Again Beryl Erickson was at the controls. With its more efficient turbosuperchargers and other engine equipment changes, the YB-36 easily outperformed the XB-36, and on 19 December, the YB-36 topped the XB-36's highest altitude mark by 3,000 feet, going to over 40,000 feet.

Designing the XB-36 and the YB-36 had been a long and complex process, clouded with indecision by the USAAF procurement staff over whether and when they wanted the big bombers in service. It is incredible that the initial production contract for the aircraft occurred roughly two years before the XB-36 made its first flight.

The government-owned Fort Worth plant, which had been erected to build B-24s, was now challenged to manufacture a machine roughly twice the size and complexity of the Liberator.

When Japan was defeated, B-36 development still languished, and B-32 production ceased. The partially-assembled B-32s on the production line were cut up for scrap, and the mile-long main assembly building at Fort Worth became a cavernous, vacant 'bowling alley.' This windowless facility was, at that time, the world's largest integrated aircraft factory.

Never mind the aircraft itself; thousands of engineering hours were required for the fabrication of tooling equipment for manufacturing quantities of B-36s. In addition, the sheer size and diversity of parts presented design and production problems never before experienced.

After eighty-nine hours of flight testing, the YB-36 was grounded for modifications on 27 May 1948. The single-wheel landing gear was replaced by the production four-wheel bogie-type undercarriage and

The Fort Worth Plant was divided into three major sections:

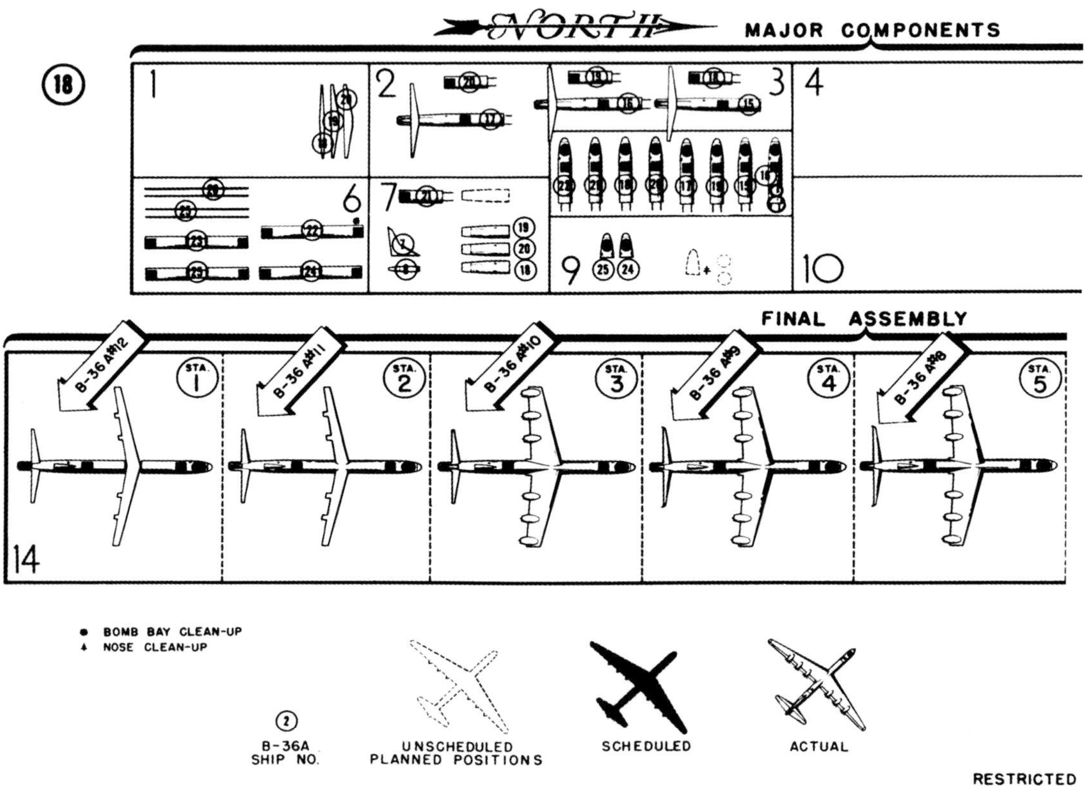

3,500-horsepower R-4360-41 engines were fitted in place of the original -25s.

Although no direct confirmation has been discovered, this undoubtedly required the same wing modifications made to the XC-99 since the first three wings had been built to the same engineering schedule. The aircraft first flew in this configuration in June 1948, and Convair made thirty-six test flights that accumulated ninety-seven and a half hours of flight time.

The B-36 assembly line would extend the entire length of the main building at Fort Worth, and it would be subdivided into three divisions: Major Components, Major Mating, and Final Assembly. Major Components was the trove of parts for the aircraft and took up roughly one-third of the south end of the building.

The Major Mating division was where the wing centre sections came together with the fuselage bomb bay section. The entire structure was cradled in a carriage so that it could be moved from the first to the second mating station. Other sub-assemblies were added in preparation for Final Assembly.

Final Assembly was divided into eleven separate aircraft position stations. As the machines progressed up the final assembly line, the landing gear, leading and trailing edges, internal systems, and six engine nacelles were installed in each airframe. Simultaneously, the adjacent engine-mount build-up assembly line was in progress, adding turbosuperchargers, inter-coolers, electrical systems, ducts and shrouding, fuel and oil fire extinguisher systems, and other equipment to the engine mount. When completed, the engine was mated to the engine mount and the cowl structure.

Engines would then be placed in the nacelles. Each Wasp Major R4360, shipped from Pratt & Whitney, was uncrated and suspended on a six-position overhead rack fixture for engine build-up at a convenient height for crews to work.

The reliability of the R-4360 was unproven, and Pratt & Whitney kept a crew of personnel at Fort Worth, giving certain flight test machines the sort of attention that came to be called the white glove treatment. The engine contractor had a big investment in the future of the B-36 programme, so due to the complexity of the engine, Pratt & Whitney wanted to be on hand to assist Convair and Air Force personnel

Major Components, Major Mating and Final Assembly. (Convair/General Dynamics)

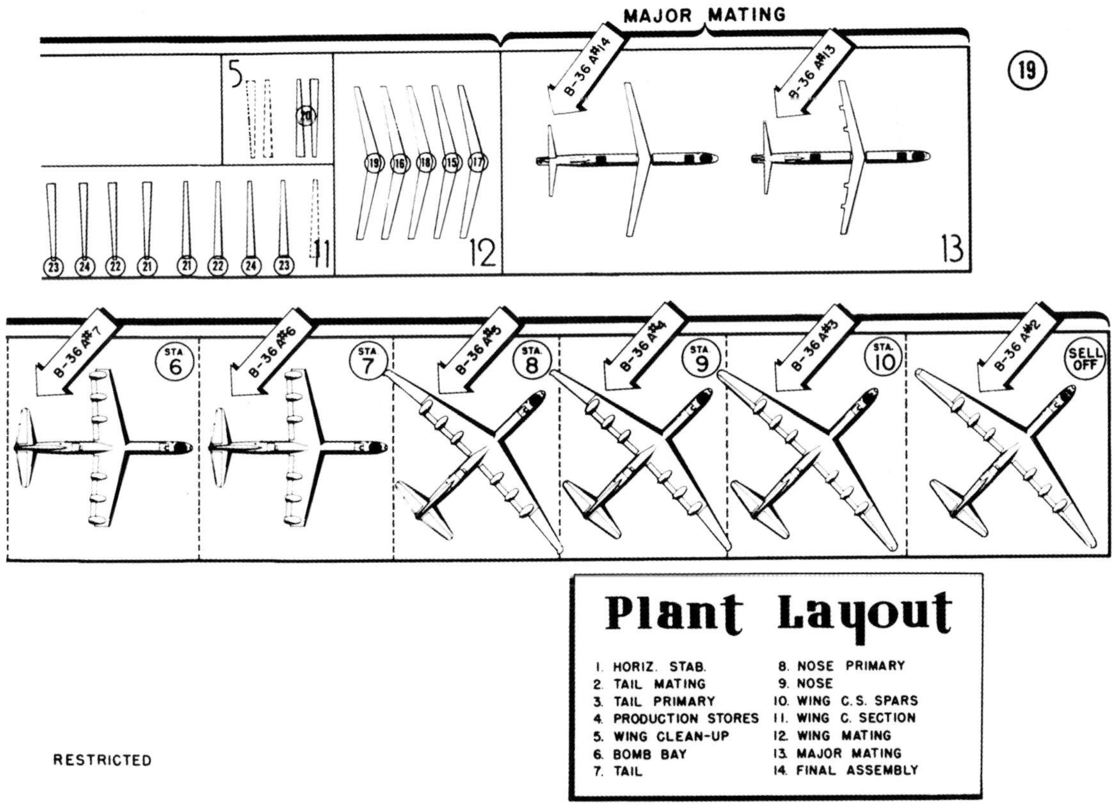

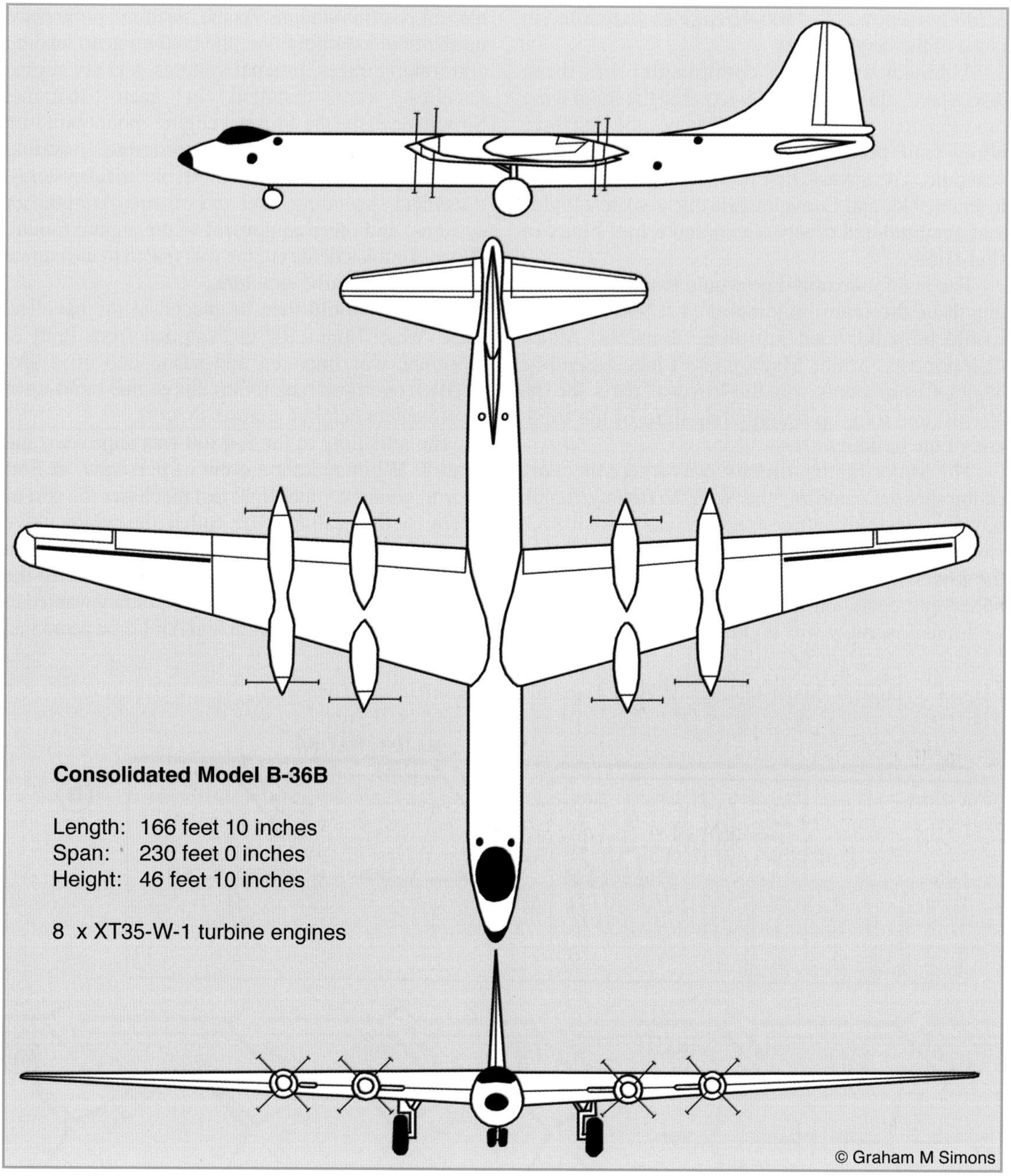

An early study for the production B-36B design. In place of six Pratt & Whitney R-4360 Wasp Major pusher engines, it would instead have used eight XT35-W-1 Curtiss-Wright gas turbines under development at the time. The turbines would have been placed in four tandem nacelles. The top speed would supposedly be 448 mph at 20,000 feet. Convair offered in February 1947 to install the gas turbines on one B-36 test plane. The installation would have cost less than $1.5 million and was to be finished by April 1948.

to learn every facet of its operation and to see that it would obtain the proper high-altitude performance. The crew from Pratt & Whitney monitored the flight testing programme throughout 1947 and 1948, developing procedural systems for proper maintenance and operation.

When the fuselage/wing assembly reached the eighth position in the Final Assembly, it was time for the installation of the outer wing panels. This required some amazing industrial gymnastics to set the B-36 at a diagonal angle so as to provide sufficient clearance in the 200-foot bay for the bomber's 230-foot wingspan. The colossal machine then moved down the remainder of the final assembly line on castored dollies. As it approached the north end of the building, the pilot's canopy, instrumentation and control surfaces were added, along with Government Furnished Equipment such as turrets, communication gear, navigational equipment, and propellers.

Finally, Air Force insignia and identification markings were applied. They were spray-painted on the aircraft by means of templates on the B-36A and B-36B models, although it has been recorded that decals were used on later models.

At the eleventh and final station, the B-36s were rolled out of the factory and moved to the Field Operations area in the north yard for clean-up and final inspection. After flight testing by Convair and military pilots, the B-36 was ready for delivery to the Air Force.

The tremendous size of the B-36 was responsible for production line problems, which grew as the programme unfolded. A major problem was when Convair tried to make the integral fuel tanks fuel-tight. Every connection, seal and joint in every tank needed a high degree of craftsmanship. Fuel leaks would plague the B-36 programme for over three years, but design refinements and technique improvements gradually brought the problem under control with the advent of Proseal, a rubber sealant developed by Convair in conjunction with the Coast Paint & Chemical Company of Los Angeles. Designed specifically for the B-36, Proseal was used to completely coat the entire inner surface of all six fuel tanks.

Another problem was the bonding of magnesium panels, primarily in secondary structures, such as wing trailing edges. Ensuring adequate quality in all bonds was gradually achieved through unique fabrication and inspection techniques. In certain areas, extensive use was made of Metlbond, a metal adhesive developed by Convair. It was of value, especially in those areas of light structure subject to vibration areas where conventional frameworks tended to concentrate the stresses at the rivet joints.

One of the most difficult problems that faced the B-36 production line was the problem of incorporating changes designed to fix other problems! At one point, nearly a dozen early B-36s filled the Field Operations area undergoing such modifications as strengthening of the wing flaps and adjustment of the flap synchronisation mechanism. The wing flaps were electrically driven, and the control mechanism - which had to prevent flaps from coming down on one side only in case of electrical malfunction - was rather complex, and it required precise setting.

Many hours of thinking went into the design and procurement of new equipment for machining, joining and installing. Various components were so large that Convair's subcontractors were unaccustomed to handling them. For example, early B-36 landing gear main struts had to be forged at the US Naval Gun Factory - the only place with a forging mill large enough and capable of the job!

What's in a name?

Officially, the B-36 never had a name, but it was not for lack of trying on Convair's part. In the 8 December 1948 issue of the employee newspaper Corvairiety, a contest was announced for all Convair employees to name the new bomber. 'Needed is a name appropriate to their size and purpose - a name which will be in keeping with the fine, historic traditions of Convair's fighting ships in days gone by, the Liberators, Catalinas, Coronados, and Vengeance

Those within Convair who 'needed to know' of the progress of the B-36 ,were kept informed by a monthly 'Restricted' Status and Progress Report (Convair/General Dynamics)

Many of the archive photographs used in this book have the original Consolidated-Vultee plates glued to them. The picture above shows aircraft number two undergoing assembly.

Left: an R-4360-41 is hung on the YB-36. (both Convair/General Dynamics)

dive bombers.' There were to be few restrictions: 'The name should be one word and should not be a 'made-up' combination. Duplication or possible confusion with other Army or Navy aircraft names should be avoided. Preference will be given to names which relate to the size, weight, power, range, purpose, and mission of the B-36.'

As 1948 came to a close, Convair established 28 February 1949 as the deadline for submitting names. A more complete set of rules was published, the most significant being that an employee could only submit one name between 5 January and 28 February 1949. The judging committee was also named - Major General Roger M Ramey, commander of the Eighth Air Force; Amon Carter, publisher of the Fort Worth Star-Telegram; and LaMotte T Cohu, president and general manager of Convair. The winner would receive a certificate, a $50 cash prize, and would '... also feature prominently in publicity attending the naming of the aircraft.' In addition, the employees from Fort Worth who submitted the top five names would be eligible for a ride in a B-36; employees from other locations were not included due to the logistics involved.

The rules also explained that the selected name would not become official until approved by the Air Force Munitions Board Aircraft Committee, which could at its sole discretion, chose any other name if desired. In an effort to be as fair as possible, Convair stated, 'If some name submitted by a Convair employee other than the winner of the contest is subsequently selected by the Munitions Board, the employee who submitted the name so chosen will also be awarded a $50 prize.' Of the 624 submissions from Fort Worth, forty-nine of them were for the name 'Peacemaker,' followed by 'Peacebinder,' 'Peace Eagle,' 'Peacekeeper,' and 'Peacemaster.' At San Diego, 11 of the 173 submissions were for 'Peacemaker.' Not surprisingly, many Fort Worth entries had a Texas theme - 'Longhorn', 'Texas', and 'Texan' being the most popular. SARG, an acronym for 'Size, Altitude, Range, and Guardian' was entered

The end of the production line. The aircraft visible - BM-025 is 4492025, the last of the B-36As built. The last few assembly stations saw the machine skewed around so as to be able to fit the outer wing panels, thus enabling a 230 foot wingspan machine to be built in a 200-foot wide space. (Convair/General Dynamics)

by R Mathis of Fort Worth. Employees at San Diego favoured 'Condor' and 'Crusader' after Peacemaker. One entry that would live long, even after it was not selected, was 'The Big Stick,' described as 'fitting the shape of the B-36 and standing for Teddy Roosevelt's words: 'Talk softly and Carry a Big Stick, you'll get far!'

It had been hoped that the winner would be named by the end of March, but the 30 March 1949 edition of Convairiety contained the note: 'Judges in the B-36 naming contest were having troubles this week, for there was no official word forthcoming as to the winners. They hoped, however, that some decision will have been reached and the names cleared for copyright before the next issue ....'

Finally, on 13 April 1949, Convairiety announced that 'Peacemaker' had been chosen by the judges and would be forwarded to the Air Force Munitions Board Aircraft Committee for approval.

According to early American history the word Peacemaker was most frequently applied to a Colt 0.45-calibre revolver often used to settle disputes in the old west. More than one entrant in the Convair contest explained that in 1949 the B-36 occupied much the same position as the famous gun and could become the world's greatest peace maker.

An entry drawing was held on 14 April between the sixty submissions to establish the $50 prize. Ray O Ryan, division manager, drew the name of G Bohn, a Fort Worth tool and diemaker. Four other names were also drawn - L McDaniel, L R Harris, G E McKenzie, and C W Cannon - to accompany Bohn on a one-hour flight in a B-36B on 15 July 1949. All sixty entrants who submitted 'Peacemaker' received

Earlier in the production assembly process, B-36s proceed straight down the line. (Convair/General Dynamics)

42-13571, the YB-36, is seen here in its original configuration with 110-inch main landing gear. By the time this picture was taken, it had been fitted with nose and tail turrets. (Convair)

certificates signed by Ramey, Carter, and Cohu. The certificates read, 'Since the ultimate purpose of the B-36 aircraft is to secure and maintain peace throughout the world, we, the undersigned judges of the contest, have unanimously selected 'Peacemaker' from more than six hundred suggestions, and have respectfully recommended that the U.S. Air Force adopt the name as official for the B-36.'

Unfortunately, objections to the name were raised by various religious groups, and the USAF deferred making any official decision. In the end, the B-36 came and went without ever being assigned an official name, although 'Peacemaker' is most often attributed to the aircraft.

Testing to Destruction.

The third B-36, and the first B-36A, carried the serial number 44-92004 and was completed in July 1947. Given the Air Force buzz number BM-004, it was the first B-36 equipped with the new four-wheel main landing gear. It was also the second B-36 to fly, edging out the YB-36 by more than three months. Ironically, it was built not for flight but for 'static and dynamic testing.'

The decision to have a structural test airframe had been made in mid-1946, after a convincing argument by General Nathan F. Twining: 'Experience has shown that we would have been unable to use our bombers efficiently had we not had this policy in effect in the past. The B-17, originally designed for a gross weight of 37,000 pounds, fought the war, flying universally at 64,000 pounds. This could never have been done without accurate knowledge of the strength of the component parts.' This policy continued on most aircraft in the USAF inventory until the 1980s when sufficient faith in computer modelling was finally gained.

The serial number, 44-92004, indicated that it - like all of the first one hundred B-36s - was part of an order placed in 1944. It carried a tail number of 492004. Beryl Erickson took the B-36A up on its first flight on 28 August, and two days later, it was ferried to Wright Field. It had been built with only the equipment necessary for the one flight. Its function was to sit in a Wright Field hangar being stretched to death to demonstrate B-36 structural integrity. Flying it to Ohio under its own power was more practical than shipping the huge components in disassembled form by rail or truck. The delivery flight of BM-004 was made by an AAF flight crew on 30 August 1947, in 4 hours and 40 minutes.

Lt Colonel T P Gerrity of AMC was the pilot; Beryl Erickson accompanied the aircraft as an observer. BM-004's flying career amounted to only seven hours and thirty-six minutes; it would never fly again after the structural integrity tests.

I think I should explain the apparent confusion about the names and location of two world-famous airfields and test centres - of course, I am talking about what is usually called 'Wright-Patterson Air Force Base' just outside Dayton Ohio.

Some sources relating to the B-36 state 'Wright-Patterson AFB, others say 'Wright Field.' Whilst it is true that today, both locations come under the same administrative grouping, they are, in fact, geographically five miles apart, with civilian land separating them.

The two locations include both Wright and Patterson Fields, which were originally Wilbur Wright Field and Fairfield Aviation General Supply Depot. Patterson Field is approximately ten miles northeast of Dayton; Wright Field is approximately five miles northeast of the same city.

Wright Field was formally dedicated on 12 October 1927 when the Materiel Division moved from McCook Field to the new site. Orville Wright

Left: 44-92005 ‘BM-005’ is in the centre of the picture - cloest to the camera is BM-004, the B-36 that was tested to destruction.

Below:B-36A-1-CF, 44-92004 the third aircraft built, seen on one of the two flights it ever made. The B-36 design needed a structural test aircraft that could be tested to destruction - and no-one could work out a way to get one to Wright-Patterson in Ohio for testing. Given the size, the best method appeared to be to fly one - which is exactly what happened

Bottom: the arrival at Wright Field Ohio. (All Convair/General Dynamics)

Once at Wright Field, the aircraft started down the road to destruction. In the colour picture above, the tail surfaces, propellers, engines and cockpit area were removed along with much of the internal equipment. BM-004 was then flipped over by overhead crane onto its back partway through testing so that loads could be applied to the bottom of the wings.

Just how big the task was can be gained from the picture above, where the stripped out airframe is just over vertical. The size of everything can be judged by the nine people standing in the open doorway in the centre of the picture. (All Convair/General Dynamics)

raising the flag over the new engineering centre.

On 1 July 1931, the portion of Wright Field east of Huffman Dam - known today as Areas A and C of Wright-Patterson Air Force Base which included the Fairfield Air Depot and the Huffman Prairie Flying Field - was redesignated Patterson Field in honor of Lieutenant Frank Stuart Patterson. He was the son of Frank J Patterson, co-founder of National Cash Register that was headquartered in Dayton. 1st Lt Patterson was killed shortly before the end of World War One when his aircraft crashed at Wright Field and he and observer 2nd Lt LeRoy Swan were killed in their de Havilland DH.4.

The area's World War Two Army Air Fields saw employment increase from 3,700 in December 1939 to over 50,000 at the war's peak. Wright Field grew from approximately thirty buildings to a 2,064-acre facility with some three hundred buildings and the Air Corps' first modern paved runways. The original field became saturated with office and laboratory buildings and test facilities. The Hilltop area was acquired from private landowners in 1943-1944 to provide troop housing and services.

The portion of Patterson Field from Huffman Dam to the Brick Quarters - including the Command Headquarters - at the south end of Patterson Field along Route 4 was administratively reassigned from Patterson Field to Wright Field. To avoid confusing the two areas of Wright Field, the south end of the former Patterson Field portion was designated 'Area A', the original Wright Field became 'Area B', and the north end of Patterson Field, including the flying field, 'Area C.'

When BM-004 reached Wight-Patterson - actually Area B (Wright Field) the engines and excess equipment were removed, and it was parked in a huge, specially-built structure known as Building 65, Static Structural Test Laboratory, located between Eleventh & Twelfth Streets in Area B that was nearly eight stories high. Ten surplus landing gear units, linked together as a hydraulic chain, pulled the forty-five-ton machine sideways into the building on castored dollies.

An inside overhead crane, on rails the length of the building, lifted the airframe into a cradle-like fixture where the testing would be performed.

In the process of the forty-five different static load tests, BM-004 was ultimately reduced to scrap. The control system was subjected to different loads on the ailerons, elevators and rudder. The pressurized cabins were tested for air-tightness and later punctured. Rubber-to-metal adhesive was used to attach tension patches and pressure pads so the rupture and breaking points could more accurately be determined.

B-36 sub assemblies.

Top: a nose-section comes together.

Above: Front and rear section connecting tubes await insertion.

Below: The pressurised rear section ready for assembly to the rest of the fuselage. (Convair)

The B-36 turbine design proposal, in both artwork and model form. The turbine itself was situated towards the rear of the nacelle, with the propeller being driven via reduction gearbox and a long shaft. (Convair)

B-36A

The B-36A was similar to the YB-36, including the 3,000 horsepower R-4360-25 Wasp Major engines. The four bomb bays could accommodate 72,000 pounds of conventional bombs, but no provisions existed for carrying atomic weapons. The maximum takeoff weight was 310,380 pounds, due mainly to structural limitations of the landing gear.

With 24,121 gallons of fuel and a 10,000-pound bomb load, the B-36A had a radius of action of 3,880 miles. The reduction in fuel required to carry the maximum 72,000 pounds of bombs resulted in a radius of only 2,100 miles. With full fuel and no weapons, the aircraft could be ferried 9,136 miles. Performance was listed as 345 mph at 31,600 feet, with 10,000 pounds of bombs and a service ceiling of 29,100 feet.

Fuel was carried in up to eight tanks. Six of these were permanently installed in the wings and were labelled No. 1 on the outboard left to No. 6 on the outboard right. These tanks were formed by sealed compartments between the front and rear wing spars inboard of each engine nacelle. The tanks could be accessed through hatches in the front spar behind hinged leading edge panels. Tanks Nos. 1 and 6 had a capacity of 2,330 gallons, but only 2,248 gallons were usable. Tanks Nos. 2 and 5 could hold 4,206 gallons with 4,073 usable, while the inboard tanks had a capacity of 4,338 gallons with 4,205.5 usable.

Total internal fuel was therefore 21,053 gallons. In addition, bomb bays No. 2 and 3 could each carry a 3,000-gallon fuel cell, expanding capacity to 27,045 gallons. Since aerial refuelling had not yet been perfected, the B-36 was not equipped for it.

In February 1949, the first Farrand hemisphere nose sight and its associated turret were installed in the YB-36 for testing. Around the same time, an AN/APG-3 tail radar and its associated turret were also installed for testing. Reports indicate that at least two of the aft sighting stations were installed but without turrets and were used simply to evaluate the sighting equipment.

The XB-36 first flew with the 3,000 hp Pratt & Whitney R4360-25 Wasp Major piston engine, and when the B-36A was ordered into production, the engine selected for it was the Pratt & Whitney R-4360-25 Wasp Major. However, the improved version of the same engine, the 3,500 hp R-4360-41, was scheduled for the last seventy-eight aircraft of the original contract. In March 1947, a still more powerful version of the R-4360 engine was proposed. It promised to deliver 4,300 hp by virtue of being fitted with the Variable Discharge Turbine (VDT). The story of the attempts to adapt the Wasp Major VDT to the B-36 is one of the most frustrating in the history of the big bomber.

The Air Force proposed the VDT engine for the Boeing B-50 and placed it into development. Convair knew this, and with support from Pratt & Whitney, proposed the VDT engine for a new B-36 model that would be designated as B-36C. Convair and Pratt & Whitney estimated that with the new VDT engine, the B-36 could have a top speed of 410 mph, a service ceiling of 45,000 feet, and a 10,000-mile range carrying a 10,000-pound bomb load.

However, to accommodate the VDT engine in the B-36, changing the propeller/engine configuration from the pusher type to the tractor type would be necessary. Although the engine would remain aft of the wing spar, its position would have to be reversed to face forward. As a result, the propeller shaft would have to extend through the entire wing and then another ten feet ahead of the wing's leading edge. Such an arrangement would present a complex engineering challenge.

In the VDT itself, exhaust gases from the engine would pass through a General Electric CHM-2 turbosupercharger with a clamshell nozzle that created jet thrust by varying the size of the turbine exit. The variable discharge nozzle was to be operated by automatic control, activated by a manifold pressure sensing device. Cooling air would be ducted through wing leading edge inlets flanking the nacelle extension. It was a cumbersome and complex design change to say the least.

The proposal to develop the new VDT engine for the B-36 was first presented by Air Materiel Command officers at a conference in Washington on 25 March 1947. Various delegates opposed the suggestion because research and development funds were too limited to be spent on the modernisation of existing weapons systems, which they felt should be

The B-36 assembly line in full swing during the winter of 1948, building B-models. It is worth noting here that the fuselage skin extends through the area that will be covered by the wing after each aircraft was fully assembled. (Convair)

reserved for developing future weapons, such as the Boeing XB-52 and the new jet-powered medium bombers, such as the North American B-45, the Boeing B-47 and Convair's own B-46.

On 6 May 1947, another conference was held in the office of General Curtis LeMay, the future head of the Strategic Air Command, who was then the Director of Research and Development. Again the agenda included the proposed VDT engine retrofit and installation. Air Materiel Command representatives provided additional data to support the recommendation made at the 25 March meeting. It was suggested that the cost of adapting the VDT engine to the B-36 could be met primarily out of procurement funds instead of research development funds, and this scheme removed the main objection to the proposal. The final rationale determined that the cost of the engine development itself could be charged appropriately against procurement funds since the VDT engine was merely an improvement of the currently procured R-4360 engine.

In later conversations with personnel from the Air Materiel Command, Convair went so far as to propose to finance the cost of the airframe modifications for one prototype B-36 with the VDT engine by reducing the contract by three machines.

With the cost now charged against procurement funds, General Spaatz, Chief of Staff approved the VDT engine's decision in one prototype B-36 and one prototype of the B-50C or B-54.

Convair suggested building an additional quantity of B-36s with the VDT engine under a new contract and the designation B36C. However, in August 1947, the Air Force's new Aircraft & Weapons Board rejected this proposal.

Once it had been decided that the B-36 was unsuitable as a workhorse bomber, even with the VDT engine, and would be used only as a special purpose bomber, there was no longer a military requirement for more than 100 of these aircraft. After all, there were not enough nuclear weapons envisioned in 1947 to necessitate more than one hundred B-36s.

Convair's proposal to increase the B-36 contract by building additional aircraft with VDT engines brought forward many interrelated issues that were not directly connected to the new engine. As a result,

Top: B-36A City of Fort Worth, 44-92015, conducts an engine power check.

Above: mechanics working on B-36s faced the intense Texas heat. Temperatures could reach 130 degrees Fahrenheit inside the aircraft.

The forty-six-foot nine-inch height of the vertical tail of the B-36 could cause problems for maintenance crews. Working four stories from ground level took skill, courage and assistance from a seat attached to a crane. (All Convair)

Above: it took a lot of fuel to fill the tanks of a B-36 - in this case BM-006! It appears that this aircraft is undergoing tank sealing, since the wing leading edges have been removed and the tank access hatches are open.

Right: B-36B 44-92057 comes together at Fort Worth. The magnesium panels on the fuselage and turret cover doors show up dark in this picture. Later they would be painted, and show up in many images as a matt finish, compared to the polished aluminium. (Both Convair)

rough days lay ahead for Convair and for supporters of the B-36 programme within the USAF.

In August 1947, when the USAF Aircraft & Weapons Board decided to cancel the one Variable Discharge Turbine powered B-36C, no B-36s beyond the first one hundred were required. This decision settled the question of a new contract, but it did not remove the funding uncertainties to complete the old contract.

Convair returned to the subject within a few weeks and submitted a proposal to install VDT engines in the last thirty-four aircraft of the 100-aircraft B-36A contract.

Meanwhile, the YB-36 was turned over to the Air Force on 31 May 1949 where it was subsequently used essentially as another B-36A.

Later, the YB-36 was returned to Fort Worth in October 1950 to be remanufactured into an RB-36E in place of the first B-36A (YB-36A) that had been tested to destruction at Wright Field.

Interestingly, this aircraft was frequently the first B-36 to go through most of the modifications programmes, such as SAM-SAC Cycle One and Cycle Two. The Air Force would add 1,952.5 flight hours to the airframe before it was retired in early 1957. The aircraft was turned over to the Air Force Museum at Wright-Patterson AFB, but it was declared surplus and scrapped when the new museum facility was built. Ralph Huffman acquired parts of the aircraft for $760. Huffman subsequently sold the remains to Walter Soplata, who kept the fuselage on his farm in Newbury, Ohio.

Project SAM-SAC - an acronym that stood for 'Specialized Aircraft Maintenance-Strategic Air Command' - came out of an announcement in June 1953 from Convair when it announced that it would be initiating 'an unprecedented program of prime importance to the entire aircraft industry - a continuing maintenance and modernisation program which eventually will encompass all B-36 aircraft.'

SAM-SAC intended to standardise the B-36 fleet around a set number of standard configurations, allowing parts to be interchanged more efficiently and for maintenance procedures to be standardised. The programme meant that around twenty-five B-36s would be undergoing heavy maintenance at Fort Worth constantly through 1957.

August C Esenwein, vice president and Fort Worth division manager, announced that 'SAM-SAC is the first contract to be awarded in keeping with the Air Force's new maintenance concept of returning a product to the manufacturer for maintenance and modernisation. That concept is based on the theory that it is more economical for the manufacturer to overhaul the airplane ...'

SAM-SAC itself was an outgrowth of Project WORTHMORE. At Convair, K A Day was the modernisation manager in charge of both WORTHMORE and SAM-SAC. He explained, 'SAM-SAC will be the accomplishment of cyclic maintenance and modernisation work to be completed in three cycles.' Bringing the aircraft through three times was meant to provide maintenance in a timely manner without keeping the aircraft out of service for a long time. The first cycle was essentially the same as the normal depot-level overhaul accomplished on most aircraft by the San Antonio Air Materiel Area (SAAMA).

Cycle One included a DIR - Depot Inspection and Repair - of the control surfaces, leading and trailing edges of the wings, outer wing panels, empennage, and engine nacelles. To accomplish this, all of the control surfaces and the engines were removed from the aircraft during the receiving inspection. The control surfaces were thoroughly washed, repainted, and balanced before being reinstalled. The turrets and fire-control systems were also removed and shipped to General Electric for modifications and refurbishment. The 20-mm cannon were refurbished locally by Convair. The refurbished turrets were mounted in test stands for functional tests, then reinstalled, bore-sighted, and harmonised.

The rest of the airframe received a full inspection, and outstanding TCTOS - Time Compliance Technical OrderS - were incorporated. In addition, the nacelles were reworked to allow engines to be installed in any position and to be interchanged between aircraft and positions without excessive rework. This was in support of the Quick Engine Change (QEC) programme that involved building an engine and accessories into a power package that could be installed quickly in the field. Applied to other aircraft, the QEC programme for B-36s ran from 1953 until 27 August 1957. At any given time, between fifty and one hundred QEC engines were available for use by SAC.

Cycle Two included a DIR of the centre wing section, fuel tanks, bomb bays, and a major inspection of the rest of the aircraft and any outstanding TCTOS incorporated. The landing gear was also overhauled, including installing new lynchpins that raised the maximum allowable gross weight of all aircraft except the J-models to 370,000 pounds. The aircraft was also repainted as necessary. Convair created twenty-three work areas at the outset of the programme, expanding it to twenty-nine after all the maintenance docks arrived from San Diego. At the peak of SAM-SAC, Convair had 5,800 employees dedicated to SAM-SAC.

Convair developed a concept where a B-36 could transport four spare engines during deployments. Each 'pod' was essentially two complete engines, and their accessories with their nacelles in place mounted front-to-front.

The tapered end at the front and rear were covers where the propellers would normally have gone. An aerodynamic beam ran between the pods and attached to the standard bomb racks in bomb bay No. 1. This concept only worked with the original sliding bomb bay doors - the later snap-action doors interfered with the attachment mechanism - and was never used operationally.

The four pictures here show at least two aircraft carrying spare engines in their transport pods. The head-on shot on the opposite page shows an aircraft with '55' on its nose. This is the Convair Assembly Line number, which translates into serial 44-92058, a B-36B-10-CF. The aircraft in the bottom left picture and above is BM-026, with Convair '23' on the nose, which is 44-92026 a B-36B-1-CF.

The two airborne shots below do not have any visible markings, but do clearly show the aerodynamic beam with the bomb-bay doors at least part-way open. As far as is known, the transport pods were not used operationally. The aircraft is thought to be 44-92026. (all Convair via Matt Black Collection)

The first aircraft to enter the SAM-SAC programme was an RB-36E, 42-13571, during early June 1953. This presented a dilemma for the workers at Fort Worth, for it was standard practice when a B-36 was at Convair to paint its assembly line number on the nose and aft fuselage to help workers more readily identify it for most of the company documentation used the assembly number, not the serial number. However, since this aircraft had begun life as the YB-36, and did not have an assembly number since it was not part of the production programme. The answer was to paint 'YB' on the nose and fuselage where the assembly number normally went. The work on the YB was completed by the end of July, and the aircraft was redelivered to the Air Force on 4 August 1953. By September 1954, 215 B-36s had been processed through Cycle One. The YB was also the first to arrive for Cycle Two of SAM-SAC, redelivered to the Air Force for the fourth time on 14 July 1955.

Part of SAM-SAC included resealing the wing fuel tanks, something that had always been somewhat of a problem on the B-36, although revised sealants and techniques had greatly reduced problems in later years. Previously, the job of removing the old sealant in preparation to reseal the tanks had been largely a manual job. During the early 1950s, it had not been unusual for an aircraft to be grounded for up to twelve weeks while its fuel tanks were being resealed.

For SAM-SAC, Convair devised a new technique. First, the wing leading edges were removed to give access to the fuel tanks. Then the nose of the aircraft was raised three feet. A chemical stripper was then sprayed through 1,140 nozzles inserted into the fuel tanks. These fan-shaped nozzles sprayed 2,280 gallons per minute of the stripper that was maintained at a constant temperature via a

refrigeration unit and heat exchanger. The dissolved material was strained and stored in a waste-water tank at the site for later disposal. After removing the old sealants, the tanks were thoroughly cleaned, and new sealant was applied. As each aircraft was delivered to Convair, the amount of fuel in the tanks was carefully measured before it was removed. When the aircraft was returned to the Air Force, exactly the same amount of fuel was filled into the tanks.

Surprisingly, given the nature and duration of B-36 flight operations at Convair, there were only two fatalities. Both occurred during a SAM-SAC test flight on 6 February 1956 when a flash fire erupted in the aft compartment of a B-36 on a test flight. The two scanners in the compartment, J E Cunningham and Fred Verrips, elected to bail out after the smoke became too thick. Unfortunately, neither man had time to pull the ripcord on his parachute before hitting the ground.

SAM-SAC used 137 acres at the Fort Worth plant with thirty-eight maintenance docks to process an average of thirteen aircraft per month. The average turn-around time for an aircraft was fifty-nine days.

On the B-36A, the physical size of the control surfaces - ailerons, elevators, and rudders - on the B-36 essentially prohibited manual control, but the final design did not use powered surfaces. Instead, when the pilot moved a control servo, tabs in the floating main surfaces moved up or down in a direction opposite of what the pilot commanded. An upward movement of the servo tab produced a downward movement of the main surface due to the air load on the displaced tab. Likewise, a down tab movement caused the main surface to move up. Control column or rudder pedal movement was only transferred to the flying servo tabs; however, the actuating mechanism was interconnected to the main surfaces through a double-acting spring to provide control feedback to the pilot. The flying servo tabs produced a small damping effect on the main surfaces in gusty conditions, creating a stability augmentation system.

Each of the four bomb bays was covered with sliding doors reminiscent of the B-24. The structurally rigid doors were mounted on rollers and moved in tracks around the fuselage contour. All of the doors were operated by electric motors through a cable arrangement. The doors on bomb bays No. 1 and No. 4 were single-piece units that slid up the left side of the fuselage. The two middle bomb bays had doors split down the centreline that slid up both sides of the fuselage - the location of the wing centre-section prevented using a single-piece design. Testing revealed that the doors were slow to operate, tended to stick in the frigid temperatures at 40,000 feet, and significantly increased drag when open.

A better solution would have to be found, but all A- and B-models would use these doors.

Thirty-six removable bomb racks of fifteen different types were provided with each aircraft. The racks and associated equipment were designed to accommodate conventional bombs weighing 500, 1,000, 1,600, 2,000, 4,000, 12,000, 22,000, or 43,000 pounds. In addition, bombs weighing 100, 115, 125,

Above: A brand new B-36B-10-CF, 44-92056 at Convair's Fort Worth facility. The '53' on the nose is its Convair manufacturing number and would be reapplied every time the aircraft visited the factory. It is worth noting that the forward turret does not have its 20-mm cannon installed.

Right: The early B-36s, plus all RB-36s, used a Norden M-9 bombsight in the extreme nose. The B-36D and later models used the newly-developed Farrand Y-3 periscopic bombsight that looked out the bottom of the fuselage instead of through the glazed nose. ———(Both Convair)

Getting B-36s out of the main Convair plant at Fort Worth involved 'raising the nose to lower the tail' on custom-built equipment.

Here are two views of of B-36B-5-CF 44-92043 being 'extracted' from the north end of Building 4. The nosewheel is about twelve feet off the concrete! (Both Convair)

250, 325, or 350-pounds could be carried at the 500-pound stations. When the three largest bomb sizes were carried, it was necessary to combine two adjacent bomb bays.

The lower portion of the bomb bay No. 1 aft bulkhead and the bomb bay No. 2 forward bulkhead (called bulkhead 6.0) incorporated a portion of the bomb bay door tracks and could be swung to the side of the fuselage when the 12,000, 22,000, or 43,000-pound bombs were being loaded and released. The same was true for the bulkhead (8.0) between bomb bays Nos. 3 and 4, although due to the 72,000-pound load limitation, only a single 43,000-pound T-12 bomb could be carried by the A-model.

The bulkheads were moved by electric motors and a push-pull rod arrangement - the motors were actuated by the movement of the bomb bay doors. The bombardier had two circuits to open the bomb bay doors - one was used for small bombs - up to 4,000-pounds each; the other for the larger bombs. The latter circuit included the automatic operation of the swinging bulkheads.

The controls allowed the bomb bay doors on No. 2 and No. 3 to be opened independently, but bomb bays No. 1 and No. 4 were slaved to operate as a pair. When the operator selected a bomb size greater than 4,000 pounds, the switch to operate 1 and 4 became inoperative, and the switches normally used to open and close Nos. 2 and 3 operated the combined large bay doors and bulkheads.

The planned AN/APQ-23 had superseded the AN/APG-7 Eagle bombing/navigation system with a radome located beneath the forward fuselage where the lower gun turrets were originally going to be located. However, delays in developing the General Electric defensive armament meant that the B-36As were delivered with incomplete fire control systems installed and without turrets or armament of any type. An incomplete B-1 system was installed on the fifth B-36A, 44-92008, in September 1948 for tests at Convair. Initially, problems with reliability prevented meaningful testing, but the aircraft was used extensively for continued testing.

Finally, one of the turrets managed to fire a twenty-round belt of ammunition without incident in November. Still, for a time, the Air Force debated scrapping the complex remote-control system and returning to manned turrets equipped with 0.50-calibre machine guns.

The crew complement of the B-36A was listed as fifteen, but this included eight gunners who had no guns and functioned mainly as spotters when they flew. The other seven crew members were a pilot, copilot, radar-bombardier, navigator, flight engineer, and two radiomen.

The B-36A suffered from many of the problems usually encountered when a complex new aircraft entered service. The fuel tanks leaked, the new alternating-current electrical system was troublesome, and engine cooling was poor. None of

B-36A-15-CF 44-92022 flies low over Lowry Air Force Base at Denver, Colorado. The spike-shaped feature at the centre of the vertical fin is sometimes seen in photos of B-36s with unpainted verticals and appears to have been skin panels that were of a different sheen than surrounding ones. (Convair)

the problems were insurmountable, and Convair engineers continued to work on solutions, but a great deal of negative press was generated.

Finally, in April 1948, the tide began to turn, and the B-36 demonstrated its potential. On 8-9 April, a B-36A 44-92013 made a thirty-three hour and ten-minute flight covering 6,922 miles, shuttling between Fort Worth and San Diego. Beryl Erickson and Arthur S 'Doc' Witchell, Jr. had remaining fuel for another 206 miles if it had been necessary. The aircraft was flown with ballast to compensate for the lack of defensive armament and carried 10,000 pounds of dummy 500-pound bombs dropped from 25,000 feet over the Air Force Bombing Range at Wilcox, Arizona, fifteen hours into the flight. Unfortunately, problems with two engines limited the average cruising speed to 214 mph.

A month later, on 13-14 May 1948, the same B-36A, again piloted by Erickson and Witchell, conducted a second long-range simulated tactical mission. Captain Wesley D Morris and First Lieutenant Richard Munday from the 7th BW were also on the flight.

The aircraft had a gross weight of 299,619 pounds, including 10,000 pounds of dummy bombs, 5,796 pounds of simulated 20-mm ammunition, and ballast to compensate for the lack of turrets and other equipment not fitted to the B-36As. The flight duration was thirty-six hours and eight minutes, during which 8,062 miles were flown at an average of 223 mph. The aircraft landed with 986 gallons of fuel remaining, which would have extended the mission by 508 miles. This was a typical high-altitude mission, with the first 369 miles flown at 5,000 feet, followed by a power climb to 10,000 feet. This altitude was maintained until thirty minutes before the target when the aircraft climbed to 25,000 feet and commenced a maximum speed bomb run, including seventeen minutes of evasive manoeuvres. The flight home was made at 25,000 feet, the B-36 demonstrating that it was a true intercontinental bomber.

Four days later another flight dropped twenty-five 2,000-pound bombs from 31,000 feet on the Naval Range at Corpus Christi, Texas. This was followed on 30 June 1948 when a B-36A dropped 72,000 pounds of bombs during a test flight, the heaviest bomb load yet carried by any aircraft.

A few weeks later, on 18-19 July 1948, 44-92013, completed a 5,983-mile flight at an average speed of more than 301 mph, making it the first machine to fly that distance at that speed. Gross take-off weight was 310,292 pounds, including full wing tanks plus a 3,555-gallon bomb bay tank, making 144,819 pounds total fuel.

Immediately after take-off, the pilot set normal rated power of 2,550 rpm and climbed to 26,000 feet. The climb took one hour and twenty-three minutes - one minute less than predicted. The flight continued 620 miles at 26,000 feet, then climbed to 30,000 feet. This altitude was achieved at a range of 2,120 miles, approximately seven and a half hours after take-off.

Fifteen minutes before reaching the target, the aircraft accelerated to 'maximum continuous speed' - about 320 mph - for 30 minutes.

Midway through this 'bombing run,' thirty-one dummy 500-pounders making 15,500 pounds of bombs were dropped. Twenty of these represented the design bomb load, while the other 5,500 pounds simulated ammunition that the cannon would have expended if they had been fitted. The target had been located, and the bombs were dropped using the radar bomb/nav system nine hours and forty-nine minutes - or 2,811 miles - after take-off. Five minutes of evasive action were taken immediately after the bomb drop, and then a climb to 32,700 feet was initiated. This altitude was maintained for about an hour; then the aircraft climbed to 34,200 feet, which was maintained for the rest of the flight back to base. The aircraft landed with the required five per cent fuel reserve. The only difficulties noted on the flight were low oil pressure indications at some altitudes and a failed turbo selector for the No. 5 engine.

Defying superstition, on 13 August - a Friday - the 13th B-36A 44-92016 made a successful shakedown flight. The first long-range flight by an all-Air Force crew was on 22 August when the 492nd Bomb Squadron took a B-36A 44-92007 on a 15,500-mile, twenty-six-hour flight that used 14,000 gallons of fuel.

On 12 September, twelve B-36s took part in Air Force Day celebrations around the country, all departing and returning to Fort Worth. Ten aircraft flown by Air Force crews logged a total of 152 hours and 45 minutes on long-distance flights; the other two aircraft were flown by Convair crews around the Fort

The Fort Worth manufacturing plant during the SAM-SAC maintenance era. All B-36s returned to Fort Worth for major maintenance in what was one of the first commercial 'outsourcing' efforts conducted by the Air Force. Instead of having military technicians at the San Antonio Air Materiel Area perform major modifications and maintenance, the Air Force elected to have the manufacturer do it. The first aircraft (RB-36E-5-CF, 42-13571) to participate in SAM-SAC arrived in early June 1953, and the last (B-36J-1-CF, 52-2216) was redelivered to the Air Force on 29 April 1957. (Convair)

Worth area. In early October 1948, Major Stephen P Dillon, chief Air Force pilot for the B-36, commanded a mission from Fort Worth to Muroc AFB carrying four 12,000-pound bombs, although one bomb would not release and had to be carried back to Fort Worth. The mission was flown at 37,000 feet, averaging 330 mph. Things were getting better, but overall performance was not exactly sparkling.

The Air Force accepted its first B-36A in May 1948, and on 18 June the aircraft was delivered to the Air Proving Ground Command at Eglin AFB for climatic testing, which lasted most of the following year. The Air Force had previously accepted the YB-36A in August 1947. Twenty B-36As were delivered during 1948 - one in May, five in June, five in July, four in August, and five in September. The 22nd and last B-36A was accepted in February 1949. The first B-36A, 44-92015, was turned over to SAC as the City of Fort Worth on 26 June 1948, and 19 more B-36As were subsequently delivered to the 7th BW based at Carswell AFB. Since the aircraft carried no defensive armament and were considered somewhat underpowered, they were used primarily for training and further flight testing. In reality, they were down for maintenance as often as not at Convair, and the Air Force worked through various problems. Fortunately, the service life of the B-36A was extremely short, the last one, 44-92017, being remanufactured into an RB-36E by July 1951.

The B-36 presented some unique challenges to maintenance workers, and specialized equipment such as dollies, jacks, and work stands proved to be in short supply. The aircraft was too large to fit in an existing hangar, and the cost of new hangars was prohibitive given the budget constraints at the time. Even ground refuelling, normally a routine process, proved cumbersome. Because of the height of the wing fuel tanks, the ground-based fuel pumps had to work harder than expected, causing them to fail frequently. As a result, new, higher-capacity pumps had to be designed and procured.

Given the location of many B-36 operating locations, including Fort Worth, maintenance work was frequently halted during periods of bad weather. In late 1949 Convair came up with a 'maintenance dock' that covered most of the wing and three engines. A pair of these docks were installed so that all six engines and both main landing gear, along with

To improve outside working conditions, Convair developed all-weather service docks. The complete dock consisted of four sections, each 36 feet in depth that enclosed 60 feet of each wing, including all of the R-4360 engines. A B-36 was towed between the two structures shown in the photo below, with the wing fitting into the slots in the sides of the buildings. A smaller dock covered the nose of the aircraft, shielding the cockpit from the sun and providing shelter for technicians working on the radar and nose turret. (Convair)

other systems mounted in the wing, could be worked on in relative comfort.

The docks included a floor at a convenient level to work on the wing leading and trailing edge, along with a metal front and roof to protect against the elements. In early versions, a canvas back covered the propellers. It provided additional weather protection but was changed to removable aluminium panels that provided better protection against the wind on later docks. Canvas continued to be used around the ends where the wing protruded through. Mobile heating units provided some warmth during the winter months, but the docks were not air-conditioned in the summer - at least their roofs kept workers out of direct sunlight. The docks were equipped with compressed air piping and electrical outlets connected to base support systems, and floodlights were also built in. Each set of docks consisted of four sections, each thirty-six feet in depth and thirty feet long. When in place, the docks enclosed sixty feet of the wing on each side of the aircraft. By the end of 1950, all of the docks had been equipped with carbon dioxide fire-extinguishing systems.

Two types of docks were eventually designed and built. The first was a permanent installation provided at the factory, Kelly AFB, and a few B-36 bases. It required only fifteen minutes for an aircraft to be towed into the dock and set up for maintenance. The second type was a mobile dock that could be moved from aircraft to aircraft. It required about thirty minutes to move a dock and install it around the aircraft to be serviced. These mobile docks were constructed to be disassembled and transported to remote operating locations as needed, but it is unclear if this ever happened. In addition, a nose dock was developed that covered the extreme forward fuselage and canopy area. Interestingly, in photographs of the damage caused by the 1952 tornado at Carswell AFB, it appears as if a great deal of it was the result of the maintenance docks impacting the aircraft.

Eventually, money was found to build some hangars. For instance, at Rapid City AFB, the Air Force constructed a hangar 314 feet long, 369 feet wide and 95 feet tall. The structure covered 3.5 acres, and eighteen miles of radiant heating pipes were buried in the floor to help combat the minus 30 deg F winters in South Dakota. Even as the last B-36 was being produced, the Air Force was completing a larger hangar (building 1050) at Carswell AFB to house them. For $2,750,000, the four-story-high hangar could accommodate four B-36s at a time.

From Technical Orders, comes this diagram of the B-36 Forward Compartment...

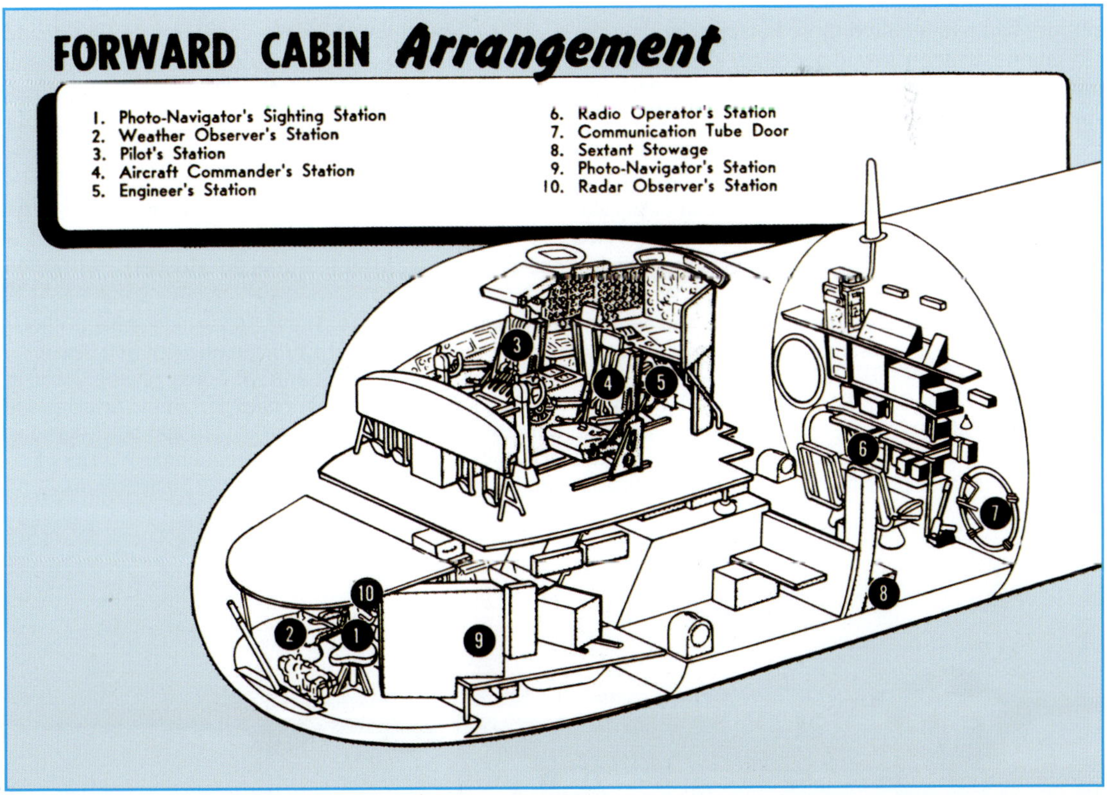

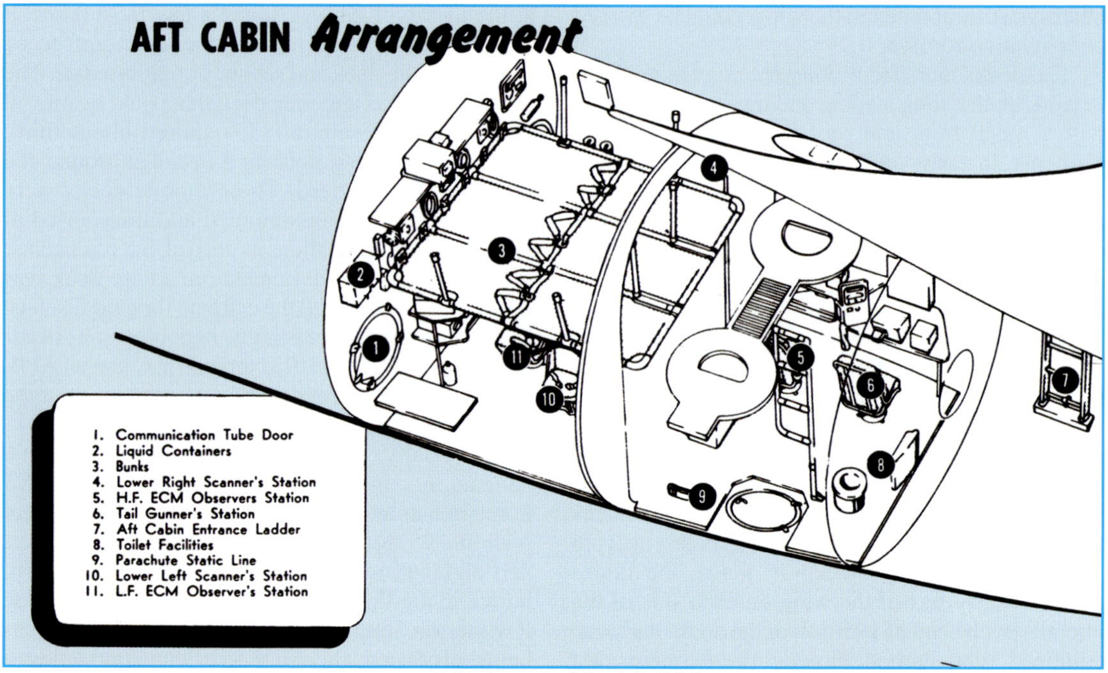

... and the layout of the Aft Cabin.

The B-36B

The B-36B was the first genuinely operational version and used uprated 3,500-horsepower R-4360-41 Wasp Major engines with water injection. These engines had five hundred more horsepower than the -25 engine, which allowed a slightly shorter takeoff distance and yielded a marginally higher cruising speeds and a higher top speed. The first B-36B made its maiden flight on 8 July 1948 with Beryl Erickson at the controls, and subsequent testing showed that its performance was generally better than expected. The top speed was up to 381 mph, and the service ceiling increased to 42,500 feet. An average cruising speed of 300 mph could be maintained at 40,000 feet.

The bomb bay arrangement was similar to the B-36A, but the B-36B could carry up to 86,000 pounds of bombs, a rather significant 14,000-pound increase. This allowed the B-36B to carry two 43,000-pound T-12 bombs, as well as various more conventional munitions. The same sliding-type bomb bay doors used on the B-36As were retained. The last fifty-four aircraft - 44-92045 through to 44-92098 - were to be equipped from the factory to carry the Mk III/IV atomic bomb in bomb bay No. 1, although only forty-nine were modified - the seven aircraft completed as RB-36Ds were not. Eighteen aircraft - 44-92045

The B-36B was the first fully operational and combat-ready model of the B-36. The B-36A included the R-4360-41 Wasp Major engines, increased bomb capacity, improved performance, and a full complement of defensive armaments. Here, B-36B-1-CF 44-92028 of the 7th Bombardment Wing of the Eighth Air Force, photographed at Carswell Air Force Base, Texas, around 1949, displays the wing's emblem on the forward part of the fuselage and bright red paint, for high visibility should the aircraft crash in arctic terrain, on the vertical tail and outer portions of the wings. This red paint was part of the Global Electronics Modification (GEM) programme, a series of modifications to better suit the B-36 and other aircraft for operating and navigating over polar regions.

Section II
Normal Procedures

T.O. 1B-36D(II)-1

CREW *Inspection* . . . . .

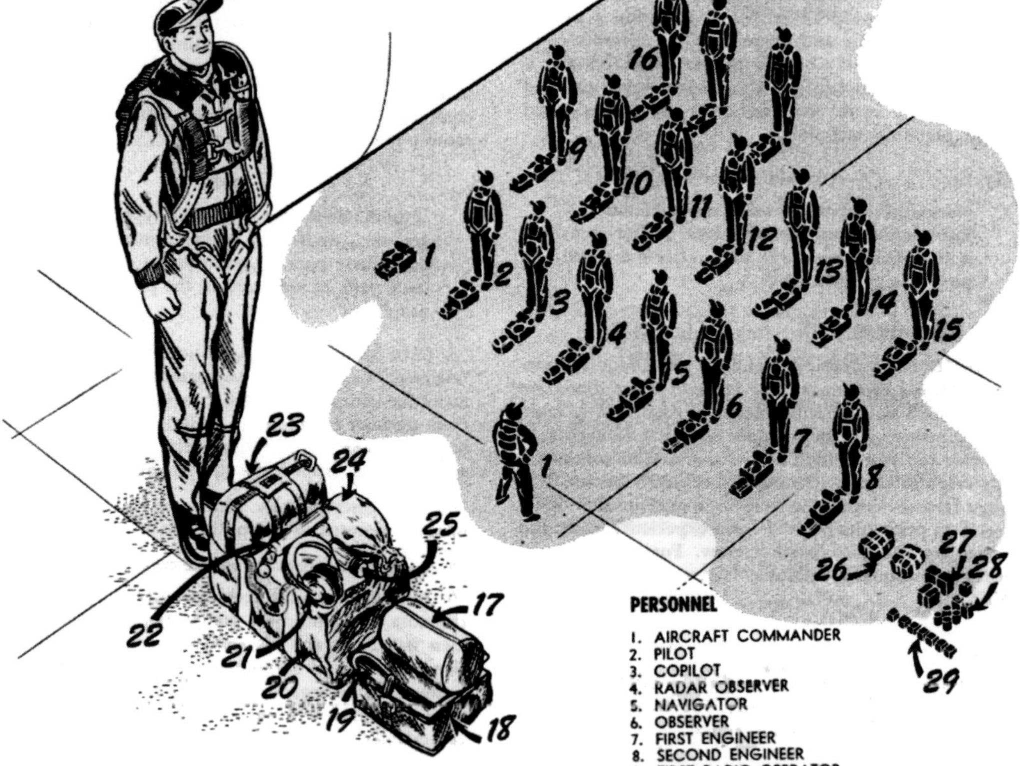

PERSONNEL

1. AIRCRAFT COMMANDER
2. PILOT
3. COPILOT
4. RADAR OBSERVER
5. NAVIGATOR
6. OBSERVER
7. FIRST ENGINEER
8. SECOND ENGINEER
9. FIRST RADIO OPERATOR
10. SECOND RADIO OPERATOR
11. UPPER AFT GUNNER (RIGHT)
12. UPPER AFT GUNNER (LEFT)
13. LOWER AFT GUNNER (RIGHT
14. LOWER AFT GUNNER (LEFT)
15. TAIL GUNNER
16. PASSENGERS

PERSONAL EQUIPMENT

17. ANTI-EXPOSURE SUIT
18. ONE-MAN LIFE RAFT
19. MAE WEST
20. A-3 BAG
21. HEADSET AND MICROPHONE
22. BAIL-OUT BOTTLE
23. CHEST-TYPE PARACHUTE
24. OXYGEN MASK AND HELMET
25. FLASHLIGHT

MISCELLANEOUS EQUIPMENT

26. EXTRA PARACHUTES, OXYGEN MASKS, AND BAIL-OUT BOTTLES(ATTACHED TO PARACHUTES)
27. FOOD AND BEVERAGE CONTAINERS
28. ALDIS LAMPS
29. FIRST AID KITS

79-115-A

Figure 2-6.

When the Hollywood movie Strategic Air Command starring Jimmy Stewart and June Allyson came out in 1955 it heavily featured the B-36.

Stewart's character is based on the real-life military career and an actual mission flown by Brigadier General Clifford Schoeffler, who crashed during an Arctic B-36 mission and survived. Brigadier General Schoeffler was on-site at Carswell Air Force Base while filming Strategic Air Command as a consultant.

One scene that many have thought to be propaganda over the years is where the aircraft commander lines up all of his crew beside the B-36 for inspection.

In fact, it is correct and the inspection is featured in the B-36 TOs, as shown here.

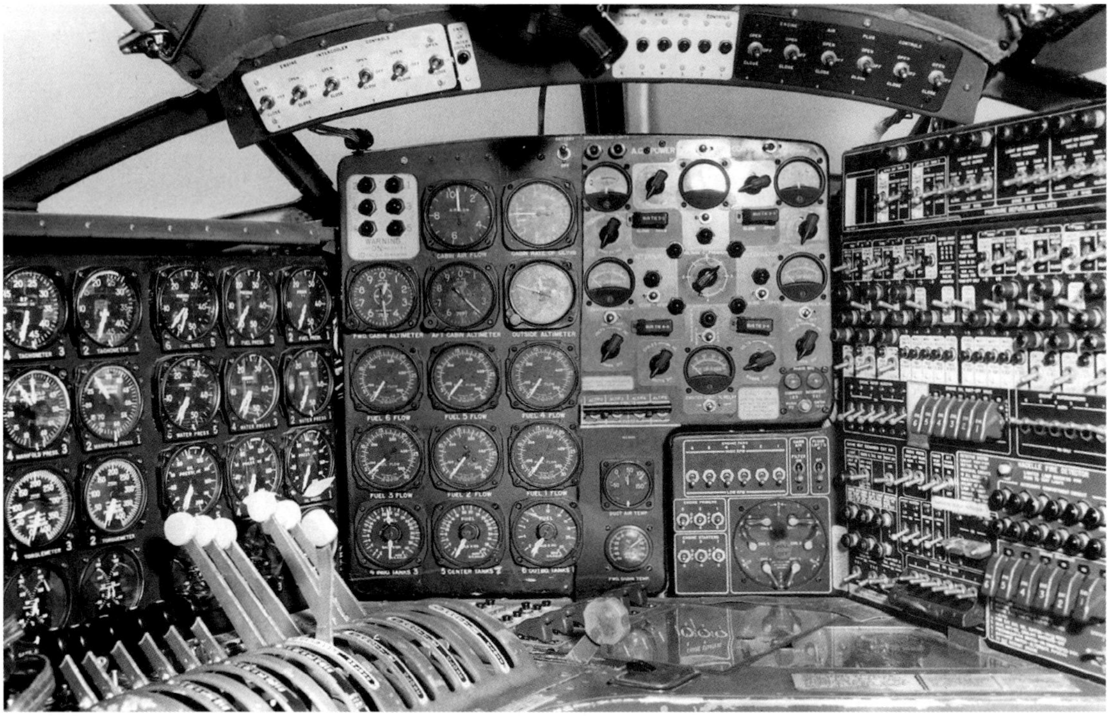

The flight engineer's station was certainly not lacking instruments and controls! He was responsible for the six engines and all hydraulic and electrical systems aboard the B-36B. He also had a duplicate set of throttle and propeller pitch levers. The panel to the left, behind the prop and throttles is the main instrument panel. In the centre is the auxilliary instrument panel, and on the right, the main control panel. Overhead, in an arc is the auxilliary control panel. The view outside is via the rear of the flight deck glazing. (Convair)

through to 44-92062 - were also equipped with guidance equipment for a pair of 13,000-pound VB-13 Tarzon-guided bombs. This was an early precision-guided munition that was controlled via radio link by an operator in the B-36 viewing a television picture from the nose of the bomb. It appears that at least the first few B-36Bs were also equipped with the mounting brackets to carry the F-85 parasite fighter, although as far as can be ascertained, no equipment was actually installed.

It was the plan to equip the B-36B with the new Farrand Y-1 retractable periscopic bombsight, but development problems resulted in the M-9 Norden being used instead. Nevertheless, the B-36B did use the newly-developed AN/APQ-24 bombing/navigation system with an improved search radar and faster computer. Finally, in November 1949, the first prototype K-1 system was installed in a B-36B-15-CF 44-92072 for testing.

In addition, the defensive armament was installed, making these the first true combat versions of the B-36. The 2CFR87B-2 system had superseded the proposed B-1 system before any units had been delivered. The major changes were all internal and included substituting an improved AN/APG-32 tail radar for the APG-3 in the B-1 system. Unfortunately, the APG-32 was delayed, and most B-36Bs were delivered with the APG-3 instead. There were six retractable remotely-operated turrets, each equipped with a pair of twenty millimetre M-24A1 cannon, plus two more twenty-millimetre cannon in nose and tail turrets. In addition, there were two retractable turrets in the upper forward fuselage, two in the upper aft fuselage, and two in the lower aft fuselage. This was the most formidable defensive armament yet fitted to any warplane and was based mainly on World War Two experience.

The guns were aimed using computing gunsights situated at two blisters on the forward fuselage and four blisters on the aft fuselage. The tail turret was directed by a gun-laying radar while the nose turret was aimed using a gunsight located in the glazed nose compartment. Bolt-on armour panels were provided to protect all but the inboard fuel tanks - they would be empty and purged by the time the aircraft was under threat - and all of the engine oil tanks.

Like the B-36A, the crew of the B-36B was usually fifteen: a pilot, copilot, radar-bombardier,

Left: the nose compartment of a B-36B, looking forward. The Norden bombsight, on the left of centre, is covered up - clearly, habits of World War Two died hard when there was a camera around! The gunsight for the nose turret was fixed to the roof of the right side of the compartment.

The layout of the interiors was something of an egonomic nightmare with little thought as to the placement of equipment and furniture. The nose compartment was fitted with somewhat basic chairs for the crewmembers, but at least they had seatbelts for turbulent weather!

Right: The forward hatch for the communications tube ran between the two pressurised compartments at the rear of the lower front compartment. Note the dixie cup dispenser on the bulkhead.

The corrugated panel behind the open hatch is the gunner's platform - it folded down, and the gunner stood on it to operate the upper gunsight. The corner of the radio operator's desk is at the lower left.

navigator, flight engineer, two radiomen, three forward gunners, and five rear gunners. Now the gunners had something to do, although continuing problems with the gun system did not allow them to do it well.

In November 1948, a B-6B flying out of Fort Worth aimed at a 'target ship' off the coast of Florida in the Gulf of Mexico. The aircraft was flown by Convair's Doc Witchell and Captain E. Crahan, an officer from the test wing at Eglin AFB, Florida. Captain Wesley D. Morris from the 7th BW was the bombardier. The 2,000-mile mission included a low-level bombing run before a group of high-ranking Air Force officers on hand for an air show at Eglin. The B-36B dropped two salvos of dummy bombs into the water as demonstrations, then scored a direct hit from 10,000 feet on a simulated target ship - in reality, a platform sitting on pilings off the coast. The dummy bombs heavily damaged the target platform load. Also on board for the flight were F Hanley and C Driskell as engineers, C Shirley and W R Camp as observers, photographer Fred Carlisle, armament engineers W N Stevenson and A D Tuttle, flight test engineer R P Scott, and navigator Lieutenant Harkness.

After the demonstration, the Air Force accepted its first B-36B, 44-92026, on 25 November 1948 and assigned it to the 7th Bomb Wing at Carswell AFB, which already operated the B-36As in a training role.

The 11th Bomb Wing would also be activated at Carswell with the B-36B, receiving its first aircraft, 44-92050, on 18 March 1949. Plans were made for other B-36 groups to be based at Rapid City, South Dakota, and Fairfield-Suisun, California. In 1947 construction began on a new SAC base at Limestone, Maine, and the installation was being built to accommodate sixty B-36s. However, the sheer size of the B-36 presented problems to the crews constructing facilities at the bases, and progress lagged behind schedule.

Everything was not working as well as it could be. The APQ-24 was neither as reliable nor as accurate in service as it had been during testing. The problem was traced to faulty vacuum tubes and inadequate training. In addition, the complex General Electric remotely-controlled turrets were prone to frequent failures. A lack of twenty-millimetre ammunition had delayed the start of operational testing until mid-1949, and the eventual results were disappointing. The entire system was unreliable, and when it did work, it was not accurate.

Although similar in concept to the defensive

The navigator's table was on the left side of the nose compartment. Instrumentation included radio and magnetic compasses, an altimeter, an airspeed indicator, and a clock. In the days before inertial guidance systems and GPS, the navigator would pore over paper charts and use a circular slide rule as a 'manual computer' to calculate where the aircraft was - or had been - at any given time. The chart-looking markings on the panel just forward of the table are the bomb bay configurations for the bombardier sitting at the Norden bombsight. (Convair)

Above: Clearly a posed photo! Convair factory workers install windshield wipers for the canopy windscreen of a B-36B. To the front of the black antiglare panel is the nose turret. Only the left 20mm cannon has been installed in the turret. The body of the turret comprised a large shield that could be turned from side to side, thus achieving traverse of the guns, and, set into the large shield, a smaller shield that pivoted to elevate or depress with the guns.

Below: Workers at Convair's Fort Worth plant place windshield wipers on another B-36B on which the nose turret has not yet been installed. Protective film on the clear panels of the canopy and bombardier's nose will be removed when the machine was completed. (both Convair)

armament installed on the B-29, the system was much more complex, a necessity to ensure it was capable of handling the ever-increasing speeds of the fighters it was designed to shoot down. The extreme cold at 40,000 feet created problems, as did the vibration of the six large engines. The APG-3 gun-laying radar for the tail turret also proved to be troublesome. As late as February 1950, the commander of the 8th Air Force was complaining that there was little point in driving a B-36 around carrying a lot of guns that didn't work.

Many of the B-36 B's initial problems resembled those of any other new and complex aircraft. Parts shortages were acute, and it was often necessary to cannibalise some B-36Bs to keep others flying. Equipment such as empennage stands, dollies, and jacks was in short supply. Because there was no funding for new equipment, maintenance crews utilised some of the tools and equipment left over from the old B-29s. The aircraft were constantly being reconfigured or awaiting modification so that operational capability was not achieved until 1952. Personnel turnover in the postwar environment also hampered progress.

Some of the problems encountered were insane self-inflicted red tape. When a part needed was manufactured by Convair, which was located a mile across the runway, the 7th Bomb Wing had to request the part from the Air Materiel Command depot at San Antonio, which in turn requested it from the manufacturer. Convair then shipped the part to San Antonio, which turned it around and shipped it to Carswell. Finally, somebody in the Air Force realised the stupidity of the situation and allowed Convair to drive the parts across the runway and deliver them to the B-36 units.

While the B-36Bs were being built, Convair was attempting to develop the re-engined B-36C to increase the aircraft's performance. When this did not work, the Air Force approved a more modest upgrade that added General Electric J47-GE-11 jet engines to the basic B-36B configuration, creating the B-36D. This change was approved while the B-36Bs were being manufactured. Convair was contracted to build 73 B-36Bs, but the Air Force directed eleven of them to be modified with jet engines on the production line. Four of the eleven appeared on Air Force rolls as B-36Ds, and seven as RB-36Ds. Therefore, Air Force records indicate that only sixty-two B-36Bs were accepted, thirty-one in Fiscal Year 49, 30 in Fiscal Year 50, and the last one in September 1950, Fiscal Year 51. For explanation, at this time the Government Fiscal Years ended in June. This disparate accounting has led to some confusion over the years.

On 15 January 1949, a five-ship formation of B-36s from the 7th Bomb Wing was flown in an air review over Washington DC, commemorating the inauguration of President Harry S Truman. In addition, several low-level runs were flown over the US Capitol, resulting in a series of photographs that have been reproduced extensively, usually in conjunction with accounts of the 'Revolt of the Admirals.'

The B-36B phase-out from service was almost as quick as that of the B-36A. Twenty-five B-36Bs were already undergoing conversion into D-models during the first half of 1951, and the last of the sixty converted B-36Bs were redelivered by February 1952. Two of the bombers had crashed before they could be converted. At least one aircraft, 44-92073, accumulated over 1,000 flight hours during twenty-two months of operation before being delivered to San Diego for conversion.

Only the first four conversions, 44-92026, 034, 053, and 054 - took place at Fort Worth, the rest were converted in San Diego. This was an attempt to relieve the workload at Fort Worth, but the decision was made after an additional 91,000 square yards of concrete pads had been poured at Fort Worth to support the conversion effort (which would have occurred outdoors). The area did not go to waste since it was later used for the various SAM-SAC, ON TOP, and ECM upgrade programmes. On the other hand, San Diego now found itself needing more ramp space - or, more specifically, more robust ramp space. The original ramp had been built to support B-24s and could not accommodate the B-36. Existing concrete and tarmac was ripped out, and almost 10,000 square yards of seven-inch-thick concrete was poured in its place. Building 3 at the plant was also extensively modified by removing various support columns to allow the large aircraft to be parked partially indoors, leaving the empennage outside the building.

When it was decided to move the B-36B conversion work to San Diego, nine all-weather maintenance docks were constructed there to facilitate the effort. Five additional docks were added later. Some other items were constructed, including horizontal stabiliser stands and two rudder stands. These were transferred to Fort Worth in July 1952 after the last D-model conversions and SAN-SAN maintenance were completed in San Diego. Fort Worth needed the docks to outfit additional Work areas in preparation for SAM-SAC and other modernisation Work. The docks were partially disassembled and shipped via rail.

The waffle-plate design of the pilots' enclosure was partially filled in by platework to keep the sun out. Enclosed in the structure was an astrodome to aid with navigation - some of these were transparent, or in the case of this example, solid. (Convair via author's collection)

Probably the only time I have ever seen the cockpit or Flight Deck referred to as the 'Pilots' Enclosure' was on the cover of this one-time Restricted monthly status report. This picture of the greenhouse under construction was taken in April 1947 and shows an A-model item before the completed assembly - both aluminium and plexiglass - was installed as a unit. (Convair via Kirk Smeeton Collection)

The two aft top turrets in the retracted position at an angle, but with the sliding doors open. In the background is the leading edge of the vertical fin. The B-36 carried sixteen of these M24A1 20mm cannon in eight turrets all operated by a sophisticated remote control system. (Convair via author's collection)

The B-36C

On 4 September, Convair called to modify a B-36A off the production line to a B-36C. Convair even went so far as to offer to deliver the last of the 34 new B-36Cs in May 1950, a delay in completing the contract of only six months. Since the primary concern in the B-36 programme now was to increase the speed of the aircraft over the target, the offer to install a more powerful engine at minimal additional cost seemed very attractive. The settlement with Convair would reduce the contract quantity from one hundred to ninety-five aircraft in place of further payment. Convair also offered to study the possibility of retrofitting the B36A and B-36B models to the B-36C standard but said they would have to answer by December 1947 to make the necessary changes in production.

The Convair proposal reached the Air Materiel Command via Maj General Lawrence C Craigie, chief of the Research & Engineering Division, and his forwarding letter expressed the fear that the engine availability schedule might be overly optimistic. He asked for comment on this, noting that the VDT engine production would have to be shared with the B-50 programme. General Twining replied that the proposal appeared feasible but that the total cost for the VDT installation and associated Government Furnished Equipment might come to as much as $15 million. Air Materiel Command reserved comment on the other part of Convair's proposal to retrofit VDT engines to the sixty-one B36As and B-36Bs until Convair could make a complete engineering and cost study.

General Hoyt Vandenberg, then Vice Chief of Staff, reminded Convair that the Aircraft & Weapons Board had rejected the VDT idea and had cancelled the VDT equipped prototype B-36 in July 1947. Vandenberg said that the Air Staff did not wish to decide on the new proposal for thirty-four B-36Cs without allowing each board member to vote.

In General Joseph McNarney's reply, he recommended approval because the performance figures, production costs, and delivery schedule

Assembled from two pages in the B-36 Technical Orders, this montage shows the location of the gunners, in relation to the turrets they were controlling.

B-36 44-92038 shows the bright red Arctic paint - not dayglo -, the polished aluminium and matt magnesium colour scheme to great effect. (USAF via author's collection)

seemed feasible. All other members of the Aircraft & Weapons Board concurred in the decision to proceed with the B-36C except General George Kenney, the commander of Strategic Air Command, the service that would 'own' and operate them.

Kenney was still fundamentally opposed to the B-36 programme and did not believe that the promised improvements would ever materialise. He felt that the usefulness of the B-36 - assuming it was useful - lay in reconnaissance, sea search, anti-submarine patrol, or as a tanker. For these roles, the speed increase promised by the VDT engines was unnecessary and not worth the extra expense.

Kenney's comments, along with the replies of the other board members, were forwarded to Vandenberg, but Kenney was overruled. With the agreement of Under Secretary of the Air Force Arthur S Barrows, General Vandenberg decided to accept Convair's B-36C proposal. On 5 December 1947, the Air Materiel Command was directed to take necessary action to get the ball rolling.

After an uphill battle lasting half a year, Convair finally got the go-ahead for the B-36C in December 1947, just as the financial outlook at the firm was becoming increasingly bleak. Convair's contracts manager, Frank Watson, described the difficult choice the company faced in gambling on completion of the contract to Brig. General H L A Shepard, the chief of the Air Materiel Command Procurement Division. Watson asserted that 'There seems to be a general awareness of the difficulties involved in attempting a five year aircraft programme on two-year appropriations. All such general discussion is no doubt meritorious and should, in due time, result in necessary action. However, this Contractor is faced with the problem immediately and seriously and is at a loss as to where to turn for some form of assurance on how to proceed.'

'Deliveries are presently scheduled through 1949. The funds expire on 30 June 1948. The Contractor has been advised very properly by Air Materiel Command that if present funds are not extended by Congress, or new funds not made available, prior to 30 June 1948, it will be necessary for Contractor to go to the Court of Claims for recovery of any amounts due and payable to subcontractors and vendors after the 30 June date.'

'It would seem a simple matter for Contractor to wait patiently until a few days before 30 June, and then if new funds have not been appropriated, to bring the programme to a close. This, however, ignores the lead times necessary in an airplane programme as complicated as the B-36 programme. The Contractor cannot wait until just before midnight on 30 June to adjust the flow of materials from subcontractors and vendors.'

Watson pointed out that the Air Force would have to make a decision, and he told Shepard that Convair was gambling on its own future. The General replied that the Air Force was fully aware of this and would resubmit an appropriation request to Congress as soon as it reconvened in January 1948.

Even as the funding discussions and new proposals were going on, the flight test programme continued. On 14 August 1947, the XB-36 had briefly reached an altitude of 38,400 feet. Soon, the first production B-36A was flown to Wright Field for its static testing, and on 4 December 1947, the YB-36 made its initial flight. It reached above 40,400 feet on its third flight, but there was little publicity.

Chapter Four

Conflict with Northrop

On 22 November 1941, Northrop Aircraft Inc was awarded a contract for two XB-35 prototypes and thirteen YB-35 flying wing aircraft with the requirement for the type to enter production via a contract for two hundred production models. The flying wing concept was novel, but was unproven and lacked a wide range of wind tunnel tests and data requirements. Nothing presented by this date could have satisfactorily assured the AAF of its success. Yet, the B-35 programme, and the later all-jet B-49, was of great relevance to the B-36 story and became increasingly so.

Such was the controversy stirred up about the Flying Wings and the B-36, it is worth looking in some detail about the development of the Northrop designs, their undoubted problems and how these problems were inflated out of all proportion by the supporters of the Convair design who at the same time played down the problems with the B-36.

Jack Northrop's flying wings - or to give them their more correct title, all wing aircraft - were some of the most spectacular, graceful and elegant flying machines ever to grace the skies.

A design as aeronautically pure as a flying wing had huge advantages over conventional aircraft design. This advantage was that drag was reduced to an absolute minimum. As a result of this minimum drag, the performance of the flying wing became unequalled in speed, range and operating economy.

For many years aeronautical designers realised that by reducing drag, that is, the net aerodynamic force acting opposite to the direction of the movement of the solid object caused by the shape or form of an aircraft as it passes through the air - that machine's performance could be greatly increased. Early steps taken in this direction brought about the changes from biplane to monoplane design; the

Right: John Knudsen 'Jack' Northrop (b. 10 November 1895, d 18 February 1981)

Below: Thought to be the first XB-35 taxying at Northrop Field. (USAF)

elimination of external wing struts and flying wires; the incorporation of retractable undercarriages and the general overall 'smoothing out' of the shape.

In spite of all these advances, the average conventional aircraft of today still has two to four times the drag of a flying wing. So in order to reduce drag to its absolute minimum, a number of aircraft designers took the drastic step of eliminating both the fuselage and tail altogether and placed the pilot, the engines and the payload completely inside the wing envelope. For the full story behind the development of the Northrop Flying Wings, see Northrop Flying Wings, Pen and Sword, 2013, by the same author.

The XB-35 received its initial start from the Army Air Corps in September, 1941, following a visit to the Northrop plant by Assistant Secretary of War

Right: an XB-35 in flight.

Below: a view of one of the XB-35s at a Northrop employee open day just after the war. Note the engine closest to the camera is fitted with a pair of three bladed propellers whilst the other three have four-bladed units. (Both USAF)

'Pulling through' the props on an XB-35 to ensure each engine was free of hydraulic locks was not an easy task. Here it takes ten men and special platform! (USAF)

Robert Leavitt, General H H Arnold, and Major General Oliver P Echols, along with General William Knudsen, the head of the War Production Board. At this time, Northrop submitted a preliminary design for the XB-35 to Wright Field. At the heart of the proposal were five essential items:

1. The low drag, high lift feature of the Flying Wing meant that, in practice, the XB-35 could transport any weight faster, farther and cheaper than an aircraft of conventional design.
2. The simplicity of construction of the XB-35 Flying Wing presented few structural complications. It cost less to build since it was built as a single unit in which the structure extended from tip to tip with no added tail or fuselage to build.
3. It had better weight distribution. Compartments along the span could distribute the bomb load and weight more evenly over the wing surface which supported it. This also would have applied to cargo if a cargo version had been built. It eliminates the need for excessive structural weight, such as is necessary for conventional bombers where the weight is concentrated in the fuselage and must be distributed over the wing from this point through heavy structural members.
4. For ease in loading and unloading, cargo could be placed in spanwise compartments where any part of the aircraft's load was easily accessible through its own cargo or bomb bay doors. This provided direct access to all portions of the cargo.
5. The XB-35 for military purposes presented a smaller target while engaged in either offensive or defensive operations. Comparisons between the Flying Wing and conventional aircraft are also illustrated by Northrop's performance figures and backed by many years of research tests in which aircraft identical in scale to the XB-35 were used. The XB-35 was built to be twenty per cent faster than conventional bomber aircraft with identical loads and horsepower.

The proposal laid out that the normal crew for the XB-35 was nine men - a pilot, co-pilot, bombardier, navigator, engineer, radio operator, and three gunners.

Cabin space was available for six more crew members, who could substitute on long-range missions. Folding bunks were built in the XB-35 to accommodate the off-duty crewmen. These fifteen men were housed entirely within the wing aerofoil itself.

Robert P Patterson, the Under Secretary of War, approved Contract No. 535 ac-21920 for 'One Air Corps Model XB-35 Airplane, Experimental, Bombardment Long Range, Mockup and Data.' The estimated cost was $2,745,285.85, with a fixed fee of $164,717.03, giving a total contract value of $2,910,000.88.

A few days later, on 1 December 1941, a Change Order was issued by the Air Corps Materiel Division at Wright Field, increasing the order by one additional aircraft. The value of this change order was $1,462,264.16 with a further $87,635.85 fixed fee for the contractor. The first was to be delivered in November 1943, the second in April of the next year. Detailed engineering began in early 1942. A fuselage-like crew cabin was to be embedded inside the wing; it included a tail cone protruding from the trailing edge. This tail cone would contain the remote sighting stations for the gunners in the production model. In the rear of the cabin, there were folding bunks for the off-duty crew on long missions. The aircraft's bomb load was to be carried in six small bomb bays, three in each wing.

Production aircraft would have a defensive armament of twenty machine guns or 20 mm cannon, carried in seven turrets, three on the aircraft's centre line, two above, and two below the outer wings. The B-35 would take advantage of a specific aluminium alloy designated 24ST devised by Aluminium Corporation of America (Alcoa) that was controlled by the powerful eastern industrialist Andrew Mellon, and at that time, Alcoa had a virtual monopoly on aluminium.

This material was considerably more robust than any alloy used previously, which in itself caused significant problems. For whatever reason, Alcoa had adopted a policy of favouring manufacturers who were building aircraft for the US government and who had been Alcoa customers in the past. Up to this time, Northrop's only major aircraft contracts had been with the Norwegians and the British for Vengeance dive-bombers.

At the time, the Reynolds Metals Company had not become a major supplier, so Northrop had no choice but to deal with Alcoa, but their continued plea for additional allotments of aluminium fell on deaf ears, and shortages at the Hawthorne plant became common.

Even at this early stage in proceedings, the protagonists were starting to express divergent opinions with the XB-35/RB-349 and B-36. Sides were taken, and both positives and negatives that each project had or experienced were amplified to score points off each other. With the passage of time, these viewpoints have become even more entrenched so that even official records have became tainted with bias, so much so that all are suspect.

Four of the most powerful piston engines were

The first XB-35 - by now fitted with single-disc prop units - flying in formation with a B-17 Flying Fortress. (USAF)

42-102367 undergoes conversion into a YB-49 at Hawthorne. The wing fences and 'vertical fins' are noticable. (USAF)

chosen for propulsion, driving pusher propellers carried on long shafts extending just behind the trailing edge. This was to be the Pratt & Whitney R-4360 Wasp Major. Known as the 'Corn-cob' because its four rows of seven air-cooled cylinders looked like one, had a swept volume of 4,363 cubic inches and promised to begin life at a rating of 3,000 horsepower, with an increase to 3,500 in prospect. With the addition of exhaust-driven turbines, it was expected that this would easily exceed 4,000 horsepower, with very low fuel consumption. Convair also chose this engine for their giant B-36, fitting six inside its vast wing - a structure even bigger than Northrop's - again driving pusher propellers.

The XB-35 had two B-4630-17 and two R-4360-21 engines installed, each with double turbosuperchargers and eight coaxial four-bladed Hamilton Standard pusher propellers. Tests were run using three-blade units but these were found to be less efficient.

A Mockup Board from Wright Field arrived at Hawthorne on 5 July 1942 to inspect a full-size wood mock-up of the centre section and a portion of the left wing. Official approval was given. Northrop built a new bomber plant at the end of the company's grounds in Hawthorne, California. This plant was completed in January 1943 and the fabrication of the parts for the first XB-35 were begun.

In size, the XB-35 would dwarf the B-17 Flying Fortress, with wing area and gross weight almost three times greater. The unconventional control system reflected years of study, wind tunnel tests, and flight test data gleaned from the the earlier Northrop N-1M and N-9M programmes.

With mock-up approval, it seemed a good idea to accelerate development and also negotiate a production order. Northrop Aircraft Inc was one of the smaller US firms, and their plant at Hawthorne was totally committed to the development and manufacture of the P-61 Black Widow.

Accordingly, the Glenn L Martin Company was awarded a contract for the detailed design of the wing and powerplant installation and a further letter of intent for the production of 200 of the eventual bomber. Martin's had previously built Boeing B-29 Superfortresses, but it was expected that these would be phased out in favour of the B-35.

Manufacture of the XB-35 began at Hawthorne early in 1943. In the course of that year, engineers from the Otis Elevator Co in New York City were called in to help complete the structural design of the wing, under Northrop and Martin supervision.

The XB-35 was completed in the first half of 1946, well ahead of the XB-36, which had been begun almost a year earlier. 42-13603 moved for the first time on its own wheels and under its own power on 16 May 1946. After dozens of high-speed taxi runs, during which speeds as high as 115 mph were attained, the aircraft seemed ready.

Like much surrounding the whole flying wing programme, there is conflicting information regarding who was on board. However, that Max Stanley was the pilot is not in doubt, although some sources say that Fred Bretcher was the co-pilot and O H Douglas the flight engineer whilst others state there was no co-pilot and Dale Schroeder was the flight engineer.

The first flight was essentially a ferry flight from

Northrop Airport to Muroc Army Air Base. The idea was to fly to Muroc with a minimum of trouble and learn about the flying characteristics of the aircraft. Stanley tested the controls with the landing gear up and down several times. The highest airspeed attained was 200 mph, as the Flying Wing, with its P-61 Black Widow chase plane in trail, cleared the mountains and began its descent to Muroc. As a precautionary measure, a no-flap approach was made, with a smooth touchdown at 112mph. The 44-minute flight was uneventful, except for erratic operation of a propeller governor. Everyone associated with the project was jubilant, anxious to press on with the flight testing and prove the design once and for all. That 'minor problem' with the propeller governor did not, as everyone expected, 'go away.' The XB-35 flew twice more in the next three months, accumulating only three hours of flight time by mid-September 1946.

Problems with the Hamilton Standard propeller governors became chronic, with the propellers continually 'hunting' around a constant speed setting and 'creeping' in fixed pitch during air operations. Additionally, there was evidence that the huge counter-rotating propellers were operating under excessive stress, leading to a restriction of eighty hours of operating time due to the danger of fatigue.

Another weakness in the XB-35 was the propulsion power train. Each engine was coupled to a remote gearbox assembly by an extension drive shaft. Two sets of four-bladed, dual rotating, reversible pitch, full feathering, Hamilton Standard propellers were mounted on dual concentric shafts extending from each gearbox. The engines were completely enclosed within the wing, an arrangement that imposed severe requirements on the aircraft's structure. Superchargers, intercoolers, oil coolers, and fans for ground-cooling and cooling at low speeds were located in the wing, as were cooling ducts and controls to diffuse the air around the engines and expel it through flaps near the trailing edge. Troubles centred around the gearbox assembly that coupled each engine to its propeller by means of a drive shaft from the engine to the gearbox and a dual concentric shaft from the gearbox to the counter-rotating propellers. Propellers and engine vibration caused frequent failures of the gearboxes. A flexible, vibration absorbing gearbox mount was a vital necessity for successful flight testing. Most of this was not the responsibility of Northrop - but it was their engineers who had to struggle with the problems.

On 17 February 1947, during a conference at Air Materiel Command, the engineering difficulties and material failures encountered in the dual rotation gearbox and propeller installation were discussed,

Only in California! The newsreel cameras are out ready to film the preparation of 42-102367 for its first departure from Hawthorne. (USAF)

Northrop test pilot Max Stanley taxies 42-102367 past the hundreds of specatators gathered alongside the 5,000 foot runway at Hawthrorne. Privately he was concerned that the runway was not long enough - he need not have worried, the aircraft took off safely with plenty of room to spare. (USAF)

and the decision was made to use single rotation gearboxes, thereby getting the XB-35 into the air at an earlier date than would have been possible by awaiting solution of the dual rotation difficulties. XB-36 single rotation props were to be cut down and used as standbys. The aircraft was grounded until March 1947, when the difficulties were largely overcome.

It was estimated that the first XB-35 had cost $14,300,000.00 up to the time of flight test. By April 1947 the cost of the two XB-35s had, through change orders, supplemental agreements, work performed by Martin and various engineering changes, increased to $25,632,259.55. On 18 November 1948 all files and data on the XB-35 were transferred from the engineering division to the procurement division.When all funds remaining on Contract W335 ac-21920 had been exhausted, additional expenditure was chargable to procurement division, which was administered by the aircraft and missiles section.

Both XB-35s were to be used for flight testing; with ground and flight vibration tests included in the programme. Problems of reduction gear and propeller operation had grounded the XB-35s for almost a year and a half, but General Spaatz stated that Northrop was not at fault in the failure to obtain adequate flight data from the XB-35s. The first flight with single rotation propellers and gearboxes was made in February 1948. However, several successive flights were terminated because of the failure of the landing gear doors. Northrop pilots believed that the performance of the XB-35 was noticeably reduced by the installation of single rotation propellers. Furthermore, these units produced excitations which resulted in cracking of the propeller housings and control surface ribs. To remedy this, strengthening of the elevon ribs was proposed. Additionally, difficulties were experienced with the engine cooling fans, forcing a re-design of the fan and ducting. At the same time, both Air Materiel Command and Northrop were conducting studies and tests to determine whether B-35 aircraft should have flexible mountings on the propeller gearboxes.

The problem of control-surface actuation on the big bomber involved developing and testing a complete hydraulic control system, as none of the aerodynamic boosts or balances developed and tested in the N-9M models had proved satisfactory. The

Max Stanley climbs away from Hawthorne. The climb out speed had to be watched, or the YB-49 could accelerate too quickly for the time taken to retract the landing gear and the doors could be torn off as happened a number of times. The huge size of the mainwheels is particularly noticable.

A YB-49 gets airborne from Hawthorne. The clouds of black smoke was a characteristic of early American jet engines, and remained so until many years later. (USAF)

system used in the XB-35 employed small valves which were sensitive to comparatively minute movements of the control cable and which, when displaced, permitted large quantities of oil to flow into the actuating cylinders. This arrangement eliminates any pilot 'feel' of the load on the control surfaces unless a deliberate arrangement for force feedback is made. Rather than undertake this, a comparatively simple force mechanism, which was sensitive to accelerations and airspeed, was developed. This device gave the pilot a synthetic feel of the aircraft which could be adjusted to any intensity required and which worked well in flight. The synthetic feel was much more satisfactory than the feedback of actual control-surface loads, particularly at high angles of attack.

Jack Northrop was well aware of the need for an auto-pilot, but there were difficulties to be overcome, particularly with those associated with the low value of detectable sideslip. 'In conventional applications, the fact that the airplane is side slipping is detected by either a lateral acceleration or an angle of bank. In an all-wing airplane neither of these indications exists except in an almost undetectable amount.'

Accordingly, it is necessary, in order to fly the airplane at zero sideslip, and therefore in the direction of its centreline, to provide a yaw-vane signal to which the pilot or automatic pilot will respond. This introduces some difficulty in automatic pilot design because for small disturbances the sideslip angle with respect to the wind, and the yaw angle with respect to a set of fixed axes, are nearly equal and opposite for a flying wing. The customary automatic pilot control on azimuth angle, tends to oppose the necessary control on sideslip. To avoid this difficulty, it is necessary only to reduce the rate of control on sideslip to approximately one-third that on azimuth.'

This modification to a conventional automatic pilot was flown on the N-9M with complete success.

The first XB-35 was ferried back to Hawthorne from Muroc on 22 November 1948 for conversion on Air Materiel Command instructions to the 'Turbodyne' engine testbed with an XT-37 engine in addition to six turbo-jet powerplants. The second XB-35 was planned to be used for the testing of flexibly mounted propellers. General Putt authorised Northrop to proceed with the Turbodyne test aircraft re-designated as the EB-35B.

Northrop had, as with Lockheed, embarked on a programme of jet engine development before America entered the war in 1941. Vladimir Pavlecka was the head of Northrop's research and design programme, which developed the 'Turbodyne' - designated T-37 - turboprop engine. On 1 July 1943, Northrop received a contract from the US Navy to build two XT-37 engines, with the first being bench-tested in December 1944 - this was the first American turboprop engine to run with a propeller fitted - but by 1945, the Navy had lost any interest in the idea of turboprop-powered aircraft.

The EB-35B was used as a flying testbed for the Turbodyne turboprop engine after it had passed ground tests and was ready for flight trials. The EB-35B was to have the six jet engines as in the other jet-powered flying wings, but this particular aircraft would have a single Turbodyne engine mounted to the left of the aircraft centreline as a pusher power plant. The jet exhaust was to be discharged through the hubs of the large counter-rotating propellers. The plans were to take-off and land using the six jet engines. Then, once the aircraft was airborne, the pilot would throttle the jet engines back and maintain flight on the Turbodyne.

Air Force planners were convinced that military strategy called for a large bomber with a 10,000-mile range for delivering the atomic bomb.

With the B-36 in increasing favour, it was natural for Jack Northrop to consider all the alternatives possible to make his flying wing fly, and be powered by his Turbodyne engine. By all accounts Jack's ultimate intention was to use twin 10,000 shp Turbodynes as the principal power source in the existing YB-49 airframe, with the further possibility of jet power boosting the performance in pods hanging from the wings like the B-36D. The idea was for the aircraft to take off using both the Turbodynes and the jets, and then shut down the jets in flight to get superior range capability. Northrop engineers planned a Turbodyne-powered flying wing designed for ranges as great as 12,000 miles, cruising at 459 mph, with a maximum of 550 mph.

Jack Northrop's firm conviction of the feasibility of such an aircraft was expressed in his observation, 'In the extremely long-range category, the turboprop comes nearer to combining the speed of the jet with the range of the reciprocating engine than any other power plant and, theoretically at least, a turboprop flying wing has adequate range and operating speed, as well as high speed, equal to, if not better, than its turbo-jet sister.'

Northrop were not totally happy with just a conversion - they submitted several design studies for a new version of the flying wing, this time with a large enough bomb bay to accommodate the nuclear weapons of the day.

One proposal would have been powered by two Northrop Turbodyne V turboprop engines, each producing 10,000 shaft horsepower, driving contra-rotating propellers. Another design study would have substituted nine of four smaller Allison turboprop engines for the two Northrop machines, also driving contra-rotating propellers. Looking at these drawings, one is struck by the similarity of both shapes to Englishman Roy Chadwick's design study that was to surface for the Avro Vulcan. All that was missing was the vertical tail. Considering that Roy Chadwick visited Northrop, one has to ask who inspired who!

When Martin withdrew from the programme, the YB-35 engineering was sketchy and incomplete. The YB-35A modernisation programme included the installation of radar standard photographic equipment, air conditioning and a tail turret - all apart from the radar being supplied from Government stores.

The YB-35s were still without the Government-supplied propellers and gearboxes and therefore could not be completed. Northrop was therefore directed to put the aircraft into storage until these items were available, which was expected to be around November. However, by then delaying factors other than propeller deliveries conspired to ground the YB-35s - the lack of co-pilot's vision glass and the shortage for the armament installation were the most serious factors. The Government Field

42-102368 in formation with a F-80A of the Flight Test Division from Muroc. The two YB-49s are notoriously difficult to tell apart - the only serials are on the upper vertical fins, just below the national insignia which, in many photographs, are hidden from view. (USAF)

Procurement Officer at Hawthorne estimated that deliveries could not start until February 1948.

There were other problems with Government supplied equipment . Such was the chronic shortage of type E-5 auxiliary power units, Northrop was forced to switch what they had from aircraft to aircraft for flight test purposes. The company had somewhat understandably assumed that the Government-provided equipment would be ready for installation when it was needed, but this was not the case. By August, eleven YB-35s were almost complete, but the basic problems - propeller and gearboxes, engine cooling fans, and maintenance of the exhaust system - remained to be solved. The good news was that the development of flexible mounted gearboxes was underway - the bad news was that it would take some time.

Trying to work out which designation applied to which aircraft became a nightmare as the modification state of each aircraft kept changing. During March 1949, Air Materiel Command finally got around to listing which aircraft was allocated which serial, and which type it was - and then promptly issued a contract to change most of them!

Headquarters Air Materiel Command in Dayton, Ohio, proposed the conversion of two YB-35s by replacing the four R-4360 engines with six J-35 turbo-jets. Washington approved this plus the conversion of the remaining nine YB-35s to J-35 engines for photo-reconnaissance work. The estimated cost of the conversion would be $13,800,800.00. In Washington, the conversion was described as a '...logical escape from an otherwise untenable position.'

A supplement to Air Materiel Command contract number W33-038 ac-21721 stated that the two XB-35s - 42-13603 that had been set aside for the Turbodyne testbed and 42-38323 which was to be used for flexible mounts - were bailed back to the company along with YB-35 42-102366 and 42-102369, which were to be stripped of all usable equipment and scrapped.

Four YB-35s; 42-102370, 42-102371, 42-102372 and 42-102373 along with three YB-35s; 42-102374, 42-102375 and 42-102377 were to be modified as YB-35Bs. The contract called for all seven modified aircraft to be flight-tested to an average of six hours each and that it would be completed in just five months.

In June 1948, a further letter was sent to Northrop from Air Materiel Command describing the work they required on the RB-49A:

1 Engineering the RB-49A airplane incorporating eight (8) J-47A engines, six (6) mounted internally and two (2) in external nacelles with space provisions for J-40 and/or T-37 engines, with a gross take-off weight of 213,500 lbs at a positive load factor of 2.
2 Designing of tools, with a complete production breakdown of the RB-49A airplane, tools to be designed at a rate of fifteen (15) per month. Tools will be fabricated for a rate of three (3) per month.
3 Partial mock up of the RB-49A airplane to include the crew compartment and installations and the engine installation.
4 Partialmaterials procurement of thirty (30)

The underside of one of the YB-49s - one of the few images that show the 'venetian blind' bomb bay doors. (USAF)

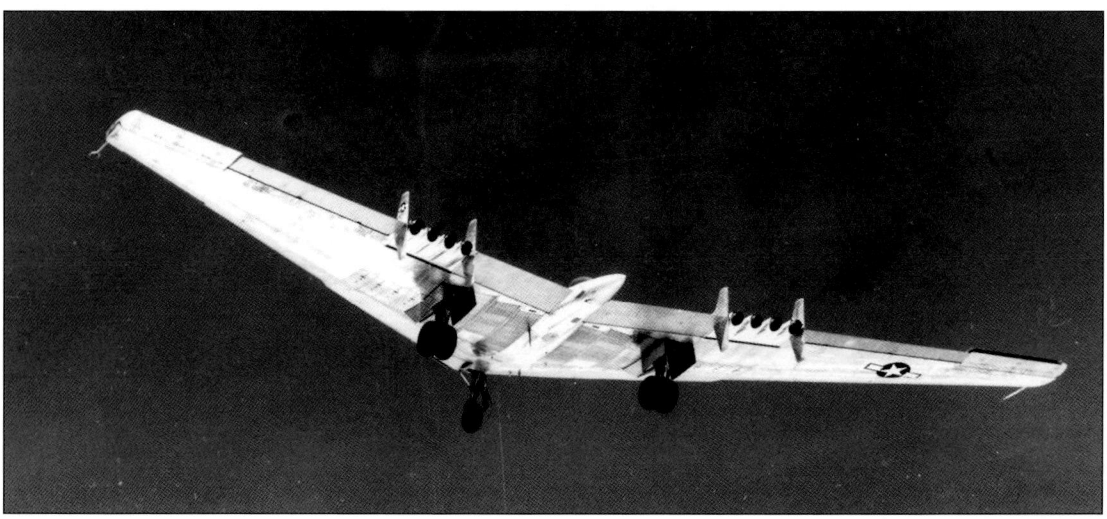

A detail view of the vertical fins on the YB-49. Contrary to popular belief they were not 'rudders.' (USAF)

RB-49A airplanes and the fabrication of one (1) static test shell.

5 Engineering and procurement to modify and flight test one (1) YB-49 airplane to the extent required to test new installations scheduled for incorporation into production RB-49A airlplane.

6 Designing of a static test jig for the testing of the RB-49A static test shell and the construction thereof.

This was the preliminary work to be undertaken for the contract for thirty RB-49s that was to be sub-contracted to Consolidated Vultee. Despite a lot of research I have failed to get to the bottom of the 'FB' designation. Under Air Force terminology, 'FB' stands for 'Fighter-bomber' whch is hardly the correct description of the all-jet flying wing! All subsequent paperwork describes this as the RB-49, which is 'Reconnaissance-Bomber', and in a stroke, did away with all the troublesome problems with vibrating reciprocating engines and propellers.

The modification of the B-35 to incorporate jet engines was not an insubstantial task. Removal of the piston engines, propellers and all associated shafting and gearboxes created a large amount of space - and since the original layout of engines, shafts, gearboxes and propellers were in a straight line, it was relatively easy to insert inlets, turbojets and exhausts in their place.

Conversion came about with Change Order 11, dated 1 June 1945, when instructions were given to convert the second and third YB-35s into YB-49 aircraft. The estimated additional cost would be $1,644,603.48, which included the fixed fee for Northrop.

From 1 December 1946 onwards, the YB-49s were administered by the Procurement division of the AMC, where the two aircraft were expected to provide important data on multi-engined jet bombers if they could be completed by an early date.

The conversion of the two bomb bays into fuel tanks ate into the bomb-load, but that was not regarded as a problem, for at an earlier conference which discussed the bomb-load, the 4,000 lb bomb had been designated as the largest bomb to be carried in the YB-49.

Then, just as with the B-35's problems with Government Furnished Equipment (GFE) the same thing arose with the B-49. The first flights of both YB-49s were delayed by deliveries of J-35-3 engines from Allison. The constant speed drives used in the B-35s were not suitable for the B-49s and a major re-design to permit functioning in the opposite direction was required before they could be used on the J-35s.

Installation of the J-35s plus all the additional equipment increased the aircraft's gross weight by 30,000 pounds. In May 1947, the automatic pilot, which was to be GFE, was deleted as it was not going to be available at the time, but the provision for it - which had already been completed in the first aircraft - was to remain.

The timescale kept slipping, and it was not until 18 September that an inspection was made, and the aircraft was described as being 'in excellent condition and complete in accordance with the detail specification.'

The YB-49 Flying Wing weighed 88,100 pounds when it was rolled out of the factory. The normal loaded weight was 205,000 pounds, which could be boosted to 213,000 pounds if necessary. A number of different dates have been recorded for the first flight of the number one prototype YB-49. Some claim it was on 1 October 1947, but the official AMC files say it occurred on 21 October when Max Stanley flew 42-102367 from Hawthorne, California to Muroc Air Force Base.

Subsequent test flights pushed the aircraft to a top speed of 520 miles per hour and placed the service ceiling at 42,000 feet. It had a fuel capacity of 17,545 gallons and a range of 4,450 miles. Thus, the YB-49 could carry over 36,760 pounds of bombs for a distance of 1,150 miles. A normal

10,000-pound load could be carried for an estimated 4,000 miles on 6,700 gallons of fuel.

The equipment situation got so bad that in FebruaryGeneral Shepard of the Procurement Division advised Washington that 'a lot of heat' was going to be put on the flying wing programme and that the Procurement Division ...was going to crack bottleneck in Government Furnished Equipment with overtime to get the YB-35s and YB-49s out and flying.'

By April 1948, the first YB-49 had completed 27 flights. Following two routine shakedown flights on the preceding days, on 26 April, a successful nine and a half-hour long-range flight was made of which six and a half hours was spent at an altitude of 40,000 feet. Both figures were believed to have been a record. The flight was completed with only one engine and one auxiliary power plant failure, so HQ USAF appeared to be well pleased with the YB-49 and the outcome of the test flight.

That same year Major Robert L Cardenas was assigned as the officer in charge of Flight Test Division projects at Muroc AB and as Chief Air Force test pilot on the YB-49 flying wing project. 'I was supposed to have flown the propeller-driven version of the Flying Wing, the XB-35. But I had told Colonel Boyd that any engineer who put a propeller on the trailing edge of a wing did not deserve his diploma. The air flowing over the top of the wing has a different temperature, velocity, and dynamic pressure than the air flowing under it, so those little propeller blades had to cut through two different air masses in microseconds, and the difference caused flutter.

The Army Air Forces decided the XB-35 needed jet engines, so Northrop converted two -35s to YB-49 all-jet flying wings. 42-102367 was instrumented for stability and control; 42-102368 was built for performance flight tests. In early 1948, my crew - co-pilot Danny and flight engineer William Cunningham - flew 368 from the Northrop factory in Hawthorne to Muroc to begin performance tests.

After completion of the Performance Phase II tests Cardenas checked out Captain Glen Edwards in the YB-49 on 20 and 21 May. Cardenas then received orders to USC for completion of his Aeronautical Engineering degree.

Over twenty months of research and flight testing had been conducted on the two YB-49 prototypes at Muroc Air Field. During this time, payload tests and endurance records were broken. Contracts were placed for thirty RB-49s and for converting the remaining ten B-35 airframes to YRB-49A strategic reconnaissance type aircraft.

The YB-49s out of all the Northrop flying wings had the habit of appearing alien and other worldly. (USAF)

During two years of flight testing, stability problems encountered in the YB-49 design had not been overcome, and further tests were planned. However, a new autopilot was to be designed and built into the aircraft that would create some form of auto-stability.

Northrop had envisioned a yaw damper /autopilot as always necessary for the flying wings, and one was flown on the N-9M in 1944. YB-49 number 2 had an autopilot installed; ship one did not, and it was only retrofitted in 1949. Initial Air Force evaluations after the premature loss of ship two, therefore, did not include a yaw damper/autopilot.

Pilot comments on the N-9 had mentioned that it was lightly damped in turbulence; it was assumed that the larger bomber, with its greater inertia, would not be as subject to responses. That was somewhat true, but once disturbed the lightly damped aircraft configuration would continue through 5-6 overshoots. Northrop predicted this, and artificial augmentation had always been planned.

Before this could be done, the first prototype crashed.

On 5 June 1948, the second YB-49 crashed, killing all on board. The event has been shrouded in mystery, with many details remaining secret, something that caused much speculation about the circumstances surrounding the accident, including the possibility of sabotage from a crewman who reported sick at the Base Hospital before the flight.

The official Air Force investigation was considerably less lurid but nevertheless uncovered much, and I looked at it in great detail on my 2013 work for Pen & Sword entitled 'Northrop Flying Wings.'

The summary of the Army Air Forces Report Of Major Accident coldly reported what was known and is pertinent to repeat here: 'YB-49 42-102368 took off Muroc AFB at 0644 PSDT for an estimated three-hour local test flight. The crash occurred approximately twelve miles NW of Muroc AFB at about 0755 PSDT. The airplane was in an inverted position at the time of contact with the ground. The nose of the plane headed about 300°. An explosion occurred almost immediately, and almost the entire wreckage was consumed by fire. The line of flight could not be definitely established. However, there appeared to be very little momentum in any direction at the point of impact. Pieces of the airplane's flaps, elevons, fins and both wingtips were scattered from the main wreckage on a line of 050° an area approximately a quarter-mile wide and nearly three miles long.'

Investigation into possible causes of the crash focused on the stall behaviour of flying wings, but the exact cause was never determined. Over the years, this has led to a common public misperception that flying wings were unstable. The successful flights of the other B-49s were largely ignored.

The known facts of the accident are limited. The flight was flown on a Saturday and did not have a chase aircraft supporting. No radio calls were received from the mishap aircraft during the accident. No instrumentation tapes were recovered from the wreckage. Two ground observers only saw the aircraft from a distance of eight to ten miles distant, apparently gyrating as it fell to earth. One observer did not observe anything until afler the smoke column appeared; he then noted a large piece fluttering to earth separately.

The other observer saw four flashes appear moving vertically downward, which he interpreted as the aircraft 'tumbling about its lateral axis.'

On board was Major Daniel H Forbes Jr, Captain Glen W Edwards, 1st Lt Edward L Swindell, along with civilians Clare C Lesser and C H LaFountain.

Despite what has been reported since the report clearly states that the thirty-year old Major Forbes was the person at the aircraft controls at the time of the accident.

The mission was planned as a performance flight, as the Air Force Phase 2 Testing (Performance) was in progress, to be followed by Phase 3 Stability Testing. The test profile called for speed power cruise

The crew, from left to right: Major Daniel Hugh Forbes, Jr - pilot. Capt. Glen Walter Edwards - copilot. Lt. Edward Lee Swindell - flight engineer. Clare C. Lesser and Charles H. LaFountain - both Air Force civilian engineers.

testing at 40,000 feet, followed by engine restarts, followed by a descent to an altitude sufficient for low power stalls, with an option for high power stalls if the low power ones were satisfactory. An Air Force flight test engineer. involved in planning the Air Force test cards theorized the altitude for these stalls as 15,000 feet but at the time of the accident, no formal stall tests had been done on the YB-49 as part of the Phase I contractor tests.

The investigation team reached a finalé with lots of ideas as to what probably happened, but no real conclusions as to what had actually happened. Numerous reports were issued, points were made, suggestions distilled, all of which generated a large amount of paperwork, but not much else.

A few days after the tragic accident at Muroc, when all seemed to be lost, Jack Northrop received a telephone call from General Joseph McNarney in Washington. The General wished to see him immediately and would be in California the next day.

General McNarney had been Deputy Chief of Staff under General George Marshall and was now Commanding General of the Air Force Air Material Command. McNarney signed purchase orders for Air Force aircraft, and his visit to Northrop was not considered an ordinary event. Jack was still somewhat depressed from the loss of the YB-49 at Muroc and wondered what other bad news was on the way.

Jack Northop welcomed General McNarney at the door of his office, and McNarney continued inside with a wide grin on his face, greeting Jack with unrestrained enthusiasm. He handed Northrop a sheaf of papers pulled from his attache case. Jack shuffled through them rapidly, returning again and again to one particular page, before looking up and returning the General's grin. Jack's smile was even bigger. The papers were a signed contract ordering thirty RB-49 flying wing bombers, with production to begin immediately. The General explained they were designated RB-49s to be used by the Air Force for photo-reconnaissance. He added, 'The order is only a drop in the bucket. Consolidated Vultee's Fort Worth bomber plant, owned by the government, will be made available to you for production of the RB-49. In large numbers.'

Jack could hardly believe what was happening. The production contract answered the lingering question of who was to blame for Captain Edwards' fatal accident - it was not Northrop's design of the flying wing. The Northrop YB-49 was the superior aircraft and the Air Force was now prepared to

Above: General Joseph Taggart McNarney (b. 28 August 1893, d. 1 February 1972) was a four-star general in the United States Army and in the United States Air Force. McNarney retired on 31 January 1952 and held executive positions with General Dynamics.

Right: Jack Northop out in the desert in front of one of the Flying Wings at Muroc AFB.

42-102368, the ill-fated second YB-49, high over the south Californian desert. (USAF)

substitute the YB-49 for the Consolidated Vultee B-36. Northrop was delighted, and as he later said, 'I felt we had, at last, won the battle.'

Washington had finally awakened to the fact that the Northrop flying wing bomber was a viable weapons delivery system - an aircraft that was not just an unorthodox experimental design of a visionary. The Air Force orders were proof of the machine's ability to outperform its B-36 competition. The YB-49 could climb at a higher rate to a higher altitude and protect itself with an array of defensive armament that was quite impressive. There would be twenty 50-calibre machine guns in four outer wing mounted turrets plus a tail cone cluster, all remotely controlled units operated electrically from four remote gunner blisters.

Perhaps the most important attribute in favour of the YB-49, when compared to the B-36, was its lower maintenance requirements. It had two fewer engines, all of the same type, not the B-36's awkward mix of piston and jet. None of this was required on the Northrop YB-49. The flying wing required less fuel to operate and, most importantly from a maintenance point of view during a war, it was simply less aircraft. The flying wing would be much easier to keep flying.

The morning after receiving the good news, Jack prepared an announcement of the new contract for distribution to Northrop employees. The engineering staff had difficulty keeping their congratulatory tours around the plant in check, knowing that hard work must now begin, the preparation for actual production in quantity of the flying wing. Two weeks later, General McNarney notified both Northrop and Consolidated Vultee of the production decision by letter: 'It is the desire of the Air Force to retain the production facilities at Fort Worth, which is now employed in the construction of B-36 airplanes. Since it is not intended to buy more than the ninety-five B-36 airplanes presently on contract, it is desired that the production of RB-49s be moved to that facility at the earliest possible date.

'An absolute minimum number of RB-49s will be built in the present Northrop facility at Hawthorne . It is requested that representatives of Northrop Aircraft and Consolidated Vultee Aircraft arrange the necessary plans for carrying out this programme with the least possible delay.'

Northrop began to plan to produce thirty RB-49 flying wing aircraft as soon as they received the letter. Eleven airframes remained at the Hawthorne plant, the unfinished portion of the original fifteen machine order for XB-35 and YB-49 bombers. Most of these could be modified for use in the new reconnaissance configuration. The majority of the new RB-49s, would be built in the plant at Fort Worth under a subcontract with Consolidated Vultee. Northrop's Hawthorne plant did not have space available at the time to produce thirty of the large flying wings, although engineering work on production jigs and tools had already been completed.

General Manager Claude Monson announced to Northrop employees that a subcontract would be negotiated with Consolidated Vultee to build the RB-49 in Fort Worth. Northrop employees would not have all the work, but they would have all the glory.

Meanwhile, Northrop's project engineer, Warren Kneriam, was sent to Fort Worth to inspect the extensive production facilities available - there would be ample room to begin B-49 production while phasing out the B-36. At first, relations between the Northrop representatives and Consolidated Vultee proceeded in a friendly and cooperative fashion.

Left: Curtis Emerson LeMay (b. 15 November 1906, d. 1 October 1990) was an American Air Force general who implemented an effective but controversial strategic bombing campaign in the Pacific theatre of World War Two. He later served as Chief of Staff of the USAF from 1961 to 1965.

Right: William Stuart Symington III (b. June 26, 1901, d. December 14, 1988) was an American businessman and Democratic politician from Missouri. He served as the first Secretary of the Air Force from 1947 to 1950 and was a United States Senator from Missouri from 1953 to 1976.

Word quickly spread through the Consolidated Vultee organisation that production of B-36s in the plant would end when the current contract was completed and Northrop's B-49 built in their place. From then on, relations were cool. John Myers and Gilbert Nettleton, John's assistant in Northrop sales, had already arrived in Texas to negotiate the subcontract.

The bad news was not long in reaching Floyd Odlum, Atlas Corporation Chairman and a major Consolidated Vultee shareholder. He was the same investor who had purchased Northrop securities at a critical time when seed capital was needed for the nascent Northrop company. In some respects, it was Floyd Odlum who may be credited with making the first security underwriting programme for Northrop a success. However, his investment company was no longer a shareholder in Northrop, having sold its stock in 1939. Nevertheless, Odlum was well aware of Jack's design capabilities and was deeply concerned over Consolidated Vultee's position as a major military aircraft supplier being challenged by upstart Northrop.

The test programme with the one remaining YB-49 aircraft continued at Muroc, soon to be renamed Edwards Air Force Base. There was nothing to indicate there would be any problem with the Air Force contract, as Northrop engineers preceded with plans for moving production to Fort Worth.

A hatchet-job to end all hatchet-jobs.

As much as there were fairly public political battles going on, other more darker battles were taking place behind the scenes.

It must be realised that during this time aircraft company relationships were akin to musical chairs; loyalties and allegiances were more associated with individual executives than companies. When an executive moved, often their assistants, underlings or bag carriers went with them. The same applied to the money men controlling the investment firms that held the purse strings for many US aircraft manufacturers: they had their 'teams' and often moved them en massé from company to company.

Much of this seems a world away from actual hands-on aircraft manufacture; to many, it is the inconsequential realm of shady deals done across the smokey boardroom table. Nothing could be further from the truth, as we shall soon see.

One pertinent example of this was Richard 'Dick' Millar was elected chairman of Northrop after the colourful La Motte Cohu resigned to become President of TWA. This association did not last long, as Cohu was unable to get along with Howard Hughes, who owned the airline. Cohu was then hired by Floyd Odlum as President of Consolidated Vultee in San Diego. LaMotte Cohu persuaded several former Northrop executives to join him, including Bob Byron, Director of Public Relations; Jack Naish, who became Director of Sales for Consolidated Vultee; and B G Reed, who advanced to General Manager of the Fort Worth production line.

Cohu did not last long in San Diego but during his tenure the Consolidated Vultee firm inherited much of Northrop's management.

It was Dick Millar who had persuaded Donald Douglas to buy Jack Northrop's company from United Aircraft in the 1930s when Millar learned Jack was leaving. Dick had been President of Vultee aircraft when Northrop arranged the Vultee Vengeance contract with the British.

Millar had left Vultee when the company merged with Consolidated in San Diego, so forming Floyd Odlum's Consolidated Vultee, which itself was part of the Atlas Corporation. This American investment firm was formed in 1928. Atlas invested in and managed many major US companies during the 20th century.

Atlas was formed in a merger of the United Corporation, an investment firm started in 1923 with $40,000, with Atlas Utilities and Investors Ltd. The corporation specialised in capital formation and management. In 1929, Atlas was a $12,550,000 investment trust. The company was able to shrewdly weather the Wall Street Crash of 1929 and continue to grow through the 1930s and 1940s. The corporation was founded by Floyd Odlum and his brother-in-law Boyd Hatch.

With Floyd Odlum as President and Boyd Hatch as vice-president, Atlas invested, managed or controlled numerous industries, including Greyhound Lines, Bonwit Teller (acquired 1934) and Franklin Simon & Co. (acquired 1936) ladies' apparel stores, Madison Square Garden, and various mines, utility companies, aviation-related businesses, and banks. After Atlas Corporation acquired the Bonwit Teller ladies apparel stores, Floyd Odlum convinced his wife, Hortense, to become involved in the store's operations. She became the first female President of a major department store chain when she became President of Bonwit Teller in 1934. In 1948, Howard Hughes acquired a controlling interest in RKO Pictures from Atlas.

Floyd Bostwick Odlum was an American lawyer and industrialist. He has been described as one of the few men in the United States who made a great fortune out of the Depression. After struggling as a corporate attorney in Salt Lake City, Odlum received an offer of a job at a New York firm, and in 1921 became vice-president of his primary client, Electric Bond and Share Company. In 1923, Odlum, a friend, and their wives pooled $39,600 and formed the United States Company to speculate in purchases of utilities and general securities. Within two years, the company's net assets had increased seventeen fold to nearly $700,000. In 1928, Odlum incorporated Atlas Utilities Company to take over the common stock of his other company.

During the summer of 1929, Odlum was one of the few industrial moguls to believe that the boom on Wall Street could not continue much longer. He sold one-half of Atlas's holdings and $9 million in new securities to investors. He had $14 million in cash and short term notes when the stock market crashed. During the next few years, Atlas Utilities bought up stock in less profitable investment companies at Depression-reduced prices. After Franklin D Roosevelt was inaugurated President of the United States, Odlum shifted gears, selling off utilities before stronger regulation set in, and switching to large-scale financing. By 1933, Odlum was one of the ten wealthiest men in the United States. Besides Atlas Corporation, he had a major stake in RKO Studios, Convair, Northeast Airlines, and Bonwit Teller, among other businesses, and was associated in the aviation business with financier George Newell Armsby. Odlum's association with Armsby provided a link to Armsby and John Cheever Cowdin's Transcontinental Air Transport, Inc.

Odlum was first married, in 1915, to Hortense McQuarrie, the first female department store head (at Bonwit Teller); they were divorced in 1935. His second wife, whom he married in 1936, was aviator Jackie Cochran. Odlum and Cochran were close friends of Amelia Earhart and her husband George P Putnam, and the Odlums were financial backers of Earhart's flying activities. They developed the Cochran-Odlum (C-O) Ranch in Indio, California, where they lived after the 1950s.

The bad news of Northrop's gain to Consolidated Vultee's loss was not long in reaching Floyd Odlum, Atlas Corporation Chairman and a major Consolidated Vultee shareholder. He was the same investor who had purchased Northrop securities at a critical time when seed capital was needed for the budding Northrop company. In some respects, it was Floyd Odlum who may be credited with making the first security underwriting programme for Northrop a success. However, his investment company was no longer a shareholder in Northrop, having sold all of its stock in 1939. Nevertheless, Odlum was well aware of Jack's design capabilities and was deeply

Left: LaMotte Turck Cohû (b. 23 September 1895, d. 10 September 1968). Cohu had many roles in the emergent aviation industry.

Right: Floyd Bostwick Odlum (b. 30 March 1892, d.17 June 1976). He was regarded as on of America's ten most wealthiest men and is seen here with his second wife, Jacqueline 'Jackie' Cochran (b. 11 May 1906, d. August 9, 1980) an American pilot and business executive.

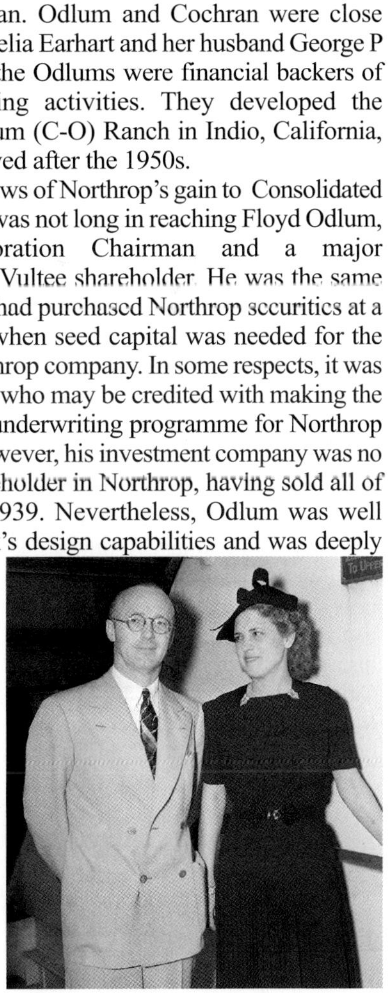

YB-49 42-102367 seen high over Muroc Air Force Base. (USAF)

concerned over Consolidated Vultee's position as a significant military aircraft supplier challenged by what he saw as the upstart Northrop.

There then followed a period of behind the scenes activity that to this day is shrouded in mystery and has been pieced together from fragments of interviews and available documents.

What is known is that on the evening of 16 July 1948, Jack Northrop was invited to meet with Secretary of the Air Force Stuart Symington at the home of John McComb in San Marino and to bring Northrop board chairman Richard Millar with him. The invitation sounded more like a summons than to a festive occasion. Symington was in town to address a meeting of the Institute of Aeronautical Sciences. He wanted to talk with Northrop about the B-49 flying wing. McComb had been a member of President Truman's Air Policy Commission. He was now the secretary's assistant and had invited Symington to stay at his house while in southern California. Northrop knew McComb, as he had previously been a member of the Joshua-Hendy firm with whom Jack had formed an ill-fated partnership to develop the Turbodyne turbine engine.

When Jack Northrop and Dick Millar arrived at John McComb's home in the late afternoon, they were surprised to find that Floyd Odlum had also been invited. General McNarney, who had personally brought the RB-49 contracts to Jack, was also in attendance.

Brigadier General Robert L. Cardenas (b.10 March 1920, d. March 10, 2022) (USAF)

The conversation began abruptly, without ceremony. Secretary Symington began by announcing that were are too many aircraft companies. The Air Force could not afford to support another large aircraft manufacturer, and they would have to cut one down.

It sounded as if Northrop had already been nominated to be eliminated. Symington followed with a request spoken as a demand, 'I want Northrop combined with Consolidated.'

Jack Northrop was shocked but asked what the alternatives were. By all accounts, Symington was blunt in his reply, 'You will be goddamned sorry if you don't.' General McNarney sounded concerned, 'Mr. Secretary, you don't mean that?' To which the Secretary of the Air Force replied, "You're goddamned right I do!"

There was little to say in response. It appeared as if Symington ordered the Northrop company to be taken over by its competitor for the long-range bomber contract. Floyd Odlum remained silent throughout the meeting. Finally, Jack Northrop asked for time to consider the implications of such a step, explaining that any decision must be referred to their board of directors, as Northrop had a majority of public shareholders. Then, they agreed to meet again at Floyd Odlum's Indio home to discuss the terms of the proposed merger in detail.

As Millar and Northrop were leaving the McComb house, Odlum denied all foreknowledge of the subject of the meeting. In turn, Symington later denied that he had arranged a meeting, saying he thought Northrop had called him to arrange a meeting while he was in Los Angeles. Symington was defensive, defending his actions for reasons unknown, offering no explanations, only denials. He said he could not remember ever saying anything about making trouble for Northrop.

Years later, when Los Angeles television commentator Clete Roberts prepared a documentary for KCET-Channel 28 on the flying wing controversy, Symington, through his attorney, Clark Clifford, threatened the station with a lawsuit if the programme was aired. The documentary was finally presented after considerable delay and no suit was filed.

Northrop clearly remembered Symington's threats at the San Marino meeting and remained puzzled by Symington and Odlum's behaviour. Northrop was deeply offended by the demand proposed by Secretary Symington, a government official. As far as he was concerned, Symington should not be making demands for corporate mergers that would affect competitive bidding on military contracts.

There was great unhappiness over the proposed deal, but Northrop and Millar decided to keep the appointment to meet with Floyd Odlum at his Indio home. They agreed that, based on the few words exchanged at San Marino, it was evident that much had gone on before they arrived. As Northrop and Millar entered Floyd Odlum's Indio home, the two aviation pioneers were aware of the aircraft personalities that preceded them on the sacrificial altar of corporate mergers and of the predatory acquisitiveness of Consolidated Vultee and its major shareholder, Odlum's Atlas Corporation. It was obvious to the duo that Northrop was next on Odlum's list for corporate assimilation.

As far as Northrop was concerned, Odlum was looking for another aircraft company to enhance his collection. It was obvious that Northrop and the RB-49 contract would be a worthy acquisition. The Air Force had let it be known that the RB-49 was the better aircraft and had already said that contracts for additional RB-49s were on the way. The military budget made it evident that only one company's aircraft would be ordered in quantity. Odlum wanted that company to be Convair, as Symington had made clear at the San Marino meeting, even if it meant that Convair would be manufacturing Northrop's RB-49.

At Odlum's home in California, the uncompromising tone of the conversation made it clear to Northrop and Millar that Odlum knew he had the backing of the Secretary of the Air Force and that President Truman's new budget did not provide for money to buy both the B-36 and the RB-49. He would drive a hard bargain to gain the entire strategic bomber contract by default, perhaps to deliberately make any corporate merger impossible. The precise terms of the proposed exchange of shares in the two companies have never been made public, but later Northrop and Millar both recalled that Northrop shareholders were to get less than one-fourth of the total shares in the merged companies. Consolidated Vultee shareholders would end up with the Northrop-developed flying wing design, all the aerodynamic

Another picture of a YB-49 departing Hawthorne. Some times the climb-out appeared fairly steep, other times it was almost flat. (USAF)

US Air Force photographers loved to take pictures of the YB-49 in flight, especially over the Californian desert and the Dry Lake area around Muroc. It's not surprising therefore that Hollywood used the YB-49 in their epic '*War of the Worlds*.' (USAF)

and production knowledge resulting from years of work by Jack, the RB-49 Air Force contracts, and all the other Northrop business, including the Northrop organization and company-owned facilities. According to Millar, Odlum never came up with any offer they could even pass on to Northrop stockholders for consideration.

When the two Northrop executives objected, Odlum became adamant, offering no alternatives. The Northrop team were amazed by the uncompromising demand from their competitor, an offer that could destroy the company. The answer was predictable. After talking about the deal next day with fellow Northrop directors, all voted to reject the offer, even if it resulted in the loss of the coveted YB-49 flying wing bomber contract.

Interestingly, Floyd Odlum and his wife, famed aviatrix Jackie Cochran, often entertained Air Force Secretary Stuart Symington at their desert home in Indio, near Palm Springs. It was a friendly relationship that was helpful to Consolidated Vultee in winning and keeping Air Force contracts. Consolidated Vultee may have learned of Northrop's being awarded the B-49 bomber contract before Northrop himself knew.

Six months after Jack Northrop said no to Floyd Odlum's demand for Northrop to merge with Consolidated Vultee and give the flying wing to his competitor, the Air Force notified Northrop that the production contract for thirty RB-49 flying wing bombers was cancelled. At the same time, Jack learned that production by Consolidated Vultee of the B-36 would continue. Work on all but one of the eleven YB-49 airframes was terminated, including the single YB-49 flying wing that was to have been used as a testbed for the powerful Northrop developed XT-37 Turbodyne engine. This project had been stopped by the Air Force earlier when Northrop was ordered to divest itself of the manufacture of the jet turbine engine. A single YB-49 was converted to the YRB-49 photo reconnaissance version, which was delivered to the Air Force in early 1951.

There were other strange goings-on. Major Robert Cardenas, command pilot of the YB-49 flying wing on its record-breaking cross-country hop to Washington D.C., had submitted a very favourable report on his flight, evaluating the 'excellent performance of the flying wing under very trying conditions, including flight with four engines out. For the full story of this flight, see Northrop Flying Wings, Pen and Sword 2013 by the same author.

Cardenas immediately flew to California to confer with Jack about the cancellation, worried that something he might have said in his report had caused the change in mind by the Air Force. Northrop reassured him that he had not but warned him not to say anything about the cancellation to anyone, for he thought it would be detrimental to Northrop Corp.

Cardenas later learned that his report had been tampered with, and excerpts from his comments about the YB-49 quoted out of context for use in other critical documents. Comparing the quoted criticism with his original document is quite revealing. It is easily seen that, if the fabricated quotes were taken as fact, there would be sufficient reasons to convince politicians that no YB-49s should be built.

It is hard to know if the confusion and misquotes were deliberate or otherwise - what is known is that despite making repeated attempts to put the record straight, Cardenas was ignored.

In the purported Cardenas test report distributed in Washington, Cardenas, who had thirty-five to forty hours in the bomber, was quoted as having said that the YB-49 was extremely unstable and very difficult to fly on a bombing mission because of continual yawing and pitching caused by the control arrangement. Also, the bomb bay doors could not be closed in flight. It was concluded that this bomber was not a good bombing platform - its directional stability was a little better but 'still not perfect, and its lateral stability was neutral. Additionally, the aircraft suffered from flap flutter.'

What Cardenas actually reported was that the aircraft had marginal stability, referring to pitch (phugoid) and the lateral directional axes (dutch roll). As the final stall test showed, it was possible to put the centre of gravity so far aft the aircraft was unstable in pitch, but that was not typically where the centre of gravity was located. Jack Northrop's Wright lecture of 1947 mentioned that the B-35 had a useable centre of gravity travel of five to seven per cent mean aerodynamic chord, compared to a conventional aircraft range of ten to fourteen per cent. However, since the chord of a flying wing was usually much larger than a conventional wing, this was not much of a problem. The real issue was not so much of marginal stability but rather of damping ratios for the axes; the flying wing was by its nature lightly damped in all axes, which could also be described as akin to marginal stability. The phugoid of the B-35 was in the order of ten seconds. In itself this was not necessarily objectionable, but the lateral directional behaviour was notably different from a conventional aircraft. The lack of a conventional tail for weathercock stability. the short moment arms for the propeller housings or vestigial tails of the B-49 and the strong dihedral effect of the swept-wing all contributed to a lightly damped system in the lateral directional axes.

Unfortunately for Northrop, critical comments such as these were taken at face value without any attempt at verification. In the actual Cardenas test flight report, none of these adverse comments was made. It is not known who authored the revised report.

The Air Force also received an adverse report from Joseph Foa, head of the propulsion branch of the Cornell Aeronautical Laboratory in Buffalo. Foa and his colleagues did analyses that differed quite considerably from those of Sears and Von Karman, which showed flying wings to be the worst possible aerodynamic configuration for jet-propelled long-range bombers. However, the success of Cardenas' cross country flight would seem to have proven otherwise.

Two of the flying wings had been redesigned to accommodate a big gas turbine engine that was developed as one of the original projects at Northrop. They had a good gas turbine, and it had passed the required fifty-hour tests at 10,000 horsepower. The turbo-prop and flying wing combination would have given Northrop an aircraft that would have carried a 10,000-pound bomb load 11,500 miles non-stop at 400 miles per hour. Symington told the company that they had no business being in the gas turbine business, and he stripped the plant of their gas turbine war work and turned it over to General Electric. The only thing that saved the company was that, for some reason or other, he did not cancel the order for F-89 fighters, and that production went on for some time and sustained the life of the company. This was the first time in Air Force history when something that was absolutely pure politics - and dirty politics at that - determined the decision of where and which aircraft should be built. It was a heartbreaker because the aircraft was unique. Its ratio of lift to drag was better than any contemporary aircraft of its time, and its ratio of payload to weight empty was apparently far better than any machine ever built. Northrop was unwilling to merge on terms considered unfair to Northrop stock-holders, and for that, they suffered vicious bureaucratic consequences.

Jack Northrop demanded an explanation of the events. When he finally reached Secretary Symington on the telephone, all the Secretary would say was, 'I have an adverse report on the airplane.' Northop had never received any such report. Shortly after Symington's statement, Northop received anonymously a photographic copy of the Air Force tests of simulated bombing runs of both the Y-49 and B-36. The recorded results in the document showed the YB-49 to be on a par with the B- 36, and, in some respects, a superior bombing platform. The company never learned the sender's identity, nor did they have any way of verifying the recorded results since the YB-49 files at Edwards were by now missing. It did appear that a friend at Edwards Air Force Base wanted them to know that the excuse regarding the YB-49s purported poor bombing performance was false.

Eventually I was able to track down the test bombing reports. A series of bombing tests were conducted in 1948 after the loss of aircraft No.2. Aircraft No.1 had to have bomb racks installed, as initially, it had no armament systems since it was planned to be the stability machine while No.2 would be the performance example. The autopilot designed for retrofit in No.1 was still unavailable as it had been lost with No. 2. The weapon bays on the B-35 were unique: there were eight side-by-side bays between the landing gear. In the YB-49, the outboard bay in each wing was sealed for fuel tank space. The bay doors were similar to a roll-top desk, being made of thin metal so they could be wound onto a drum when opening. Designed for a propeller-driven aircraft with a top speed of 350mph, they had difficulty coping with the increased speed of a jet. The doors often refused to operate and were a source of irritation to the Air Force evaluators.

The tests were conducted bombing from 10, 20, and 30,000 feet. There was urgency in evaluating the aircraft as a bombing platform as soon as possible. The bombsight employed was a World War Two era Norden device.

A memo from 1949 states the RB-49 would be equipped with the K-1 optical radar bombing system, as it was felt the high altitude and high speed of the flying wing would be too much for the Norden sight; but that was what was used in the tests, comparing the results with a B-29 also using the Norden bombsight.

The results were extremely disappointing. The Circular Error Possible (CEP) of bombs dropped from the YB-49 was approximately twice that of the B-29. What was emphasised more was that the stability of the YB-49 was marginal and that as it was flown, it was unsatisfactory for the bombing or reconnaissance missions. The bombardier took not less than four minutes to make a B-49 bombing run; on the B-29, no run exceeded forty-five seconds.

For those unfamiliar with the operation of the then-secret Norden bombsight, this is how it operated. The bombsight was an analogue computer,

Jack Northrop - fourth from the left - joins a routine YB-49 test flight. Northrop test pilot Max Stanley is on the extreme left.

using gears and shafts to solve the bombing triangle of releasing a bomb to hit a target. The bombardier entered the type of bomb, aircraft height and speed using micrometre scales on the sight. He then looked through a gyro stabilised telescope pointed at the ground, which had an illuminated travelling grid of lines that travelled at a constant rate controlled by a manual knob and potentiometer. He pointed the telescope at an obvious point on the ground some distance ahead of the aircraft. He then swivelled the sight in yaw so that the object travelled straight down vertical lines scribed on the glass. In this way, he found the drill angle of the aircraft. He then rotated the knob to match the speed of the travelling grid to the object's motion through his field of view; gears translated this into the ground speed of the aircraft, which was then translated by more gears into a computation of the bomb release range and the angle of the sightline to the target when at the release range. The bombardier then swivelled his telescope to find the actual target; once he found it, he put the crosshairs of the telescope on it and tracked it, now continuously refining the drift and travelling grid knobs.

A PDI (Pilot's Direction Indicator) was provided for the pilot, but this was difficult to follow, so the Norden bombsight was generally coupled to the autopilot on the bomb run. When the angle of the crosshairs (on the target) reached the pre-computed release range angle, the bombs were automatically released.

The lightly damped dutch roll of the YB-49 resulted in considerable oscillation of the optical telescope line of sight after the rollout from the turn onto the bomb run. It took considerable pilot effort to damp out the motion on the unaugmented YB-49 no. 1; the Air Force bombardier reportedly became airsick looking through the sight. As a result of this extra motion, the YB-49 crew had to struggle to measure the ground speed and drill initially. In addition, without a coupled autopilot, the YB-49 pilot had to rely on manually chasing the needles driven by the bombsight. Turns to follow the PDI would excite the dutch roll once again.

Moreover, the lightly damped phugoid required continuous pilot attention to maintain the constant speed and altitude the bombsight solution was computed on; the bombardier had to manually adjust the sight if the airspeed varied by more than five miles an hour. All these factors contributed to the lengthy bomb runs. Bombing errors were both along-track and cross-track. For the limited samples flown the CEP of the YB-49 was over 1000 feet, while the B-29's was just under 600 feet.

Further tests were done later in 1949 after an autopilot had been installed. The Norden bombsight was used once again. The aircraft was easier to operate on the bombing run with an autopilot/yaw damper installed - the reported instability having been fixed.

By 1949 the B-49 was not considered a viable contender as a bomber. The small weapons bays of the 1942-vintage flying wing design could not carry the larger conventional Grand Slam bombs developed during the war. The Mk-5 Atomic Bomb, developed from the Nagasaki Fat Man weapon, was five feet in diameter and required voluminous bays, which the B-49 did not have. By 1949 the B-49 was being considered only for use as a strategic reconnaissance aircraft. One RB-49 was ordered to be built, with four engines in the wing and two externally mounted jets, similar to the outboard B-47 jet pods, allowing more fuel tanks in the wing; the cameras and radar were mounted in a bulged after centre body.

When Northrop sales representative Nettleton asked Senator Carl Hayden, chairman of the Senate Armed Services Committee, for an explanation of the flying wing contract cancellation, he was told that President Truman had personally ordered the cancellation of Northrop's YB-49 bomber contract because of a shortage of funds. Hayden said it was Truman's understanding that Northrop's flying wing still needed additional expensive development and had to be dropped in favour of the B-36. The bomber command would then receive operational B-36s before the B-49 could be accepted. Apparently, Secretary of the Air Force Symington had spoken to the President before flight test reports were completed and convinced him that the B-36 was the machine the Air Force preferred. President Truman had been apparently misinformed about the successful YB-49 flight testing programme at Edwards, and corroborating files were then removed to prevent anyone else from knowing the facts about Northrop's flying wing.

In addition to the Secretary's close association with Odlum and his conflict of interest regarding the B-36 vs B-49, there is little doubt that another factor played an important role in predisposing the Secretary in favour of the B-36 in its competition with Northrop's B- 49. A dispute had arisen between the Air Force and the Navy over allocation of scarce defence dollars appropriated for the two services.

Secretary Symington had apparently found it quite easy to persuade Louis Johnson, President Truman's Secretary of Defense and a former director of Consolidated Vultee, to terminate construction of the large supercarrier United States, because the budget would not permit both the completion of the aircraft carrier and production of the number of bombers desired by the Strategic Air Command.

At a Washington meeting organized by Secretary Symington, invited executives of military aircraft manufacturers Douglas, Boeing, Lockheed, and others testified to what they took to be the possible superiority of the Consolidated Vultee B-36 bomber.

At this point, the Air Force made a sudden discovery. It announced the finding that jet fighters were unable to intercept the B-36 at altitudes above 40,000 feet. The Air Force allegedly learned of this new ability of the B-36 during extensive interception tests conducted at Edwards Air Force Base in California. The timing of the discovery was interesting - the Air Force had already finalised its procurement programme for fiscal 1949 in early May of the previous year, and not a single B-36 was included in the programme. As a result, the B-36 had been considered a dead duck in military circles. Now, the Secretary was informed that interception tests proving the invulnerability of the B-36 had been going on for about three months.

At the same time, the USAF was awarding contracts for the construction of the YB-49 to Northrop and buying more of Northrop's deadly night fighter, the jet-powered P-89 Scorpion. This was a fighter with a service ceiling of 51,000 feet, leaving some critics to wonder what kind of intercepting aircraft they were flying at Edwards that could not fly higher than 40,000 feet?

So Northrop's flying Wing YB-49 slipped into history, a dream destroyed. If not for political and budgetary considerations, military aircraft and commercial air travel today could well have been very different. Our airliners might have been flying wings. The demise of the Northrop flying wing was a step backwards for the Air Force and the US aerospace industry of the time.

But that was by no means the end of the politics.

Chapter Five

Politics and Rivalry

During World War Two, there existed broad wartime presidential authority to reorganise the armed forces under the War Powers Act of 1941, but this authority was due to expire six months after the end of the war, so in April 1944, the US Congress began considering legislation for a post-war organisation.

Here lay the origins of the 'military-industrial complex' a phrase that describes the relationship between a nation's military and the defence industry that supplies it, seen together as a vested interest that influences public policy. A driving factor behind this relationship between the government and defence-minded corporations is that both sides benefit from obtaining war weapons and from being paid to supply them. The term is most often used about the system behind the military of the USA, where it is most prevalent due to close links between defence contractors, the Pentagon and politicians.

In the context of the USA, the appellation was extended to the military-industrial-congressional complex adding the US Congress to form a three-sided relationship termed an iron triangle. These relationships included political contributions, political approval for military spending, lobbying to support bureaucracies, and oversight of the industry; or more broadly, to have the entire network of contracts and flows of money and resources among individuals as well as corporations and institutions of the defence contractors, private military contractors, the Pentagon, the Congress and executive branch.

History shows that from 1797 to 1941, the US government relied on civilian industries while the country was actually at war. The government owned their own shipyards and weapons manufacturing facilities which they relied on upon through World War One. With World War Two came a massive shift in the way that the American government armed the military. President Roosevelt established the War Production Board to coordinate civilian industries and shift them into wartime production. Throughout World War Two, arms production in the United States went from around one per cent of the annual GDP to forty per cent of the GDP. In addition, various American companies, such as Boeing, Consolidated and General Motors, maintained and expanded their defence divisions.

In response to the forthcoming legisation from Congress, the Joint Chiefs of Staff, the wartime body consisting of the most senior uniformed leaders, decided that it would need to prepare a submission, as they and their various advisory committees were themselves ad hoc wartime creations. On 9 May 1944, it appointed a Special Committee for Reorganisation of National Defense under the chairmanship of Admiral James O Richardson, a former Commander in Chief, United States Fleet, consisting of Major General William F Tompkins from the War Department General Staff, Major General Harold L George from the USAAF, Rear Admiral Malcolm F. Schoeffel and Colonel F Trubee Davison, a former Assistant Secretary of War for Air.

The committee reported to the Joint Chiefs of Staff on 11 April 1945. It endorsed the unification of the War and Navy Departments into a single department of armed forces headed by a civilian secretary, with three equal services through the creation of an independent air force. During the war, the United States Army Air Forces (USAAF) had achieved a degree of de facto independence from the United States Army itself and was eager to become a fully-fledged armed service on an equal footing with the Army and the US Navy. Richardson dissented, favouring the status quo over creating a new department, but he accepted the proposal to perpetuate the organisation of the Joint Chiefs of Staff by statute.

This created a controversy over strategy and weapons when the US Army Air Forces (AAF) was fighting to become an independent service. Gen. of the Army Henry H Arnold, Commanding General of the US Army Air Forces; General Carl A Spaatz; and Lt. Gen. James H Doolittle emphasised that all

Top officials of the National Military Establishment meet in Key West, Florida in March 1948. Front row, left to right: Admiral Louis E Denfeld, USN, Chief of Naval Operations; Fleet Admiral William D Leahy, USN, Chief of Staff to the Commander in Chief; James Forrestal, Secretary of Defense; General Carl Spaatz, USAF, Chief of Staff of the Air Force; and General Omar N Bradley, USA, Chief of Staff of the Army.
It was these men that held the future of the US military establishment in their hands, including the B-36.

forms of airpower's demonstrated effectiveness made the AAF the lead service in the American defence phalanx. General Doolittle, testifying before the Senate Military Affairs Committee, pointed out that the Navy was no longer the first line of defence for the United States. The US required an independent Air Force featuring an in-being strategic atomic force that could deter any aggressor from initiating conflict. This would be the country's strategic concept in the postwar era, and it was supported by President Harry S Truman and Army Chief of Staff Gen. Dwight D Eisenhower, among others.

Senior Navy officers, including Fleet Admirals William D Leahy, the Chief of Staff to the Commander in Chief, Ernest J King, the Commander in Chief, United States Fleet and Chester W Nimitz, the Commander in Chief, US Pacific Fleet, regarded the committee's recommendations as radical. They opposed the idea of a single secretary of National Defense, which they felt was too much responsibility for one man. It interposed a civilian head between the Joint Chiefs of Staff and the President of the United States, which might diminish the Navy's power and influence. They also feared the possible loss of the Navy's air arm, as had happened to the Royal Navy when the Royal Naval Air Service was absorbed into the Royal Air Force upon the creation of the latter in 1918.

The Navy feared it might lose its air element to an independent Air Force and that even the Marine Corps might be lost. Moreover, the naval leadership, convinced that the Navy required everything to make it self-supporting in pursuit of its mission, opposed Truman's and Eisenhower's concept of mutually supporting services under unified command. In the Congressional hearings on unification, General Eisenhower emphasised that the economy would be a driving force in postwar defence matters. The nation could not afford the Navy's concept of autonomous forces in the World War Two form.

The Senate Committee on Military Affairs formed a subcommittee to draft legislation, with Major General Lauris Norstad, the Assistant Chief of the Air Staff of Plans, and Rear Admiral Arthur W Radford, the Deputy Chief of Naval Operations (DCNO) for Air, as its advisors. Radford was considered a hardliner in his opposition to unification even within the Navy, and in July 1946, James Forrestal, the Secretary of the Navy, and Nimitz, now the Chief of Naval Operations (CNO), replaced him with the DCNO for Operations, Rear Admiral Forrest Sherman. Although also a naval aviator, Sherman did not oppose unification. He and Norstad drew up an agreement that the Joint Chiefs of Staff endorsed and forwarded to President Truman for approval on 12 December 1946.

This became the basis for the National Security Act of 1947, which created the National Security Council (NSC), Central Intelligence Agency (CIA), an independent United States Air Force (USAF), three civilian military department heads, and the National Military Establishment, a unified command with a cabinet-level Secretary of Defense to oversee the service departments and the Joint Chiefs of Staff. The Act left the Navy with the autonomy it sought and control of its own Naval and Marine Corps Aviation, effectively legitimising four military air forces. The act appeared to end the debate, although none of the services was completely happy with it.

It was clearly a compromise. The Act and the so-called 'functions paper' - actually, Truman's Executive Order - failed to resolve roles-and-missions disputes among the services. The new Air Force and the Navy – at conferences at Key West, Florida, and Newport, Rhode Island, in the spring and summer of 1948 – could not work out their differences over the strategic atomic mission and other functions questions.

The Air Force was set to rely on the B-36 intercontinental-range bomber to accomplish the strategic mission supporting the Truman Administration's policy of deterrence.

Immediately, criticism of the B-36 began appearing in newspapers and journals. Some of this criticism came from Hugh L Hanson, a Navy employee with the Bureau of Aeronautics, who had also contacted Forrestal, then the Defense Secretary, and several Congressmen. The Secretary of the Air Force, Stuart Symington, complained about this to the Secretary of the Navy, John L Sullivan. Nevertheless, the attacks continued.

William Stuart Symington III was an American businessman and Democratic politician from Missouri. He served as the first Secretary of the Air Force from 1947 to 1950 and was a United States Senator from Missouri from 1953 to 1976.

Born in Amherst, Massachusetts, Symington worked as an executive in his uncle's iron products company and for other companies before becoming president of Emerson Electric. He resigned from Emerson in 1945 to take various positions in the administration of President Harry S. Truman, becoming the first Secretary of the Air Force in 1947. He was elected to the Senate in 1952, defeating incumbent Republican Senator James P. Kem. He joined the Senate Armed Services Committee and the Senate Foreign Relations Committee, and emerged as a prominent critic of McCarthyism.

In 1948 and 1949, the Air Force made several decisions that led to Strategic Air Command's reliance on the B-36 for the SAC atomic deterrent mission until the B-52 long-range bomber could enter the operational inventory. In 1948, following the Soviet-inspired Communist coup in Czechoslovakia and the Soviet Union's blockade of Berlin, the possibility of war increased. The Air Force emphasised that the B-36 was the only aircraft capable of delivering the atomic bomb from bases in the US.

In early 1949, SAC Commander in Chief General Curtis E LeMay recommended to General Hoyt S Vandenberg, USAF Chief of Staff, that the Board of Senior Officers review the B-54 programme because B-36 tests with jet pods had been outstanding. Compared to the B-54, the B-36 with jet pods was faster, operated higher, and had

Left: James Vincent Forrestal (b. 15 February 1892 – d. 22 May 1949).

Right: Hoyt Sanford Vandenberg (b. 24 January 1899 – d. 2 April 1954) was a USAF general. He served as the second Chief of Staff of the Air Force, and the second Director of Central Intelligence. He denied that the Air Force was 'putting all its eggs in one basket', disclosing that only five per cent of USAF bombers were B-36s and also strongly denied that the USAF wanted to take over US naval aviation.

greater range and bomb-carrying capacity. Subsequently, the B-54 was cancelled. Symington informed Secretary Forrestal that the B-36 could fly from the US and could, 'because of its speed and altitude, penetrate enemy country without fighter escort, destroy the strategic target, and return nonstop to its base on this continent.'

Navy Secretary James V Forrestal took the lead in promoting the maritime strategy of depending on larger and faster carriers and opposing the creation of an independent Air Force.

Forrestal, a former naval aviator who came from a strict middle class Irish Catholic family, had been a successful financier on Wall Street before becoming Under Secretary of the Navy in 1940. He became Secretary of the Navy in May 1944 upon the death of his superior, Frank Knox. President Roosevelt requested that Forrestal take the lead in building up the Navy. In 1947, after the end of the war, President Harry S. Truman appointed him the first Secretary of the newly created Department of Defense. Forrestal was intensely hostile to the Soviet Union, fearing Communist expansion in Europe and the Middle East. Along with Secretary of State George C. Marshall, he strongly opposed the United States' support for the establishment of the State of Israel, fearing that this would alienate Arab nations which were needed as allies, and whose petroleum reserves were vital for both military and civilian industrial expansion. John L Sullivan, formerly the Assistant Secretary of the Navy (Air) succeeded him as Secretary of the Navy; Kenneth C Royall, the Under Secretary of War, became the Secretary of the Army; and Stuart Symington, who had been the Assistant Secretary of War for Air, became the first Secretary of the Air Force. As the Navy had wanted, the Secretary of Defense had a coordination role, and lacked the authority and resources to exercise effective control over service departments and their chiefs. Forrestal hoped that with unification accomplished, the services would set aside their parochial differences.

Following the end of World War Two, the US Government was concerned about the large deficit spending that had been necessary for the war effort, which reached 119 per cent of the gross domestic product in 1946. Deficit spending had lifted the US out of the Great Depression, but now Truman and his economic advisors were concerned about the prospect of inflation, which rose to 14.4 per cent in 1947 after wartime price controls were removed and embraced austerity. So as to reduce expenditure, the armed services had to demobilise and return to a peacetime military quickly. Defence budgets declined from $81 billion in fiscal year 1945 to $9 billion in fiscal year 1948, representing a decline from thirty-seven and a half per cent of GDP to three-and-a-half per cent. The services were reduced

President Harry S Truman with Secretary of the Air Force Stuart Symington and Chief of Staff of the Air Force Hoyt Vandenberg.

Presidential photo-call! President Harry S Truman poses for the media in the side hatch of B-36A 44-92010. (USAF)

from eighty-nine army and six marine divisions to twelve; from 213 air groups to sixty-three - only eleven of which were operational, with some existing only on paper; and from 1,166 warships to 343. Meanwhile, $13 billion went into the Marshall Plan, which commenced in 1948.

US war plans were drafted for a potential conflict with the Soviet Union. It was considered unlikely that the Soviet Union wanted to start a war, but the plans were prepared for the possibility that one might break out as a result of a miscalculation. The Soviet Union had fifty divisions in Germany and Austria to the US Army's one, enough to quickly overrun Europe east of the Rhine. This was a major barrier, but it was not considered that it could be held for long, forcing a retreat to the Pyrenees. In view of the Soviet Union's overwhelming superiority in conventional forces, the planners felt that the United States had no alternative means of striking back other than a strategic air offensive employing both conventional and nuclear weapons.

Admiral Louis E Denfeld, who had succeeded Nimitz as CNO on 15 December 1947, was critical of the war plan, which he regarded as deeply flawed. He noted that abandoning Western Europe without a struggle ran counter to the US Government policy of building up the democracies there. It also meant accepting the loss of the Mediterranean Sea. The plan called for using the Karachi area as a base for the strategic air campaign, but this would involve an enormous logistical effort to sustain, and it would not support other elements of the war plan. Moreover, there was no fallback in case the strategic bombing campaign failed. He was willing to sign off on the plan only as a temporary one for short-range planning and advocated a more aggressive strategy in which the Rhine and the Middle East were held. None of the three services had the resources to implement the short-term war plan, much less the more ambitious one.

In the years leading up to World War Two, the United States Army Air Corps had developed a doctrine of strategic air bombardment, which the Air Corps Tactical School promulgated. During World War Two, the experience of strategic bombing revealed major flaws in the Air Corps' precision bombing doctrine. Unescorted bombers were found to be highly vulnerable to fighters and took high losses. Improvements in anti-aircraft guns drove the bombers to higher altitudes, from which accurate bombing was difficult. None of the principal targets of the bombing offensive in Europe was destroyed or even suffered severe disruption, and only the oil campaign was ultimately regarded as successful. Air raids on Japan encountered weather and flying conditions that made daylight precision bombing from high altitude even more difficult than in Europe, resulting in a switch of tactics to low-level area bombing of cities with incendiaries. The wartime Chief of the USAAF, General of the Army Henry H Arnold, contended that the conventional bombing had destroyed Japan's ability to wage war, and the atomic bombing of Hiroshima and Nagasaki had given the Emperor of Japan an excuse to end the war.

The advent of nuclear weapons gave the strategic bombardment theorists encouragement that the factors that had limited the effectiveness of strategic bombing during the war could be overcome. Colonel Dale O Smith wrote that:

'The most effective air siege will result by concurrently attacking every critical element of the enemy's economy at the same time. This will result in a general disintegration of all industry that will, in turn, prevent reconstruction. Oil, transportation, power, vital end products, and weapon factories, if destroyed concurrently, would leave a nation in such a devastated state as to preclude repair since the capability for repair would have been lost as well. When our bombs were constructed of puny TNT this concept was questionable because we did not have sufficient power and we were forced to look for panacea targets, Achilles' heels, and short cuts ... If all the critical industrial systems could be destroyed at one blow, so that recuperation were impossible within any foreseeable time, there seems little question but that a nation would die just as surely as a man will die if a bullet pierces his heart and his circulatory system is stopped.'

The bombing campaign called for in the war plans was both nuclear and conventional. By June 1948, components for about fifty Fat Man and two Little Boy bombs were on hand. These had to be assembled by specially trained Armed Forces Special Weapons Project assembly teams. Only Silverplate Boeing B-29 Superfortress bombers were capable of delivering nuclear weapons, and of the sixty-five that had been made, only thirty-two were operational at the start of 1948, all of which were assigned to the 509th Bombardment Group, which was based at Roswell Army Airfield in New Mexico. Trained crews were also in short supply; at the beginning of 1948 only six crews were qualified to fly atomic bombing missions, although enough personnel had been trained to assemble an additional fourteen in an emergency. But up to twenty per cent of the target cities in the war plan were beyond the 3,000-nautical-mile range of the B-29, requiring a one-way mission, which would expend the crew, bomb and aircraft. There were also doubts about the ability of the B-29 to penetrate Soviet air space; as a propeller-driven bomber, it was highly vulnerable to the new Soviet jet fighters, even at night. The Boeing B-29 was the mainstay of the bomber fleet in 1948, the year the Convair B-36 Peacemaker was introduced into service.

As we have already seen, in the early part of World War Two, German victories had led to apprehension that the United Kingdom might be overrun. Therefore, the Air Corps invited design proposals for an intercontinental bomber to reach Germany from bases in the USA.

From this came two ultra-long-range designs, the Northrop B-35/49 and the Consolidated B-36. Both aircraft pushed state of the art at the time, but both soon ran into development and schedule problems and lost priority to the B-29. They were not cancelled as such, and in 1943 when it looked like bases in China - the only ones in Allied hands within B-29 range of Japan - might be overrun, an order was placed for one hundred B-36s.

Most aircraft orders were cut back or cancelled in 1945, but the B-36 order was left untouched. Many Air Force officers were sceptical of the value of the B-36. Still, in tests conducted between April and June 1948, the B-36 outperformed the Boeing B-50 Superfortress, the improved model of the B-29, in long-range cruising speed, load capacity and combat radius. The commencement of the Berlin Blockade in June 1948 led to increased concerns about the aggressive stance taken by the Soviet Union and demands for an intercontinental bomber. The B-36 was not yet atomic capable; deliveries of atomic-capable B-36s commenced in 1949. In service, it suffered from a host of problems, as was usual for new aircraft. An intrinsic one was that it was a piston-engine aircraft in the era of jets. It was therefore accepted as an interim aircraft, pending the introduction of the jet Boeing B-52 Stratofortress, but this was not expected to occur before 1952.

The 80th Congress adjourned in August 1948 without passing a bill authorising a seventy-bomb group peacetime air force, but the Chief of Staff of the Air Force, General Hoyt Vandenberg, took the provision of the first increment of funds for the purpose as a mandate and commenced the acquisition process for the 2,201 aircraft required with the funds on hand. This included the remaining ninety-five B-36s from the original contract, along with ten of the new Boeing B-47 Stratojet bombers, 132 B-50s, 1,457 jet fighters and 147 transport aircraft. In 1948, the services began preparing their budget submissions for fiscal year 1950. The Air Staff requested $8 billion, which would cover the seventy-group programme. But after word got around that budgets would be cut proportionately,

Symington arbitrarily increased the submission to $11 billion. The resulting service requests, when tallied in July, came to $29 billion.

There was no reason to believe that this would be available. The Bureau of the Budget had originally forecast a $5 billion surplus in the fiscal year 1950. Still, the recession of 1949 resulted in a drop in revenue and a revised forecast of a $2 billion deficit. Forrestal cut the defence request to $23.6 billion in October 1948, but the Budget Bureau convinced Truman to set a $14.4 billion ceiling on defence expenditure in the fiscal year 1950. The Joint Chiefs estimated that in a war, this would reduce the USA's reaction to a strategic bombing offensive from the UK. The Joint Chiefs of Staff divided the $14.4 billion between the three services, giving $4.834 billion to the Army, $4.624 billion to the Navy, and $5.025 billion to the Air Force.

It meant that the air force would have to cut back to just forty-eight groups. Vandenberg convened a senior officers' board chaired by General Joseph T McNarney to determine a structure. It decided to reduce Strategic Air Command to fourteen Bombardment Groups. Its Commander, Lieutenant General Curtis LeMay, stated that the atomic mission required four groups of bombers, which he said should be equipped with B-36s. The B-36 could cover ninety-seven per cent of targets in the Soviet Union from bases in North America. In the conventional role, it could carry thirty-nine tons of bombs over medium distances. He endorsed a proposal to improve the performance of the B-36 by adding twin jet pods. Of the remaining ten bombardment groups, five would be equipped with B-50s, two with the new B-47s, and three with B-29s. The B-36 programme benefited from the cutbacks because $269,761,000 was recouped from cancelling orders for other aircraft. LeMay also recommended that the Boeing B-54, an improved version of the B-50, be cancelled and the funds used to purchase thirty-six more B-36s and five more B-47s. Forrestal signed off on this recertification of

Three B-36s overfly the Capitol Building in Washington DC in 1949. There seems to be some confusion regarding this. Some sources - almost certainly correct - state that five machines overflew Washington durng the inauguration of President Harry S Truman on Thursday 20 January 1949. Other sources say that during during the Congressional debate over its performance and effectiveness a number of B-36 flew down the Mall and over the Capitol Building. (USAF)

President Truman with Secretary of State Dean Acheson, left and Secretary of Defense Louis A Johnson on the far right. (USAF)

funds in March 1949. That month the board also recommended that the B-36 acquisition be limited to what was required for four Groups, after which production would be switched over to the B-52.

US Naval Aviation.

The US Navy acquired its first aircraft carriers in 1922, when it commissioned a converted collier as the USS Langley. Carriers accompanied the fleet, and were tasking the aircraft with scouting, observation and attacking enemy vessels. Between 1910 and 1930, twenty per cent of all naval officers went into naval aviation. These included Forrest Sherman, Arthur Radford, Gerald F Bogan and Daniel V Gallery, who all rose to flag rank in the wartime Navy. Crucially, and in contrast to the Army, where corps loyalty was paramount, the Navy taught that every officer was a naval officer first and a specialist second. It was bolstered by a long-standing ethos of creating a 'balanced fleet' in which all specialists played a part. While some naval aviators became zealous advocates of naval airpower, they expressed no desire to separate from the Navy.

In order to operate from carriers, aircraft needed tailhooks and strengthened undercarriages, which made them heavier and less manoeuvrable than similar land-based aircraft, but fears that they could not compete against land-based fighters proved ultimately groundless; between 1 September 1944 and 15 August 1945, US Navy Grumman F6F Hellcat and Vought F4U Corsair fighters destroyed 2,948 Japanese fighters for the loss of 191 of their own. However, like strategic bombing, the record of aircraft carriers was not as clear cut as the enthusiasts suggested.

Only two battleships were sunk by US carrier aircraft alone: the giant Yamato and Musashi. US carrier aircraft accounted for four of the eighteen Japanese heavy cruisers that were sunk, six of the twenty-five light cruisers, and twenty-seven of the one hundred and twenty-seven destroyers. They were particularly lethal against other aircraft carriers, sinking eleven of the nineteen Japanese carriers sunk in the war. In the post-war drawdown, the aircraft carrier fleet was reduced to the three Midway-class and eight Essex-class.

One role the Navy could play in a conflict with the Soviet Union was participation in strategic bombing. In December 1947, Gallery wrote a top-secret memorandum on the subject. The idea was that instead of building a bomber with a range of 5,000 nautical miles, Gallery argued that it was a better idea to build one with a lesser range that could be launched from an aircraft carrier. Radford noted that any target in the world was within 1,500 nautical miles of the sea. A carrier could be deployed quickly in a crisis and did not require expensive overseas bases. Gallery even went further than most Navy officers in arguing that strategic bombing with nuclear weapons should be the primary mission of the Navy. In forwarding the memo to Sullivan, Denfeld wrote: 'I not only consider Rear Admiral Gallery's initiative in preparing the paper was commendable and proper, but that the paper itself demonstrates the type of constructive thinking that the Navy tries at all times to encourage.' The memo was leaked to a syndicated newspaper columnist, Drew Pearson, who published it in The Philadelphia Inquirer and the Philadelphia Bulletin. Denfeld gave Gallery a private reprimand for making 'an extensive and somewhat uncontrolled distribution of a classified document.'

This concept had severe practical limitations in 1948. The characteristics of nuclear weapons were not widely known at the time. Still, the Navy did have some expertise in officers who had served with the wartime Manhattan Project, principally Deak Parsons, John T Hayward and Frederick L Ashworth. Twelve Lockheed P2V Neptunes were configured for the atomic mission, and a squadron, VC-5, was formed under Hayward's command. A Fat Man atomic bomb was sixty inches wide and weighed 10,000 pounds, and there was no aircraft in the Navy's inventory that could carry a bomb that wide, but the P2V could carry the slimmer twenty-eight-inch Little Boy bomb. It was demonstrated that the P2V could take off from the three large Midway-class aircraft carriers with the aid of jet-assisted take-off JATO rockets. The ability to land on one was less certain and never attempted. This meant a one-way mission expending bomb, aircraft and crew.

On 7 March 1949, Hayward flew a simulated atomic bombing mission against California in a P2V launched from the USS Coral Sea off the East Coast. He dropped a pumpkin bomb on the Salton Sea test site near El Centro, California, and then flew back across the country to land at NAS Patuxent River in Maryland. A more suitable aircraft, the North American AJ Savage, was under development.

Symington's action had angered the Navy. In a hearing before the House Armed Services Committee, Admiral Arthur Radford, a thirty-year Navy flyer and commander of the Pacific Fleet, supported by a panel of expert witnesses, testified, 'The unescorted B-36 is unacceptably vulnerable, and the plane could not hit precision targets from very high altitudes under battle conditions.' Admiral Radford denounced the B-36 as a 'symbol of a theory of warfare - the atomic blitz - which promises a cheap and easy victory.' The Navy appeared to be fighting the Air Force, not so much because they felt their programme of supercarriers was being unduly proscribed, but because it was their conviction that conventional warfare, not atomic bombing, was more likely to occur in the future. In view of this interdepartmental wrangling, which directly involved Secretaries Symington and Johnson in 1948 and 1949, it would have been difficult for them to be objective in choosing the YB-49 over the B-36. They were already firmly committed to the B-36, even if they had not had any conflict of interest outside their

One of the eighteen B-36Bs part of the GEM programme at Carswell, 44-92031 is seen over the Guadaloupe Mountains in west Texas on 13 April 1949. (USAF)

President Truman signs the National Security Act Amendment of 1949, which created the United States Department of Defense. Secretary of Defense Louis A Johnson leans over the desk. Behind him is Admiral Louis Denfeld, General Omar N Bradley, and General Hoyt Vandenberg.

official cabinet positions.

Forrestal considered the notion of a single service having a monopoly on nuclear weapons to be misguided. He convened a conference at Key West from 11 to 14 March 1948 attended by the Joint Chiefs of Staff and one deputy each to discuss the roles of the different services. The resulting Key West Agreement assigned primary responsibility for the strategic bombing to the Air Force, but the Navy was not prohibited from participating. Navy leadership doubted that wars could be won by strategic bombing alone. Some naval officers had a moral objection to relying upon the widespread use of nuclear weapons to destroy the major population centres. Most felt that atomic bombs were best used against targets like submarine pens and logistical hubs rather than cities and industrial facilities. The Gallery memorandum led some senior leaders in the Air Force to fear that the Navy wanted to take over the strategic bombing mission. Still, the real agenda for naval aviators was to justify their own existence.

Since 1945, the Navy had been working on the design of a new class of aircraft carrier. Its principal proponent was Admiral Marc Mitscher, Radford's predecessor as the DCNO for Air and the skipper of the USS Hornet during the 1942 Doolittle Raid when USAAF North American B-25 Mitchell bombers were launched from that aircraft carrier. Mitscher proposed the construction of an aircraft carrier that would have been ideal for that mission. He wanted a flush deck to operate sixteen to twenty-four large bombers weighing up to 100,000 pounds and carry enough fuel and bombs for one hundred sorties to be flown without rearming or refuelling. The 1946 Operation Crossroads nuclear tests highlighted another advantage of the flush deck: it was less susceptible to the shock waves produced by a nearby nuclear explosion.

The flush deck carrier was given the designation Project 6A. Since the bombers would be too large to fit in a hangar, Mitscher suggested that it be dispensed with, but the designers added one to carry eighty McDonnell F2H Banshee jet fighters. They calculated that 24 Douglas A3D Skywarrior bombers would require a flight deck of 1,125 feet long and 132 feet wide; this was reduced to 1,050 by 113 feet so it would fit into the Navy's largest dry docks. It was estimated that a carrier of this size would have a full load displacement of up to 81,000 tons. Although the proposed 6A carrier was only 100 feet longer than the Midways, its size and radical appearance led the media to refer to it as a 'supercarrier.' The plan was that the Navy's aircraft carriers would operate in four carrier strike groups, each with a 6A, a Midway-class and two Essex-class aircraft carriers. Four 6A carriers were slated to be built, with one laid down each year from 1949 to 1952, all being operational by 1955. Nimitz approved the ship's characteristics on 2 September 1947 followed by the acting Secretary of the Navy, W John Kenney, the following day.

The first 6A represented a $189 million item in a $14 billion defence budget, and that was inevitably going to attract the attention of the Bureau of the Budget. On 16 December 1947, its director, James E. Webb, stated that he was opposed to the 1949 shipbuilding programme due to its cost. Sullivan offered to cancel the battleship USS Kentucky and battlecruiser USS Hawaii to assure funds for the 6A carrier, and Webb informed Sullivan that he and Truman had accepted the shipbuilding programme on that basis on 19 December.

The Joint Chiefs' approval was not sought in 1947 because the new unification law had not yet been enacted. In testimony before Congress in May 1948, Sullivan and Denfeld said that the 6A carrier had the approval of the Joint Chiefs, the Secretary of Defense and the President. General Carl Spaatz, the retired Chief of Staff of the Air Force, objected; the Joint Chiefs had never approved it. Forrestal then submitted it to the Joint Chiefs for their approval on 26 May 1948. Leahy, Denfeld and the Chief of Staff of the Army, General Omar N Bradley, approved it; Vandenberg refused to do so. Congress funded the 6A carrier as part of the shipbuilding programme on 24 June 1948, and Forrestal gave his approval on 22 July, giving the first 6A carrier the designation CVA-58. Truman authorised the shipbuilding programme the following day. The ship's keel, named the USS United States, was laid at Newport News, Virginia, on 18 April 1949.

When he became the Defense Secretary, Forrestal showed himself to be a weak coordinator, unable under the new law to step in and resolve the many differences among the services. Forrestal did not support Truman's 1948 Presidential campaign; instead, he met with Truman's opponent, Thomas E Dewey. He discussed the possibility of remaining in the cabinet in a Republican administration. It angered Truman, and on 2 March 1949, after he won the election, he announced that Forrestal was being replaced by Louis A Johnson, a former assistant secretary of War and who had raised $1.5 million for Truman's re-election campaign. Having failed to provide strong support to Truman's 1948 political campaign, Forrestal's influence waned significantly. At the same time, his health began to fail.

He resigned in March 1949, in deep mental distress, and on 22 May jumped to his death from a window on the sixteenth floor of the National Naval Medical Center in Bethesda, Maryland. Several biographers characterised his death a suicide, but rumors and conspiracy theories that persist to the present day allege the US government murdered Forrestal.

Johnson had no qualms over supporting Truman's military budget reductions and fiscally preferred the Air Force's argument. His idea of an executive was someone who gave orders, and those orders were to be carried out immediately and without question. When the naval officers questioned his decisions on weapons and strategy - such as the cancellation of the United States - he took that as a sign of insubordination. When attacks appeared against his character, he wanted those responsible punished.

Secretary Johnson began by reviewing military procurement programmes and quickly focused on the Navy's flush-deck supercarrier United States on which construction was to start in April 1949. The Navy estimated the cost of the carrier at $190 million, but this figure failed to include the thirty-nine additional ships required to complete the task force. Total construction cost was $1.265 billion, a staggering sum in 1949.

Johnson sought the opinions of General of the Army Dwight Eisenhower, the three service secretaries and the Joint Chiefs on the advisability of continuing the construction of the United States. Bradley and Vandenberg urged its cancellation, although Bradley had favoured the carrier the previous year.

Admiral Louis E Denfeld, Chief of Naval Operations, defended the supercarrier, calling it necessary in the interest of national security. General Omar N. Bradley, Army Chief of Staff, and General Vandenberg, Air Force Chief of Staff, strongly opposed the construction, arguing that the supercarrier would duplicate the function of the Air Force's land-based bombers. Eisenhower also opposed building the carrier.

On 23 April 1949, Johnson cancelled the United States; Truman concurred with the decision. This vessel was the symbol and hope for the Navy's future, and its cancellation greatly demoralised the service.

Navy officials were outraged at not being informed of the decision. Navy Secretary Sullivan met with Truman on 25 April and resigned in protest, emphasising that the decision could have far-reaching and tragic consequences. Rumours immediately surfaced within the Navy's high command that Johnson was pro-USAF and was determined to cut the Navy down to size.

Johnson did not seem disturbed. His decision to cancel the United States provided him with an economy in the military budget needed to meet his budgetary goals while demonstrating that he was in firm control of the military and could make difficult decisions.

To replace Sullivan, Johnson recommended Francis P Matthews for the position of Secretary of the Navy. A lawyer from Omaha, Nebraska, served as a director of the United Service Organizations (USO), a service organisation that entertained the troops. He came to the attention of Johnson by assisting him with political fundraising for the 1948 Truman campaign. Matthews admitted the nearest he had come to naval experience was rowing a boat on a lake. He was sworn in on 25 May 1949. Another change that month was the departure of Radford, who became Commander in Chief Pacific (CINCPAC), and was replaced as VCNO by Vice Admiral John D. Price. On 10 August, Truman signed amendments to the National Security Act, which created the new position of Chairman of the Joint Chiefs of Staff, and appointed Bradley to the post.

The stage was now set. This bitter confrontation, precipitated by the Navy and its advocates, had been foreseen by General Eisenhower. 'Someday we're going to have a blowup,' he predicted in January 1949. 'God help us if ever we go before a Congressional committee to argue our professional fights as each service struggles to get the lion's share. Public airing of grievances... someday will go far beyond the bounds of decency and reason, and someone will say, 'Who's the boss? The civilians or the military?'

High-ranking naval officers, determined to make a case for the supercarrier and against the B-36, took action. The Navy's Op-23 research and policy office had been formed in December 1948 by Denfield to advise him on unification. Capt. Arleigh A Burke, a World War Two destroyer commander and future Chief of Naval Operations, took charge of this office in early 1949. He placed Op-23 under tight security, causing the press to speculate that it was involved in shady business and directed his people to collect detrimental data on the B-36 while amassing positive information on the supercarrier.

Going public, naval officers criticised the B-36 as being too slow and vulnerable to enemy defences. This, however, was only the beginning of what turned out to be a vicious campaign to discredit not only the B-36 but also the top leadership of the fledgling Air Force.

In April 1949, what became known as the Anonymous Document appeared and made its way around Washington, DC, charging that Symington, Johnson, and Floyd B Odlum, chairman of the board of Convair, had put the heat on the Air Force to buy B-36s, in spite of all the bomber's deficiencies. It pointed out that before his posting as Secretary of Defense, Johnson had been on the board of directors of Convair, the manufacturer of the B-36 bomber, and was the head of Convair's law firm. The document highlighted his apparent conflict of interest in representing the government with this manufacturer. It claimed that the B-36 was a 'billion-dollar blunder' and alleged 'fraud' on the part of B-36 contractors regarding costs, capabilities and test results.

The document was sent to Glenn L Martin, the chairman of the Glenn L Martin Company, and several members of Congress.

At first, there was little sign that Congress would investigate the Anonymous Document. Senator Millard Tydings, the Chairman of the Senate Armed Services Committee, was a close friend of Martin's but was wary of the contents of the Anonymous

Admiral Arthur W Radford, Commander of the US Pacific Fleet, the man who called the B-36 'a billion dollar blunder.' He charged the Air Force with neglect of defence and tactical aviation due to its emphasis on strategic bombing.

Carl Vinson (b. 18 November 1883, d 1 June 1981) was an American Democratic politician who served in the US House of Representatives for over fifty years and was influential in expanding the US Navy.

Document. Carl Vinson, the Chairman of the House Armed Services Committee, had concerns about the ongoing publicity campaigns of the Navy and Air Force, particularly the leaking of classified information. It included the publication by a United Press reporter, Charles W Corddry, that the United States was targeting seventy Soviet cities for strategic bombardment. With the influential Tydings unwilling to act, Republican Congressman James Van Zandt, a Navy advocate with wartime naval service, introduced a resolution in the House of Representatives on 25 May 1949 calling for an investigation of contract awards and cancellations. Vinson saw this as a challenge to his authority. On 1 June, he submitted his own resolution that the House Armed Services Committee be authorised to conduct an investigation into the procurement of the B-36. The House adopted Vinson's resolution on 8 June. Thus began one of the most fractious public confrontations in US military history.

The first phase of the House Armed Services Committee hearing and investigation on 'Unification and Strategy' was held from 9 to 25 August 1949. The focus was on the allegations of fraud and corruption emanating from the Anonymous Document.

Brig. Gen. Joseph F Carroll, director of Air Force Special Investigations, traced the anonymous document to Cedric R Worth, a former Hollywood scriptwriter who had served with the Navy during the war and was now an assistant to Dan A Kimball, under Secretary of the Navy. Glenn L. Martin, an aircraft manufacturer whose bombers had lost out to the B-36, had provided Worth with considerable data. A Navy court of inquiry subsequently determined that Commander Thomas D Davies, Op-23 deputy to Captain Burke, had also fed material to him.

At first, there was little sign that Congress would investigate the Anonymous Document. Worth was called as a witness and testified before the House Investigating Committee. Senator Millard Tydings, the Chairman of the Senate Armed Service Committee, was a close friend of Martin's but was wary of the contents of the Anonymous Document.

Obviously, the Secretary's close association with Odlum and his conflict of interest regarding the B-36 vs B-49, meant that there could be little doubt that Secretary Symington had apparently found it quite easy to persuade Louis Johnson, President Truman's Secretary of Defense and a former director of Consolidated Vultee, to terminate construction of the large supercarrier United States, because the budget would not permit both the completion of the aircraft carrier and production of the number of bombers desired by the Strategic Air Command.

Remarkably, the committee found no substance to charges of improper interest in aircraft procurement on the part of Johnson or Symington. The Air Force was exonerated of all charges of wrongdoing. At the conclusion, the committee recommended that Worth be fired. Following a naval court of inquiry, Worth was dismissed. The apparent vindication of Secretary Johnson and inappropriate work by Worth was an embarrassment to the Navy.

The Navy's supporters in the press held back nothing. Hanson Baldwin, the military editor of the New York Times and a graduate of the Naval Academy, described Symington as one of the nastiest politicians in Washington, someone who had ganged up on Forrestal. Baldwin charged that Symington had played dirty pool and dirty politics, and was 'a two-faced goad who most people in the Air Force did not respect.' Baldwin even went so far as to claim that Symington was the only service secretary not asked to be a pallbearer at Forrestal's funeral because the family believed he had contributed to Forrestal's death.

On hearing word of proposed cuts to the Navy budget, a naval aviator serving on the Joint Staff,

USS United States (CVA-58) was to be the lead ship of a new design of aircraft carrier. On 29 July 1948, President Harry Truman approved construction of five 'supercarriers', for which funds had been provided in the Naval Appropriations Act of 1949.

The keel of the first of the five planned postwar carriers was laid down on 18 April 1949 at Newport News Drydock and Shipbuilding. The programme was cancelled a few days later, United States was not completed, and the other four planned carriers were never built. (both Tom Brewer USAF Museum)

Captain John G Crommelin, called an impromptu press conference in which he claimed that unification had been a mistake and that Johnson was out to destroy the Navy. Denfeld did not respond directly to Crommelin's remarks, assuming that naval officers were free to express their personal opinions. Matthews felt differently; he issued a statement to the effect that Crommelin's actions rendered him unfit to continue serving on the Joint Staff. Accordingly, he was transferred to a billet on Denfeld's staff, normally held by a rear admiral. Matthews was furious, and Denfeld quickly moved Crommelin to a more junior post. Matthews and Denfeld then issued a guidance memorandum that stated that speeches and articles for public release had to be cleared through the Office of the Secretary of the Navy.

Matthews had requested advice from senior personnel on issues facing the Navy that might come up in hearings, so Bogan, now the Commander of the First Task Fleet in the Pacific, wrote to Matthews on 20 September to inform him of the state of morale in the Navy, which he described as 'lower today than at any time since I entered the commissioned ranks in 1916', and he expressed support for Crommelin's views. The letter was confidential, but Radford, as CINCPAC, and Denfeld, as CNO, reviewed the letter as it was routed through official channels to Matthews's office. In his endorsement, Denfeld concurred with the sentiments that Bogan expressed.

In October, a second hearing focused upon the proposed reduction in the Navy and the cancellation of the United States and the soundness of the proposed expansion of the strategic bomber forces. They were given added urgency by Truman's announcement on 23 September that the Soviet Union had tested its first nuclear device. Matthews announced that no Navy man would be censored or penalised for the testimony he offered at the hearing. This should have been unnecessary since it was illegal to threaten witnesses to testify before Congress or take action against them afterwards.

Nevertheless, when Vinson opened the hearings on 6 October, he declared: 'It is the intent of the Committee that all testimony given shall be frankly and freely given and be given without reprisals in the Department of Defense against any individual presenting testimony during the course of these hearings. The committee will not permit nor tolerate any reprisal against any witness in these hearings nor will it permit or tolerate any shepherding of the testimony being presented. We want these witnesses to speak what is in their minds, to put their cards on the table, and to do so without hesitation or personal concern. We are going to the bottom of this unrest and concern in the Navy. And the committee expects full cooperation in this from the Department of Defense. '

The naval officers called to testify were expected to support Secretary Matthews. Still, instead, officer after officer arose to testify that the Air Force reliance on the B-36 was inadequate and that the entire strategy of atomic bombing was immoral and misguided. Among the officers testifying from 6 to 17 October were the naval leaders of World War Two: Fleet Admirals Ernest King, Chester Nimitz and William Halsey, Admirals Raymond Spruance and Thomas Kinkaid, and General Alexander Vandegrift, the wartime head of the Marine Corps. Burke had run tests which showed the Navy was already in possession of a fighter aircraft, the F2H Banshee, that could reach high enough altitudes to intercept bombers like the B-36, and he knew it would be unreasonable to assume that an opposing major world power would not also have developed such an aircraft. In that case, the B-36 would need to be accompanied by long-range fighter escorts with the requisite range and ceiling to complete its mission, and the Air Force had no such fighter available in their inventory. In his testimony, Denfeld broadly supported the Navy officers who had testified before him.

In a hearing before the House Armed Services Committee, Admiral Arthur Radford, supported by a panel of expert witnesses, testified that the unescorted B-36 was unacceptably vulnerable and that the aircraft could not hit precision targets from very high altitudes under battle conditions. Admiral Radford denounced the B-36 as a 'symbol of a theory of warfare - the atomic blitz - which promised a cheap and easy victory.' The Navy appeared to be fighting the Air Force, not so much because they felt their programme of supercarriers was unduly proscribed, but because it was their conviction that conventional warfare, not atomic bombing, was more likely to occur in the future. In view of this inter-departmental wrangling, which directly involved Secretaries Symington and Johnson in 1948 and 1949, it would have been difficult for them to be objective in choosing the YB-49 over the B-36. They were already firmly committed to the B-36, even if they had not had any conflict of interest outside their official cabinet positions.

Symington and Vandenberg rebutted the admirals' testimony, point by point, on 18 and 19 October. Regarding the United States, Vandenberg commented: "I accept the military capability of this ship as stated by the Chief of Naval Operations. My opposition to building it comes from the fact that I can see no necessity for a ship with those capabilities in any strategic plan against the one possible enemy.' Symington denied that the Air Force favoured the bombing of civilians or that it believed that an atomic blitz offered a 'quick, easy and painless war.'

Vandenberg testified that 'Veterans of the Eighth, the Fifteenth, the Twentieth and other historic Air Forces know very well that there are no cheap and easy ways to win great wars.' He said that during World War Two, bombers had always managed to get through to their targets and that technological improvements since then made it still more likely. He was optimistic in his testimony, although he had a reason for concern, having received a memo from Major General Gordon P Saville that only one B-36 had so far attempted a radar-controlled bombing run from 40,000 feet.

The remainder of the testimony before the House Armed Services Committee was from former President Herbert Hoover, Johnson, and Generals of the Army Marshall, Eisenhower and Bradley on the merits of unification. Bradley noted that he had participated in the two largest amphibious operations in history, namely the invasions of Sicily and Normandy, and confidently predicted that 'large-scale amphibious operations, such as those in Sicily and Normandy, will never occur again.' He made no attempt to hide his contempt for the Navy's methods during the case, and he accused senior naval officers of poor leadership and disloyalty: 'Our military forces are one team – in the game to win regardless of who carries the ball. This is no time for 'fancy dans' who won't hit the line with all they have on every play unless they can call the signals. Each player on this team – whether he shines in the

The Air Force put one B-36A-5-CF, 44-92010 on display at Andrews Air Force Base in February 1949, along with a B-45, B-47, F-82 and YB-49 flying wing. (USAF).

spotlight of the backfield or eats dirt on the line – must be an all-American.'

The House Armed Services Committee found a number of actions taken by the administration and by the services involved to be overstepping. It held that evaluation of the B-36's worth was the responsibility of the Weapons Systems Evaluation Group and that the services jointly should not pass judgment on weapons proposed by one service. On cancellation of the supercarrier, the committee questioned the qualifications of the Army and Air Force chiefs of staff, who had testified in support of Johnson's decision, to determine vessels appropriate for the Navy. In disapproving of Johnson's summary manner of terminating the carrier and his failure to consult congressional committees before acting, the committee stated that 'national defense is not strictly an executive department undertaking; it involves not only the Congress but the American people as a whole speaking through their Congress. The committee can in no way condone this manner of deciding public questions.'

Making the Air Force case.

Vinson's committee held hearings on B-36 procurement in August and on strategy and unification in October 1949. In June, Symington appointed W Barton Leach, an Air Force Reserve colonel and Harvard Law School professor, to coordinate and direct the Air Force case for the B-36. Leach had served with Army Air Forces and had earned a reputation for incisive analysis of AAF operations in Europe.

He proceeded to organise the Air Force case by analysing the charges, preparing replies to the allegations, making a study of the aircraft industry, preparing a memo on Symington's policies relative to the aircraft industry, collecting all Air Force statements on the heavy bomber programme chronologically, analysing all Inspector General reports on the B-36, and preparing an explanation of Air Force action on the B-36.

The result of Leach's massive effort was A History of B-36 Procurement, which Vinson had requested and which formed the foundation of the Air Force's presentation to the committee. In early July 1949, the Air Force Association's third annual National Convention, held in Chicago, also helped counter the Navy's charges by disseminating material on the B-36 Peacemaker's mission and operational characteristics. At 45,000 feet, this intercontinental bomber was anything but vulnerable.

Each day during the AFA meeting, seven B-36s flew up from Fort Worth, Texas, circled the fair area at low level, and returned nonstop to Carswell AFB, Texas.

In regard to B-36 procurement, Symington informed the committee that 'at no time since I have been Secretary has any higher authority attempted to recommend in any way the purchase of any airplane. Every aircraft that was purchased by the Air Force during my tenure was recommended to me by the Chief of Staff of the Air Force and his staff.' Modifications in the B-36 programme were approved by Symington only after recommendations had been made by General Vandenberg, Lt Gen. Lauris Norstad, and Gen. Joseph T McNarney. Symington also strongly denied that he had ever discussed forming a large aircraft combine with Floyd Odlum or any aircraft manufacturer.

General George C Kenney, a former SAC commander in chief, testified to the committee that, although he initially opposed production of the B-36, the bomber had been modified to be 'the fastest, longest-range, best altitude-performing, and heaviest load-carrying bomber in the world.' Had he changed his view under political pressure? 'No', replied Kenney. 'If the bomber had the performance and would do the job that I was charged with carrying out, I would buy it.'

Symington revived the matter with General LeMay, who had become commander of SAC. He replaced General George C Kenney, an enthusiastic booster of the YB-49, who at one time expressed serious misgivings about the B-36, even suggesting in 1946 that the B-36 contract be cancelled. LeMay admitted that he had never wanted the Northrop flying wing, as it was designed before the atomic bomb had been thought of, wasn't large enough, and could not accommodate the number and size of bombs required by the SAC to mount an effective strategic deterrent.

LeMay was wrong about the atomic bomb-carrying capacity of the B-49, but there was no one at the time with adequate knowledge of the highly secret atomic bomb to challenge him. LeMay had never expressed an interest in Northrop's radical flying wing concepts, preferring traditional aircraft. He had convinced himself - and almost everyone else for that matter - that the conventional B-36 could do the job better. When he appeared before a review board of senior Air Force officers to give them his opinion, he found vocal support for his views. None of the generals were interested in advancing the state of the art in aircraft design. They thought only of immediate requirements, of aircraft that would be flown while they were still in command.

Years later, General LeMay went on record saying that he did not recall having taken part in any conference in which cancellation of the flying wing was decided upon: 'We had a shortage of funds, and were in the hands of Congress as to what we could afford. Because the B-36 was further along and more conventional, which required less costly further development work, we preferred to buy it rather than the YB-49 bomber. Also, I remember hearing that a YB-49 had crashed at Edwards, killing Captain Edwards and his crew, and this played a part in my opinion. I had not heard of any plan to merge Northrop with Convair at the time a decision to cancel the big wing was made. At this time jet engines were being introduced, and I thought that to make the best use of jet engines, a thin wing would be necessary. The YB-49 had a very thick wing to carry the crew and bomb load, and therefore it would not be suitable for supersonic speeds when equipped with jet engines.'

General LeMay also took the stand, saying, 'I expect that, if I am called upon to fight, I will order my crews out in those airplanes, and I expect to be in the first one myself.' Van Zandt questioned LeMay closely, but the SAC commander in chief insisted that the B-36 was the only bomber that could accomplish the intercontinental mission.

Even then, the Air Force had not yet allocated all its appropriated funds. It still had $197 million left, but it still awarded no B-36 contracts. At this late date, and with newly discovered and questionable information in hand, the Air Force wanted to change their mind. Toward the end of the year, they decided to finalise themselves again, reviving the Consolidated B-36 programme.

The semi-annual Washington economy drive, then in full swing in 1949, threatened to knock $800 million out of the Air Force budget for the coming year. Faced with the multi-billion dollar federal deficit, the Truman administration and Congress had three alternatives: lapsing into deficit financing, increasing taxes, or slashing expenditures. The last was the least distasteful to Congress, and it was the Air Force would be the principal victim. The reason given at the time was that the President's budget, which called for a forty-eight Group Air Force, was now emphasising long-range bombing, a somewhat weak explanation. Anyone who has ever been exposed to Air Force publicity knows that the United States Air Force never subordinates strategic bombing. If the seventy-five B-36s they now wanted to buy from Consolidated had been included in the programme at the outset, or if money had been reserved for them, pending complete evaluation of the Air Force's interception tests would have saved about ninety per cent of its termination reserve monies. The puzzling question remains; Why did they find out in December what wasn't known in May? Why was the Consolidated B-36 suddenly the best aircraft?

There was no money to buy the seventy-five expensive Consolidated B-36 bombers unless practically everything else was cancelled. Symington issued the orders to do so, cancelling contracts in force for aircraft already being constructed at a loss of $71 million in contract termination costs.

The eight cancelled contracts involved 480 fighters and bombers and ten transport helicopters, including orders for the last 100 Republic F-84s not yet delivered, fifty-one North American B-45C four-jet bombers, eighty-eight Curtiss-Wright F-87 night fighters, 118 North American F-93-1 jet fighters (a modified F-86 powered by an advanced model of the British Nene engine), forty-three Boeing bombers, an advanced type Superfortress powered with piston engines, ten Kellett H-10 helicopters, thirty Northrop C-125B Raider trimotor assault transports, and thirty Northrop RB-49 reconnaissance flying wings. All these contract cancellations were issued in order to buy seventy-five B-36 bombers from Consolidated Vultee, including modification costs to add four turbojet engines to each plane in addition to the six-piston engines for which the bomber was designed. The remainder of the funds available were allocated to purchase Northrop F-89 Scorpion jet night fighters, Boeing B-47 turbojet bombers, Lockheed F-94 jet night fighters, and Fairchild T-31 trainers, in addition to the modification of Boeing B-50s for aerial refuelling.

The committee expressed solid support for effective unification but stated that 'there is such a thing as seeking too much unification too fast' and observed that 'there has been a navy reluctance in the inter-service marriage, an over-ardent army, a somewhat exuberant air force ... It may well be stated that the committee finds no unification Puritans in the Pentagon.'

During the hearings, public opinion shifted strongly against the Navy. Time magazine noted: 'Even so staunch a friend of the Navy as the New York Times Annapolis-trained military analyst Hanson Baldwin wrote that he himself did not consider the cutbacks in the Navy programme disastrous.' Baldwin added dryly: 'Some of the Navy's interest in morality as applied to strategic bombing seems new-found.'

After the hearings, Secretary Matthews set about punishing those officers who had testified and were still actively serving in the Navy in defiance of his public promise not to do so. Denfeld was first to go; he was summarily relieved by Truman on Navy Day, 27 October 1949. Matthews explained that he and Denfeld disagreed widely on strategic policy and unification. Denfeld retained his rank and was offered Commander in Chief of the Naval Forces in the Eastern Atlantic and Mediterranean. Still, he declined and elected to retire instead. Matthews selected Sherman as his new CNO. Bogan was given command of Fleet Air at Naval Air Station Jacksonville, a position usually filled by a rear admiral. He, too, elected to retire rather than face assignment to a position of lesser authority. Crommelin continued to speak out openly and was forced into retirement by Sherman.

One of Sherman's first actions as Chief of Naval Operations was to disband OP-23, but not before the Naval Inspector General's office seized all documents searching for evidence tying it to Crommelin's disclosures or breaches of security. Matthews and Johnson attempted to block the promotion of Burke by crossing out his name on the promotion list, but this was seen and reversed by Truman. The House Armed Services Committee condemned Denfeld's dismissal, concluding that: 'the removal of Admiral Denfeld was a reprisal against him for giving testimony to the House Armed Services Committee. This act is a blow against effective representative government in that it tends to intimidate witnesses and hence discourages the rendering of free and honest testimony to the Congress; it violated promises made to the witnesses by the Committee, the Secretary of the Navy, and the Secretary of Defense; and it violated the Unification Act, into which a provision was written to specifically prevent actions of this nature against the Nation's highest military and naval officers.'

The Truman administration won the conflict with the Navy, and civilian control over the military was reaffirmed. Military budgets following the hearings prioritised the development of Air Force heavy bomber designs. These were deployed across the country and at dozens of overseas bases. Frank Pace, who as Director of the Bureau of the Budget had been a driving force behind defence cuts, was appointed Secretary of the Army, and Leon Keyserling, a Keynesian economist, replaced Edwin Nourse as the chairman of the Council of Economic Advisers when the latter quit over the administration's failure to cut spending. Johnson authorised the modernisation of two Essex-class aircraft carriers, increasing the Navy's projected aircraft carrier strength in the fiscal year 1951 to seven. Still, a committee he established to look for other economies suggested another $929 million in cuts to the fiscal year 1950 budget, mainly at the expense of the Army and Navy budgets, which were cut by another $357 million and $376 million, respectively. While most of Johnson's cuts came at the expense of the Navy, it was the Army that was affected the most. After a year with Johnson at the helm, the Army had lost 100,000 men, and only one of its ten divisions was at full strength. Truman still talked about cutting the defence budget to $9 billion. Unwilling to support further cuts, Symington

A flight of four B-36Bs seen over Lake Michigan, approaching Chicago on 3 July 1949. (USAF)

submitted his resignation in April 1950.

The Secretary of the Air Force, having decided the Air Force wanted seventy-five B-36s, and having spent all its money, was forced to chop the other contracts. It was a very strange way to run an Air Force, and was hardly calculated to bring credibility to the military planners and politicians involved. It would not be until ten years later, when the giant Boeing B-52 strategic bomber was operational, that it could be said the Strategic Air Command was in a position to defend the United States adequately. Politics and corporate machinations had taken their toll on professional soldiers and airmen.

The official reason for the cancellation of Northrop's RB-49 was that a shortage of funds prevented the Air Force from supporting both the B-36 and the RB-49 programmes. By implication, the public was allowed to assume that the B-36 was a much better strategic bomber, even though B-36 maintenance reports show otherwise. The six B-36 engines were always overheating, often catching fire in flight. A retired mechanic commented, 'One-week maintenance was routine for each hour of flight.' Even worse, fighter pilots said Soviet MiG's of the time would have had no trouble shooting down a B-36. The Air Force said the B-36 was successful because it kept the United States out of war.

No physical evidence, no files, no engineering drawings, few reports remain to prove otherwise. The FBI report on Major Cardenas' accusation of sabotage on the cross-country YB-49 flight disappeared. The airman who failed to fill the oil tanks at Wright-Patterson was killed in an unexplained accident.

There is something of an interesting footnote to all of this. General Cardenas had a piece published in July 2009 edition of the Smithsonian Air and Space Magazine, as he told to James P Busha about his testing of the flying wings. The article apparently rubbished the wings - or did it? Unfortunately, the piece is far too large to reproduce in its entirety here, but this is a flavour.

'Each test had its own set of problems - some minor, some that almost killed me. On my first takeoff, the airplane accelerated too rapidly, causing the gear doors to blow off. I could either pull the Flying Wing up at a high angle of attack on takeoff or pull back on the power and wait the 90 seconds for the gear to retract. The problem was that the jet-powered Wing was designed around the propeller-driven XB-35, which operated at slower speeds. Northrop had simply swapped prop engines for jets, and of course the speed of the aircraft increased.'

I may be wrong, but that sounds like a veiled admission that the pilot let the aircraft get away from him, but was twisted around to blame the aircraft, thus seemingly 'setting the record straight' to make

Cardenas' words match with the then-current narrative. The entire 2009 article is worth seeking out.

The Consolidated B-36 bomber, already obsolete when delivered, never reached full-scale production as anticipated by the Secretary, and Boeing's superior jet-powered B-52 eventually became the Strategic Air Command's firstline operational bomber. Even the transitional Boeing YB-47 had its problems with yawing on bomb runs, but the Air Force showed no hesitation in paying additional monies to design and install advanced automatic pilot equipment for the B-47, something Jack Northrop also requested of the Air Force. Northrop, however, was denied additional funding for design of an advanced auto-pilot for his YB-49. The Northrop YB-49 bomb-bay doors were the same as originally designed for the slower YB-35, yet when Jack requested additional monies to modify the twice-as-fast YB-49 bomb-bay doors so dropped bombs would not tumble, the Air Force refused his request.

High-speed taxi tests of the YB-49 were run by the Air Force with a full gas load, with the flying wing at maximum gross weight, across the dry lake beds of Muroc, carving ruts across the desert floor that could still be seen many years later. The unusual behaviour was akin to someone telling the pilot to drive the flying wing across the desert until it was destroyed - which it was, in a fiery collapse of the nose wheel, the second of two flying wings destroyed at Edwards. It was a strange way to run taxi tests. It was almost as if the Air Force was insisting that the flying wing fail.

A few years later, Floyd Odlum made the first contribution of $100,000 to Stuart Symington's abortive campaign to win the Democratic nomination for President. Odlum was the last chairman of Consolidated Vultee, by then called Convair. When the newly organised General Dynamics Corporation assumed controlling interest in Convair from Odlum's Atlas Corporation, they reorganised the company into the Convair Division of General Dynamics, taking over the B-36 production contract. General McNarney, procurement officer for the Air Force, who offered no objection to the demands made of Northrop by Symington at the San Marino meeting, later retired from the Air Force to become President of Convair headquarters in San Diego.

On 25 June 1950, the Korean War broke out, and the administration was forced to confront the crisis with the forces it had on hand. The Truman administration immediately decided not to use the nuclear arsenal and sought to check the North Korean advance with conventional forces. The war discredited the proponents of austerity and vindicated the hawks that had called for increased defence spending. As an initial response, Truman called for a naval blockade of North Korea and was shocked to learn that such a blockade could only be imposed on paper since the Navy no longer had the warships to carry out his request. Faced with public criticism of his handling of the Korean War, which opened with a series of setbacks and defeats, and wishing to deflect blame from the peacetime defence economy measures he had espoused, the President decided to ask for Johnson's resignation on 19 September 1950. He needed a Secretary of Defense that had the confidence of all three services, preferably one with significant military experience, and nominated George Marshall. Matthews resigned on 31 July 1951 to become the US Ambassador to Ireland.

The Korean War compelled a reluctant Truman to loosen the purse strings. The administration did not decide between military and civilian spending; it found that it could afford both. No solution for inter-service rivalry or any process for the resolution of competing budgetary claims emerged. The rivalry between the services was not ended; what ended was a competition over a zero-sum budget. Defence outlays quadrupled between 1950 and 1953. In 1951, the Army had double the workforce called for in Johnson's budget; the Navy increased its carrier force from fifteen to twenty-seven; Air Force grew from forty-eight Wings to eighty-seven. Fears of inflation proved unfounded; although it increased to eight per cent in 1951, it dropped back to below one per cent the following year. Between 1954 and 2002, annual defence outlays averaged $317.7 billion in 2002 dollars, about one and a half times the average between 1947 and 1950. Between 1948 and 1986, the Air Force's share of the defence budget was thirty-five per cent, the Navy's thirty-one per cent, and the Army's twenty-eight per cent.

The Navy did get a supercarrier; Johnson approved its construction on 22 June 1950. Launched in October 1955, the USS Forrestal, at 61,000 tons, was one and a half times the size of the Midway-class aircraft carriers. It featured an armoured flight deck just large and sturdy enough to land a heavy bomber carrying a small nuclear bomb. The ship was also equipped with steam catapults to assist the heavier nuclear bombers in getting airborne. The flight deck was angled, allowing the new carrier to launch and recover aircraft simultaneously and obviating the need for a flush deck.

Chapter Six

Four Burning, Six Turning

Convair devised a method to increase the speed of the B-36. On 5 October 1948 the company proposed installing a pair of turbojet engines underneath each outer wing panel. These engines could be used during takeoff and for short bursts of speed at critical times and would have only a minimal effect on range, more due to the additional drag than the relatively small amount of fuel used by the jet engines.

Unlike the extensive changes needed to install the VDT engines, only relatively minor modifications would be required to mount the jet nacelles. Convair was confident that a prototype B-36 with jet engines would be ready to fly less than four months after Air Force approval. The Air Force did not question the apparent merits of the Convair proposal. However, approval was delayed due to budgetary restrictions looming in December 1948 and the decision to convert the B-36As into RB-36E reconnaissance aircraft a month before. It should be noted that as originally planned, the RB-36Es did not include jet engines - they were remanufactured B-36As with photo and radio-intercept reconnaissance capabilities.

Colours and Markings

The YB-36 and all B-36A aircraft were delivered in natural metal finish, revealing the two different materials, shiny aluminium and dull magnesium, used for their skins. The doped fabric control surfaces were painted an aluminium colour that closely matched the dull finish of the natural magnesium. National insignia were located on both sides of the aft fuselage and the upper left and lower right wing surfaces.

Large 'buzz' numbers were painted on the forward fuselage - BM was the B-36 code, plus the last three digits of the serial number. Some aircraft also had the buzz number painted on the lower left wing.

The B-36B introduced having 'USAF' painted on the lower left and upper right wing surfaces, displacing the lower buzz number. The USAF and national insignia were much further inboard, almost adjacent to the outboard R-4360 nacelle than on later aircraft when the markings were moved outboard of the jet nacelles. As part of Project GEM, most B-36Bs, and a few B-36As had the top, and bottom surfaces of the outer wing panels and both horizontal and vertical stabilisers painted a bright red to aid visibility in the white-out conditions experienced during Arctic operations. The first B-36Bs left the factory without the red paint, and it was added in the field. Later B-36Bs were painted on the assembly line. The area around the serial numbers, 'USAF', and national insignia were left unpainted. Sometime in 1950, most of the standard markings were applied in decal form instead of being painted.

At some stage during B-36B production, the buzz numbers disappeared from the forward fuselage, replaced with 'UNITED STATES AIR FORCE' in nine-inch letters on the forward fuselage just aft of the forward turret compartment. The marking appeared insignificant given the size of the fuselage. Some aircraft included both the small UNITED STATES AIR FORCE and the buzz numbers.

As the red markings disappeared, the round 'numbered Air Force' insignia and geometric tail

Proof of concept aircraft B-36B-10-CF 44-92057. The jet pods were different from production units, no lower sculpting and sway bars. At this time the nose turret still had the guns installed. (Convair)

Proof of concept demonstrator B-36B-10-CF 44-92057 gets airborne with four burning and six turning. Clear in this shot is that the jet pods have no lower sculpting and no anti-sway bracing. (Convair via author's collection)

code (triangle, circle, etc.) began to appear on both sides of the vertical stabiliser. At least two of 'red tails' had triangle markings and the 8th Air Force insignia on the vertical stabilisers. Later, a letter representing the specific Bomb Wing would appear inside the geometric marking.

If aircraft were assigned to a specific squadron within a wing, the squadron colour was often applied to the tip of the vertical stabiliser, the nose gear doors, and infrequently to the front of the jet pods and the propeller spinners. When two Bomb Wings were assigned to the same Group, one of the Wings used striped colours while the other used solid colours. Buzz numbers began to return late during B-36D production but now omitted the 'BM' and just used the last three or four digits of the serial number.

B-36D

The most apparent change for the B-36D was two pairs of 5,200-pound thrust General Electric J47-GE-11 turbojets in pods underneath the outer wing panels. To save money and simplify production, the pods were basically the same as those developed for the inboard engines on the Boeing B-47 Stratojet. The outrigger landing gear and some supporting structure were deleted, although the aerodynamic fairing and taxi light on the bottom of the pods were retained. Initially, the struts and pods were even manufactured by Bell Aircraft Company on the same Buffalo, New York, production line used to make B-47 pods. In May 1951, the pods were manufactured in a new Bell facility located twelve miles from the Convair Fort Worth plant. Special collapsible aerodynamic covers were installed over the engine inlets to minimize drag when the engines were not operating. About five per cent of the normal airflow was allowed to pass through when the covers were closed, mainly to keep the compressor turning to prevent it from freezing. Hot air from the anti-icing system could also be ducted to the turbojets to prevent freezing when operating at extreme altitude.

Like the R-4360s, the General Electric jet engines were government-furnished equipment. Once the engines, struts and pods arrived at Fort Worth, they were assembled in an area separate from normal B-36 production. The complete units were then taken to the final assembly line, where they were hung on the wings. The turbines were modified to burn

The production version of the jet-pods showing the lower sculpting between the two engines. (Convair via author's collection)

The paired J-47 engines provided the B-36 with an additional 20,800 pounds of thrust for take-off as well as some flight conditions. (Convair via author's collection)

standard aviation fuel instead of jet fuel so that the B-36 could feed them from the existing fuel supply. This resulted in the engines producing slightly less power, but the trade-off was considered worthwhile.

Very little structural modification was required to support the new engine pods, a tribute to how strong the basic B-36 wing was. The jet engines' control was mounted on a separate panel above the pilots' heads, while instrumentation was spread across two subpanels added below the main instrument panel. The flight engineer station received essentially no changes due to the jet installation. Additional twenty-gallon oil tanks were installed in the outer wing panels to hold thirteen gallons of the special oil the jet engines required. Engine operating time was limited by the amount of oil available, but this seldom presented operational problems.

The reciprocating engines remained the same 3,500-hp R-4360-41 Wasp Majors that had powered the B-36B, although they would be updated to -41A models with the same horsepower sometime during the service life of the aircraft. The maximum gross weight was increased to 357,500 pounds, a figure that would remain constant across all models until the advent of the B-36J. Another major improvement was that most of the flying surfaces were now covered with magnesium skin instead of doped fabric. The retractable tail 'bumper' that had been installed on the A and B models was deleted on new-builds, but it appears that the bumper was retained on at least the B-36Bs completed as D-models.

The B-36D was supposed to use an improved K-3 bombing and navigation system. However, development problems prevented the K-3 from being delivered to equip the first B-36Ds, which used a K-1 unit that was little more than a refined version of the APQ-24 used in the B-36B. The Farrand Y-1 retractable periscopic bombsight had run into development problems. In its place, Farrand developed a non-retractable version called the Y-3, and this was installed in most B-36Ds. It remains unclear if the B-36Bs completed as B-36Ds initially carried the Y-3 or the Norden sight. The substitution of the Y-3 for the Y-1 in the K-

B-36 powerplant 'eggs' stored vertically, awaiting fitment to an airframe. (Convair via author's collection)

Introduced on the B-36D, the four J-47 engines in paired pods, seen here on an aircraft at Biggs AFB, were designed by General Electric and owed much to the Whittle engine from the UK when developed as the TG-190. Reflecting the early stage of jet engine design, when introduced, it had a life of 150 hours between overhaul, increasing to 1,700 hours by 1956. This photograph shows the segmented covers over the jet intakes that provided streamlining when they were not in use, yet allowed enough airflow through to prevent icing up.(USAF)

system resulted in a new K-3A designation. All B-36Ds were eventually retrofitted with the K-3A. Since the Y-3 bombsight used a small periscope protruding from the right side of the forward fuselage bottom, the flat glazed panel in the nose was often covered over with aluminium. Of course, on aircraft still equipped with the Norden bombsight - and all RB-36s - this panel was still glass, complete with its own windshield wiper.

An AN/APG-32A gun-laying radar replaced the APG-3 to direct the tail turret. It appears that at least the B-36Bs that were completed on the production line as D-models were initially equipped with the APG-3 and were later modified with the newer unit.

The B-36D was fitted with 'snap-action' bomb bay doors, called 'clam shell doors' by Convair at the time, as opposed to the sliding fit type fitted to the preceding B-36A/Bs. These doors could open and close in only two seconds, minimizing the drag penalty usually associated with getting ready to drop bombs over the target. The doors were hydraulically actuated and proved to be more reliable than the earlier cable-operated sliding doors. Only two sets of doors were provided, one set covering the forward bomb bays Nos. 1 and 2 and the other covering the aft bays Nos. 3 and 4. All B-36Ds were delivered with the ability to carry a Mk III/ 4 atomic bomb in bomb bay No. 1 - this was chosen because the bombs still had to be armed in flight, and the forward bomb bay was the most accessible. Conventional bomb capacity was generally similar to the B-model.

Two additional 4,800-gallon auxiliary fuel tanks were added into the inboard section of the wings, bringing the total to eight tanks carrying 36,622 gallons. These new tanks consisted of four interconnected bladder-type fuel cells made of rubber impregnated nylon fabric and were not self-sealing or armoured. Instead, removable bullet sealing pads could be installed on the wing's undersurface between the engine nacelles to protect the main fuel tanks. The flight manual contained a warning that these auxiliary fuel tanks differed in size from aircraft to aircraft, often by as much as 100 gallons. On most aircraft, the fuel piping was deleted from bomb bay No. 2, and only a single 3,000-gallon tank could be carried in bomb bay No. 3. However, the paperwork is confusing because different issues of the flight manuals for B-36s show bomb bay fuel tanks in one, two, or all four bomb bays. The plumbing was likely changed during various ON TOP or other modification programmes.

The job descriptions for the B-36D's fifteen crew members changed slightly: aircraft commander, two pilots, two engineers, navigator, bombardier, two radio operators, and forward observer; and five gunners aft. In fact, one of the radiomen operated the ECM equipment, the other handled the nose turret, while one of the pilots and the observer operated the forward upper gun turrets. Although the aft cabin of all B-36s had always contained six bunks for crewmembers, it was discovered that in service, the crew in the front cabin rarely, if ever, went aft and slept in their seats instead. Convair devised a way to mount two fold-down bunks in the forward cabin, and this change was made during the D-model production run. Kits were provided that allowed the operational units to add the bunks to aircraft already delivered. One bunk was hung from the top of the radio operator's compartment and was high enough to not interfere with the work of other crewmembers. The second bunk folded up flat against the top of the navigator's compartment when not in use. Convair had investigated using hammocks that could be strung up but rejected the concept as less than ideal.

The main instrument panel from B-36D 44-92096. The jet engine instrumentation was split between two sub-panels next to the centre pedestal, with the controls, switches, and circuit breakers located on the overhead panel. Note the fans provided in front of each seat to help cool the pilots. Six red warning lights are located at the top of the main panel, indicating an uncommanded propeller reversal. Usually, each control wheel had a lacquered 'horn button' in the centre with the Consolidated Vultee logo on it - both seem to be missing when this photo was taken, possibly due to souvenir hunters! (Convair via author's collection)

B-36D, 49-2701 overflies Boulder Dam. (USAF)

The modification of B-36B 44-92057 to include the jet engines was authorised on 4 January 1949, and the aircraft made its first flight on 26 March 1949. Due to the unavailability of J47 engines, it had four Allison J35-A-19 engines in the pods under the outer wing panels. The pods on this aircraft differed somewhat from production models by not having the sculpted lower surface that housed the outrigger landing gear and landing light on the B-47. The production pods delivered by Boeing were externally identical to their B-47 counterparts, although they deleted some internal structure, and the landing gear doors were locked in the closed position. In addition, the prototype installation did not include the sway-brace between the pylon and lower wing surface used on production examples to correct a small vibration problem.

A second B-36B, 44-92046, was also equipped with J47-GE-11 engines for additional high-altitude testing. Neither of these aircraft was equipped with the other changes specified for the B-36D, and both were among the last B-models converted to the full B-36D configuration. The first aircraft was also used to evaluate the potential use of 16-foot, four-bladed propellers in place of the standard three-bladed units. This was intended to mitigate a vibration problem that had long plagued the B-36. The tests were reportedly inconclusive but led, at least indirectly, to developing a revised square-tip, three-bladed propeller that would be introduced on the B-36H.

As usual for a B-36 first flight, Beryl Erickson and Doc Witchell were at the controls of 44-92057 when it made its first flight with the jet pods. Also on board were William 'Bill' P Easley, J D McEachern, MSgt. G S Fish, R O. Garlington, and Robert Moller. Although the first flight took place at 17:50 hours on a Saturday, several thousand Convair employees turned out to watch it. The flight lasted 3 hours and 15 minutes.

The last eleven B-36Bs were equipped with the jet engines on the assembly line, with seven becoming RB-36Ds and four being completed as B-36Ds prior to delivery. All of these aircraft were completed to the full D-model standard on the line. On 19 January 1949, the Air Force issued a new contract, AF33-038-2182, to Convair to cover the production of 39 additional B-36s beyond the ninety-five on the original contract. By October 1949, the contract had increased to seventy-five new aircraft and would ultimately be extended to cover two hundred and five aircraft up through most of the B-36H models.

The original order for 100 (later reduced to 95) B-36s was based on a unit cost of $4,692,392 per aircraft, of which nearly fifty per cent was government-furnished equipment. The breakdown was: airframe, $2,530,112; engines (installed), $589,899; propellers, $184,218; electronics, $55,974; ordnance, $30,241; armament, $747,681. Modification of these aircraft to RB-36E and B/RB-36D standard added $1,556,294 per aircraft, for a total of $6,248,686. The second increment of seventy-five B-36s cost $4,732,939 per aircraft, including a new bomb/nav system and upgraded engines. Part of this reduction was based on the write-off of the production tooling costs after the initial production run. The breakdown of these later aircraft was about 58.2 per cent GFE and 41.8 per cent Convair. Including the $435,623 cost to design the bomber and $39,475,234 for the two experimental models - the XB-36 and YB-36 - the first ninety-five B-36s cost the government $988,506,574 in Fiscal Year 49 dollars.

The third B-36D, 44-92090, was used for an accelerated service test programme and flew 500 hours during the first seventy-three days. The aircraft underwent a thorough inspection that required a seven-day down period every 120 hours during this period. Each flight was a simulated tactical mission that was accomplished as close as practical to how a regular Air Force unit would fly the aircraft. The missions attacked ‘targets’ that ranged from the Dakotas to Florida and from the Pacific to the Atlantic. Most of the simulated bombing runs were conducted at 40,000 feet. Flights averaged approximately twenty-five hours each, although one lasted over thirty-nine hours.

The programme evaluated how various components behaved under extended operation at high altitudes and long ranges. The flights also served two other purposes. First, they allowed many Air Force personnel an opportunity to train on long-range flights, with Convair engineers offering advice. Second, the flights also allowed engineering and design personnel the chance to familiarise themselves with the problems that occurred during long-duration missions. The last flight of the programme was in mid-November 1950, completing 1,008 flight hours.

The first new-build B-36D, ordered initially as a B-model, flew on 11 July 1949, and the Air Force

An early-model B-36 - notice the lack of jet pods - overflies downtown Cinncinati. Note also the exhausting staining of the horizontal tail surfaces from the two inboard engines. (USAF)

B-36 under construction. Note the leading edge access panels moved up and the protection carpets on the upper surface of the wings. The outer wing panels still have to be fitted. (Convair)

accepted its first B-36D, 49-2653, on 22 August 1950. Although officially assigned to the 11th BW at Carswell, the aircraft was immediately sent to Eglin AFB for testing. The twenty-six new-build B-36Ds were delivered five in August 1950, five in September, one in October, two in November, one in December, three in January 1951, six in March, two in April, and the last one in August 1951. This last aircraft carried an early serial number, 49-2655, but a very late block number (35) and was delivered substantially after its production linemates. Convair had used this aircraft as the prototype for various 'crew comfort' items that would be introduced on later models, explaining its late delivery.

A decision was made to retrofit the jet engines to all existing B-36Bs, so becoming B-36Ds and the B-36As became RB-36Es. The Air Force authorized the conversions as an extension of contract AF33-O38-2182, the current production contract.

The Fort Worth plant was already busy building new B-36s and remanufacturing the B-36As, so after the first four B-36Bs, 44-92026, 034, 053, and 054 were converted, the modification effort was transferred to San Diego. At either location, each aircraft was completely overhauled, and new control surfaces, jet engines, and the snap-action bomb bay doors were added. The effort was extensive - all of the control surfaces were removed, the outer wing panels were taken off to be strengthened to accommodate the jet pods, the engines and all accessories were removed and sent to Kelly AFB, the existing fuel tanks were resealed, and the new auxiliary fuel tanks were added into the inner wings. In addition, the electronics were brought up to date. Still, it was much less effort than required to remanufacture a B-36A into an RB-36E. Most disassembly occurred outdoors in the new work docks, but reassembly was accomplished with four aircraft at a time, mostly enclosed in Building 3 - the building could not accommodate all but the empennage. The aircraft were reassigned later block numbers, although some overlapped block numbers were applied to the new-build D-models.

A head-on image, showing the nose turret, offset gunsight and a good view of the glazed area.

The first B-36B, 44-92043, arrived at San Diego on 6 April 1950 and made its initial flight as a B-36D on 5 December 1950. The aircraft made two additional test flights, on 10 and 16 December, before being re-delivered to the Air Force the following day. The last modified aircraft, 44-92081, was re-delivered to the Air Force on 14 February 1952. Before beginning test flights at San Diego, modified aircraft had their engines run-up, navigation equipment checked, and the guns were fired into a special gun butt built across the runways from the Convair plant. Each gun fired approximately 50 rounds of nonexplosive ammunition, and the first test was conducted on 21 November 1950. Similar tests were conducted on each B-36 at Fort Worth prior to delivery. In fact, by the end of 1950, B-36 tests had fired 50 tons or 200,000 rounds of 20-mm ammunition in the gun butt at the north end of the Fort Worth facility.

The performance benefit from the jet engines was significant. Although originally the Air Force claimed the jet engines boosted the top speed to 439 mph at 32,120 feet and the service ceiling to 45,020 feet, this was later revised to 406 mph at 36,200 feet and a service ceiling of 43,800 feet. Whether this discrepancy was due to miscalculation, some overzealous public relations as the Congressional hearings were underway at the time, or changes in the aircraft themselves is not certain. The jet engines reduced the takeoff run by almost 2,000 feet and effectively doubled the standard rate of climb to 900 feet per minute. The B-36 flew well on four or even three piston engines, so it was common to shut down some of the engines during the cruise. The turbojets were usually used only over the target area or for takeoff and climb out.

Although still a great deal lower than the performance expected from the B-52, the B-36 was no longer considered a 'sitting duck' and could outrun most contemporary fighters at high altitudes. For the record, the speed quoted for an aircraft is usually at its best operating altitude; for contemporary fighters this was about 20,000 feet. The fighters generally lost a lot of speed by the time they got to 40,000 feet if they could get there at all. The Air Force was satisfied to rely on the B-36 until the development of the new Boeing B-52 was completed.

On 16 January 1951, six B-36Ds were flown from Carswell to the UK, landing at RAF Lakenheath after having staged through Limestone AFB, Maine. The flight, dubbed Operation United Kingdom, was led by Colonel Thomas P Gerrity, commander of the 11th BW. The flight returned to Carswell on 20 January, marking the first time that B-36s had deployed outside the USA.

The long missions usually flown by the B-36 caused a great deal of fatigue for the crew. To improve the environment inside the aircraft, during mid-1951 Convair began installing sound deadening panels inside each pressurized compartment. Different sized panels made of wool and fibreglass were designed that snapped onto bulkheads inside the aircraft and were installed as the aircraft rotated through San Diego or Fort Worth for upgrades. There were ninety-seven panels in the forward compartment and fifty-nine in the aft cabin. Although each panel began by being cut from a template, each was tailored to the particular aircraft into which it was installed. In addition, thirty pieces of vinyl carpeting were installed on the floor. These modifications also provided a certain amount of thermal protection inside the aircraft, further increasing crew comfort. Unfortunately, these would be among the items removed during the Featherweight programme.

By this time the Air Force and Convair were also installing additional crew comfort items, including expanded galleys, better bunks complete with mattresses, blankets, and pillows, and a variety of storage areas for personal items. The new galley, equipped with two electric burners, was located in the aft compartment and included skillets, pots, pans, and lids for cooking, along with knives, forks, spoons, and ladles. Two plug-in hot cups were provided for heating soups, coffee, and other liquids, and an electric oven allowed baking bread or other foods. A small refrigerator was provided to store perishable foods.

Two folding tables were installed along the sides of the aft compartment where the lower bunks could be used as chairs. This allowed up to four men to eat in relative comfort. A special container was provided that allowed hot meals to be transferred to the forward cabin using the normal dolly. Strung between the bunks were small racks for storing personal items, and new storage compartments near the top of the cabin were provided for kit bags and other items that were previously stored on the floor. The aft cabin lavatory facilities were upgraded with a sink, mirror, commode, and privacy curtains. A smaller, but similar, lavatory was added to the forward compartment.

A flight to French Morocco was made on 6 December 1951 when six B-36s of the 11th BW

B-36F 44-92683 in formation with another F, 44-92680. (USAF)

Significant changes to the flight engineer's station on the B-36H and J reflected the need for two seats. On earlier models, there was only one despite the presence of two engineers. The throttles and instruments for the jet engines were retained at the pilot's station. (National Museum of the United States Air Force via Roger Deere)

and modified in San Antonio and Fort Worth. The bad luck surrounding the F-model's introduction to service continued on 5 August 1952; gasoline overflowed from the No. 3 tank vent on a B-36F 49-2679 and was ignited by the exhaust from a B-10 power unit on the ramp. Three crew members sustained minor injuries, and the aircraft from the 7th BW/ 436th BS was a complete loss.

B-36G

The B-36G designation initially applied to a swept-wing, jet-powered version of the B-36F. Two machines, 49-2676 and 49-2684 were ordered converted to B-36Gs, but the designation was changed to YB-60 before being built.

B-36H

First announced on 5 November 1950, the B-36H was the major production version of the B-36, with eighty-three being built. The initial contract, an extension of AF33-038-2182 for fifteen B-36H and eight RB-36H aircraft, was announced on 5 September 1951. However, the contract had been signed over a year earlier, resulting in the aircraft having FY50 serial numbers. An additional forty-four bombers and thirty-nine reconnaissance variants would be ordered in FY51, with twenty-four more B-36Hs and twenty-six RB-36Hs ordered in FY52.

The B-36H was substantially similar to the B-36F that preceded it but relocated the K-system electronic components into the pressurized compartment to facilitate in-flight maintenance and featured a rearranged flight deck with a second flight engineer station. In addition, the revised flight deck featured a new instrument panel for the pilot and co-pilot and improved night lighting at all four crew stations. The mockup of the new flight deck arrangement had been inspected during August 1950, at essentially the same time as the first B-36D was delivered. Despite the attention to detail paid during the development of the new flight deck, Air Force evaluators found a few items to criticize once the aircraft entered service. For instance, the pilot's gyro horizon was considered too small and was unreliable. Somewhat surprisingly, the co-pilot's was found to be adequate in all regards. The space available on the flight deck was considered highly unsatisfactory. It was recommended that the flight engineer's panel be moved aft about twelve inches and the pilot's pedestal shortened by six inches to 'enhance the emergency escape of the co-pilot and assistant flight engineer.'

The twelve B/RB-36H-1 machines were

equipped with the same C-2 defensive system as the later B-36Fs. However, beginning with Block 5 aircraft, a new C-3 system was introduced that incorporated dynamic gun mounts designed to eliminate further the fire dispersion problem that had plagued the B-36 since the beginning. This consisted of a spring cushion arrangement that allowed the cannon to move back and forth on tracks along the line of fire, allowing some of the shock to be absorbed by the springs instead of being transferred to the turret.

A new AN/APG-41 gun-laying tail radar was introduced on 51-5742. This improved unit used twin tail radomes and was essentially two APG-32s coupled together, allowing one radar to track an immediate threat while the second continued to scan for other threats. The left-hand unit - when facing the tail - could scan from sixty degrees right to eighty degrees left; the right-hand unit could scan eighty degrees right to sixty degrees left.

The engines were six R-4630-53s and four J47-GE-19s, the same as on the B-36F. Slightly improved ECM equipment was included, as were two A-6 or A-7 dispensers carrying 1,400 pounds of chaff to confuse enemy radars.

The B-36H made its first flight on 5 April 1952, although deliveries to operational units did not begin until December 1952. One of the reasons deliveries were held up was that an RB-36F had suffered a pressure bulkhead failure while flying at 33,000 feet. The accident was traced to a defective bulkhead, and all B-36s were restricted to altitudes below 25,000 feet until the entire fleet could be inspected and defective bulkheads replaced. While the accident investigation was ongoing, the Air Force declined to accept any new aircraft from Convair.

The B-36's original propeller blades had structural limitations that resulted in flight restrictions which hampered performance. There were also concerns over propeller-induced vibrations and buffeting against the fuselage sides and the horizontal stabiliser. This had been recognised even before the first flight of the XB-36, leading to investigations of using sixteen-foot, four-bladed propellers instead of the normal nineteen-foot, three-bladed units. Similar propellers had been test-fitted on the XB-36 before its roll-out and had been flight tested on a B-36B 44-92057 during 1950. Since the B-36 could cruise with some of the engines shut down, many pilots opted to shut down the inboard engines and feather the propellers, easing the vibration on the fuselage and buffeting on the stabiliser. However, the evaluations of the four-bladed propeller were apparently inconclusive, and the decision was made to develop a new three-bladed unit.

A revised blade, made by a special flash-welding process, had a slightly broader chord and less pitch

Another view of the flight engineer's station. (National Museum of the United States Air Force via Roger Deere)

to minimise the buffeting. The new propeller could be used freely except for landing and takeoff. The obvious difference was the use of square blade tips instead of the original rounded tips. This blade weighed an extra twenty pounds each, but its greater efficiency promised to compensate for the small loss in aircraft range. Additional blades were subsequently ordered and retrofitted to most earlier aircraft, including the XC-99.

The Air Force accepted thirty-two B36Hs in FY52 - seven in December 1951, five in January 1952, three in February, five in March, and four in each of the next three months. It received forty-three B-36Hs in FY53 - four in July 1952, four in August, seven in September, three in October, four in November, two in December, four in January 1953, and three during each of the next five months. Eight B-36Hs were accepted in FY54 - three in July 1953, three in August, and two in September.

The B-36H cost $11,321 more than the B-36F. Airframe costs were lower, but the price of the engines showed an increase, as did armament, electronics, and propellers. The new costs were: airframe, $2,077,785; engines (installed), $874,526; propellers, $214,186; electronics, $80,272; ordnance, $30,241; and armament, $872,436.

A B-36 deployment on 2-21 February 1953 turned out to be particularly tragic. As part of a simulated tactical mission - Operation Styleshow - to RAF Fairford in the UK, eighteen B 36s from the 7th BW flew from Carswell to the staging base at Goose Bay, Labrador on 2 and 3 February. One B-36 developed mechanical problems and returned to Carswell. On 6 February, the remaining seventeen aircraft departed Goose Bay headed for Fairford, encountering severe weather en route. Although sixteen aircraft managed to land safely, one B-36H, 51-5719, commanded by Lt Col Herman Gerick, ran out of fuel after holding for excessive time and executing two missed Ground Controlled Approaches (GCA). According to Air Force records, the fourteen-man crew baled out and landed across Oxfordshire, Wiltshire and Berkshire. The reports suggested that the by now crewless aircraft flew on for thirty or so miles before coming down in Nethermore Woods, near Pitters Farm, Sandy Lane, Lacock, Wiltshire. Luckily, none of the crew or anyone on the ground was injured.

Later investigations revealed that the GCA centre at Fairford was understaffed and staffed by inexperienced controllers, which undoubtedly played a role in the crash.

For the next week, the B-36s flew training missions out of Fairford. Fourteen B-36s departed for Goose Bay on 13 February; two B-36Hs remained in the UK for special weapons training. Unfortunately, on 13 February, the GCA controllers at Goose Bay misdirected one B-36H 51-5729, being flown by Clifford Schoeffler, so that it flew into a hill sixteen and a half miles southwest of Goose Bay while attempting to land. Two of the seventeen crew members aboard - in the rear compartment - were killed and the aircraft destroyed. The thirteen remaining aircraft eventually returned to Carswell, with the last arriving on 21 February. The two aircraft that had stayed at Fairford returned to Carswell on 23 February.

Although unusual, the B-36 could be safely landed with very few engines running. On 27 March 1954, Captain Berry H Young from the 7th BW/ 9th BS successfully landed his B-36H at Carswell with all three R4360s on the right wing and all four jets inoperative. A hydraulic failure meant that the landing gear had to be lowered manually, and the flaps were inoperative to complicate matters further. Nevertheless, the landing proved uneventful, and the crew and aircraft were intact. Around Carswell, this became known as the 'miracle landing.' The crew was presented the Carswell Crew of the Month award and also received a personal commendation from General LeMay.

TANBO XIV

One B-36H - 51-5706 - was converted into a prototype in-flight refuelling tanker. The heading name needs some explanation. Searching for a tanker that could refuel jet aircraft at higher altitudes and speeds, in late 1951, Strategic Air Command became interested in a readily convertible B-36 TANker-BOmber, or TANBO. The 'XIV' refers to the Mark XIV refuelling reel that was installed. On 15 January 1952, the Air Force authorised Convair to equip one B-36 with a probe-and-drogue refuelling system for tests. The modification contract was approved in February 1952, and the work was completed in May. A large reel for the refuelling hose was bolted into bomb bay No. 4, and bladder fuel tanks to hold jet fuel were permanently installed in the other three bomb bays. The removable portion of the design consisted of a framework mounted in bomb bay No. 4 that supported a Mark XIV reel, fuel transfer pumps, and an extendable hydraulically-operated boom. Removing the reel would allow atomic weapons to be carried in bomb bay No. 4, but the other bomb bays were unavailable since the jet fuel tanks were permanently installed. A windmill-type power source was mounted on the boom to feed the fuel pumps and to provide a means of extending the refuelling hose away from the aircraft.

The refuelling boom could be retracted entirely within the aircraft, and when extended, the bomb bay doors formed a tight seal around the boom. As a result, there were almost 16,000 gallons of fuel available for transfer at a rate of 600 gallons per minute. This was equivalent to a B-47's internal and external fuel, but more probably could top up two or three B-47s on the way to their target. In addition, the converted B-36H tanker had a crew of nine and could be returned to a bomber configuration in twelve hours.

Testing began in March 1953 using an F-84 as a receiver. However, due to difficulties with the British-made reel mechanism, the non-availability of adequate hose, and problems with governing the propeller transferring power to the fuel pumps, the tests were suspended on 27 May. The problems were not addressed before the advent of the Boeing KC-135 Stratotnker, which eliminated the need for the TANBO concept. The Tanbo B-36H was released to the Rascal production programme on 6 July 1954, and on 21 July, the Air Force officially cancelled the Tanbo XIV project.

Two views of the navigator's station of a B-36J.

This compartment could get crowded for it held not only the navigator, but also a photo-navigator, radar observer and a nose gunner/weather observer.

(National Museum of the United States Air Force via Roger Deere)

Two views of the navigator's compartment of a B-36J, showing the radar observer's station

(National Museum of the United States Air Force via Roger Deere)

Items in the nose areas of a B-36J.

Left: the 'little boys room' in what was charmingly called the 'roomette.'

Above: coffee pots with electrical connections become hot cups in the radio operator's area.

Below: The start of the pressurised tunnel back to the rear area.

(National Museum of the United States Air Force via Roger Deere)

The scale and size of the B-36J bomb-bays in the National Museum of the United States Air Force's example. (Dr Harry Friedman)

B-36J

The B-36J was the final production version of the B-36. It had an additional fuel tank in each outer wing panel that increased the fuel load by 2,770 gallons, bringing total fuel capacity with bomb bay fuel tanks up to 36,396 gallons. The aircraft had a more robust landing gear that permitted a gross takeoff weight of 410,000 pounds, resulting in a slightly degraded top speed of only 411 mph. A new AN/ARC-21 high-frequency command radio was also installed. The only external change was a single elongated radome to cover the twin antennas of the APG-41A gun-laying radar in the tail, introduced during B/RB-36H production.

The first B-36J made its maiden flight in July 1953. Flight testing soon discovered an unsatisfactory aileron control characteristic that resulted in the rerigging of the control cables. The Air Force accepted twenty-eight B-36Js in FY54: two in September 1953 and two in October, then three each month from November 1953 through March 1954, none in April, four in May, and five in June. Five more B-36Js were accepted in FY55: four in July 1954 and one in August. The final fourteen of the thirty-three B-36Js were completed as Featherweight III aircraft. These were the only Featherweight aircraft to be completed as such on the production line, all the other H-models were modified after production.

The last B-36J, 52-2827, was rolled out on 10 August 1954 and was delivered to the Air Force on 14 August. 'This last B-36 will join others to become an integral part of the nation's insurance that we are in business to keep the peace but prepared to bring defeat to those who might be so stupid as to break it.' Those were the closing words of Major General Francis H. Griswold, Vice commander of SAC, just before the last B-36 roared into the skies on the way to its home at Fairchild AFB, Washington. Over 11,000 people were on hand to watch the end of an era at Fort Worth. Major Laurence Nickerson piloted the aircraft, but also on board were three men who had been on the first flight of the XB-36 eight years earlier: Gus Green, D McEachern, and Joe Hefley.

The B-36J cost half a million dollars less than the preceding B-36H: airframe, $1,969,271; engines (installed), $639,651; propellers, $214,186; electronics, $77,691; ordnance, $32,036; and armament, $707,379. Featherweights cost approximately $100,000 less, mainly because they did not carry the 20-mm cannon or turrets. By the time the B-36 production programme was completed, the Air Force had spent over $1,000 million on the aircraft.

The Featherweights

Even with the great range of the B-36, there had to be compromises between the weapons that could be carried and the distance to the targets that could be attacked. In the early 1950s, it was not yet evident that high-yield thermonuclear weapons would eventually become fairly small and lightweight. Thus, devising a means to extend the range of the bombers became vitally important. Interestingly, although in-flight refuelling was just emerging, and would become standard on almost all Air Force aircraft - including some B-29s and most B-50s - it never seems to have been seriously considered for the B-36 fleet.

As an alternative, on 28 January 1954, the Air Force approved the first phase of Project Featherweight to increase the operational altitude and range of the B-36. The major objective of the Featherweight programme was to eliminate the need to hold aircraft in readiness at the pre-strike stage.

Calculations on flight paths and range showed that operations from only one base, at Limestone

AFB, Maine, could support direct operations from the Continental United States to deep inside the USSR, where most of the targets were located.

This meant that all other standard B-36s were forced to the pre-strike stage in order to have sufficient range to attack 'significant targets' in the Soviet Union regardless of the route chosen. This meant flying from their home base to another airfield closer to the USSR to reduce the range to target. Such pre-strike staging was vulnerable, time-consuming, costly in terms of prepositioned materiel and airlift, and subject to adverse weather conditions. In addition, strike missions mounted from some of the more remote pre-strike bases required a sacrifice of bombing altitude. The Pentagon was also getting increasingly concerned over the cost and dubious strategic advanages of the pre-strike bases - most of which were located outside the United States - might be rendered unusable by political or hostile action.

It became evident to the Air Staff and SAC planners that a requirement existed for an aircraft that could strike through the Arctic without pre-strike staging or attack from more remote pre-strike bases without a corresponding sacrifice in altitude, or attack significant targets with pre-strike and post-strike staging through North American bases.

The only aircraft available in early 1954 that could meet these requirements was a modified B-36. The idea was to remove enough weight from each aircraft so that maximum fuel could be carried on all missions - previously, most missions had been flown with less fuel due to gross takeoff weight restrictions based on landing gear limitations. TANBO XIV may have considered converting the B-36 into a tanker, but unfortunately, the concept of refuelling the B-36s in flight at the edge of American airspace does not appear to have entered anyone's head.

With an already unprecedented range, other means were sought to increase the range and the flight duration of bombing missions, and this is where the B-36 Featherweight programme came in.

A major problem was altitude at remote pre-staging bases and the revised doctrine of how to wage a global war involving nuclear weapons fell parallel to the determination that, with the more lightweight thermonuclear devices that were becoming available, each aircraft would become more 'productive' by carrying a much heavier punch and more than one atomic weapon.

It was simultaneous with the decision to build a force of intercontinental ballistic missiles that SAC, which would have responsibility for those as the second leg of the deterrent from the end of the decade, sought a solution that only the B-36 could provide. The Boeing B-47 medium bomber had aerial refuelling, which the B-36 did not. Still, the overall capacity of the aircraft to deliver more range was a real possibility due to its size and weight. A large and heavy aircraft can provide more weight reduction than can a smaller and lighter aircraft.

In early 1954, just as decisions were being made about the overall configuration of SAC after the B-36 was retired and a new generation of weapons would become available by the end of the decade, a strongly contested debate developed over the balance between missiles and manned aircraft, introducing the phrase 'push-button warfare' from those already involved in the balance of procurement, seeking increased efficiencies through the use of unmanned strike systems and fewer maintenance and support personnel than required for aircraft.

The two sides of the argument were contested by General Bernard Schriever, who campaigned for a greater reliance on rockets and missiles, and General Curtis LeMay, who sought to prioritise the manned air fleets that had been essential for winning the Second World War. Schriever would get his missiles at the cost of manned air fleets of tankers and bombers, which would be reduced. However, that was in the future, and in 1954 there was all to play for. So it was that a concerted effort began to put the B-36 through a significant weight reduction programme, expand the aircraft's demonstrated capability, and further validate its existence.

Three configurations were considered for the Featherweight programme. Configuration One involved the tactical unit - usually the Bomb Wing - removing all the retractable turrets, auxiliary bomb racks and crew comfort items immediately before a retaliatory strike. This tactic was rejected because of the potential delay of possibly several days in the unit being able to undertake missions. Eventually, all aircraft went through a general housekeeping process in the field. In addition, many unused or unneeded brackets and spare parts were removed during routine maintenance at the squadron level.

Configuration Two - called a Tactically Stripped Featherweight - involved removing all the extraneous equipment from each aircraft, except the guns, ECM equipment, auxiliary bomb racks, and crew comfort items. The turrets were reconfigured to allow their rapid removal if required. In addition, as many external protuberances as possible were removed from the aircraft to decrease drag.

Periscopic sextants and high-altitude operating equipment were added, and flush covers for all six sighting blisters were procured but not normally installed. These modifications were accomplished at the depot level - either Convair or San Antonio - and resulted in a weight reduction of 4,800 pounds. If needed, the tactical unit could quickly remove the turrets and install the flush blister covers to eliminate several thousand additional pounds.

These modifications increased the range by twenty-five per cent with guns and thirty-nine per cent without guns. This programme was applied across all types of B/RB-36s. The aircraft had a '-II' suffix appended to their designation, sometimes written as '(II)' in the manner of B-36D-II or B-36D(II) being equivalent.

The ultimate Featherweight 'conversion' was Configuration Three, also conducted at the depot level. Under this programme, all defensive armament except the tail turret and its radar was deleted, as were the forward and upper aft sighting blisters. The lower aft blisters were retained on most aircraft since they provided a convenient location for crewmembers to observe the engines for oil leaks, etc. On some aircraft, these blisters were replaced by flat Plexiglas, providing another small decrease in drag. The chaff dispensers and ECM gear were retained, and brought up to a later standard. Most of the remaining crew comfort equipment - bunks, galley, sound deadening, carpet - was also deleted, along with the astrodome on top of the cockpit. On bombers equipped with the -53 engines - since they could attain higher altitudes due to the use of fuel injection instead of carburettors - five additional oxygen bottles were installed in the area previously occupied by the upper forward turrets.

Without guns, the crew could be reduced, usually, by two of the aft gunners. The forward gunners generally had other duties, such as navigating and were retained. Since most of the insulation had been removed from the pressurized compartments, the temperature at high altitude would be unbearable, so provisions for heated flying suits were installed. The new flying suits contained integral communications equipment, so the fixed intercom system and speakers were removed. These modifications gave a weight reduction of 15,000 pounds, that resulted in a range increase of between twenty-five and forty per

The End is near!

Left: The aft fuselage for the last B-36J. Even at this stage of production the censor has scratched out the production number (the white blotch at the extreme right). Note the man on top of the radome fairing.

Below: The censors continued their work, this time on the nose with a black marker, in this famous picture of the roll-out of 52-2827.
(Both Lockheed Martin)

cent, depending on the B-36 model over the Featherweight Two configuration.

The weight and drag reduction increased the top speed of the modified B-36Ds to 418 mph, and modified B-36Hs increased to 423 mph. More importantly, the weight reduction allowed an increase in operating altitude - officially up to 47,000 feet and well over 50,000 feet, according to many former crew members. These aircraft had a '-III' appended to their designations.

In addition, both configurations of Featherweight aircraft had their main landing gear pivot shafts beefed up, the 'large bomb fitting' on the rear wing spar modified to withstand additional gust load factors, and bulkhead twelve in the aft fuselage strengthened by adding a layer of fibreglass cloth to its aft face. Various navigation and radio equipment was also updated. The B-36 had been built with removable armour panels surrounding the integral fuel tanks in the wings - Featherweight removed these. The anti-ice and fuel tank purging systems were also deleted.

The entire B-36 and RB-36 fleet underwent Featherweight modifications. Where possible, the Air Force accomplished other modifications while the aircraft was being converted to Featherweights - including improved thermonuclear capabilities, SAM-SAC, ON TOP Phases 8-10, and the K-system recycling effort. From the onset, the plan was to bring some aircraft up to the full Featherweight III configuration while leaving others in Configuration II to conduct missions where defensive armament might be necessary. For instance, of the one hundred and four B/RB-36s assigned to the Fifteenth Air Force, only thirty-two were scheduled for the full Configuration III modifications, and this included the ten aircraft being modified into GRB-36D FICON carriers. All B-36 changes were to be completed by December 1954, with all RB-36s following by March 1955. The last fourteen B-36Js were manufactured to the Featherweight configuration III.

At the same time as the Featherweight modifications, in conjunction with ON TOP Phase 10, all RB-36s were returned to a primary bombardment mission. However, the aircraft retained a dormant reconnaissance capability that could be used in what was termed 'the exploitation phase of conflict or peacetime operations.' The ferret ECM equipment and associated radomes were relocated from between bulkheads eight and nine to between bulkheads ten and twelve in the aft fuselage. Also, as part of ON TOP Phase 10, some B and RB aircraft received a ten-inch scope for the APS-24 at the bombardier's station instead of the original five-inch scope. On bomber aircraft, the five-inch scope was relocated to the navigator's station.

There was some disagreement between SAC and the Air Force Systems Command over removing the second photographer from the standard crew list. AFSC suggested retaining the second crew member and removing the split vertical and forward oblique camera installations to achieve an equivalent weight reduction. SAC argued that since the aircraft no longer had a primary reconnaissance role, the second photographer was not needed, although why all the camera equipment was retained was not stated. In the end, the cameras were retained, and the second photographer was not manifested for strike missions. SAC also began postponing reconnaissance training and instead concentrated on sending RB-36 crews through the regular bombardment training.

The only major challenge experienced during the Featherweight conversions was a shortage of altimeters. Initially, a new C-19 altimeter had been specified that measured between zero and 60,000 feet. Unfortunately, the vendor could only supply thirty-five units per month, while up to eighty-six B-36s were being modified in some months. Ultimately, the Air Force decided that some aircraft - usually the Configuration II bombers - could be equipped with modified C-12 units capable of measuring between zero and 55,000 feet. The first Featherweight Configuration II aircraft began its modification in February 1954 and was redelivered in August 1954. The last modified bomber was redelivered in November 1954, with the last reconnaissance version following six months later.

Beginning in late 1954, most, if not all B and RB aircraft received high altitude camouflage paint under ECP-2309B. This involved painting the bottom of the fuselage and most of the lower wing surface with anti-flash white. The painting was accomplished concurrently with the aircraft undergoing ON TOP Phase 10, Featherweight, or SAM-SAC Cycle 2 modifications. The first few aircraft were painted in the Experimental Building, but most later aircraft were painted out-of-doors on a secluded part of the ramp. A few machines also had the top of the forward crew compartment painted white, although no record of an ECP that authorized this could be found. At the same time, any aircraft that still had fabric-covered ailerons was modified (ECP-2315) with metal-covered surfaces. Bomber aircraft also had their bomb-spotting camera relocated from just behind bulkhead nine to just behind bulkhead 10.0 for undetermined reasons.

Chapter Seven

Strategic Air Command

Cold War Planning

Exactly how serious was the threat of World War Three in the late 1940s only became apparent when documents were released in the 1990s after the end of the Cold War.

The geopolitical situation at the end of the 1940s was as tenuous as it had been at the beginning of the decade. The Cold War was rapidly deepening, China was in turmoil with a pro-Soviet government seizing power, and the Soviet Union held half the Eurasian landmass under its control. What is more, Soviet leader Josef Stalin had announced a policy to expand his empire wherever possible. A Third World War, including attacks on the USA, was seen as a genuine possibility.

While the USSR had retained its massive land army - the largest in the world built during World War Two, the United States had rapidly demobilised to a mere skeleton force. All the United States had to its advantage was airpower. The United States had nuclear weapons - which the Soviets would not possess until 1949 - and it had what would become the best long-range bomber force in the world. This was the Strategic Air Command, known worldwide by the acronym SAC, pronounced 'sack.'

The military planners had done what they could to plan for the feared eventuality. Today, it is easy to chart the course of the development of the B-36s against the backdrop of information to which men like Vandenberg, Twining and LeMay - but few others - were privy. In late 1945, the Joint Chiefs of Staff authorised work on a contingency General War Plan for operations against the Soviet Union. The plan, code-named Pincher, was completed on 18 June 1946.

The upshot of events that were geared to implementation of Operation Pincher included Operation Broadview of August 1946, the defence of the North American continent against a Soviet invasion; Operation Griddle the counterattack against a Soviet invasion of Turkey; Operation Caldron, the retaliation against a Soviet invasion of the Middle East; and Operation Cockspur , the counterattack against a Soviet invasion of the Italian Peninsula.

That, however, is getting slightly ahead of the narrative. SAC was initially established in the US Army Air Forces on 21 March 1946, acquiring part of the Continental Air Forces (CAF) personnel and facilities (the World War Two command tasked with the air defence of the continental United States (CONUS). At the time, CAF headquarters was located at Bolling Field in the District of Columbia, and SAC assumed occupancy of its headquarters facilities until relocating SAC headquarters (HQ SAC) to nearby Andrews Field (Maryland) as a tenant activity until taking control of Andrews Field in October 1946.

SAC initially totalled 37,000 USAAF personnel. In addition to Bolling Field and, seven months later, Andrews Field, SAC also assumed responsibility for Roswell AAF (New Mexico) and Smoky Hill AAF (Kansas). SAC also had seven other CAF bases transferred on 21 March 1946 which remained in SAC through the establishment in 1947 of the US Air Force as an independent service. Those installations were Castle Field (California), Clovis AAF (New Mexico), Fort Worth AAF (Texas), Davis-Monthan Field (Arizona), Rapid City AAF (South Dakota), MacDill Field (Florida) and Mountain Home AAF (Idaho). On 31 March 1946, Kirtland Field (New Mexico) was also assigned to SAC. Under the first SAC Commander in Chief, General George C Kenney, initial units reporting to the Strategic Air Command headquarters on 21 March 1946 included the Second Air Force, the IX Troop Carrier Command and the 73d Air Division.

The Fifteenth Air Force was assigned to SAC on 31 March, while the IX Troop Carrier Command was inactivated on the same date, and its assets were redistributed within SAC.

With postwar demobilization still underway, eight of the ten assigned Bomb Groups were inactivated before the Eighth Air Force was assigned to SAC on 7 June 1946.

In the wake of the successful employment of air-dropped nuclear weapons against Hiroshima and Nagasaki to effectively end World War Two, SAC became the focus of the nation's nuclear strike capability, to the extent that Joint Chiefs of Staff (JCS) Publication 1259/27 on 12 December 1946 identified that, '..the 'air atomic' strategic air force should only come under the orders of the JCS.'

In addition to the strategic bombing mission, SAC also devoted significant resources to aerial reconnaissance. In 1946, SAC's reconnaissance aircraft inventory consisted of F-2 photo variants of the C-45 Expeditor support aircraft, but by 1947 SAC had acquired an F-9C squadron consisting of twelve photo-reconnaissance variants of the B-17G Flying Fortress. An F-13 squadron, the F-13 later re-designated as the RB-29 Superfortress, was also established. SAC conducted routine aerial reconnaissance missions near the Soviet borders or the twelve-mile international waters limit, although some missions penetrated Soviet airspace. The flight profiles of these missions, above 30,000 feet and in excess of 300 knots,

Commanding generals of the newly reorganized Air Forces, March 1946. Standing left to right: Lt Gen Nathan F Twining, Maj Gen Donald Wilson, Maj Gen Muir S Fairchild. Seated, left to right: Lt Gen John K Cannon, General George C Kenney, Commanding General of the Army Air Forces Carl A Spaatz, Lt Gen. Harold L. George, Lt Gen George E Stratemeyer, and Maj Gen Elwood R Quesada. (USAF)

A good view of the Strategic Air Command shield and sash on RB-36H-35-CF, 51-13735. All the reconnaissance aircraft had glazed panels for the Norden bombsights. (Lockheed Martin)

made interception by Soviet air forces difficult until the Soviet's 1948 introduction of the MiG-15 jet fighter. Project Nanook, the Cold War's first Top Secret reconnaissance effort, used the first RB-29 missions for mapping and visual reconnaissance in the Arctic and along the northern Soviet coast. Later missions were Project Lepopard along the Chukchi Peninsula, followed by Projects Rickrack, Stonework, and Coveralls.

It should be recorded that in 1946, the US possessed only nine atomic bombs and twenty-seven B-29s capable at any one time of delivering them. Furthermore, it was later determined that an attack by the 509th Composite Bomb Group during the 1947 to 1948 time frame would have required at least five to six days just to transfer custody of the bombs from United States Atomic Energy Commission (AEC) sites to SAC and deploy the aircraft and weapons to forward operating bases before launching nuclear strikes.

Unfortunately, postwar budget and personnel cuts had had an insidious effect on SAC as its Deputy Commander, Major General Clements McMullen, implemented mandated force reductions. This continued to wear down SAC as a command and morale plummeted. As a result, by the end of 1947, only two of SAC's eleven Groups were combat-ready.

In terms of overall Air Force basing and infrastructure, SAC acquired an ever-increasing share of USAF infrastructure and the USAF associated budget. In 1947, before the USAF was established as an independent service, construction commenced on Limestone AAF (Maine), a new SAC installation specifically designed to accommodate the B-36 Peacemaker. Fort Dix AAF (New Jersey), Spokane AAF (Washington) and Wendover Field (Utah) were also transferred to SAC between 30 April and 1 September 1947. Following the establishment of the USAF as a separate service, an additional forty-six bases in the United States were added to SAC.

In addition to bases under its operational control, SAC also maintained tenant wings at several bases under the control of other USAF MAJCOMs. These non-SAC bases with SAC tenants included Amarillo AFB (Texas), Eglin AFB (Florida), Lowry AFB (Colorado), Mather AFB (California), Robins AFB (Georgia), Seymour Johnson AFB (North Carolina), Sheppard AFB (Texas) and Wright-Patterson AFB (Ohio). SAC also often maintained a presence at former SAC bases that the command subsequently relinquished to other MAJCOMs, including but not limited to Altus AFB (Oklahoma), MacDill AFB (Florida), Homestead AFB (Florida) and Travis AFB (California).

The 99th Strategic Reconnaissance Wing at Fairchild AFB, Washington State, used film strips around the globe to emphasize its reconnaissance role. Note the checkerboard on the nose gear door. (Lockheed Martin)

Above: B-36D, 49-2658 on the tarmac at Lakenheath. This was the first appearance of the B-36 bomber in Europe. In a press release, Pilot Horton said that dummy bombs were dropped en route and that when he approached the coast of England, as many as twenty British Vampire and Meteor jets zoomed around his B-36 at one time. He remarked, to the press, that he had not used the B-36's four auxiliary jets to increase speed during interceptions.

Below: Clearly a posed shot of a British Gloster Meteor jet fighter with B-36D, 49-2658, done for the inevitable size comparison photograph. (both USAF)

On 15 May 1947, Joint War Plan JWPC-474.1 was issued, which discussed a major Soviet invasion of Western Europe, and concluded that there could be no realistic land defence. From this realisation, the concept of the requirement for B-36s operating from bases in North America originated. Meanwhile, supplemental War Plans dealt with other theatres. Operation Drumbeat discussed the prospects for (the defence of the Iberian Peninsula and Operation Moonrise both of August 1947 discussed the American intervention in the Chinese Civil War in response to the Soviet intervention therein and a subsequent land war in Asia. The most worrying was Operation Deerland of September 1947, a contingency plan for a campaign against a Soviet invasion of the Northeastern United States via Canada.

On 8 November 8 1947, the Joint Chiefs of Staff completed Strategic Plan Broiler (GSPC-496.1). It was the first in a series of outlines for fighting World War Three using the American military assets as they existed in 1947 at their post-war low point. The plan relied heavily on nuclear weapons delivered by the SAC B-29s, B-50s and B-36s.

SAC re-organised itself in 1947 which was accomplished under new Deputy Commander, Maj. General Clements McMullen from the Eighth Air Force. Faced with an austere defence budget, which forced the Air Force to adopt a 55 Group

Two weapon specialists load 20 mm rounds into the twin nose guns of a Ramey RB-36. SAC badge is prominent on the aircraft's nose. The unit insignia was usually painted on the right-hand side. (USAF)

rather than its planned 70 Group programme, General McMullen reorganised the Command, trimmed manpower at all levels, and centralised command jurisdiction functions at Headquarters Strategic Air Command.

SAC combat units began reorganising under the Hobson Plan in October and December. This was an organisational structure established by the USAF in 1948. Known as the 'Wing-Base' plan, it replaced the 'Base Plan' used by the United States Army Air Forces, the predecessor organisation of the USAF.

Under the Wing-Base plan, the operational combat squadrons were assigned to a Combat Group. The support squadrons on the station were assigned to a Maintenance and Supply Group, an Airdrome Support Group, and a Medical Group. The four Groups were assigned to a Wing, a new level of Command which unified all of the components, flying and support. The Group Commanders were subordinate to the Wing Commander, an experienced combat flying leader. The Wing would assume the historical numerical designation of the assigned Combat Group. A Base Commander was established to handle the Wing Commander's administrative duties and coordinate with the various Group commanders. In this, known as the Hobson Plan, the Support Groups and the operational flying Combat Group and the Wing became one unit. The Wing-Base organisation was formalised in Air Force Regulation (AFR) 20-15, Organization Principles and Policies for the US Air Force.

Organisations known as Wings had existed in the Air Force since 1918, and new Wings were created in the 1920s and 1930s. During World War Two numerous wings existed; some provided training in the United States, others controlled combat groups and support organisations overseas. However, the USAF Wings established in 1947 were new organisations and shared no lineage or honours with the Wings formed under the Army. In 1948 and afterwards, some AAF wings were re-designated as Air Divisions, and placed immediately above the USAF Wings and below the Numbered Air Forces in the USAF organisational pyramid.

Another major change implemented by the Hobson Plan was the standardisation of designations. For example, the 1st Fighter Wing, established at March Air Force Base, would consist of the 1st Fighter Group (its Combat Group); the 1st Maintenance and Supply Group, the 1st Combat Support Group (to operate base facilities and services), and the 1st Medical Group. Subordinate to the groups were the 1st Field

The 11th Bombardment Wing (Heavy) had a flock of long-range geese on their shield. The motto underneath the shield translates to 'Progress without fear or prejudice.' (Lockheed Martin)

Convair B-36D-45-CF, serial number 44-92080 was photographed on the runway at San Diego soon after its conversion from a B-36B-20-CF to a D mode|. This bomber was redelivered to the USAF in the latter part of 1951 and was assigned to the 92nd Bombardment Wing. The aircraft did not have a long career: on 29 January 1952, it landed short and crashed while approaching Fairchild AFB, near Spokane, Washington. Although the crewmen all survived, the aircraft was written off. (Convair)

Maintenance Squadron, 1st Supply Squadron, 1st Engine Squadron, 1st Security Police Squadron, and so on. Operational flying Squadrons retained their historical designations and were assigned to the Combat Group. Units assigned to the base as tenant units, under the Command of other Wings, would also retain their designations.

SAC flew its first maximum effort mission in 1947, making simulated attacks on major American cities such as Kansas City, Chicago, and New York. The most significant flight was over New York City on May 16, when 101 B-29s theoretically dropped their bombs in a maximum effort strike. However, another thirty B-29s remained at their bases, unable to take off because of maintenance and supply problems.

SAC Colours and Markings

In 1954 the Strategic Air Command began painting the familiar 'star-spangled band' down each side of the nose, with the SAC shield on the left side. The right side was usually unadorned except for the band, but some aircraft displayed the wing insignia over the band.

During late 1955, the small 'UNITED STATES AIR FORCE' on the forward fuselage was replaced with thirty-six-inch-high 'U.S. AIR FORCE' markings. It left no room for the buzz numbers, and they were usually deleted, although a few aircraft moved them forward of the new markings.

The 'high altitude camouflage' white undersides also began to appear. In reality, this was an anti-thermal white paint meant to provide a small amount of additional protection against the thermal pulse of a nuclear detonation. The paint added almost 200 pounds to each airframe. At the same time, the aircraft was given a coat of acrylic paint to inhibit corrosion, particularly on the magnesium skin. The fuselage generally used a clear coat, but the wings were often painted with an aluminium colour that obscured the natural metal finish. The 'USAF' marking on the lower left wing was usually deleted at this time. Since most of the units changed to a consolidated maintenance squadron, the individual colour markings disappeared. However, the large buzz numbers continued on some aircraft, usually written in front of the U.S. AIR FORCE in the same size.

Other aircraft had the last four digits of their serial numbers written in twelve-inch letters on the forward fuselage above the white demarcation line under the crew hatch.

The Convair production number was frequently left painted in nine-inch numbers on the extreme forward fuselage and the aft fuselage. Even if the units removed these, Convair repainted them the next time the aircraft went through maintenance or modification. Oddly, many photographs have these numbers scratched out by the censors, although the serial numbers were left intact. There were, of course, many variations to these markings.

Assigned Resources as of December 1947:
Personnel: 49,589 (5,175 officers, 39,307 airmen, and 5,107 civilians.)
Tactical Aircraft: 715 (319 B-29s, 230 P-51s, 120 P-80s, 9 C-54s, and 35 F-2, F- 9, F-13 and FB-17 aircraft. There were no B-36s yet; B-36A No.1 had just been flown in August, and the YB-36 took to the air for the first time in December.
Bomber Units: 11 Very Heavy Bomb Groups, 6 equipped with B-29s, and 5 with no aircraft assigned.
Active Bases: Sixteen SAC bases in the USA.

1948 was a year of changes and important events, a big year for SAC. On 19 October, the command leadership changed, with Lt. General Curtis E LeMay assuming Command, replacing General Kenney, who was reassigned. Brig. General Thomas S Power became Deputy Commander of SAC a week later. Also, Headquarters Strategic Air Command was moved from Andrews AFB, Maryland, to Offutt AFB, Nebraska, effective 9 November 1948.

The first of the postwar bombers, the Boeing B-50, an improved version of the B-29, was delivered to SAC's 43rd Bomb Wing at Davis Monthan AFB on 20 February 1948.

On 26 June, the first B-36 was delivered to the 7th Bomb Group at Carswell AFB, Texas. The introduction of the B-36 as an operational aircraft changed the designation of bombardment aircraft. The B29s and B-50s, which had been designated as 'very heavy,' were redesignated 'medium' aircraft, while the new B-36 was designated a 'heavy' bomber. The term 'very heavy' was dropped.

After the 1948 Bikini Atoll nuclear tests, the 'Half Moon' Joint Emergency War Plan developed in May 1948 proposed dropping fifty atomic bombs on twenty Soviet cities, with President Harry S. Truman approving 'Half Moon' during the June 1948 Berlin Blockade (Truman sent B-29s to Europe in July). SAC also ordered special ELINT RB-29s to detect improved Soviet radars and, in cooperation with the 51st Air Force Base Unit, SAC also monitored radioactive fallout from Soviet atomic testing on Novaya Zemlya.

On 17 March 1948, the Joint Chiefs of Staff issued Plan Frolic (JCS-1844.1), a short-range Emergency War Plan for engaging the Soviet Union. Operation Halfmoon superseded this plan, later renamed Doublestar (JCS-1844.4), which made the defence of Western Europe the key part of fighting a war against the Soviet Union from 1948 to 1949. Meanwhile, on 8 March 1948, Joint Chiefs of Staff planners completed JSPG-500.2, which outlined Operation Bushwacker, the general plan for fighting World War Three in or after 1952.

Bushwacker called for a massive nuclear air offensive to hold the Soviet forces down, while the United States began the slow process of mobilising for conventional warfare.

Air Force planning for Bushwacker continued to

An RB-36D takes off from Walker AFB, New Mexico, on its second mission during the 1953 SAC Bombing and Navigation Competition. The 92nd Bomb Wing won the Bombing Competition and the Fairchild Trophy. (USAF)

evolve into 1949 via War Plans Fleetwood and Trojan, which set a goal of stockpiling 400 nuclear weapons by 1 January 1953. Much of the evolution of the SAC did take place during this time, including the development of the B-36 and eventually the huge build-up of B-47s, can now be understood more clearly in the context of these plans.

Bushwacker was succeeded by War Plan Dropshot (JCS1920.1), which outlined the strategy for a global nuclear and conventional war to be conducted in or after 1957. Dropshot was accompanied by Offtackle, a near-term emergency War Plan designed for implementation immediately and with the limited resources - including B-36As and B-36Bs - that were available in 1949.

Confronted with severe manning, supply, and administrative problems throughout its first two years of existence, SAC was unable to devote much time to bombing practice, so bombing accuracy fell far below desired standards.

The first air refuelling units were activated-the 43rd and 509th Air Refueling Squadrons at Davis Monthan, receiving their first tankers, modified B-29s, in late 1948.

A major international event occurred in 1948 with the Soviet blockade of the city of Berlin in late June, which heightened Cold War tensions. SAC deployed two B-29 squadrons to Goose Bay, Labrador, in preparation for deployment to Germany. Two other B-29 units were placed on alert, one ready to deploy within as little as three hours. The rest of the Strategic Air Command was placed on 24-hour alert status. Later in the month, two units were moved to England to RAF stations located at Marham in Norfolk and Waddington in Lincolnshire.

From 7 to 9 December 1948, a B-36 from the 7th Bomb Wing, piloted by Maj. John D Bartlett completed a round-trip flight from Texas to Hawaii. The flight, on the 7th anniversary of the Pearl Harbor attack, was undetected and caused quite a reaction from Hawaiian authorities.

Assigned Resources of December 1948:
Personnel: 51,965 (5,562 officers, 40,438 airmen, and 6,365 civilians).
Tactical Aircraft: 837 (35 B36s, 35 B50s, 486 B-29s, 131 F-51s, 81 F-82s, 30 RB-29s, 24 RB-17s, 4 RC-45s, and 11 C-54s). Total B-36s assigned was 35 aircraft.
Bomber Units: Two Heavy Bomber Groups, one

B-36s of the first mass B-36 flight to the Far East, named Operation Big Stick. The bombers visited air bases during August 1953, including Japan, Okinawa, and Guam. Flown by the 92nd Bomb Wing, 15th Air Force. (USAF)

Above: B-36A-15-CF flies low over Lowry Air Force Base at Denver, Colorado. The spike-shaped feature at the centre of the vertical fin is sometimes seen in photos of B-36s and appears to have been skin panels of a different sheen - or even material - than surrounding ones.

Right:B-36A-10-CF serial number 44-92014 runs up its 3,000-horsepower Pratt & Whitney R-4360-25 Wasp Major engines prior to takeoff. The buzz number BM-014 includes the iast three digits of the serial number. (Both USAF)

equipped with B-36s and one without aircraft, 12 Medium Bomb Groups, 11 equipped with B-29s, and one equipped with both B29s and B-50s. Active Bases: 21 SAC bases in the continental United States. This increase reflected the change, effective 13 January 1948, that all US Army airfields be redesignated US Air Force bases.

The run-up to Korea and start of the Cold War. SAC transferred to the United States Air Force on 26 September 1947, concurrent with the latter's establishment as a separate military service. Units directly under SAC HQ included the 8th and 15th Air Forces, as well as the 311th Air Division, 4th Fighter Wing, 82nd Fighter Wing, 307th Bomb Wing, and two reconnaissance units, the 311th Reconnaissance Wing and the 46th Reconnaissance Squadron. The 56th Fighter Wing was subsequently assigned to SAC on 1 October 1947.

Following the establishment of the USAF, most SAC installations on US territory were renamed as 'Air Force Base' during late 1947 and into 1948, while non-US facilities were renamed as 'Air Base.'

In May 1948, in an exercise versus Air Defense Command's 'Blue' force, a SAC' 'Red' strike force simulated attacks on Eastern Seaboard targets as far south as Virginia. After a scathing 1948 Lindbergh review of SAC operations in the air and at six SAC bases, General Kenney was removed as Commanding General on 15 October 1948 and replaced on 19 October 1948 by 8th AF's commander, Lieutenant General Curtis LeMay. Upon Lemay's assumption of command, SAC had only sixty nuclear-capable aircraft, none of which possessed a realistic long-range capability against

The B-36B was the first fully operational and combat-ready mode of the B-36. Improvements included the R-4360-41 Wasp Major engines, increased bomb capacity, better performance, and a full complement of defensive armaments. Here, B-36B-1-CF serial number 44-92028 of the 7th Bombardment Wing of the Eighth Air Force, photographed at Carswell Air Force Base, Texas, around 1949, displays the Wing's emblem on the forward part of the fuselage and bright red paint, for high visibility should the plane crash in Arctic terrain, on the vertical tail and outer portions of the wings. This red paint was part of the Global Electronics Modification Program, a series of modifications to better suit the B-36 and other aircraft for operating and navigating over polar regions. (USAF)

the USSR.

The B-29D, which had become the B-50 in December 1945, was first delivered to SAC in June 1948. This was followed by SAC's first Convair B-36 Peacemaker arriving at Kirtland AFB, New Mexico in September 1948.

In November 1948, LeMay had SAC's headquarters, and its command post moved from Andrews AFB (Maryland) to Offutt AFB (Nebraska). At Offutt, the command moved into 'A Building' a three-storey facility which the Glenn L Martin Company had previously used during World War Two. Concurrent with establishing this new headquarters facility, Lemay also increased SAC Radar Bomb Scoring (RBS) runs the same year to 12,084. In addition, SAC also enhanced its organic fighter escort capability by initiating the replacement of its World War Two vintage piston-engine F-51D Mustang and F-82E Twin Mustang fighter aircraft with F-84G Thunderjets.

In January 1949, SAC conducted simulated raids on Wright-Patterson AFB. Assessments of these raids by 'LeMay's entire command...were appalling,' despite the SAC deputy commander, Major General McMullen, having instructed all bomber units to improve their effectiveness.

The practice mission was a total failure, confirming LeMay's fears upon taking over the command just two months earlier. General LeMay was quoted as saying, 'You might call that just about the darkest night in American aviation history. Not one airplane finished that mission. Not one.'

To motivate crews and enhance operational effectiveness command-wide, SAC established a competition, the first so-called 'Bomb Comp' in 1948. Winners of this inaugural event were the 43rd Bombardment Group (unit) and, for aircrew award, a B-29 team from the 509th Bombardment Group.

Given its global operating environment, SAC also opened its own survival school at Camp Carson, Colorado in 1949, it moved to Stead AFB, Nevada in 1952 before transferring the school to the Air Training Command in 1954.

SAC also created Emergency War Plan 1–49 (EWP 1-49), which outlined the means for delivering 133 atomic bombs, '..the entire stockpile...in a single massive attack...' on 70 Soviet cities over a thirty-day period.

The first Soviet atomic bomb test occurred on 29 August 1949 and the Joint Chiefs of Staff (JCS) subsequently identified SAC's primary objective was to damage or destroy the Soviet Union's ability to deliver nuclear weapons. The JCS further defined SAC's secondary objective was to stop any Soviet advances into Western Europe, and its tertiary objective was the previous EWP 1-49 industrial mission.

Red-tailed birds

As the USAF and SAC pondered the use of strategic bombers as a deterrent force and as a potential asset in fighting World War Three, the B-36 came to be seen as a vitally important weapon. The B-36 was the only aircraft that could fly from North America without aerial refuelling, strike deep into the heart of the Soviet Union and not have to depend on European bases as a place to land after the mission.

As any strike against the Soviet Union would be flown across the North Pole, basing the B-36s as far north as possible, such as in Alaska, Labrador or Maine, would put the bombers closer to the targets, and thus extend the range. However, in 1948, the B-36 fleet was based in Texas.

The B-36 had proven its ability to carry huge bomb loads over very long distances, but to be part of SAC's global counterstrike strategy, it would have to prove itself in the extreme weather conditions of the arctic. This led to the development of the Gem programme, aimed at the evaluation of B-36 operational capabilities in extreme cold weather areas. The bases chosen for the Gem evaluation would be Goose Bay, Labrador, Limestone, Maine, and Fairbanks, Alaska.

The 7th Bombardment Wing assigned eighteen aircraft and crews to Gem. These B-36s would then have their tails and wingtips painted bright red for identification purposes. If the aircraft were forced down in the Arctic, their natural metallic colour would blend in with the terrain and make them hard to locate, especially in low-visibility conditions: the red would be much easier to spot. When it was known why the tails were painted as they were, the red-tailed aircraft became symbolic of the SAC's growing intercontinental power to reach a potential enemy across the North Pole.

The first B-36 to be assigned to Gem was B36A 44-92007, the fourth B-36A off the production line. It was flown to Eglin AFB, Florida, on 18 June 1948, for testing in the climatic hangar, where extremely low temperatures could be evaluated in controlled conditions. Aircraft were placed in this heavily insulated chamber. Measurements and readings were taken as the temperature was lowered in ten degrees increments every three hours, down to a low of minus seventy-two degrees Fahrenheit. The purpose of these tests was to evaluate the effect of extreme temperatures on bomb bay doors, turrets, landing gear and other movable components. During the cold early months of 1949, the red-tailed B-36Bs underwent cold weather field tests at Ladd and Eielson AFB, near Fairbanks, Alaska.

The Gem programme was only one aspect of preparing the B-36 for its role in the much-feared Third World War. Long-duration flights, which had been little more than demonstrations in 1948, became routine as General Curtis LeMay began to mould SAC into a potent fighting force.

By 1949, the training missions were averaging twenty-four hours. Few lasted less than ten hours, and thirty-hour missions were fairly common. However, the longest B-36 flight ever flown was made by a Convair crew flying an RB-36, 44-

A dramatic downward-looking view of this red-tail B-36B escorted by a pair of Air Force F-80s. (USAF)

92090. This record endurance flight lasted for 51 hours, from 9:05 am on 14 January 1951 to 12:25 pm on 16 January.

By 1949, B-36 crews were running 'maximum effort' training missions, in which the maximum number of bombers available would be launched in as short a time as possible. The idea was to prepare crews for immediate action if an enemy launched a sudden surprise attack.

As the 7th and 11th Bombardment Groups accelerated training received additional aircraft and flew more and more maximum effort sorties and other simulated combat missions, in-flight difficulties became more frequent. The readiness that LeMay demanded of SAC would come at a high cost.

Engine problems would be a significant theme in hindering the operational readiness of the B-36 fleet. In a July 1949 incident, a 436th Bombardment Squadron machine suffered an engine fire at 40,000 feet. The fire was so severe that the engine burned entirely out of the wing trailing edge.

Electrical controls of the other two adjacent engines were disrupted and they were shut off. Captain Harold L Barry turned the aircraft for Carswell only twenty miles away and made a safe, smooth landing with only three of the aircraft's six engines - all on the same wing. Ironically, the engine that dropped off came to rest near the small Texas town of Drop.

Captain George Benedict's B-36 was struck by lightning in February 1949 on the way to participate in the B-36 fly-over during the Presidential Inauguration. This rare occurrence burned a ten-inch hole through the fuselage, but the damage was minor, and the crew considered themselves lucky.

The first major B-36 tragedy occurred at Carswell AFB on 15 September 1949, during a maximum effort training mission. As the second aircraft - 44-92079, flown by Maj Troy Husband - roared down the runway at 7:45 pm, it failed to pick up the speed necessary to become airborne. The aircraft ran off the end of the runway, crashing into Lake Worth, killing one of the thirteen men aboard. Four others were knocked unconscious by the impact and drowned. It was the first fatal crash of a B-36 after more than five thousand hours of successful flights.

The inquiry revealed that two propellers had been in reverse, serving as a brake on the B-36's take-off speed. To prevent such an accident from occurring again in the future, the SAC initiated a procedure of releasing the brakes slightly while checking out each propeller, from the outboard to inboard.

On the early B-36s, the only way to check whether a propeller was in reverse was to have a mechanic stand in front of it and feel the air movement. One ground crew run check was to reverse numbers one and six - the outer engines - two and five, and three and four - the inboard engines - running up in front of each engine to feel the wind. Before a B-36 take off, one of the crew members up in the forward compartment would jump out and see if all engines were blowing in the same direction- towards the tail. If it was all right, he would hop back in and off they'd go. In later B-36 models, propeller reverse lights were installed.

During March 1948 it was announced that the 7th Bombardment Wing (Heavy at Carswell AFB - on the other side of the runway from the Convair plant - would become the first operational unit for the B-36. The Strategic Air Command notified the 436th bomb Squadron that it would transfer six of its B-29s to the 93rd Bombardment Group at Castle AFB, California, to make room for the new

The 15th Air Force insignia on this RB-36F-1-CF, 49-2704, is located further from the fin leading edge than was usual. The quantity of platforms and staging needed to service the rudder and fin is noticable. (USAF)

Fifteen B-36s at low level. The ground must have shook with the cacophony of ninety Pratt & Whitney R-4360 engines. (USAF)

aircraft. The 7th BW responded by sending four flight engineers and five crew chiefs to Convair for training. Training equipment for the B-36 began arriving at Carswell by early April.

On 1 November 1949, the Second Air Force was activated at Barksdale AFB, Louisana, and on 7 November, Headquarters Fifteenth Air Force began operations at March AFB, California, having moved there from Colorado.

The Strategic Air Command then consisted of three Air Forces, the Second Air Force, the Eighth Air Force, and the Fifteenth Air Force.

On 12 March, a 7th Bomb Group B-36 set a long-distance record when it completed a 9,600 mile flight in 43 hours and 37 minutes without refuelling. This flight also began and ended at Carswell.

Assigned Resources as of December 1949:
Personnel: 71,490 (10,050 officers, 53,460 airmen, and 7,980 civilians.)
Tactical Aircraft: 837 (36 B-36s, 99 B50s, 386 B-29s, 67 KB-29s, 26 RB-29s, 28 RB-17s, 19 C-54s,10 C-82s, SYC-97s, 80 F-86s, and 81 F-82s.) Total B-36s assigned was 36 aircraft.
Bomber Units: Three Heavy Bomb Groups, one equipped with B-36s and two in the process of equipping with B36s; 11 Medium Bomb Groups, eight fully equipped with B-29s and three partially equipped with B-29s and B-50s.
Active Bases: 17 SAC bases in the continental USA.

The outbreak of war on the Korean peninsula was the major event for SAC in 1950. Three B-29 Groups soon proved to be insufficient to carry out strategic bombing and provide more immediate tactical support to ground troops.

Two more SAC B-29 Groups, the 98th and 307th Bomb Groups, were offered to Supreme Commander Allied Powers, General Douglas MacArthur, by the Joint Chiefs of Staff.

By late September, the strategic bombing offensive was finished. The FEAF Bomber Command had destroyed all significant strategic targets and enemy airfields in North Korea. B-36s. were not used in Korea, and remained at their home bases in the United States as a deterrent force.

Assigned Resources as of December 1950:
Personnel: 85,473 (10,600 officers, 66,600 airmen, and 8,273 civilians)
Tactical Aircraft: 961 (38 B36s and 20 RB-36s, 195 B-50s, 282 B-29s, 130 KB-29s, 19 RB-50s, 46 RB-29s, 27 RB-45s, 4 C-82s, 14 C-97s, 19 C-

The Carswell Air Force Base sign. (NMUSAF)

124s, and 167 F-84s). Total B/RB36s assigned was 58 aircraft.
Bomber Units: Two Heavy Bomb Groups equipped with B-36s; one Heavy Reconnaissance Group equipped with RB-36s; 12 Medium Bomb Groups, four equipped with B-50s, seven equipped with B-29s, and one equipped with a combination of B-29s and B50s; three Medium Strategic Reconnaissance Groups, one equipped with RB-45s, one with RB-29s, and one with RB-29s, RB-50s, and C-82s.
Active Bases: nineteen bases in the USA, and one overseas in Puerto Rico.

1951 saw continued participation in the Korean War; delivery of two new aircraft to SAC, the all-jet B-47 medium bomber and KC-97 tanker; and the first B-36 overseas flights to England and French Morocco.

Command leadership continued with General LeMay and Maj. General Power, Deputy Commander. Lt. General LeMay was promoted to General on 29 October 1951.

Throughout the year, the 98th and 307th Bomb Wings remained in the Far East under the operational control of the FEAF Bomber Command. Their B-29s were engaged primarily in attacking bridges, marshalling yards, supply and troop concentrations, and various other tactical targets.

The 306th Air Refueling Squadron at MacDill AFB, Florida, received SAC's first KC-97E tanker on 14 July 1951. Outfitted with a 'flying boom,' the four-engine, propeller-driven tanker could fly fast enough to match the minimum speed of the new B-47 medium bomber. It transformed the B-47 into an intercontinental bomber. Each KC-97 squadron was authorized twenty aircraft.

First flown in 1947, the B-47 all-jet medium bomber was committed to production in 1949. It made its first appearance in the Strategic Air Command in the 306th Bomb Wing at MacDill AFB on 23 October 1951. The authorized complement was forty-five aircraft for each wing, compared to thirty for B-36 wings. On 16 January, the first B-36s arrived in England. Six B-56Ds of the 7th Bomb Wing at Carswell AFB, Texas, landed at RAF Lakenheath in Suffolk, having staged through Limestone AFB (later, Loring AFB), Maine. The flight returned to Carswell on 20 January.

On 3 December 1951, the first B-36s landed in French Morocco. Six B-36s of the 11th Bomb Wing arrived at Sidi Slimane, French Morocco, having flown non-stop from Carswell. The flight resumed on 6 December.

With the abatement of the threat of World War Three developing out of the Korean conflict, the bombing competition was resumed and expanded. To stress the importance of navigation and to enable reconnaissance wings to compete, navigation was included as a separate phase of the meet. MacDill AFB, Florida, served as the competition headquarters, as well as the staging base for medium aircraft. Carswell was the staging base for heavy aircraft. Held 13-18 August, the third meet was attended by forty-five SAC crews representing twelve bomb wings and three reconnaissance wings, flying B/RB-36s, B/RB-295, and B-50 aircraft. Two Royal Air Force crews using standard B-29s also participated.

Assigned Resources as of December 1951:
Personnel: 144,525 (19,747 officers, 113,224 airmen, and 11,554 civilians).
Tactical Aircraft: 1,165 (96 B363 and 63 RB—56s, 216 B-50s, 346 B-29s, 10 B47s, 185 KB-29s, 22 KC-97s, 40 B/RB-45s, 40 RB-50s, 32 RB-29s, 4 C-82s, 36 C-124s, and 75 F-84s). Total B/RB-36s assigned was 159 aircraft.
Bomber Units; Three Heavy Bomb Wings, two equipped B-36s and one in the process of converting from B-29s to B-36s; twenty Medium Bomb Wings, eight equipped with B-29s (including two TDY with FEAF,) four equipped with B-50s, four in the process of being equipped with B-50s, one with both B-29s and B-50s, four in the process of being equipped with B-29s, one equipping with B-47s, and two with no aircraft assigned. Two Heavy Reconnaissance Wings equipped RB-36s; three Medium Reconnaissance Wings, one equipped with RB-50s, RB-29s and C-82s, one with R/RB-45s, and one equipping with RB-29s.
Active Bases: twenty-two SAC bases in the USA and eleven overseas.

During 1952 the war dragged on in Korea, more B/RB-36s were delivered to SAC, and the SAC insignia was officially adopted.

Command leadership continued with General LeMay and General Power, with the position of Deputy Commander changed to Vice Commander in October. Brig. General Richard M. Montgomery became Chief of Staff in September, relieving Maj. General August M. Kissner, who had held the position since 1948.

On 4 January, Headquarters USAF approved an insignia for the Strategic Air Command. The insignia evolved out of a contest conducted in late 1951.

With a $100 U.S. Defense Bond as the prize,

A far from unusual view from a SAC B-36 - one engine stopped and feathered in flight. It was fairly common procedure to feather the inboard pair when in the cruise to ease the turbulence vibration created by the propeller wash close to the rear fuselage. (USAF)

the contest drew entries from sixty military and civilian personnel scattered throughout the command. The judges, Generals LeMay, Power, and Kissner, selected the design submitted by Staff Sergeant R.T. Barnes, who was assigned to the 92nd Bomb Wing, Fairchild AFB, Washington.

Operations continued with the B-29s of the 98th and 307th Bomb Wings, and RB-29s of the 91st Strategic Reconnaissance Squadron supporting the United Nations efforts in Korea.

On 29 July, an RB-45C from the 91st SRW, commanded by Maj. Louis H Carrington, made the first non-stop, trans-Pacific flight from Elmendorf AFB, Alaska, to Yokota Air Base, Japan. The flight was made possible by two KB-29 in-flight refuellings, and earned Maj. Carrington and his two-man crew the MacKay Trophy for 1952.

For the second consecutive year, the Strategic Air Command had the lowest aircraft accident rate in the Air Force. It received the Daedalian Trophy.

The fourth SAC Bombing Competition was held October 13-19, involving ten B-29, five B-50, and four B-36 Wings. Medium bombers staged out of Davis Monthan AFB, Arizona, and the heavy bombers operated out of Walker AFB, New Mexico. The Royal Air Force entered the meet with four crews, two flying Washington (B-29) medium bombers and two Avro Lincoln bombers. The Eighth Air Force's 97th Bomb Wing and the Fifteenth Air Force's 93rd Bomb Wing tied for the Fairchild Trophy, and Maj. General Thomas S Power, Vice Commander of SAC, flipped a coin to decide which Wing would gain possession of the trophy for the first half of the ensuing year. The 93rd won the privilege.

Another SAC competition was organized in 1952; planned as an annual the event, the initial SAC Reconnaissance, Photo, and Navigation Competition, was held between 23 October and 1 November. Twelve crews representing four Wings, two RB-36, one RB-50, and one RB-45, participated. The 28th Strategic Reconnaissance Wing, an RB-36 unit of the Eighth Air Force, had the highest score in the combined areas of photo-reconnaissance and navigation. The 28th won the P T Cullen Award, named in honour of Brig. General Paul T. Cullen. Prior to his death in a C-124 crash on March 23, 1951, General Cullen had been one of the leading photo-reconnaissance authorities in the United States.

Assigned Resources as of December 1952:
Personnel: 166,021 (20,282 officers, 134,072 airmen, and 11,667 civilians).
Tactical Aircraft: 1,638 (154 B-36s and 114 RB-36s, 62 B-47s, 224 B50s, 417 B-29s, 39 RB-50s, 18 RB-29s, 22 RB-45s, 36 C-124s, 4 C-82s, 179 KB-29s, 139 KC-97s, and 230 F-84s). Total B/RB-36s assigned was 268 aircraft.
Bomber Units: Four Heavy Bomb Wings, three equipped with B-36s and one in the process of being equipped with B-36s. Four Heavy Strategic Reconnaissance Wings, two equipped with RB-36s and two in the process of being equipped with RB-36s; 21 Medium Bomber Wings, five equipped with B-50s,11 equipped with B-29s (including two TDY with FEAF, three being equipped with B-47s, and two with no aircraft assigned; Four Medium Strategic Reconnaissance Wings, one equipped with RB-50s and C-82s, one with RB-45s, one B/RB-29, and one without aircraft assigned; four Strategic Fighter Wings equipped with F-84s.
Active Bases: twenty-six SAC bases in the USA and ten overseas.

Although SAC continued to grow throughout

Security was strict on SAC bases, and cameras were not allowed, so most photographs were offical in nature. Here is seen the radio operator with his hand on the telegraph key for sending Morse Code. In the upper right is a gun sighting station in a plexiglass dome. (USAF)

B-36D-35-CF 49-2664 of the 436th Bomb Squadron, 7th Bomb Wing after suffering a main landing gear failure at Kirkland Air Force Base on 15 October 1951. The damage to the aircraft was minimal, and it was returned to service. (National Museum of the United States Air Force)

1953, this growth was tempered somewhat by the Air Force Wing programme being reduced from a goal of 143 to 120 combat Wings. Important events included the cease fire in Korea, deployment of the first B-47 Wing, the first B-36 overseas flight to the Far East, and conversion of SAC's F-84s to a fighter-bomber with a nuclear bombing capability. Also, 1953 saw SAC reach its planned goal of ten B/RB-36 wings, located at eight bases.

Effective 20 January 1953, SAC's four fighter-escort Wings (the 12th, 27th, 31st, and 508th) were redesignated strategic fighter Wings in recognition of their new mission of developing an atomic bombing capability. Two additional F-84 strategic fighter Wings were activated during the year.

The 98th and 307th Bomb Wings and the 91st Strategic Reconnaissance Wings continued to combat with the FEAF Bomber Command until the fighting ended in Korea on July 27, 1953.

Swift deployment of F-84G Thunderjets across the Atlantic became equally crucial to SAC operations, mainly since the F-84 had been converted to a fighter-bomber carrying nuclear weapons. Appropriately nicknamed Operation "Longstride," the first mass non-stop fighter flight over the Atlantic Ocean was a dual mission conducted by the 31st and 508th Strategic Fighter Wings, located at Turner AFB, Georgia. In addition, three in-flight refuellings by KC-97s were required to get the fighters across the Atlantic.

The first B-47 Wing deployment was made between 22 January and 20 February by the first B-47 Wing, the 306th Bomb Wing. In an exhaustive exercise, 'Sky-Try', the B-47 was successfully tested under simulated combat conditions in preparation for its overseas deployment. Shortly after the completion of Sky Try, SAC decided the 306th was ready for its first 90-day rotational training exercise to England. The B-47s staged through Limestone AFB, Maine, where they remained overnight before going on the next day. They stayed at RAF Fairford between 4 and 6 June. This initial deployment set a precedent for B-47s in England. SAC would maintain at least one B-47 wing in England at all times, continuing into early 1958.

The first mass B-36 flight overseas to the Far East occurred in August and September 1953. The 92nd Bomb Wing, out of Fairchild AFB, visited bases in Japan, Okinawa, and Guam. Nicknamed operation 'Big Stick', this 30-day exercise came shortly after the termination of hostilities in Korea and demonstrated US determination to use every means possible to maintain peace in Asia.

The fifth SAC Bombing Competition was held between 25 and 31 October. Seventeen bomb Wings sent two crews each to the competition. The B-47 made its first appearance in the competition, with seven participating Wings staging out of Davis Monthan. Walker AFB, New Mexico, was the staging base for ten Wings - four B-36, four B-50, and two B-29. Results of the competition for the coveted Fairchild Trophy were extremely close, with the winner not being decided until the last mission was flown. In the end, a B-36 unit won the trophy for the first time, the 92nd Bomb Wing of the Fifteenth Air Force. The 92nd edged out its nearest competitor, a B-50D wing, by twenty points. The B-47 wings fell below expectations in several aspects, particularly navigation. Most of the B-47 wings wound up in last place.

The Second Reconnaissance competition was staged out of Ellsworth AFB, South Dakota, held between 18 and 27 October. The fourteen competing crews represented seven wings (four RB-36, one RB-50, one RB-29, and one YRB-47). The 5th Strategic Reconnaissance Wing, Travis AFB, California, a Fifteenth Air Force RB-36 unit, won the prestigious Paul T Cullen Award for its contributions to photo and signal intelligence

The lower forward compartment of the B-36 could get kind of cosy when all the crew were at their stations, especially when wearing their parachute harnesses and packs. (National Museum of the United States Air Force)

collection. It was the first time RB-36s won the competition.

1953 was a banner year for the B-36, having won the two most important competitions that year.

Assigned Resources as of December 1953:
Personnel: 170,982 (19,944 officers, 138,782 airmen, and 12,256' civilians).
Tactical Aircraft: 1,902 (185 B-363 andr127 RB-36s, 329 B-47s, 138 B50s, 110 B-29s ,38 RB-50s, 8 RB-29s, 88 YRB-47s, 11 RB-47s, 359 KC-97s, 143 KC-29s, 49 C-124s and 235 F84s). Total B/RB-36s assigned was 322 aircraft.
Bomber Units: Six Heavy Bomb Wings, equipped with B-36s; four Heavy Strategic Reconnaissance Wings, equipped with RB-36s; 23 Medium Bomb Wings, eight equipped with B47s, one partially equipped with B-47s, five with no aircraft assigned but scheduled to receive B-47s, four equipped with B-50s, two equipped with B-29s (both TDY with FEAF,) and three partially equipped with B-29s. There were four Medium Strategic Reconnaissance Wings, one equipped with RB-50s, one partially equipped with RB-29s, and two partially equipped with YRB-47s. Six Strategic Fighter Wings, five equipped with F-84s and one with no aircraft assigned.
Active Bases: twenty-nine SAC bases in the USA and ten overseas.

1954 was when the B-36 reached its highest number of aircraft assigned to the Strategic Air Command; doubling of the B-47s in SAC and the first nonstop B-47 flight to Japan; the first B-36 wing rotation overseas, and RB-36s given a primary mission of bombing. It also was the year of peak B-36 strength. By the year's end, all B-29 aircraft had been phased out of SAC and retired to Davis Monthan AFB.

Command leadership changed, with General Power reassigned and replaced in May by Maj. General Francis H. Griswold as Vice Commander of SAC. General LeMay continued to serve as Commander-in-Chief of SAC.

In early 1954, Headquarters USAF directed that FEAF Bomber Command be discontinued, and its three B-29 wings return to the USA and re-equip with B-47s. On 18 June, concurrent with the deactivation of FFAF Bomber Command at Yokota Air Base in Japan, Headquarters 3rd Air Division was activated at Andersen AFB, Guam, and assigned to SAC. The new division was primarily manned by personnel from the FEAF Bomber Command.

On 16 June, SAC's four RB36-equipped heavy strategic reconnaissance wings were given a primary mission of bombing. However, they retained limited reconnaissance as a secondary mission.

With the doubling of B-47s, SAC operations increased tremendously. Approximately 142,000 air refuelling hookups were affected during the year. Training flights were conducted throughout the world. Records were established and broken. Teamed with the KC-97 tanker, the B-47 became an intercontinental bomber, challenging the B-36.

On 21 June 1954, a flight of three 22nd Bomb Wing B-47s, led by Maj. General Walter C Sweeney made a non-stop flight from March AFB, California, to Yokota Air Base, Japan, a distance of 6,700 miles, in less than fifteen hours.

The flight was supported by two KC-97 in-flight refuellings and marked the first appearance of the B-47 in the Far East.

During the summer of 1954, SAC cooperated in the filming of the Paramount film 'Strategic Air Command' and relaxed security at both Carswell and McDill AFB. The film featured both the B-36 and B-47 in glorious flying sequences. The movie was a huge hit and a great promotion explaining the B-36 mission.

On 15/16 October, the 92nd Bomb Wing returned to the Far East to be deployed for a 90-day rotation training assignment to Guam. This was the first time an entire B-36 wing had been deployed to an overseas base.

Assigned Resources as of December 1954:

Personnel: 189,106 (23,447 officers, 151,466 airmen, and 14,193 civilians).

Tactical Aircraft: 2,640 (209 B36s and 133 RB-36s, 795 B47s, 78 B-50s, 265 RB-47s, 12 RB-50s, 54 C-124s, 592 KC-97s, 91 KB-29s, and 411 F-84s.) Total B/RB-36s assigned was 342 aircraft, the highest number of B-36s in service with SAC at one time.

Bomber Units: Six Heavy Bomb Wings equipped with B-36s; four Strategic Reconnaissance Wings equipped with RB-36s; 24 Medium Bomb Wings, 17 equipped with B-47s, two with YRB-47s, two with B/RB-50s, and three equipped with B-47s. Five Medium Reconnaissance Wings, four equipped with RB- 47s and one in the process of equipping with RB-47s; Six Strategic Fighter Wings, four equipped with F- 84Fs, one with F-84Gs, and one converting from F-84Gs to new swept-wing F-84Fs.

Active Bases: thirty SAC bases in the USA with eleven overseas,.

Probably the most important event for SAC during the year 1955 was the introduction of the Boeing B-52 Stratofortress all-jet bomber, which spelled

Below: B-36D-1-CF 44-92096. A canvas cover is over the gunners position aft of the cockpit, and the huge bomber is tied down to prevent wind damage. (USAF)

Right: The artwork for the 42nd Bomb Wing (Heavy) at Loring Air Force Base in Maine. The motto is translated as 'The Skies For Us.' (Lockheed Martin)

Above: B-36D-1-CF 44-92096 cruises above a break in the clouds. (USAF)

Left: The SAC shield on RB-36D-20-CF 49-2702. The just visible checkboard nosewheel doors on the bottom right was a popular marking. (Lockheed Martin)

the beginning of the end for the B-36 Peacemaker. Build up of the B-47 force continued, and all B-50s were phased out.

Command leadership was the same, with General Richard M. Montgomery, Chief of Staff, promoted to Maj. General in December.

In 1955, the New York-New England area became increasingly important to SAC operations. Dow and Loring Air Force Bases, Maine, had been supporting F-84 and B-36 Wings, respectively, for some time; Westover AFB, Massachusetts, which became a Strategic Air Command installation on 1 April 1955, was being groomed to support tankers and bombers; and new B47/KC-97 bases were being built at Portsmouth, New Hampshire, and Plattsburg, New York. In line with this expansion, SAC realigned its three numbered air forces's bases and units, effective 13 June, and moved Headquarters Eighth Air Force from Carswell AFB, Texas, to Westover. SAC's numbered air forces were generally responsible for units and bases in the following geographical sections of the country: Second Air Force, the Southeast, including Texas; Eighth Air Force, the Northeast and the Central United States; and the Fifteenth Air Force, the South-west and West.

SAC reorganized its air refuelling wings during 1955 and established two tanker wings, the 4060th at Dow AFB and the 4050th at Westover. KC-97s were assigned to each wing. The establishment of these two wings signalled the beginning of a programme to concentrate air refuelling strength in the Northeast. The build-up would continue well into the 1960s, and would provide SAC with increased B-47 deployment mobility over the North Atlantic.

The 93rd Bomb Wing, located at Castle AFB, California, was the first wing to be equipped with B-52 Stratofortresses. On 29 June, Brig. General William E Eubank, Jr., flew the first aircraft (a B model, SN 528711) from the Boeing factory in Seattle, Washington, to Castle. Most of the B-52Bs produced were assigned to the 93rd Bomb Wing during the period from June 1955 to March 1956.

With the phase-out of all B-50s starting in late 1954, there were now only two types of bomber aircraft in the SAC inventory. So, just B-47s and B-36s competed in the seventh SAC Bombing Competition held August 24-30. March AFB was the staging base for 23 B-47 wings. The ten B/RB-36 wings staged out of Fairchild. Each wing was again represented by two crews. The most significant factor in this competition was the tremendous improvement made by B- 47s in both bombing and navigation. For the first time, a B-47 unit, the 320th Bomb Wing, won the Fairchild Trophy.

With the conversion of all RB-36 aircraft to bombers, the reconnaissance competition became an all-B-47 affair. The Eighth Air Force's 91st Strategic Reconnaissance Wing won the P T Cullen Award.

Throughout the early 1950s, the Strategic Air Command became more and more involved in the development of missiles as a means of increasing its long-range striking power. By 1955, the Snark, a subsonic intercontinental missile, and the Rascal, an air-to-ground missile designed to be launched from a bomber, had undergone encouraging tests. Tests had been conducted dropping the Rascal from a B-36. After President Dwight D. Eisenhower had placed the highest national priority on the development of ballistic missiles, Headquarters USAF accelerated the development of the Snark and the Navaho, another intercontinental missile, and the Atlas, an intercontinental ballistic missile (ICBM.) In November, Headquarters USAF told SAC to work closely with the Air Research and Development Command to establish an 'initial operational capability' for ICBMs. They would be turned over to SAC for operational use.

Assigned Resources as of December 1955:
Personnel: 195,997 (26,180 officers, 151,595 airmen, and 18,222 civilians).
Tactical Aircraft: (205 B-36s and 133 RB-36s, 1,086 B-47s, 18 B-52s, 234 RB-47s, 12 RB-50s, 51 C-124s, 679 KC-97s, 82 KB-29s, and 568 F-84s.) Total B/RB-36s assigned was 338 aircraft.
Bomber Units: Seven Heavy Bomb Wings, six equipped with B-36s and one equipped with B-52s; Four Heavy-Reconnaissance Wings, equipped with RB-36s; 27 Medium Bomb Wings, 22 equipped with B-47s and five equipping with B-47s; five Medium Reconnaissance Wings, equipped with RB-47s; six Strategic Fighter

Magnesium Overcast - a B-36 in flight. (National Museum of the United States Air Force)

Above: Something of a mystery picture - a B-36H with it's landing gear down, dropping a unidentified object by parachute. (USAF)

Left: the Wing insignia of the 6th Bomb Wing at Walker Air Force Base, New Mexico. This is a B-36F-5-CF photographed at Convair Fort Worth, during servicing, something of a common event. Note also the striped nosegear doors. (Lockheed Martin)

Wings, all equipped with F-84Fs; one Strategic Reconnaissance Wing, Fighter, equipping with RB-84Fs and RB-84Ks; and one Light Strategic Reconnaissance Squadron, with no aircraft assigned.
Active Bases: thirty-seven SAC bases in the USA and four overseas bases.

1956 saw SAC respond to the Suez Crisis; the last KC-97, a G model, delivered, and the first RB-57, a C model, introduced into the Strategic Air Command, as well as the first B-36 unit converting to B-52s.

Command leadership continued with General LeMay, Commander-in-Chief; Maj. General Griswold, Vice Commander, and Brig. General David Wade replaced General Montgomery as Chief of Staff.

The B-52 conversion programme continued in 1956, and by the end of March, the 93rd Bomb Wing at Castle AFB, California, was fully equipped with thirty B-52s (later reorganised to operate forty-five B-52s). The 42nd Bomb Wing at Loring AFB, Maine, was the second Wing to be equipped with B-52s, with the first aircraft delivered in June. The 42nd was also the first B-36 unit to convert to the new all-jet heavy bomber. The 99th Bomb Wing, Westover AFB, Massachusetts, became the third B52 Wing, receiving its first Stratofortess in December.

In reacting to the Suez Crisis, caused by Egypt closing the Suez Canal, SAC took several actions to place its force on alert and demonstrate to the world the high degree of readiness maintained by its bomber force. The crisis, which lasted from mid-November to mid-December 1956, prompted the Strategic Air Command to concentrate its large tanker task force to key bases in the northern United States and overseas in Greenland, Newfoundland, and Labrador. Two B-47 Wings and one B-36 Wing were left overseas on alert during their normal overseas rotational training.

Operations Power Block and Road Block were two closely related exercises in which 1,000 B-47s and KC-97s flew gigantic simulated combat missions over North America and the Arctic. It was SAC's largest and most complex B-47 exercise to date. The exercise utilised the KC-97s placed on alert and strategically positioned because of the Suez Crisis. The B-47 was now in the spotlight; the B-36 had no such spectacular demonstration,

It is hard to imagine the devastation at Carswell caused by tornadoes that hit on 1 September 1952. The weather forecast was for thunderstorms and gusting winds. Fortunately, it happened on Labor Day when few people were on the field. Before they broke, anemometers at the base recorded winds as high as 91 mph. Many aircraft were undergoing maintenance and were not tied down.A few fuel tanks ruptured as the bombers were torn apart, but a very quick-thinking duty officer at the 7th BW managed to get all electrical power to the flight line turned off before any fuel ignited. Note the missing vertical stabiliser and damaged wing on the aircraft near the top centre of the photo. It was fortunate that the storm was at Carswell since the Convair plant was close enough to provide immediate support, and it was easy to get the damaged aircraft to the plant. Even so, one aircraft was virtually destroyed, and an incredible eighty-two were damaged, including ten at the Convair plant. (USAF)

Something of mystery picture - maybe eight B-36 Peacemaker bombers under the glow of ramp lights at an unknown location, possibly Carswell Air Force Base in Texas. The B-36 in the foreground carries the 'Triangle J' markings belonging to the 7th Bomb Wing at Carswell. In the back, at least three bombers have the 'Circle W' markings of the 92nd Bomb Wing assigned to Fairchild Air Force Base in Washington. These tail markings had evolved from the group markings used in World War Two and were found on SAC aircraft into the early 1950s. In 1953, tail marking schemes were dropped. (AFMC History Office)

at least as far as is known.

On 1 May, the first RB-57, a reconnaissance version of the British-designed B-57 Canberra light bomber was delivered to the 4080th Strategic Reconnaissance Wing at Turner AFB, Georgia.

On 16 November, the final KC-97G was delivered to 98th Air Refueling Squadron, Lincoln AFB, Nebraska.

The eighth SAC Bombing Competition grew along with SAC, and in 1956, the largest one to date was held, with forty-two Wings participating in a combined bombing, navigation, and reconnaissance meet. It was held from 24 to 30 August, with Lockbourne AFB, Ohio, hosting 27 B-47 and five RB-47 Wings. Loring AFB, Maine, served as the base for eight B/RB-36 and two B-52 Wings. Each participant sent two crews, similar to the year before. The B-36s of the 11th Bomb Wing, Second Air Force, won the Fairchild Trophy back, beating out the B-47s. It was a triumph for the B-36 crews, besting its jet competitors, including the new B-52 units. However, B-47s would win nearly all the significant events against B- 36 crews the next year.

GRB-36Ds from the 99th Strategic Reconnaissance Wing at Fairchild AFB Washington State teamed with RF-84Ks of the 91st Strategic Reconnaissance Squadron, Larson AFB, Washington, were phased out in 1956 after less than a year of operation since the FICON project became operational in 1955.

Assigned Resources as of December 1956:
Personnel: 217,279 (27,871 officers,169,170 airmen, and 20,238 civilians).
Tactical Aircraft: 3,188 (247 B/RB-36s, 97 B-52s, 1,306 B-47s, 254 RB-47s, 16 R-57s, 51 C-124s, 750 KC-97s, 74 KB-29s, 336 F-843s, and 57 RF-4Fs). Total B/R36s assigned had been reduced to 247 aircraft, the beginning of the end of the Peacemaker's operational service.
Bomber Units: 11 Heavy Bomb Wings, seven equipped with B/RB-36s, one with B-52s, and three in the process of equipping with B-52s; 28 Medium Bomb Wings, 27 equipped with B-47s, and one in the final stages of equipping with 47s; five Medium Reconnaissance Wings, equipped with RB-47s; one Light Strategic Reconnaissance Wing being equipped with RB-57s; five Strategic Fight Wings equipped with F-84Fs; one Strategic Fighter Reconnaissance Wing being equipped with RF-84s.
Active Bases: 36 SAC bases in the continental United States and 19 overseas, a total of 55 bases.

It was a year of change for SAC in 1957. General LeMay left as the command's longtime Commander-in-Chief, to become Air Force Vice

Chief of Staff in June; General Thomas S. Power moved up from Vice Commander to succeed LeMay; more bases were acquired, particularly overseas; the 15 minute ground alert concept was developed, by which SAC would maintain one-third of its aircraft on ground alert ready for take off; the last B-47, an E model, was delivered; the first KC-135 jet tanker was also delivered; the first high-altitude U-2 went into service; retirement of all KB-29s was completed; and a non-stop, around-the-world, 24,325 mile flight of three B-52s led by Maj. General Archie Old, Jr., was accomplished from 16 to 18 January. The record-breaking, 45 hour and 19 minute flight, named Operation Power Flite, won the MacKay Trophy as the outstanding flight of 1957.

But 1957 was a quiet year for what remained of the B-36 fleet. It was now a B-47 and B-52 show. For the first time, there were more B52 wings than B-36 Wings. Also, SAC decided that its strategic fighter Wings were no longer necessary because of technological advances, changes in tactics, and the programmed phase out of the relatively slow moving B-36s. Four Wings were transferred to the Tactical Air Force, and two were deactivated.

B-36s did compete in the ninth SAC Bombing Competition held between 30 October to 6 November. Pinecastle AFB, Florida, was the staging base for twenty-eight B-47 and five RB-47 Wings, while Carswell AFB, Texas, provided the same services for five B-36 and five B-52 Wings. After several years of absence, the Royal Air Force entered the competition with two Vulcan and two Valiant bombers and crews. With the exception of the crew and wing navigation awards, which were won by a B-36 wing, the B-47 units won all the major events in which they were pitted against B-36s. The Fairchild Trophy was won by the 321st Bomb Wing, a B-47 unit.

Assigned Resources as of December 1957:
Personnel: 224,014 (29,946 officers, 174,030 airmen, and 20,038 civilians).
Tactical Aircraft: 2,711 (127 B/RB-36s, 243 B-52s, 1,285 B478, 216 RB-47s, 24 RB-57s, 50 C-124s, 742 KC-97s, and 24 KC-1355). Only 127 B/RB-36s were assigned, B-52s outnumbering B-36s for the first time.
Bomber Units: 11 Heavy Bomb Wings, four equipped with B/RB-36s, five equipped with B-52s, and two in the process of equipping with B-52s; one Heavy Strategic Wing with no aircraft assigned; 28 Medium Bomb Wings equipped with B-47s; four Medium Strategic Reconnaissance Wings equipped with RB-47s; one Light Strategic

It's hard to decide which is of the greatest interest - the B-36 or the cars! They certainly help date this picture, which was allegedly taken at Biggs AFB. An American friend has told me that the cars are, from left to right, a 1957 Chevrolet 210 Series four-door station wagon, a 1954 Buick Special or a Century four-door sedan, a 1957 Chevrolet Bel Air four-door hardtop sedan, a 1956 Mercury Custom two-door hardtop, a 1959 Buick Le Sabre four-door Sedan and partly visible in the lower right corner is a 1956 Dodge Sierra station wagon.

Reconnaissance Wing equipped with RB-57s and U-2s; one Strategic Missile Squadron (ICBM - Snark) with no missiles yet assigned.
Active Bases: thirty-eight SAC bases in the USA and thirty overseas.

1958 was the twilight year for the Peacemaker; only 33 aircraft remained in SAC, most of them the featherweight B-36J model, the last production model of the B-36. Actually, counting two H models assigned to the 4925th Test Group (Atomic), the total B-36sin the Air Force Inventory was 35 aircraft. Several record-breaking flights by both B-52s and the new KC-135 jet tanker-replacement for the KC-97 - occurred during the year. By the end of 1958, there were more B- 52s in SAC than there had ever been B-36s. Only two B-36 wings were operational during 1958. Strategic Air Command would soon become an all-jet bomber force, with the B-52 heavy bomber and B-47 medium bomber supported by KC-135 tankers. Both bombers, through in-flight refuelling, were now able to achieve intercontinental range, once only possible by the B-36 earlier in the decade.

The B-36 made its last appearance in the tenth annual SAC Bombing Competition, held between 13 and 18 October. B/RB-47s and the RAF's Valiants staged out of March AFB in California. B-52s and B-36s staged out of Castle AFB, also in California. SAC participants included four crews from the 38 Bomb Wings (two B-36, twenty-six B-47 and ten B-52), and one RB-47 strategic reconnaissance wing. The Royal Air Force sent eight crews. Once again the competition was dominated by B-47 Wings, which won the first three places in combined bombing and navigation. The Fairchild Trophy went to the Second Air Force's 306th Bomb Wing. The B-36s were shut out. It was the end of the glory days for the B-36.

Assigned Resources as of December 1958:
Personnel: 258,703 (34,112 officers, 199,562 airmen, and 25,029 civilians).
Tactical Aircraft: 3,031 (22 B-36s, 380 B-52s, 1,367 B-47s,176 RB-47s, 19 RB-57s,182 KC-135s, 780 KC-97s, 51 C-124s, and 54 F-86s). 1958 was the last year of B- 36 operations, with the sole wing remaining in Texas. Only a few aircraft were in service by the end of the year.
Bomber Units: Eleven Heavy Bomb Wings, eight equipped with B-52s, two getting ready to receive B-52s, and one, the last B-36 Wing (the 95th Bomb Wing, Biggs AFB, Texas), was in the midst of phasing out its B-36s; Fiurteen Strategic Wings, two equipped with B-52s, one partially equipped, and eleven were in various stages of development; twenty-eight Medium Bomb Wings equipped with B-47s; three Medium Strategic Reconnaissance Wings equipped with RB-47s; one Combat Crew Training Wing equipped with B/RB-47s; one Light Strategic Reconnaissance Wing equipped with RB-57s and U-2s; three Atlas D squadrons and one Snark squadron, none of which were equipped yet with missiles.
Active Bases: Thirty-nine SAC bases in the continental United States and twenty-five overseas.

This was the final year of B-36s being flown by the Strategic Air Command, and it was only 43 days into the new year. The last B-36, a H model, was retired from the 95th Bomb Wing at Biggs AFB, Texas, and flown to Fort Worth on 12 February to become a memorial to the men and women who built and flew the Peacemaker. The B-36 era had officially ended. SAC had a slogan in 1956/7, 'A Decade of Peace through Global Airpower,' and the B-36 certainly had been an essential contributor to the accomplishment of that fact.

SAC continued to grow in 1959, reaching the highest number of bomber aircraft ever assigned in its history by the end of the year. It had 3,207 aircraft, including 488 B-52s and 1,366 B-47s, taking over the mission that the B-36 once had accomplished for SAC. It was now becoming a combination bomber and missile force. Air refuelling had developed into an essential part of SAC operations, giving the B-52 and B-47 intercontinental striking capability. SAC had come a long way from its beginnings in 1946, and the B-36 had played its role in making SAC the world's most potent deterrent force.

SAC continued its deterrent role throughout the 1960s, 1970s, and 1980s. With the end of the Cold War, the Strategic Air Command was deactivated in 1992, after forty-six years of global operations, keeping the peace for America.

Chapter Eight

Strategic Reconnaissance

General Curtiss LeMay strongly influenced the decision to produce a reconnaissance version of the B-36. He had flown B-17 strikes in Europe and commanded B-29 strikes against Japan in World War Two and was disturbed by the lack of a reconnaissance capability that could photograph the same targets the bombers could attack. One of his first actions upon taking command of SAC was to insist on an up-to-date supply of strategic reconnaissance aircraft. The B-36 was chosen as a reconnaissance machine for much the same reasons as it was for a strategic bomber - altitude and range. All of the original SAC bombers had reconnaissance variants at General LeMay's insistence. Initially, there was even a reconnaissance variant of the B-52 specified. However, very few were produced before SAC decided to have more bombers and rely on the Lockheed U-2 and other assets for intelligence gathering. The remanufacturing of the B-36As into RB-36Es ahead of the production of RB 36Ds attested to the urgency of the SAC Commander's request. With the B-36, just over one-third - 142 machines - were configured for reconnaissance. The aircraft was assigned to the 5th Strategic Reconnaissance Wing (SRW) at Travis AFB, 28th SRW at Rapid City (later Ellsworth) AFB, the 72nd SRW at Ramey AFB Puerto Rico, and the 99th SRW at Fairfield-Suisun (later Travis) AFB, California. Although new RB-36 deliveries continued until late 1953, by 1954, all of them were being reconfigured for a primary nuclear strike capability, with reconnaissance left to the much faster but shorter-ranged RB-47s.

The B-36 reconnaissance programme was proposed and approved during early 1948, and a mock-up of the camera installation was completed on 17 March 1949 before being reviewed and approved by the Air Force. The RB-36D and RB-36E programmes progressed almost simultaneously, with the largest difference being the fact that all the RB-

An often-used photo of 49-2688, a RB-36D-I 0-CF that shows the original location of the ferret ECM radomes under the fuselage. All reconnaissance variants were manufactured with the radomes in this location. The contrast between the matt magnesium skin and the shiny aluminum skin also shows up well. When bomb bay No. 4 was converted to carry nuclear weapons, the FECM radomes and equipment were moved under the rear fuselage below the forward edge of the tail. At the same time the bomb bay doors were reconfigured. (Lockheed Martin)

36Ds would be new-builds while the twenty-two RB-36Es were remanufactured from the YB-36 and twenty-one of the B-36As.

There was little difference between the aircraft other than their production heritage. The two types proceeded down the production line interspersed. The official explanation of the RB-36 missions was 'to carry cameras and electronic equipment which would gather information about the enemy in case of war.'

The reconnaissance variant was inspected by the 689 Board beginning on 21 November 1949. This group of Air Force officers and civilian specialists inspected all new Air Force models before they entered series production. This board was headed by Brigadier General George W Munday from the Air Materiel Command and consisted of seventy-five members from Air Force Headquarters, AMC, SAC, the Continental Air Command, and the Air Proving Ground. The Convair project engineer, Norm B Robbins, headed the group of Convair engineers who answered the board's questions during the five-day inspection.

The RB-36 was outwardly similar to the bomber version but carried a crew of twenty-two. The additional crew members were needed to operate and maintain the photographic and electronic reconnaissance equipment. The area that usually contained bomb bay No. 1 was converted into a sixteen-foot long pressurised compartment that contained fourteen K-17C, K-22A, K-38, and K-40 cameras, as well as a rudimentary darkroom that allowed the film cartridges to be reloaded in flight. Adding the compartment involved changing the forward and aft bulkheads into pressure domes, reconfiguring the bomb bay doors, and changing the exterior skin around this area to aluminium since magnesium could not tolerate the pressure cycles. This provides easy identification of the reconnaissance aircraft. Several camera windows were installed on each side and the bottom of the compartment, each covered by a sliding door.

The standard photo-reconnaissance configuration included seven camera positions inside the pressurised compartment that could accommodate up to fourteen cameras. Five of the stations - the trimetrogon, vertical, split vertical, multi, and forward oblique - were remotely controlled from the photographer's station in the photo compartment or the photo-navigator's station in the nose of the aircraft.

Trimetrogon is an aerial photographic survey method that involves the use of three cameras in one assembly. One camera is pointed directly downwards, and the other two are pointed to either side of the flight path at a thirty-degree depression angle. The images overlap, allowing the use of stereographic interpretation of the topography. The name comes from the Metrogon cameras used in the original montages.

The left- and right-side oblique cameras were controlled by switches at their respective stations by the photographer. The vertical camera could be used for night photography when photo-flash bombs illuminated the target. A photocell trip unit was installed that caused the camera shutter to be tripped when the photo-flash bomb went off after being dropped from bomb bay No. 2. The desired photographic overlap could be obtained with the remotely-controlled cameras through a combination of airspeed, altitude, and intervalometer settings. A vacuum system, defrosting system, and electrically-operated camera doors formed an integral part of

This was the original internal arrangement for all RB-36 models, except D-models and early B-36Fs did not have chaff. Later the Ferret ECM equipment and radomes would be moved into the aft fuselage and bomb bay No. 4 reactivated to carry nuclear weapons. (Convair, via author's collection)

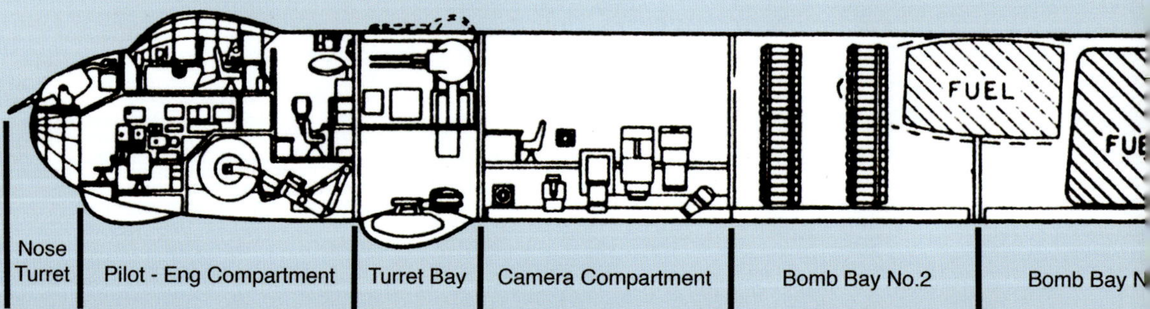

each camera system. In addition to the cameras in the photo compartment, a pair of C-1 radar scope cameras were carried, as was a single A-6 motion picture camera - the photo-navigator could use both in the forward fuselage.

The K-40 camera, with a forty-eight-inch focal-length lens, had been an an early requirement for the RB-36 but quickly ran into development problems. Development had been initiated in late 1948, and the first experimental model was delivered in June 1950. But as late as March 1951, the camera was still undergoing service testing and had not made it to the operational fleet. Nevertheless, the camera continued to be listed as a B-36 asset until the last RB-36 was retired.

The bomber models' communication tube that allowed crew members to travel between the forward and aft pressurised compartments was substantially modified in the RB-36s. Instead of a single tube extending from the aft of the forward compartment through both turret bays and all four bomb bays to the front of the aft compartment, the RB-36 featured two tubes. The first tube extended from the forward pressurised compartment through the forward turret bay into the new photo compartment. Since this tube was comparatively short, it did not include a movable cart. The second tube ran from the back of the photo compartment through the three bomb bays - or two bomb bays and electronics compartment - and the aft turret bay to the pressurised compartment in the aircraft's rear. However, this tube still used the cart.

Initially, the RB-36 was not equipped to carry bombs. Bomb bay No. 2 was modified to carry eighty one hundred-pound T86 or M46 flash bombs, and bomb bay No. 3 generally contained an auxiliary fuel tank but could carry flash bombs instead. As originally delivered, a single set of thirty-three foot eight-inch long doors covered the two middle bomb bays, a substantial difference from the bomber versions. Since the aircraft were not equipped as bombers, the K-system (K-1 or K-3A, as appropriate for the model) was not installed, although the aircraft continued to carry the APQ-24 search radar. The reconnaissance models were not equipped with either Norden or periscopic bombsights.

As built, the last bomb bay (No. 4) was deleted from the reconnaissance variants, and this area instead contained a special pallet that held ferret ECM (FECM) equipment. Three large radomes were mounted on the bottom of the fuselage where the aft bomb bay doors were normally located. Operators onboard the RB-36 could record and analyse radar and communications signals using the ferret equipment while the aircraft flew close to Soviet territory. In deleting the last bomb bay, Convair took the opportunity to lighten the aircraft slightly by using different bulkheads on each end of the area that did not contain the reinforcements necessary to mount bomb racks. In addition, certain parts of the aft wing spar and some fuselage frames were also lightened. All of this would mean significant rework was required when it was later decided to use the RB-36s as bomb carriers. The normal defensive armament of sixteen 20-mm cannon was retained on all production RB-36s.

The operations for the reconnaissance version did not differ significantly from the bomber version. Instead of the normal bombardier, a photo-navigator sat in the glass nose where he had nearly unrestricted views in front and to the side of the aircraft. As the aircraft approached the photo target, the pilot turned the steering controls over to the photo-navigator, just

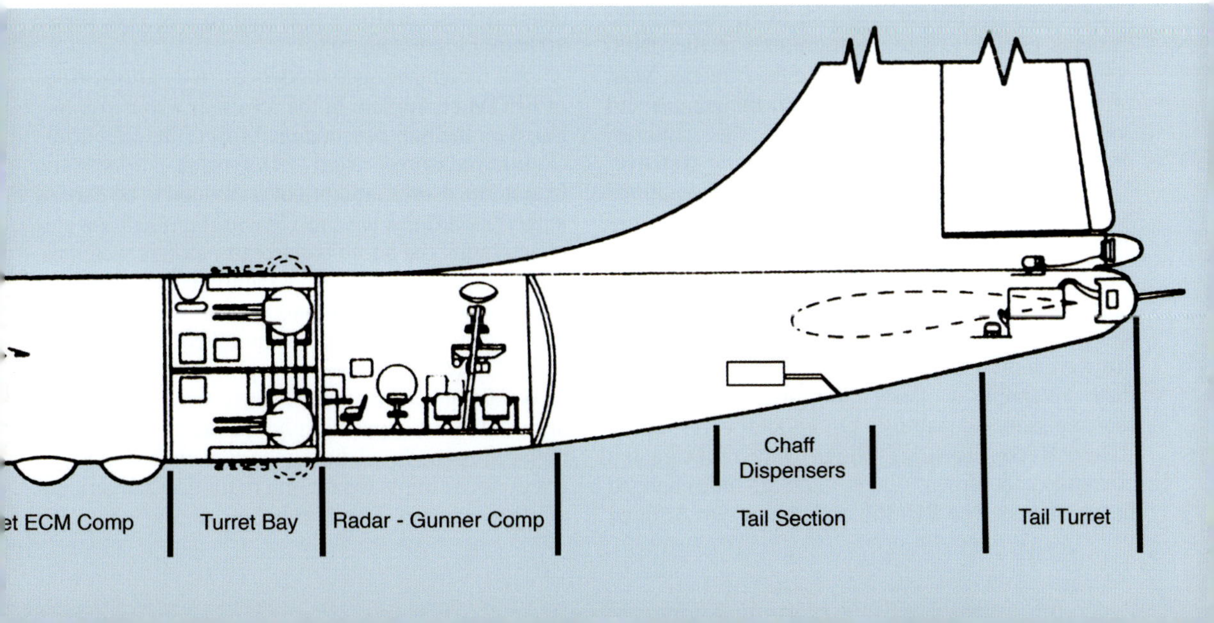

An interesting photograph of RB-36H-25-CF, 51-13720, after the successful completion of flight tests with Ford-built R-4360 engines. The picture provides a good look at the shiny aluminium skin used around the pressurised photo compartment in the area that was bomb bay No. 1 on the bombers and the nose compartment. The matt-looking area is the magnesium covered un-pressurised zones of bomb bay No.2 and the turret compartment. Both the side-oblique and forward-oblique camera doors may be seen in their closed positions. (Lockheed Martin).

as was done for a bombardier when a B-36 was starting a bomb run. The photo-navigator steered the aircraft into the proper position, then operated the cameras remotely. The photographer in the photo compartment did little operating of the cameras. Most of his time was spent loading film magazines and ensuring the proper operation of the cameras, pressurisation, and heating/dehumidifying systems.

On 16 June 1954, SAC's four RB-36-equipped heavy Strategic Reconnaissance Wings were assigned a primary mission of strategic bombing, with reconnaissance becoming a secondary capability. By now, the Air Force had shifted most strategic reconnaissance to the RB-47, and the RB-36s were more useful as nuclear deterrents, although they retained a fairly comprehensive latent reconnaissance capability. On 1 October 1955, the RB-36 Reconnaissance Wings were redesignated Heavy-Bombardment Wings, although little changed but the name. The RB-36s underwent two or three concurrent modification programmes to provide a nuclear delivery capability. However, the primary changes were performed as part of ON TOP Phase 10 beginning in late 1954.

All reconnaissance models carried various types of FECM equipment in the area that was bomb bay No. 4 on the bomber models. Most of the Electronic Countermeasures and Defensive Electronic Countermeasures equipment continued to be carried in the forward fuselage, just like the bombers. As part of activating the bomb bay to carry atomic weapons, this equipment was moved into the aft fuselage between bulkheads ten and twelve, the three large radomes were relocated simultaneously. To save weight, bulkheads seven, eight and nine in the reconnaissance aircraft had been redesigned and were not capable of supporting bomb racks. These were replaced or modified during the conversion, although it was not a simple matter and required a fair amount of disassembly. The bomb bay doors were also changed to more closely match the bomber models - Nos. 3 and 4 were covered by a single set of new near thirty-three feet long doors, while bomb bay No. 2 was protected by a set of sixteen-foot doors that were modified from the original set of doors.

Most RB-36s also received the weather reconnaissance modification that allowed them to collect rudimentary meteorological data during flight. A weather observer's station was added in the lower part of the extreme nose compartment. The station included a humidity indicator, clock, altimeter, and a new radio altimeter instrumentation. The antennas for the radio altimeter were flush-mounted on the underside of the horizontal stabilizer, and the electronics were added to the unpressurized area of the aft compartment. A barometric pressure, temperature, and humidity probe was added to the right side of the extreme nose just behind the glazed panels. A radiosonde equipment rack was added at the intermediate frequency ECM operator's station at bulkhead ten in the aft compartment. The dispenser itself was installed in the floor on the centreline of the rear pressurised compartment where the strike camera was carried in the bombers.

Controls for the dispenser were installed at the high-frequency ECM station on the right side of the aft compartment and also at the right lower gunner's blister. The Featherweight programme initially removed this equipment, only to have it reinstalled under ECP 2310 a few months later.

Not surprisingly, little is known about the missions flown by RB-36s, even after all these years. It is fairly certain that the aircraft never performed overflights of the Soviet Union, at least not from the European side. What it did on the Pacific and Arctic sides is much less clear - still, direct overflights of interior targets are unlikely. It is, however, entirely possible that RB-36s flew peripheral signal gathering missions along the Pacific and Arctic coasts of the Soviet Union.

One deployment that is known involved two RB-36s from the 5th Strategic Reconnaissance Wing from Travis AFB during March 1954. For two weeks, the aircraft flew missions out of Thule, Greenland, to determine if clandestine Soviet communications activities existed in an area of interest along the northeastern coast of Greenland, between latitudes 080-00N and 070-00N.

The RB-36s, from the 23rd and 72nd Strategic Reconnaissance Squadrons each flew two

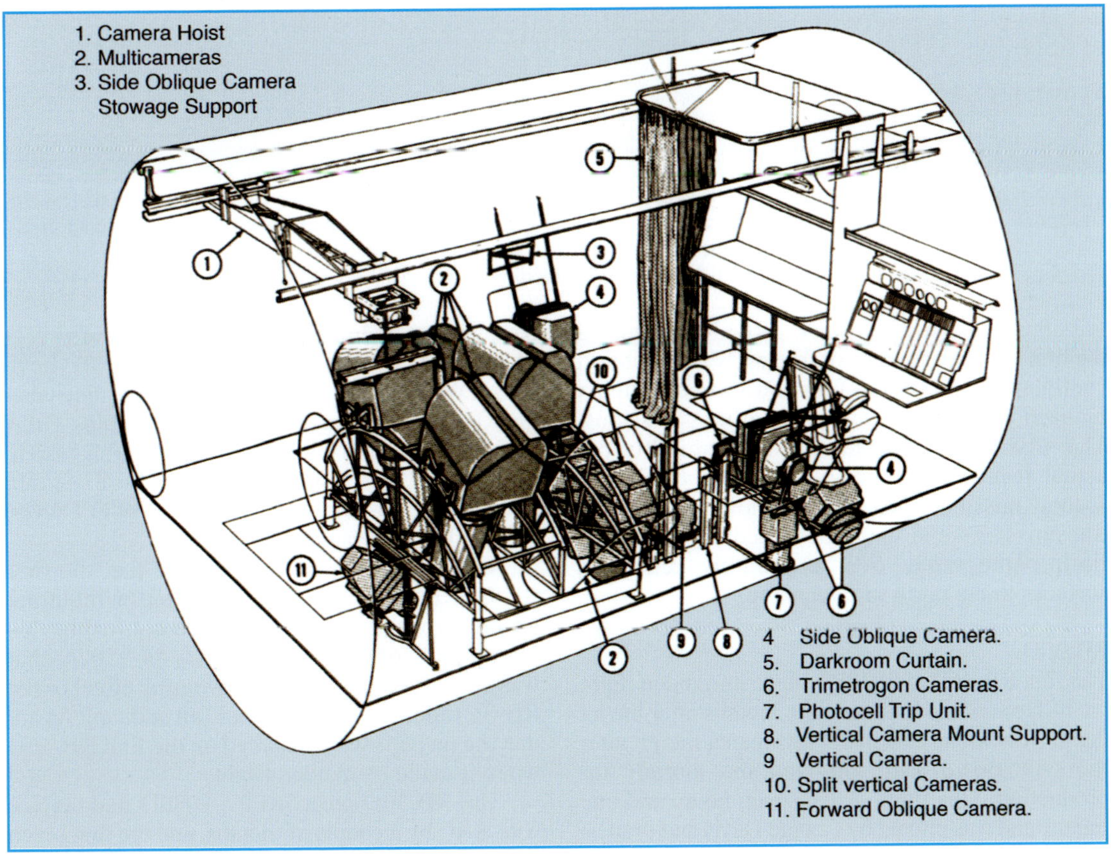

The photographer's position in an RB-36. The photographer did very little operating of the cameras - they were normally controlled by the photo-navigator in the nose. From here, the photographer monitored the operation of the cameras and their associated systems, reloading them if required.
(National Museum of the United States Air Force)

missions in support of Project 54AFR-11. During the first mission, the area of interest was monitored continuously for twenty-four hours - twelve hours by each aircraft - to detect Soviet transmissions. The mission was considered successful, but the actual results could not be ascertained. On the second mission, each aircraft monitored Soviet transmissions and also conducted experimental flash photography over the highly reflective surfaces to the north of Greenland.

RB-36D

The first RB-36D, 44-92088, made its maiden flight on 14 December 1949, only six months after the jet demonstrator had flown and less than a month after the 689 Board had approved the aircraft for production. This flight lasted seven hours and one minute and was piloted by George Davis and Francis Keen. Other members of the crew included J D McEachern, William 'Bill' P Easley, S A Mayfield, Bert L Woods, and C J Driskell. Observers included the RB-36 project engineer Norm B Robbins, Gil A Hofeller, Captain R G Newbern, Captain R E March, Captain L LeCouvre, Lieutenant H F Smith, Lieutenant D B Ingram, Lieutenant P W O'Dwyer, and Sgt P R McNamara.

Various reports have suggested that the first flight of the RB-36D was conducted without the jet pods, but researchers may be confusing this with photos of the single B-36B, 44-92026, that was used to evaluate the aerodynamic effect of the RB-36 radomes. Nevertheless, all indications are that the jet pods were installed on the first RB-36D when it made its maiden flight.

The RB-36D preceded the B-36D into service with SAC by a couple of months, and the first seven

RB-36Ds came off the production line before any bomber-versions of the jet-augmented design.

All of the 24 RB-36Ds were new-builds, although the first seven had been initially ordered as B-36Bs and were completed on the production line and delivered as RB-36Ds. None of the B-36Bs that had been delivered without jet pods were converted into RB-36Ds because of the extensive rework required.

All RB-36Ds were delivered to the 28th Strategic Reconnaissance Wing at Rapid City AFB, North Dakota (now Ellsworth AFB). Three RB-36Ds were delivered in June 1950, and the remaining twenty-one were delivered between July 1950 and May 1951. Due to various materiel shortages, the RB-36Ds did not become operationally ready until June 1951, although several operational reconnaissance missions had apparently been flown as early as July 1950.

Convair established a photo test target at the south end of the Fort Worth plant to demonstrate the camera equipment aboard the RB-36s during flight tests. This target consisted of a series of white lines of varying size against a black background. The target took up part of the south parking lot near the Grant's Lane entrance, and employees were reminded not to park in the area.

RB-36D-1-CF 44-92088 showing the two camera ports on the side of the fuselage. The large square aperture with a man in the side oblique port usually carried a K-22A camera with a twenty-four-inch focal length. Also of interest is the deployed 20-mm turret on the upper fuselage. This gives a good look at how the turret bay doors slid down the fuselage. Interestingly, this particular RB-36D, identifiable by the 'Ship 85' marking, above the radome and just forward of the dull grey magnesium of the turret bay skinning, was later modified to carry the 240-inch focal length Boston Camera and was redesignated ERB-36D. (Lockheed Martin).

The performance of the RB-36D was similar to its bomber counterparts with a few differences. First, since the reconnaissance version generally took off with fewer bombs but more fuel, it tended to be a little faster and fly a slightly higher early in the mission. But because it did not drop its primary payload - the reconnaissance gear - it was a little heavier on the return flight than the bombers, so it was a little slower.

The longest known B-36 flight was made by a Convair test crew flying an RB-36D, 44-92090. The flight took off at 09:05 on 14 January 1951 and landed at 12:35 on 16 January - precisely fifty-one and a half hours in the air. Although this flight was unusual, most B-36 flights lasted more than ten hours, and it was not unusual for missions to last thirty hours. The average training mission was scheduled for twenty-four hours. At least one aircraft from the 717th SRS at Rapid City managed to log 200 hours in a single month - January 1951. During March 1951, the 28th SRW managed to fly over 1,000 hours with their RB-36s, a milestone recognized during a ceremony at Rapid City AFB on 15 May.

The first RB-36D, 44-92088, spent its entire career as a reconnaissance testbed and was reportedly redesignated ERB-36D. At one point, the aircraft was modified to carry a so-called 'Boston Camera' with an incredible 240-inch focal-length lens.

The Boston Camera, also known as Pie Face and officially classified as the K-42 Camera Model, was a prototype airborne photo reconnaissance camera manufactured for the USAF by Boston University in 1951. The lens had an f/8 stop and used a 1/400 second shutter speed, and could photograph a golf ball from an altitude of 45,000 feet. The lens was designed in 1947 by Dr James Baker for installation in a camera designed by the Boston University Optical Research Laboratory. It seems that the camera weighed about three tons, and eight hundred pounds of lead shot were required to balance it.

Even the B-36 could not carry a camera over twenty feet long, so the lens used a set of mirrors to achieve the 240-inch effective length. A large opening was cut in the left side of the camera compartment, and the camera was meant to shoot sideways from a long standoff distance. A much smaller opening was cut further back on the fuselage to allow a small aiming-telescope the same basic field-of-view as the Boston Camera. Each negative measured eighteen by thirty-six inches, and was made up from two eighteen-inch 'squares' on two rolls. The modifications began on 7 December 1953, and the aircraft was delivered to the Air Force on 2 March 1954. The camera was tested for about a year before being removed from the RB-36D in 1955 and installed in a C-97. There are reports that the RB-36 took a picture of New York's Central Park from seventy-two miles away, and the photo interpreters

The Boston Camera on display under the B-36 at the National Museum of the US Air Force near Dayton, Ohio. (Roger Deere via National Museum of the United States Air Force)

Another posed 'groupshot', this time at Edwards Air Force Base, California. In the foreground is the X-4 and XF-92A. (Convair/General Dynamics)

could make out people walking there.

The Boston Camera was plagued with problems that caused it to vibrate and produce smearing on the newspaper-sized negative, so that photo interpreters would see several smeared frames along with several clear ones. The camera was never used operationally and was donated to the Air Force Museum, now the National Museum of the US Air Force near Dayton, Ohio in 1964. After the Boston Camera was removed, the Air Force determined it would cost $200,000 to bring the aircraft back to production standards. Since it was the oldest RB-36D in the fleet, the Air Force decided to retire the aircraft instead. The engines and other equipment were removed and returned into the spares inventory, and the aircraft was scrapped at Kelly AFB in late 1955.

RB-36E

In an effort to gain intercontinental reconnaissance capability as quickly as possible, General LeMay ordered the B-36A fleet converted into RB-36Es. The Air Force authorised the conversions as an extension of contract AF33-038-2182, the current production contract. Since the YB-36A, the first B-36A, had been destroyed during structural testing at Wright Field, the original YB-36, 42-13571, was also modified to RB-36E standard to give the Air Force twenty-two aircraft. As originally envisioned, these were RB-36Bs in that the aircraft would be brought up to B-36B standard and be equipped for surveillance. The decision to install jet engines on the last few B-36B production aircraft and call them B-36Ds resulted in the same changes being extended to the RB-36E configuration.

Although generally described as a modification, the RB-36Es were remanufactured, not converted. The process began with the aircraft arriving in Fort Worth, where what little operational equipment remained on board was removed. The aircraft was stripped of all other equipment and engines before being stored on an isolated portion of the Convair ramp for several months.

Eventually, they were disassembled even further, being broken down into their major manufacturing components. These were refurbished, brought up to the B/RB-36D standard, and reintroduced onto the production line interspersed with D-models. On the production line the RB-36Es were treated just like any other new-build B-36, and at the end of the line the RB-36Es were rolled out for a second time. Strangely, and for unlocated reasons, there was a single exception to this - one aircraft, 44-92008, was neither the first nor the last to be remanufactured, went through the remanufacturing process in the

Technicians work on one of the powerplants - note the protective matts on the wing surface so as to prevent damage to the surface. (Convair)

open air on the ramp next to Building 4.

As completed, the R-4360-25 engines were replaced by R-4360-41s, and the aircraft were also equipped with the four J47-GE-19 jet engines. The same reconnaissance cameras and electronic systems scheduled for the RB-36D were used, although in common with the RB-36D, the planned forty-eight-inch K-40 camera was not available until late 1951. The aircraft was also fitted with the 20-mm defensive armament that had not been ready when they were initially built, and they also received the new snap-action bomb bay doors used on the RB-36Ds. The first remanufactured aircraft made its maiden flight on 7 July 1950. The first RB-36E was delivered to the 28th SRW at Rapid City AFB on 28 July 1950, and the last conversion was completed on 27 April 1951.

RB-36F

The 13 April 1949 order for thirty-six additional B-36s from Convair under the same contract AF33-038-2182 that initiated B-36D production included nineteen RB-36Fs and five more were ordered the following year. The RB-36F made its maiden flight on 30 April 1951. The first four RB-36Fs were accepted in May 1951, with the last being delivered in December 1951. The reconnaissance equipment was similar to the RB-36D, while the other aircraft systems were the same as the B-36F.

During early 1952 an RB-36F suffered a pressure bulkhead failure while flying at 33,000 feet. The accident was traced to a defective bulkhead, and all B-36s were restricted to altitudes below 25,000 feet until the entire fleet could be inspected and defective bulkheads replaced. While the accident investigation was ongoing, the Air Force declined to accept any new aircraft from Convair. Eventually, Convair traced the fault to a minor manufacturing flaw and instituted a fix for all affected aircraft.

RB-36H

The Air Force bought seventy-three reconnaissance versions of the B-36H. The initial contract - an extension of AF33-O38-2182 - for fifteen B-36H and eight RB-36H aircraft was announced on 5 September 1951, although it had been signed over a year earlier, meaning that the aircraft carried FY50 serial numbers. An additional thirty-nine reconnaissance variants would be ordered in FY51 and twenty-six more in FY52. Twenty-three RB-36Hs were accepted during the first six months of 1952; forty-two others were delivered between July 1952 and June 1953, and the last eight were accepted during FY54 - three in July 1953, three in August, and two in September. The camera and ECM/ ferret equipment was generally similar to the earlier RB-36s, while all other systems were identical to the B-36H.

Chapter Nine

Nuclear Bomb Testing

Before the banning of testing air-dropped atomic weapons following the Limited Test Ban Treaty, nuclear tests were supported by B-36 aircraft in some manner.

The Limited Test Ban Treaty (LTBT), also known as the Partial Test Ban Treaty, was a treaty that prohibited nuclear weapons tests in the atmosphere, outer space, and under water. Negotiations for this agreement began when the Soviet Union proposed the ban of nuclear weapons tests at a meeting of the Subcommittee of Five (the United States, the United Kingdom, Canada, France, and the Soviet Union) of the United Nations Disarmament Commission in May 1955. Then, from October 1958 to January 1962, the USA, the United Kingdom, and the Soviet Union held trilateral meetings known as the Conference of the Nuclear Weapon Tests to discuss a treaty. These meetings, given new urgency after the 1962 Cuban Missile Crisis, resulted in the formation of the LTBT. The treaty opened for signature on 5 August 1963 and entered into force on 10 October 1963. Since then, more than 120 states have signed the treaty.

Without a doubt, the B-36 as a type participated in numerous tests, but conclusive documentation, including identities, is somewhat thin on the ground. In many of these instances, the B-36 dropped the weapon being tested, but there were other detonations where the aircraft that dropped the device could not be ascertained. In addition, various other B-36s were used as 'sampler' aircraft to measure the radiation released from the tests and 'effects' aircraft to measure overpressures. SAC's B-36s may not have dropped any bombs in anger, but they did drop some - it was a dangerous job.

At least five B-36s were dedicated for long periods to the atomic test mission. A single Featherweight III B-36D-5-CF, 49-2653, was used as an 'effects' aircraft for almost all of the early tests. Four B-36Hs - 50-1083, 50-1086, 51-5726, and 52-1386 - were used extensively by the 4925th Test Group (Atomic) at Kirtland AFB, New Mexico, in support of atomic testing. In addition, two RB-36H-15-CFs - 51-5748 and 51-5750 - were modified with a series of upward-looking cameras to photograph the mushroom clouds at high altitudes.

The B-36 was chosen for use in the atomic tests for two reasons. Firstly, they were still the mainstay of the strategic deterrent fleet, although it was apparent they were on their way out as the B-47 and B-52 came online. Second, they were large enough to carry meaningful equipment over long distances and were among the only aircraft that could fly high enough to obtain some of the data the Los Alamos scientists needed. Surprisingly, the Air Force was concerned about the effects of atomic detonations on fabric control surfaces. The B-29 and B-50 still used fabric - most B-36s had been converted to metal surfaces during various modification programmes, and the few that still had fabric rudders were quickly modified.

When high-yield nuclear weapons - both fission and fusion - began to be developed, both the Atomic Energy Commission and the Air Force were concerned about the potential effects on the delivery aircraft. Largely to determine the maximum yield weapon that could be delivered by an aircraft and have it survive to return home, the Air Force agreed to fly instrumented B-36, B-47, and B-50 aircraft near various atomic tests. These would be known as 'effects' aircraft to determine what effects the heat, blast, and overpressure of a nuclear detonation had on a machine. The best estimates using theoretical data indicated that the B-36 should deliver weapons in the megaton range, while the B-47 would probably be limited to about half of that. Operational considerations meant that the B-50 would likely never be called upon to deliver high-yield weapons, and the type was removed from testing after Operation Ivy.

A single Featherweight III B-36D-5-CF serial 49-2653 was modified at Wright-Patterson AFB between 9 May and 15 June 1952, including the addition of a metal rudder - an approved modification for the B-36 fleet, but one that had not been universally implemented. The aircraft was heavily instrumented with thermocouples to measure heat, accelerometers to measure movement, strain gauges, recording meters, and oscilloscopes. All of the data was recorded aboard the aircraft using either photographs of the oscilloscopes or on wire recorders.

This was before telemetry was a widely-used concept, and the electromagnetic pulse of the detonation would likely have rendered any telemetry unusable in any event. Calibration of the sensors was completed on 15 August, and the aircraft was flown to Carswell AFB for maintenance. On 21 September 1952, the machine arrived at Kwajalein Island in the Pacific, followed by a B-47B on 2 October 1952 that would be used for similar tests.

Operation Texan

This was a full-scale rehearsal for Operation Ivy conducted from Bergstrom Air Force Base, near Austin, Texas, on 13 August 1952. A target ship was positioned in the Gulf of Mexico at the same distance - 425 miles - from Bergstrom that the Eniwetok test site at Runit Island was from the Kwajalein airfield. A total of thirty-nine aircraft participated in simulated bomb drops, sampling missions, drone control, and cloud-tracking tasks. Of these, three were B-36s - the dedicated B-36D effects aircraft, and two B-36H drop aircraft. One of the H-models would drop a live device during Operation Ivy, while the other served as a sampler control aircraft with scientists from Los Alamos aboard to direct the efforts of the sampler fleet. The device dropped during Operation Texan was a modified T-59 training shape that simulated the Mk 18 that would be dropped at Eniwetok. The device was sixty inches in diameter, one hundred and twenty-eight inches long, and weighed 8,600 pounds.

Operation Ivy

In mid-October 1952, the Wright Air Development Center (WADC) published a report that attempted to specify the minimum safe altitudes to be used by a B-36D for both surface-burst and air-burst weapons. In all cases, the B-36 was assumed to be travelling at high speed in level flight when the weapon was dropped, with some scenarios including an immediate sharp breakaway turn. None of the weapons was parachute retarded.

The first tests of devices with yields more significant than a megaton were undertaken during Operation Ivy in the autumn of 1952, sponsored by the Los Alamos National Laboratory. Two devices were tested: a liquid-fuelled thermonuclear device during Shot Mike and an Mk 18 fission device during Shot King.

For Shot Mike, the effects B-36D was flown from the airfield at Kwajalein and was fifteen miles away at an altitude of 40,000 feet at the time of detonation on 1 November 1952. The Mike device was too heavy to be air dropped and was detonated on the ground. The 10.4 megaton detonation created a crater 164 feet deep and 6,240 feet in diameter and a fireball three and a half miles in diameter. When the shock wave arrived at the B-36D, the aircraft was at 38,500 feet at a slant range of twenty-five miles from the detonation. The aircraft had a true airspeed of 278 knots and a true ground speed of 254 knots, away from the blast. The B-36D experienced a temperature of 93 deg F on the wingtip nearest the explosion and a peak overpressure of 0.33 psi - a reading that was only sixty-two per cent of the design limit. This data was considerably less than expected and yielded little helpful information.

One of the conclusions from Shot Mike was that the B-36 was not fast enough to escape the potentially disastrous effects of a thermonuclear device unless

The results of Shot King, part of Operation Ivy. The B-36 that dropped the weapon escaped serious damage, but this explosion led to major changes to SAC nuclear bombers. (USAF)

the bomb was equipped with a retarding parachute that gave the bomber extra time to escape. Unfortunately, Strategic Air Command strongly opposed the use of parachutes on nuclear weapons, but eventually, they relented and allowed the use of retarding parachutes on almost all atomic weapons.

The Shot King device was a prototype of the Mk 18 super oralloy bomb (SOB). This was a nuclear bomb design that was the highest yield fission bomb produced by the US. The Mark 18 had a design yield of 500 kilotons.

The device consisted mostly of standard stockpiled components. It was based on the stockpiled Mk 6D bomb but used the ninety-two point implosion system developed for the Mk 13. In addition, the normal uranium-plutonium composite core was replaced by a new design made up of approximately one hundred and thirty-two pounds of highly enriched uranium, known as oralloy, in a natural uranium tamper. The complete bomb weighed 8,600 pounds.

A dry run for Shot King was held on 8 November 1952, with a modified T-59 training shape being loaded into the B-36H drop aircraft. The next morning the shape was dropped into the ocean near the Shot King surface target, northeast of Runit Island in Eniwetok Atoll. Most of the other aircraft and ships scheduled to support the actual test were involved in this dry run. All went well.

The actual Mk 18 prototype had arrived on Kwajalein via Douglas C-124 on 7 November. Following the successful dry run on 12 November, the device and all of its components were checked out and loaded in the B-36H. The next day the aircraft took off, but the drop was cancelled because of a solid overcast over the test area. The weapon was unloaded from the B-36H, underwent minor maintenance, and reloaded 16 November. Following a 06:30 departure, the B-36H conducted practice bombing runs over the target for three hours. In this case, the target consisted of a series of brightly-painted oil drums mounted on pilings that provided a good optical target from twenty-five miles. Radar reflectors had also been installed, providing a radar target that was visible at a range of sixty miles. The bombardier used the optical sight and dropped the device from 40,000 feet. He missed the mark by a remarkably small two hundred and fifteen feet, and fifty-six seconds after release, the device exploded at an altitude of 1,480 feet with a yield of 500 kilotons.

The effects B-36D was about 28,000 feet out of position during Shot King and provided little useful data. The B-36H drop aircraft, however, sustained minor damage from the blast. Unfortunately, the H-model was not instrumented, but engineers later calculated that the empennage had been exposed to approximately eighty per cent of its design limit. One of the results of this test was the development of a thermal protection device for the inside of the glazed panels on aircraft. The original curtains were made from aluminized asbestos, but these could only be used once due to a severe blackening of their exposed surfaces. Subsequently, an improved material was selected - a white duck fabric similar to canvas - that could be used multiple times. The B-36s participating in Shot Mike were equipped with the aluminized asbestos curtains, and these would remain through the end of Operation Castle when the updated material finally replaced them. Another change that resulted from the Operation Ivy tests was the decision to develop a highly reflective white paint to help protect the delivery aircraft. Eventually, almost all SAC nuclear bombers would have their bottom surfaces coated with a special heat-resistant white paint. However, the local units experimented with various white paints for the remainder of the Pacific test series, and the areas covered differed considerably from the later operational schemes.

Operation Upshot-Knothole

This operation was conducted at the Nevada Test Site and consisted of eleven atmospheric tests conducted between 17 March and 4 June 1953. There were three air-drops, seven tower tests, and one air-burst.

Today known as the Nevada National Security Site - and as the Nevada Test Site until 2010 this is a United States Department of Energy reservation located in southeastern Nye County, Nevada, about 65 miles northwest of Las Vegas. Formerly known as the Nevada Proving Grounds, the site was established in 1951 for the testing of nuclear devices. It covers approximately 1,360 square miles of desert and mountainous terrain. Nuclear weapons testing at the site began with a one-kiloton-of-TNT bomb dropped on Frenchman Flat on 27 January, 1951. Over the subsequent four decades, over 1,000 nuclear explosions were detonated at the site.

During the 1950s, the mushroom clouds from the one hundred atmospheric tests could be seen from almost a hundred miles away. The city of Las Vegas experienced noticeable seismic effects, and the mushroom clouds, which could be seen from the downtown hotels, became tourist attractions. Westerly winds routinely carried the fallout from above-ground nuclear testing directly through St. George, Utah and southern Utah.

The purpose of the tests included validating new theories using both fission and fusion devices.

Approximately 21,000 Department of Defense military and civilian personnel participated in Operation Upshot-Knothole as part of the Desert Rock V exercise. Unfortunately, Operation Upshot-Knothole, particularly Shot Harry, drew a great deal of criticism as resultant fallout levels produced increased offsite radiation exposures. The tests comprising the 1953 Operation Upshot-Knothole included:

Shot	Date	Launch	Type	Yield
Annie	17 March	tower	weapons related	16 kilotons
Nancy	24 March	tower	weapons related	24 kilotons
Ruth	31 March	tower	weapons related	200 tons
Dixie	6 April	air drop	weapons related	11 kilotons
Ray	11 April	tower	weapons related	200 tons
Badger	18 April	tower	weapons related	23 kilotons
Simon	25 April	tower	weapons related	43 kilotons
Encore	8 May	air drop	weapons effects	27 kilotons
Harry	19 May	tower	weapons related	32 kilotons
Grable	25 May	Cannon	weapons related	15 kilotons
Climax	4 June	air drop	weapons related	61 kilotons

The B-36 did not participate in all of these tests. However, twelve B-36s, part of a fifty-three aircraft armada participated in Shot Nancy on 24 March 1953. The lead B-36 was commanded by Brigadier General Joe W. Kelly, commander of the 19th Air Division from Carswell. The predawn detonation was used to provide first-hand knowledge of what an atomic explosion looked and felt like. The B-36s were from various squadrons, but all landed at Carswell AFB following the explosion.

The tests included Shot Ruth of 31 March, the first UCRL device, a uranium deuteride core meant to explore deuterated polyethylene mixed with uranium as thermonuclear fuel and if successful, to lead also to a compact thermonuclear primary. The predicted yield was one and a half to three kilotons, while the maximum theoretical was twenty kilotons. However, the device fizzled - that is, the deuterium moderated, meaning slowed down the neutrons more than expected and so quenched the reaction. This was embarrassing for designers, especially as it left two hundred feet of the tower still standing.

The blast-induced loads obtained during the two Operation Ivy shots had been too low to provide adequate verification of the blast load theory at levels approaching the maximum capabilities of the aircraft. In addition, the response data from IVY showed that the aft fuselage and empennage of the B-36 were more vulnerable than had previously been predicted. As part of the tests, the effects B-36D (49-2653)

Operation Upshot-Knothole's Shot Grable saw the use of 'Atomic Annie' the M65 atomic cannon. The test was attended by the Chairman-delegate of the Joint Chiefs of Staff, Admiral Arthur W. Radford and United States Secretary of Defense Charles Erwin Wilson; it resulted in the successful detonation of a 15 kiloton shell (W9 warhead) at a range of seven miles. This was the first and only nuclear shell to be fired from a cannon. B-36 components were exposed to blast and radiation effects during Operation Upshot-Knothole.

received additional instrumentation after it had returned to Wright-Patterson Air Force Base on 21 November 1952, but the instrumentation could not be calibrated entirely prior to departing for Kirtland Air Force Base.

Nevertheless, the aircraft was exposed to Shot Encore as part of Project 5.3 over the Nevada Proving Grounds. The aircraft crew included aircraft commander Lieutenant Colonel Jerry Hunt, radar operator Lieutenant Colonel Harold Upton, and flight engineer Major Samuel Baker. In order to more accurately simulate an operational aircraft, this time, the B-36D was loaded with 25,000 pounds of dummy bombs in the Number One bomb bay. The effects aircraft had to fly a widely separated formation with the drop aircraft to ensure it was in the proper position when the device dropped. The shot was detonated on 8 May 1953, but again the data was not truly satisfactory, partially because the instrumentation had not been adequately calibrated. After this test, the aircraft was sent to Fort Worth, where Convair performed a complete instrument calibration with assistance from the Cook Research Laboratories.

On 4 June 1953, an unidentified B-36H dropped a high-yield Mk 7 atomic device over Area 7 of the Nevada Proving Ground for Shot Climax. This was the eleventh and final test of Operation Upshot-Knothole. Interestingly, since the B-36 was not usually equipped to handle the tactical Mk 7, a bomb rack from an F-84 fighter was temporarily installed on the B-36 for the test. The 1,334-foot altitude detonation was 172 feet west and 232 feet north of the designated ground zero. The predicted yield of this device was 50-70 kilotons, and the actual 61 kiloton yield was the highest of any US continental test up to that time. This test was meant to test the 'Cobra' core that was subsequently used as a primary in the TX-14, TX-17, and TX-21 thermonuclear devices fired during Operation Castle.

In addition to airborne support, the B-36 design also participated in Operation Upshot-Knothole on the ground. The Air Force wanted to expose various portions of an aircraft structure to higher blast effects than could be safely obtained by a manned aircraft in flight. Therefore, various assemblies - box beams, tension ties, stabiliser and elevator assemblies, outer wing panels, and parts of bonded metal structures - were manufactured in triplicate and placed on the ground near the detonation. One was shielded from the blast effects, one from thermal radiation, and the other was unshielded and exposed to the full force of the detonation. In addition, the stabiliser, elevator, and outer wing panels were placed under load to simulate flight conditions. These components were exposed to both Shot 9 and Shot 10 of Operation Upshot-Knothole as part of Project 8.1a. The data collected was considered satisfactory.

The tests resulted in a wide range of damage. For temperatures of approximately 350 degrees Fahrenheit, the tests showed that waffle panels were less vulnerable to skin buckling than flat panels. Honeycomb core panels were the most susceptible due to bonding release, with failures occurring as low as 300 degrees Fahrenheit. The overpressure required to produce panel buckling on the B-36 stabiliser and elevator assembly was found to be between 1.2 and 3.2 psi (at 13,000 feet from the detonation). An over-pressure of 5.7 psi caused the wing panel, positioned 4,774 feet from ground zero, to fail.

Operation Castle

This nuclear test series was conducted between February and May 1954 at Eniwetok, in the Pacific Marshall Islands.

The effects B-36D 49-2653 was flown on all six tests as part of Project 6.2a with the call sign of 'Elaine 1.' The aircraft was operated by crew S-36 from the 42nd Bomb Squadron, 11th Bomb Wing at Carswell AFB, with Lieutenant Colonel George J. Savage as the aircraft commander for each flight. For the first five shots, the aircraft was positioned in such a manner as to simulate that it had just dropped the weapon being detonated - that is flying away from the blast. On the last Shot, the aircraft flew towards the blast in order to acquire data for this orientation. On five of the shots, the yields of the detonations were such that good data were obtained - the unexpectedly low yield of Shot Koon provided no useful information. Shot Yankee provided the highest thermal and gust loading, sixty-four per cent and seventy-six per cent, respectively, of the theoretical aircraft limit. A 322-degree thermal pulse buckled the elevator skin in four places. It blistered a large portion of the paint off the lower surface of the horizontal stabiliser - despite newly added gloss white with a clear overcoat. Shot Bravo resulted in over-pressures in excess of one hundred per cent of the theoretical limits and resulted in significant damage to various parts of the aircraft skin, although no primary structure was damaged.

In addition, two B-36Hs, 50-1083 and 50-1086 were used as sampling aircraft during the tests, and a single RB-36H was used as a sampler controller, directing the sampling aircraft into the correct areas of the cloud. The sampling B-36s reached 55,000 feet, although it often took them over two hours of climbing to do so. The crew wore partial pressure suits, but even so each aircraft was limited to

Operation Castle nuclear test series was conducted between February and May 1954 at Eniwetok, in the Pacific Marshall Islands.

Shot	Date	Expected Yield	Actual Yield	Altitude	Slant Range
Bravo	01 Mar	4-8 megatons	15 megatons	33,000	60,580
Romeo	27 Mar	1.5 - 7 megatons	11 megatons	37,000	63,580
Koon	07 Apr	0.33 - 2.5 megatons	0.11 megatons	40,000	56,570
Union	26 Apr	1-6 megatons	6.9 megatons	37,000	62,700
Yankee	05 May	6 -10 megatons	13.5 megatons	40,000	56,990
Nectar	14 May	1 - 2.5 megatons	1.69 megatons	33,000	126,380

approximately 90-100 minutes above 50,000 feet before encountering either crew or equipment problems.

Some of the aircraft damage was recorded in the Operation Castle final report: 'The effects B-36 flew during the six Operation Castle shots to collect definitive blast and thermal response data near the aircraft's design limits so that the B-36 weapons delivery handbook could be completed.

'The yield of the first Operation Castle shot, Bravo, was approximately one hundred and fifty per cent greater than the positioning yield used for the effects studies of aircraft in flight. The weapons effects program B-36D - the same plane used during Operations Ivy and Upshot-Knothole was exposed to overpressure load, which caused mechanical damage that required replacing the bomb bay doors, all four lower plexiglass scanners' blisters, and the radar antenna radome.

'The undersides of all six engine nacelles and the landing gear and lower aft gun turret bay doors were also damaged. The radome was 'dished in' about seven inches, both bomb bay doors were buckled, the skin on the nose wheel doors was cracked, the main landing gear 'canoe' doors were dented, and several access doors were either blown off or unlatched by the blast.'

'Considerable thermal damage ensued. The heat pulse from the explosion buckled several small, unpainted inspection panel doors, scorched the left wing root fabric filler, blistered and scorched the paint at the wing roots, peeled. Blistered paint on the middle of each horizontal stabiliser, blistered the paint and buckled metal on the elevator trim and servo tabs, burned and charred black rubber padding inside the two lower aft scanner's blisters, the upper blisters were covered over and damaged many other components, including retracted gun turrets, propeller spinners. Even the bomb bay communications tunnel between the forward and rear crew compartments.

'The crew reported seeing an intense bright red glow through the thermal curtains that had been pulled shut just before the blast. On all shots, the crew saw two distinct light pulses near the beginning of the thermal pulse. The thermal pulse lasted about fifteen seconds.

'Shortly after the Bravo burst, the aft crew compartment was filled with smoke from blister padding, miscellaneous lubricating fluids, and charred components outside the crew cabin. Fire warning lights on four of the reciprocating engines lit up for about four seconds as thermal radiation impinged on sensors located in the engines and all jet engine exhaust temperature gauges pegged, but the engines returned to normal operation.

'Thermal effects on this airplane during the 13.SMT Castle Yankee shot were also considerable: a 322 degree Fahrenheit thermal pulse buckled the elevator skin in four places and blistered and peeled a large portion of the paint on the lower surfaces of the horizontal stabiliser and elevators, despite the plane's underside having been painted with a protective coat of clear lacquer over white enamel to improve the reflecting properties of the skin. The thermal pulse was accompanied by a twenty-second duration radiation pulse.

The damage from the first Castle flight had required 818 man-hours to repair. Somewhat laconically, the final project report for Castle noted that these phenomena also had a deleterious effect on the mental attitude of the crew.

The report concluded that 'for the relatively slow-speed, propeller-driven aircraft such as the B-36, the effects of the blast wave resulting from the detonation of a nuclear weapon may very well limit the operational capabilities during a strategic mission.'

Information gathered during the Operation Castle tests resulted in a B-36 weapons delivery handbook being developed. The preferred delivery flight began at 345 knots at 40,000 feet, which was about the maximum speed possible, followed by a violent turn away from the target immediately after the weapon was dropped. It was estimated that the aircraft could survive a surface burst from a 10.8 megaton free-fall or 100 megatons parachute-retarded bomb. If the bomb was set to explode at 6,000 feet, these figures dropped to 1.5 and 35 megatons, respectively.

Operation Teapot

Several operational B-36 crews participated as observers during Operation Teapot as part of Project 40.4. Shot Turk on 7 March and Shot Met of 15 April was observed by crews from the 7th BW at Carswell as part of Project 40.0. These were considered operational training missions to verify 'nuclear bomb delivery and escape procedures from the SAC [weapons] delivery handbook for the B-36' The B-36s both used the call sign 'Powder Burn.' For the 45- kiloton Shot Turk, the aircraft was one mile east of ground zero, tail-on, flying eastbound at 250 mph and 23,000 feet. The aircraft was directly overhead at 26,000 feet and 250 mph for the twenty-four-kiloton Shot Met.

After experiencing the effects of the detonation, the aircraft returned to Carswell. When the data was analysed, it was determined that the radiation exposure was essentially nil - each crew member received less than three millirem - or one-thousandth of a rem - of neutron exposure and twenty-seven millirem of gamma exposure. In each case, this was less than what would trigger the film badges worn by the crew during the missions, and the recorded crew dose was zero.

As part of Shot Wasp on 18 February, an unidentified B-36 dropped a Mk 12 (TX 12) case being used to test a 1.2-kiloton air defence weapon using the venerable Ranger Able uranium core in a new compact, lightweight implosion system. The test was at Area 7 of the Nevada Proving Grounds. The detonation had been scheduled for 07:30 hours but was postponed until 12:00 noon when the B-36 take-off was delayed and again by clouds over the test location.

Approximately thirty-five major experiments were conducted during the detonation, all for either weapons development or civil effects (Plowshare) purposes. The implosion system was a sphere twenty-two inches in diameter but only weighed one hundred and twenty pounds. The total device weight was 1,500 pounds. The unretarded (free-fall) device detonated at 762 feet altitude.

On 25 March 1955, primarily to test procedures of the nuclear test four days later, a B-36 dropped a non-nuclear high-explosive device from an altitude of 30,000 feet over Yucca Flat, Nevada. The device detonated against a background of intricate smoke trails and puffs positioned just before the burst by six F-86s and another B-36. The smoke provided photo reference points.

The Wasp test was largely repeated as part of Shot Wasp Prime on 29 March 1955. The unretarded Mk 12 case was dropped from 15,000 feet and exploded at approximately 740 feet. About forty Air Force aircraft participated in the test, mostly performing cloud sampling missions. Within five minutes of the detonation, the cloud had topped 30,000 feet altitude and had largely vanished within twenty minutes. This device used a slightly higher yield core for weapons development purposes. The yield was about the same as predicted. As something of a footnote - this Shot

The infamous Shot Bravo during the Castle series of tests. The yield from this explosion was three times what was expected. (USAF)

was fired 5 hours and 5 minutes after Apple-1, the first time in US history that two nuclear explosions were set off in one day.

Shot HA (high altitude) was on 6 April 1955 over Yucca Flat. This B-36H airdrop was a test of a 3.2-kiloton air-to-air missile warhead similar to the Wasp Prime device - a seventeen-inch spherical system weighing one hundred and twenty-five pounds in a 1,085 pounds Mk 5 ballistic case. The device was dropped from 42,000 feet, and was parachute retarded to permit the B-36 to escape to a safe distance, marking the first parachute weapon drop conducted at the Nevada Proving Ground. The device was still at 32,650 feet when it detonated. The B-36H dropped a series of radiosondes to record air pressure before dropping the HA device. In addition, thermal and radiation sensors were installed in the aft fuselage. Two RB-36s were used during Shot HA to collect radioisotope samples from the cloud, but one bomber could not climb high enough to obtain useful samples.

Operation Redwing

This test series was conducted between April and July 1956 at Eniwetok, in the Pacific Marshall Islands and included the first air drop of a US thermonuclear weapon. Originally, a B-36 was going to be used to drop the TX-51-X1 from an altitude of 40,000 feet. However, further analysis determined that the B-36 was too slow to escape the expected thermal effects of the device, and a B-52B, 52-013, was ultimately selected for the Shot Cherokee drop aircraft. A B-36 was used to drop diagnostic canisters in support of Cherokee.

A B-36 was used to drop the low-yield TX-28 device used in Shot Osage on 17 June 1956. The device detonated at an altitude of 670 feet within 180 feet of the desired target and yielded seventy kilotons. This was a proof test of the W-25, a lightweight, low yield plutonium warhead intended for air defence and other tactical applications. This spherical implosion device had a diameter of 17.4 inches, was 25.7 inches long and weighed 174.6 pounds. It was dropped in an instrumented Mk 7 drop case, which had a total weight of 3,150 pounds. This was the last nuclear test in which a B-36 participated.

Operation Miami Moon

This was an operation to gather radioisotope samples from the British nuclear weapons tests conducted during Operation Grapple on Malden Island, south of Hawaii, in May and June 1957.

Four specially-equipped RB-36s from the 5th BW were modified with four large external sampling pods, two on either side of the fuselage ahead of the wing. The pods held removable fine-mesh paper filters to trap the radioactive particles, which were later analyzed on the ground — no in-flight analysis was conducted. Originally four sampling flights were to be conducted during each of the four planned British tests, but ultimately the British only tested three devices and the Air Force could only afford to fly two sampling missions per test. A 17-hour calibration mission was flown on 11 May 1957, and two missions were flown on 15 May, two on 31 May, and two on 19 June, all from Hickam AFB, Hawaii. Each sampling mission lasted nineteen hours, with approximately two and a half hours spent inside the mushroom cloud at an altitude of 40,000 feet.

Operation Old Gold

A similar programme was flown to gather data from Soviet nuclear tests, although the aircraft would necessarily not be able to fly as near to the cloud. During late 1957 and early 1958, two RB-36s from the 5th BW deployed to Eielson AFB, Alaska. This time each aircraft only carried two sampling pods mounted on the side of the fuselage at the side-oblique camera position. A door in each pod opened at particular times during flight, exposing small tubes inside the pod that collected slipstream air and ducted it to containers located inside the camera compartment. The pods had originally been mounted parallel to the aircraft but were later angled slightly to correspond to the wing angle-of-attack. This was done to solve a problem where the pods were subjected to excessive aerodynamic forces because the B-36 tended to fly slightly nose high - in fact, one pod had been ripped off an aircraft as it departed Fairfield-Suisun Air Force Base. The flights were flown along the edges of Soviet airspace for several days following each of the Soviet tests.

Cosmic Rays

Although not a part of the atomic test series, one of the EB-36Hs (51-5726) from the 4925th Test Group (Atomic) at Kirtland AFB was used by the University of California Radiation Laboratory at Berkley during an investigation into the number and energy of cosmic ray neutrons in the upper atmosphere. The project began in November 1956 and continued until 1 February 1957, when the aircraft was scheduled for periodic maintenance. The tests were considered very successful and were later continued using a B-52.

Decontamination

As a result of supporting these nuclear tests, at least four B-36s (49-2653, 50-1083, 50-1086, and 52-

The light from an atomic bomb test explosion during Operation Redwing is reflected in the waters of Enewetak Atoll in the Pacific. (USAF)

1386) were heavily contaminated with radioactive material. Initially, the Air Force attempted to use normal maintenance personnel to decontaminate the aircraft. They were not totally successful. In one report it stated 'From experience gained following Shot Bravo in decontamination of B-36 aircraft, it was apparent that the techniques and utilization of personnel and equipment must be revised. Entirely too much time was used to decontaminate the aircraft and excessive radiation exposures were being accumulated by B-36 maintenance personnel who participated in the process. Decontamination is not 100% effective due to the nature of radioactivity and the inherent problem of completely cleaning all aircraft surfaces and engines.

The initial attempt after Operation Castle Shot Bravo was indeed manpower intensive. After the completion of a mission the two B-36Hs were parked in an isolated area and allowed to radioactively 'cool' for twenty hours. Work stands were positioned, and engine cowlings removed. Then a 1:5 ratio mixture of Gunk - a propriety engine cleaner and degreaser - and kerosene was applied over the exterior surfaces of the aircraft and engines.

These surfaces were thoroughly scrubbed using brooms while the mixture was applied. A warm water and detergent mixture was applied to remove the emulsion formed by the gunk fluid, followed by a fresh water rinse to remove all residue. The aircraft was then allowed to drain for thirty minutes before radiation measurements were taken. The procedure was repeated three times. The entire procedure required seventeen personnel who took four to five days and used 5,200 gallons of water, 220 gallons of Gunk, and a thousand gallons of kerosene for each aircraft.

After Operation Castle Shot Romeo, the Air Force decided to allow the aircraft to cool for forty-four hours. Twenty-six additional personnel were assigned to wash each aircraft, this time using 2,350 gallons of water, 83 gallons of Gunk, and 321 gallons of kerosene. The warm water was heated and a couple of small drain holes were drilled in each engine cowling to prevent trapping contaminated water.

Overall, this was considered a much better way to decontaminate aircraft in the field, and these procedures were used for the duration of the Operation Castle tests.

On 30 September 1954, the Air Force awarded Convair a contract to figure out how to decontaminate the aircraft. The contract had two purposes: 'To reduce the radioactive contamination of three B-36 airplanes to a level the Air Force considers safe for operating personnel, and, to modernize each airplane to conform with the current SAM-SAC Cycle I configuration.'

The decontamination task had never been attempted before and forced Convair to overcome several unique problems. First, special facilities had to be constructed at Fort Worth to handle the disposal of contaminated wash water and particular liquid and solid waste materials. It was necessary to thoroughly train each worker in the proper methods of handling radioactive parts and materials to ensure personal safety. This included the need to wear protective clothing, showering each day before going to lunch or before going home, and observing special precautions during smoke breaks and trips to the restroom. These precautions effectively limited each eight-hour shift to six hours of productive work. The men were not ptovided with decontamination suits, but merely wore weat-weather protection clothing.

Each aircraft was largely disassembled and thoroughly washed. A few badly contaminated skin sections were replaced, as were many rubber and plastic components. The aircraft were redelivered to the Air Force on 1 April, 17 June, and 19 August 1955, respectively.

Following that test series, the four RB-36s used during Operation Miami Moon were decontaminated at Hickam Field, Hawaii. Each aircraft was parked in a remote section of the field and allowed to cool for three days. The decontamination process was generally similar to that performed after Operation Castle, using Gunk and kerosene.

Broken Arrow

The US Department of Defense has several terms to address nuclear weapon incidents or mishaps. They are stated on the Nuclear Weapon Accident DoD Directive 5230.16. The incidents involving an un-sanctioned release of an atomic ordinance include the accidental or unauthorized launching of a weapon, an unauthorized nuclear detonation, the non-nuclear burning of a nuclear warhead or one of its components, and radioactive contamination and the jettison of an atomic payload due to accidental causes. The term that applies here is Broken Arrow.

On an April afternoon in 1981, the DoD and the US Department of Energy released its once top-secret Narrative Summaries of Accidents Involving US Nuclear Weapons: 1950 to 1980. In a gripping and detailing matter, the report described thirty-two incidents involving atomic warhead releases during those three decades. Of that number, only two involved B-36 operations.

The first occurred over the Canadian Pacific Ocean coast, near British Columbia. On 14 February 1950, a B-36B, tail number 44-92075, part of the 7th Bomb Wing stationed out of Eielson Air Force Base, Alaska, was on a routine, cross-continent simulated combat flight pattern from Eielson to Carswell AFB, Texas, when, six hours into its mission, the bomber developed engine problems that forced the crew to shut down three engines.

Flying at 12,000 feet with ice forming on its wings and half of its engines out of commission, 44-92075 had problems maintaining level flight. The pilot decided to turn the big bomber away from land and towards the relative safeness of the ocean to drop its nuclear ordnance, a Mk 4, Fat Man-type of weapon, over open waters. The release occurred from 8,000 feet. At around 3,800 feet, the altitude on which the weapon's detonator was pre-set, the high explosive on the warhead detonated, causing a bright flash followed by a shock wave. After release, the aircraft turned south-east, towards Princess Royal Island, where the crew of seventeen bailed out offshore. Two days later, the entire wreckage of the plane washed up on Vancouver Island.

The second Broken Arrow incident involving a B-36 occurred almost seven years later. Although, not as detailed as the previous deployment, the report did relate the story of a B-36A ferrying a Mk 17 nuclear bomb from Biggs AFB in Texas to Kirtland AFB, New Mexico. On 22 May 1957, this machine - with no tail number posted on the incident memo - took off from Biggs for its mission. At exactly 11:50 am, Mountain Standard Time and while on approach to Kirtland at an altitude of 1,700 feet, the aircraft's bomb bay door began to give way, releasing the weapon, along with the entire bay structure, two minutes later, just under five miles south of Kirtland's control tower. The weapon's parachute mechanism opened, but due to the low operational ceiling, it did not ultimately deploy.

The high explosive material inside the Mk 17 detonated on impact. The explosion destroyed the weapon and left a gaping crater twelve feet deep and twenty-five feet in diameter. Such was the violence of the detonation that the Armed Forces Special Weapons Program, the assessment unit assigned to the investigation of the accident, found debris fields as far as a mile outside the contact zone. The final incident report blamed the crewman who removed the weapon's firing pin - a procedure used to secure the ordnance before the final bomb run - by snagging a piece of his clothing against the bomb's parachute release wire for its partial deployment.

Chapter Ten

Parasites

The concept for parasite aircraft was not new by the 1950s. Although several countries had investigated the idea, perhaps the most successful application was the US Navy's Curtiss F9C Sparrowhawk biplanes from the 1930s. First ordered in June 1930, the F9C was less than 20 feet long with a wingspan of only 25.5 feet. A single 420-hp Wright R-975 engine could propel the 2,000-pound fighter to a top speed of 175 mph. When the Navy began building two large airships - Akron and Macon - it was decided that each airship would be equipped with a small hangar deck that allowed up to five Sparrowhawks to be carried. The original XF9C-1 prototype was modified with a hook device in front of the canopy and tests were conducted using the airship Los Angeles beginning on 23 October 1931. Six production F9C-2 Sparrowhawks had been ordered a week earlier.

By all accounts, the little fighters were quite successful as parasites. Unfortunately, the Akron was lost on 4 April 1933, followed by the Macon on 12 February 1935, effectively ending the programme. A decade later, the US military would try again.

XP-85 Goblin

The first jet fighters introduced near the end of World War Two had insufficient range to escort the long-range B-35 and B-36 bombers then on the drawing boards, it was doubtful they could escort B-17s. As one possible solution to this problem, the Army Air Forces revived the parasite fighter idea of the early 1930s. They proposed that the long-range bombers carry their protective fighters with them. On 29 January 1944, the Army Air Forces invited the industry to submit conceptual proposals for parasite jet fighters.

On 3 December 1942, the USAAF sent out a Request for Proposals (RfP) for a diminutive piston-engined fighter. By January 1944, the Air Technical Service Command refined the RfP, and, in January 1945, the specifications were further revised in MX-472 to specify a jet-powered aircraft. Although several aerospace companies studied the feasibility of such aircraft, McDonnell was the only company to submit a proposal to the original 1942 request and later revised requirements. The company's Model 27 proposal was completely reworked to meet the new specifications.

The McDonnell Aircraft Corporation was the only company to respond, and proposed a small fighter aircraft to be carried partially inside a parent B-29, B-35, or B-36 heavy bomber. However, the AAF rejected this plan in January 1945, concluding that the fighter would have to be carried entirely inside the B-35 or B-36.

The XB-35 Goblin on its ground handling trolley. Intended to get airborne after being carried aloft inside the B-36, it only ever took to the skies inside a B-29, and then, not for long! (National Museum of the United States Air Force)

Since the XF-85 never flew with a B-36, there are no photos of the pair together. However, in July 1946, the XP-85 - this was before the P-pursuit designation was changed to F-fighter - mock-up inspection at McDonnell plant in St. Louis used a mock-up of a B-36 bomb bay to demonstrate how the concept would work. Note that the bomb doors bear little resemblance to reality - they were neither the old-style sliding doors nor the new snap-action doors. Unlike the RF-84Ks used in the later FICON programme, the XF-85 was designed to fit entirely inside a single bomb bay - meaning that, in theory, a B-36 could carry more than one parasite.

The initial concept for the Model 27 was for the fighter to be carried half-exposed under the B-29, B-35, or B-36. The USAAF rejected this proposal, citing increased drag and reduced range for the composite bomber-fighter configuration. On 19 March 1945, McDonnell's design team led by Herman D. Barkey submitted a revised proposal, the extensively redesigned Model 27D. The smaller aircraft had an egg-shaped fuselage, three fork-shaped vertical stabilizers, horizontal stabilizers with a significant dihedral, and 37° swept-back folding wings to allow it to fit in the confines of a bomb bay. The miniature aircraft measured 14 feet 10 inches long; the folding wings spanned 21 feet. Only a limited fuel supply of 112 US gallons was deemed necessary for the specified 30-minute combat endurance. A hook was installed along the aircraft's centre of gravity; in flight, it retracted to lie flat in the upper part of the nose. The aircraft had an empty weight just short of 4,000 pounds. So as to save weight, the fighter had no landing gear. During the testing programme, a fixed steel skid under the fuselage and spring-steel 'runners' at the underside of the wingtips were installed in case of an emergency landing. Despite the cramped quarters, the pilot was provided with a cordite ejection seat, bail-out oxygen bottle, and high-speed ribbon parachute. The aircraft had a pressurized cockpit, an ejection seat, and the eventual armament was to be four 0.50-calibre machine guns in the forward fuselage sides.

The engine was to be a 3,000 pound Westinghouse J34-WE-7 (later a -22) axial-flow turbojet with a nose intake and a straight-through exhaust. The top speed was over-optimistically estimated at 648 mph. It would be launched and recovered from a trapeze-like structure that would be extended from its parent aircraft.

With the trapeze fully extended, the engine would be air started, and the release from the mother ship was accomplished by the pilot pulling the nose back to disengage from the hook. In recovery, the aircraft would approach the mother ship from underneath and link up with the trapeze using the retractable hook in the aircraft's nose. The anticipated production shift would see a mixed B-36 fleet with both 'fighter carriers' and bombers employed on missions. There were plans that, from the 24th B-36 onward - the first B-36B - for provisions to be made to accommodate one XF-85, with a maximum of four per bomber envisioned. Up to ten per cent of the B-36s on order were to be converted to fighter carriers with three or four F-85s instead of a bomb load. Despite later events, it appears that the first few B-36Bs actually had the mounting brackets for the trapeze included in bomb bay No. 1.

Conditional upon the results of flight trials with the XP-85, the Army Air Forces had intended to order an initial batch of thirty production examples. However, before completing the first prototype, this plan was shelved in favour of a more cautious approach in which only the two experimental aircraft would be acquired. If flight tests were favourable, more could be ordered later.

No conventional landing gear was fitted since the XP-85 was to be launched and recovered from a retractable trapeze underneath its parent bomber. Instead, a retractable hook was installed on top of the fuselage in front of the cockpit. The XP-85 would approach its parent bomber from

These two pictures show the XP-85 with its wings folded vertically (above) and extended (left) with the tiny aircraft nested completely inside the bomb-bay mock-up.

The wings could be extended using the power cables that ran into the belly of the fighter. The power was also used to raise and lower the canopy. (Convair)

Right: another view of the XP-85 mock-up. Note how this version had the 'original' wings, without extensions. The XP-85 Goblin was not specifically designed for the B-36, but the huge bomber provided the right mission envelope, so that when the contract was awarded in 1945, it was the only sensible application. (Convair)

Below: The first attempted hook up with the trapeze on the EB-29 resulted in turbulence and one of the legs somehow smashing through the diminitve aircraft canopy. It resulted in a forced landing on a dry lake bed.

underneath during recovery, and the hook would engage the trapeze. Once attached, the aircraft would be pulled up into the bomb bay. If an emergency landing were necessary, the prototypes were provided with a retractable steel skid underneath the fuselage, and steel runners protected the wingtips. These would have been deleted from any production aircraft.

A mockup of the parasite fighter and the B-36 bomb bay was constructed at the McDonnell facility in St. Louis in June 1946. Since a B-36 could not be spared for the project, a Bell/Atlanta-built B-29B-65-BA, 44-84111, was modified with a special launch-and-recovery trapeze for use in the initial testing. With wry humour, the B-29 was named Monstro, after the whale that swallowed Pinocchio.

The first flight, using 46-524, was on 23 August 1948 but as the XF-85 attempted to return to the carrier aircraft the trapeze smashed through the canopy, and pilot Ed Schoch was forced to make an emergency landing using the belly skid.

A few more test flights were made with the XP-85, but the recovery operation proved to be much more complicated than expected, forcing several emergency landings using the retractable steel skid.

Due to the turbulence encountered as the XF-85 approached the trapeze, only three of the seven free flights ended in a successful hookup. The other four flights ended in skid landings on Rogers dry lakebed at Edwards AFB. The second Goblin to fly (46-0523) made its only captive flight on 19 March 1949 and its only free flight, the last flight of the programme, on 8 April 1949.

The Air Force reluctantly concluded that since the recovery operation was so difficult a job for even experienced test pilots, it would probably be far beyond the capabilities of the average squadron pilot.

In addition, it was projected that the performance of the XF-85 would likely be inferior to that of foreign interceptors that would soon

Above: A XF-85 hanging from the trapeze on the EB-29 mothership. It was this operation that was fraught with danger, especially the retrieval stage. It is worth noting that the wingtips are in the extended position. (USAF)

Left: whereas this picture shows wings in the flight position, but the tips are stowed 'vertical.' (McDonnell)

enter service. Furthermore, a budget crunch in the autumn of 1949 led to a severe shortage of funds for developmental projects. Consequently, the Air Force terminated the XF-85 programme on 24 October 1949. Both aircraft survive to this day.

FICON

The FICON (FIghter CONveyor) project was essentially a follow-up to the earlier XP-85 experiments. It was reasoned that many of the difficulties encountered with the XP-85 were due to that aircraft's unique shape, largely dictated by the requirement that it fit entirely into the bomb bay of a B-35 or B-36. If that requirement was relaxed, a more conventional fighter configuration could be used. Accordingly, a straight-wing Republic F-84E Thunderjet was chosen as the subject of the next round of experiments.

The idea was relatively simple and much like the Goblin concept. The F-84 had a probe and hook attached to the extreme nose. The B-36 would lower a large trapeze structure so that it was well clear of the bomber. The F-84 would fly up under the B-36 and insert the probe into a funnel at the end of a boom hanging from the trapeze. Once the fighter was locked into place at the nose, the boom would rise until latching pins aft of the cockpit slipped into a saddle on the fighter and locked. This would secure the F-84 at three points. Then the entire structure would be raised mostly into the bomb bays on the B-36.

On 19 January 1951, Convair was authorised to use an RB-36F 49-2707 to carry the F-84E parasite. The bomb bay of the JRB-36F was

One of the strangest Cold War weapons put to use by SAC was the FICON F-84 and B-36 combination. (USAF)

extensively modified, and the usual bomb racks were replaced by a retractable H-shaped cradle securely fastened to the rear wing spar.

Major Clarence E 'Bud' Anderson was selected to fly the F-84. However, just before the testing began in early 1952, the Air Force project engineer, Ben Hohmann, decided one more safety feature needed to be added - explosive bolts. Hohmann worried that the redundant locks on the trapeze could fail in such a way that Anderson would not be able to unhook if necessary in an emergency. It took a bit of convincing, but ultimately the new emergency safety system was installed.

F-84E, 49-2115, from the 31st Fighter Group, was used to test the basic concept by engaging its nose in a large basket on the end of the cradle. The first test was to push the nose of the F-84 into a funnel attached to the cradle to evaluate the turbulence during the rendezvous manoeuvre. The first attempt proved somewhat difficult, and as the F-84 pushed into the funnel, the fighter began bucking and porpoising. On the next flight, it was decided to go ahead and try to fight through the bucking and lock the aircraft in place. Anderson managed to link up with the boom, but the fighter turned grossly unstable, and so Anderson attempted to release the hook. Nothing happened. The emergency safety system worked - the explosive bolts fired, and the aircraft separated cleanly.

The engineers decided that the boom was not rigid enough, so the solution was to redesign the boom and trapeze. The boom was shortened by one hundred inches, and a snubber and self-centring device was installed to keep the boom from tilting. In addition, the hook on the F-84 was moved from the nose to a location on top of the fuselage just ahead of the cockpit. It would mean the fighter would have to fly closer to the bomber, but hopefully, the entire structure would be more rigid.

The first test of the revised system seemed to work well. The F-84 successfully engaged the trapeze without any unexpected problems. But as the trapeze operator in the B-36 began to raise the F-84 into the bomb bay, Anderson heard a loud bang and the F-84 lurched hard to the right. One of the two-inch diameter aft locking pins had sheared. Again, Anderson executed an emergency release. The entire incident had taken 3/24ths of a second from the initial bang to the fighter falling away free. Unfortunately, the F-84 was falling at less than its stall speed, and Anderson had shut down the engine after he was solidly connected to the trapeze. Fortunately, even with only 10,000 feet of altitude to play with, Anderson managed to get the engine restarted and made a safe landing at Carswell.

Anderson reported that the docking procedure was too tricky and thought the entire programme should be cancelled. In response, several other fighter pilots were brought in for further tests - all agreed it was difficult but could be made workable if the mating technique was simplified. Convair responded by devising a better method for making initial contact. Finally, after a dozen or so flights with the revised hardware, everybody agreed the concept could be made to work.

There was less emphasis on using the FICON concept for fighter escorts by this time, but a new need had developed. Soviet air defences were making it increasingly difficult for large strategic reconnaissance aircraft to penetrate Soviet airspace. The Air Force was not as worried about bomber formations penetrating since the two nations would be at war by that time, and fleets of bombers could assist in protecting each other. However, reconnaissance aircraft penetrated one at a time, hopefully without being detected. The FICON concept offered a way to transport a relatively small reconnaissance aircraft near the Soviet border to be released, make its reconnaissance run, and return to the waiting carrier aircraft. Given the 10,000-mile range of a B-36 and the 2,000-mile range of a fighter-reconnaissance aircraft, the system would have an effective range of almost 12,000 miles. The new Republic RF-84F Thunderflash was selected since it could also carry a small atomic weapon if the need ever arose.

In 1953, the first swept-wing YF-84F, 49-2430, was modified much the same way as the F-84E except that its horizontal stabiliser, relocated in the swept-wing version, was sharply modified canted downwards to clear the bottom of the B-36 during launch and recovery. Early tests revealed an unacceptable amount of flutter around the empennage of the F-84 when it was stowed. Changing the contours of what remained of the B-36 bomb bay doors cured the problem.

The project was revealed to the public in August 1953, and the aircraft performed at the National Aircraft Show in Dayton, Ohio, over the Labor Day weekend. For three days, the JRB-36F and YF-84F flew demonstrations where the F-84 was launched from the carrier at an altitude of several thousand feet. Ray Fitzgerald was at the controls of the B-36 and Major C E Good was at the controls of the F-84. There was no lack of B-36 participation in the air show. In addition to the FICON aircraft, two B-36s landed at the show after a thirty-three-hour nonstop flight from Japan. Two other bombers landed after a flight from England, although the jet stream had forced these to land twice en route to refuel. The FICON concept would also be demonstrated to the public at Eglin and at Carswell in the next several months.

In January 1954, Convair announced that the Air Force had awarded a contract to modify ten RB-36Ds and twenty-five RF-84Fs - 52-7254 through to 7278.

The B-36s were scheduled to be modified to the Featherweight III configuration, receive the ECM Phase II modifications and go through SAM SAC maintenance at the same time. This was far below the number of aircraft SAC originally had in mind: thirty RB-36s and seventy-five RF-84s. Convair did not tool up to make large numbers of parts given the small number of aircraft being modified, and each GRB-36 was essentially modified using hand-built assemblies. The B-36 modifications would be performed concurrently with SAM-SAC maintenance, although the bombers would be out of service a little longer than normal due to the substantial changes required. The modified aircraft were redesignated GRB-36D-III and RF-84K, respectively. The first GRB-36D-III, 49-2696, carrier made its initial flight on 28 July 1954, piloted by Ray Fitzgerald, with Fred B. Petty as copilot. At this point, the aircraft had been equipped with the trapeze but had been otherwise unmodified. Initial testing was to be complete by 22 September 1954, but an RF-84K was not available until 17 December, causing considerable delays in the programme. Perhaps it was just as well; in the interim, the main trapeze jack failed during ground tests and needed to be redesigned. This slipped the beginning of production flight tests until 1 April 1955, which proceeded smoothly. Despite this, the first GRB-36D was delivered to the Air Force in February 1955, six months ahead of the first parasite RF-84K.

As a concept, FICON operations were simple. If desired, carriers and parasites could fly out of different bases, and the parasite could be picked up in midair en route to the target area. Alternatively, the pair could be mated on the ground before takeoff.

Convair designed a particular set of loading ramps that could elevate the back end of the B-36 to allow the parasite to be loaded on the ground. Then, in a more permanent solution, a special loading pit was constructed at Fairchild AFB at the cost of $55,000 - the fighter was towed into the pit, and the B-36 was positioned over it so that the fighter could be lifted into position.

In a typical mission, the RF-84K was ferried about 2,800 miles and released at an altitude of 25,000 feet. After completion of the mission, the RF-84K would be recovered by the GRB-36D and returned to base. The idea was that the RF-84K would be released about 800-1,000 miles from the target and within a relatively safe area. The pilot of the RF-84K would continue to the target, obtain the high- or low-level photographs, then return to the waiting carrier aircraft.

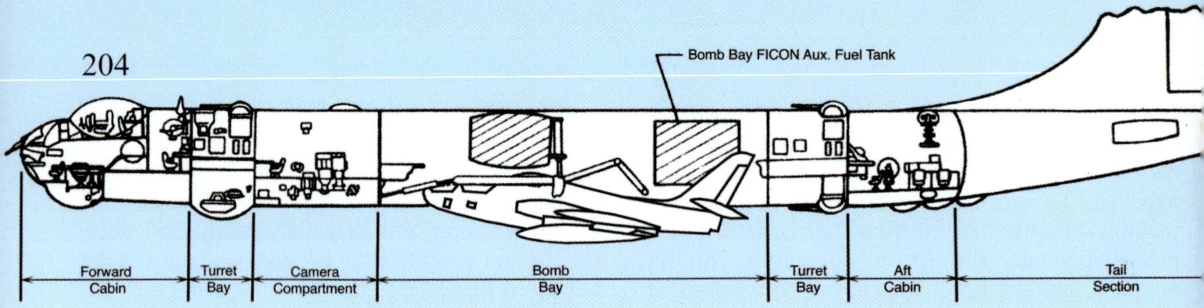

The general arrangement of the GRB-36 mothership retained the original areas of the bomb-bay with the addition of fuel tanks for the fighter. (Convair, via author's collection)

On a typical FICON mission, the B-36 would take off from Fairchild AFB, Spokane, Washington, with its little RF-84 rider leaving its base at Moses Lake, less than 100 miles to the west. The two aircraft would rendezvous and the RF-84K would be hoisted inside the B-36 for the long haul to the photo site.

Once secured aboard the B-36, the pilot of the RF-84K could enter the bomber via a catwalk. Hours later, he would climb back into the cockpit of his F-84 and be launched for the mission.

The GRB-36Ds were modified with plug-and-clearance doors instead of bomb bay doors. The clearance doors fitted tightly around the parasite during flight, while the plug doors filled the hole that remained when the RF-84K was not being carried. The doors consisted of an aluminium honeycomb core, internal extruded tubing, and external aluminium skins to form a sandwich panel assembly. The lower cradle assemblies that formed the bottom of bulkheads seven and eight were removed to make way for the RF-84K to be hoisted into the bomb bays. The ECM compartment in what should have been bomb bay No. 4 was removed, and the electronics and radomes moved into the aft fuselage the same as other RB-36s. The lower section of bulkhead nine was strengthened to accommodate the attachment of the aft end of plug-and-clearance doors.

The boom and trapeze - consisting of an upper drag strut, lower drag strut, drag strut positioning jack, main jack and yoke, snubber jack, forward and aft latch assemblies, boom assembly, probe receiver and shaft, and a boom-positioning cylinder - were installed to catch and release the RF-84K. The hydraulic parts - mainly the jacks and cylinders - were off-the-shelf commercial items purchased from outside vendors. The rest of the assemblies were manufactured by Convair in Fort Worth. The boom was considered the critical piece and consisted of two extruded aluminium sections welded together. Bulkheads six and eight were strengthened to support the trapeze assembly, while fittings for the main jack were installed on the rear wing spar. The front wing spar was modified with fittings for the forward latch assembly. Two independent hydraulic systems were installed for trapeze operation and door actuation.

A trapeze operator's station was installed facing aft on bulkhead six in the camera compartment. This involved the relocation of the lower bunk and safety straps, strengthening bulkhead six for trapeze snubber jack fittings, relocating the bomb bay light switch, mounting lights for trapeze operation, installing the trapeze

The RF-84F is seen fully retracted into the 'shoe' containing the upper part of the parasite's upper fuselage with the cockpit that could be entered and exited in flight. (USAF)

A trio of images showing the hook-up of a SAC GRB-36 with RF-84K - clearly from the markings and serials they are two different events, but they do show how the process occurred. (USAF)

operator's window in bulkhead six, and the installation of the control panel and seat. The access door in bulkhead six was made larger to allow a fully-suited RF-84K pilot to enter the camera compartment.

Special night and rendezvous lighting was installed on the horizontal stabilisers and under the fuselage, and an APX-29A IFF/rendezvous set was installed. The bomb bay was equipped with a catwalk, safety wires, and handholds so that the RF-84K pilot could ingress/egress during flight. Since the B-36 did not usually carry jet fuel as its own jet engines were modified to run on aviation gas, a 1,140-gallon fuel tank filled with JP-4 was carried offset to the left side to clear the RF-84 K's tail in bomb bay No. 4 so that the RF-84K could be refuelled while mated. This tank was constructed of a riveted sheet metal structure with welded and riveted skins. Access doors were provided so that the rubber fuel bladder inside could be inspected. The GRB-36D could also supply the parasite with electrical power, preheat air, and pressurisation air during flight.

The operational Air Force crews began training at Convair in late 1955 when thirteen pilots from

Above: With it's main landing gear jacked up to allow the RF-84F to be positioned, 49-2696 shows how the fighter is located towards the restrain and deploy mechanism.

The image below shows the considerable remodelling of the bomb bay area to make it all practicable.
(Both Lockheed Martin)

Fairchild AFB arrived. After initial daylight training at Convair, the pilots returned to Fairchild, where more extensive training, including night and high-altitude operations, continued. The GRB-36D carriers saw limited service with the 99th Strategic Reconnaissance Wing (SRW) based at Fairchild AFB, operating with RF-84Ks from the 91st Strategic Reconnaissance Squadron of the 71st SRW initially based at Great Falls AFB, Montana, then moved to Larson AFB, Washington that later became Boeing's Moses Lake facility.

In at least one case, the GRB-36D proved to be an adequate emergency landing field. On 12 December 1955, an RF-84K piloted by Captain F P Robbinson was practising night operations when his hydraulic system began to fail. The pilot suspected he did not have sufficient time to return to base but radioed a GRB-36D that was nearby and explained the situation. Major Jack R. Packwood, the pilot of the bomber, arranged to rendezvous with the fighter and a hookup was made without incident. The mated pair returned to Fairchild AFB without further incident. The Air Force quoted Captain Robbinson: 'The GRB-36 was the best emergency alternate I ever heard of. If it hadn't been there, it's a cinch I would have had to bail out.' The same bomber crew had made nineteen other hookups and drops earlier in the day during routine practice. The bomber belonged to the 348th B5 of the 99th BW.

A story that went around Washington State for a while that told of a junior duty officer at Larson AFB in Moses Lake who did not know the nature of the then-secret FICON flights. His consternation was understandable when, early one morning, the pilot of an RF-84K requested clearance for a sixteen-hour mission with no stops or refuellings listed. The Washingtonians say that only by waking his commanding officer was the FICON pilot able to get his seemingly impossible flight cleared!

Other stories have circulated about new operations personnel at Larson being confused by RF-84K pilots that filed forty-eight-hour long flight plans with no stopovers listed.

Few details have been released concerning the missions flown by the FICONs, but rumours have persisted over the years that the RF-84Ks made several overflights of the north-eastern Soviet Union on reconnaissance missions before the Lockheed U-2 became available. No available documentation supports these rumours, but not a great deal has been released about the operations of the 99th SRW during that time period. Once the U-2 had proven its ability, the FICONs were quickly phased out of service.

TIP TOW and Tom-Tom

The XP-85 and FICON were not the only bizarre experiments performed during the late 1940s and early 1950s to evaluate enhancing the range of jet fighters by having them carried into the combat zone by bombers or other large aircraft.

Perhaps the most unusual of these range-

The alternative to jacking up the main landing gear to allow the RF-84F to be positioned. A pit was dug to allow the RF-84F to be rolled underneath. This is a particularly good image of the restrain and deploy mechanism. (Lockheed Martin)

extension experiments were Projects TIP TOW and Tom-Tom, where jet fighters were attached to the wingtips of B-29s and B-36s. I covered the B-29 experiments in my book B-29 Superfortress: Giant bomber of World War Two and Korea, Pen & Sword 2012. The concept was first put forward by Dr Richard Vogt, a German scientist who came to America after World War Two, recruited by the US Air Force under Operation Paperclip, a secret US intelligence programme in which more than 1,600 German scientists, engineers, and technicians were taken from former Nazi Germany to the US for government employment between 1945 and 1959.

Vogt worked as a civilian employee for the Research Laboratory of the US Air Force in Dayton, Ohio from the beginning of 1947 to 1954. He intended to use the idea to increase the range of an aircraft by attaching two 'free floating' panels to carry extra fuel. This could be done without unnecessary structural weight penalties if the extensions were free to articulate and were self-supported by their own aerodynamic lift. In addition, the panels would effectively increase the aspect ratio of the overall wing, providing a significant reduction in wing drag. The theory suggested the extra fuel was being carried 'for

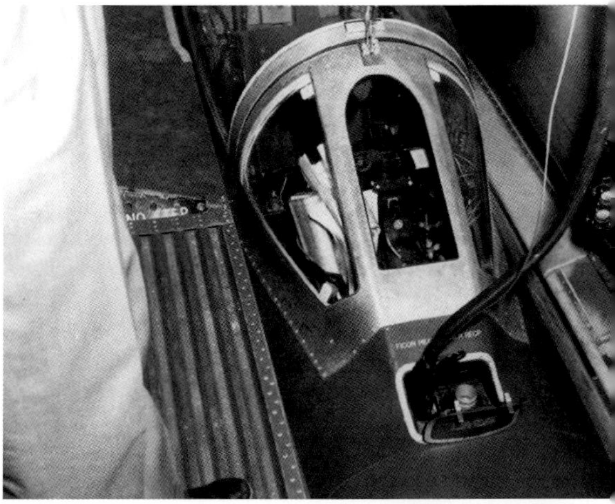

Two more views of the GRB-36/RF-84K combination, showing left, the cockpit area of the parasite fighter enclosed within the bomb-bay.

Below: 52-7269 on the beam on 692 in the pit at Fairchild AFB. (USAF)

free' by the more efficient wing, and the range of the aircraft was increased by the extra fuel.

Other uses for this concept became apparent. However, the one that sparked the most interest was for a bomber to carry two escort fighters, one on each wingtip. The Germans had experimented with the concept during late 1944 and early 1945.

During 1949, initial US experiments had successfully used a Douglas C-47A and Culver PQ-14B trainer. These tests involved a coupling device which was a single-joint attachment that permitted three degrees of freedom for the PQ-14. A ring was placed on a boom attached to the right wingtip of the C-47. Only local structural

The trapeze configuration for carrying an RF-84F seen here in the five positions, along with an explanation of 'what went where;. (Convair, via author's collection)

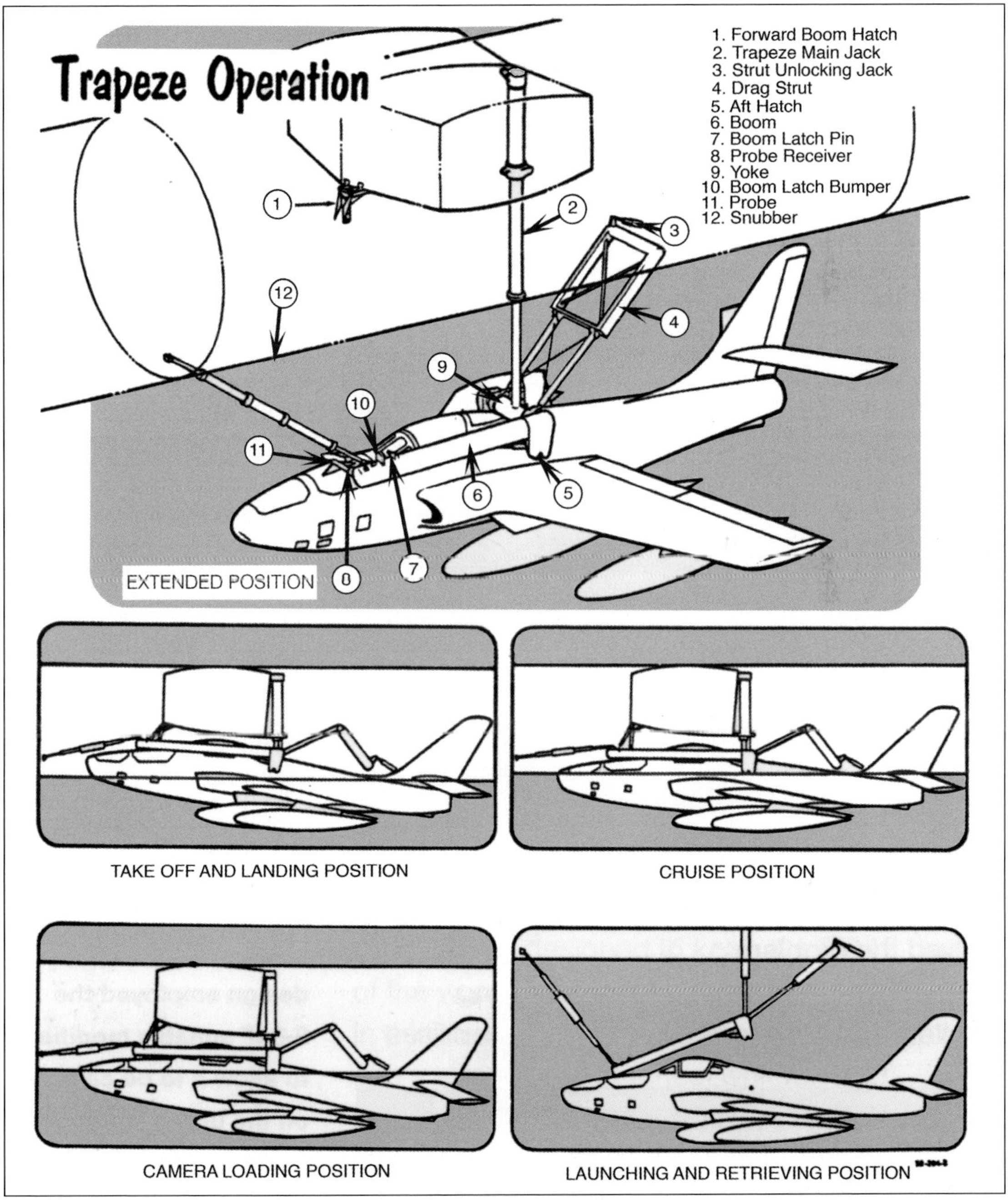

Ten RB-36Ds were converted to GRB-36D-111 FICON operational carriers in the mid-1950s. Here, GRB-36D-111 49-2694 has an RF-84 slung underneath. The GRB-36D-111 was assigned to the 99th Strategic Reconnaissance Wing at Fairchild Air Force Base. (USAF)

reinforcement was required since its lift would support the PQ-14. A lance was mounted on the left wingtip of the PQ-14, and by facing the lance rearward, no locking mechanism was required since drag would keep the aircraft in place. The PQ-14 would position itself slightly ahead of the C-47 and essentially reverse the lance into the ring. To uncouple, the PQ-14 would accelerate away. The first attempt at coupling was made on 19 August 1949 over Wright Field, Ohio. Wingtip vortex interference was encountered, forcing the engineers to re-evaluate the concept and moving the ring further away from the C-475 wingtip. Finally, on 7 October 1949, a successful coupling was made with Major C.E. 'Bud' Anderson at the controls of the PQ-14B.

At the same time as the C-47/PQ-14 experiments, a full-scale programme was initiated using a B-29 to tow two straight-wing F-84 fighters. Republic Aviation Corp was awarded a contract to design, build, and evaluate the combination under Project TIP TOW. Two F-84D-1-REs, 48-641 and 48-661, were modified for the initial TIP TOW tests under the designation EF-84D. The wingtips of the EF-84Ds were modified to be attached to flexible mounts fitted to the wingtips of a specially modified EB-29A, 44-62093. This idea proved to be highly dangerous, although several successful link-ups were made. Tragically, midway through the planned test series, the entire three-plane EF-84D/EB-29A/EF-84D array crashed as a unit on 24 April 1953, killing everybody on all three aircraft. TIP TOW was immediately cancelled. The cause was

Project TIP TOW used a pair of EF-84Ds, 48-611 and 48-661, and EB-29A 44-62093 to validate the concept of free-floating panels attached to the wing tips. Tragically, the entire TIP TOW formation would be lost, effectively ending the programme. (USAF)

Tom-Tom test aircraft JRB-361-CF 49-2707 had orange and blue trim painted on the nose, and wing tip pods. The aircraft was also fitted with a test boom on the extreme nose. (Lockheed Martin)

subsequently traced to one of the EF-84Ds going out of control during the link-up and flipping over onto the wing of the B-29.

Around the same time a project was undertaken with a pair of RF-84F-5-REs, 51-1848 and 51-1849, attached to wingtip hook-up assemblies on the JRB-36F, 49-2707 - the initial FICON testbed. The B-36 was formally assigned to the Tom-Tom project on 8 May 1954. An interesting aside, here, is that according to sources, the Tom-Tom codename was derived from the first names of two men - Major General Tom Gerrity and Convair contract manager Tom Sullivan - which is supposedly why it is not written in all capital letters.

The B-36 system included provisions to launch and retrieve the fighters in flight and to provide fuel, pressurization, and heating air to the parasites while coupled. In addition, the wing structure of the B-36 and F-84s were substantially strengthened to tolerate the expected stress of coupled flight. The Thieblot Engineering Company accomplished the design of the Tom-Tom mechanisms under subcontract to Convair. A fixed mockup of the coupling mechanism was attached to the wing of the JRB-36F, and one RF-84F and seven hours of proximity flight tests were completed on 30 September 1954. Each of the F-

Early Tom-Tom flight tests were made with simplified mock-ups of the attachment hardware. Neither of these installations was capable of actual operation, but they were sufficient to allow pilots to attempt the docking manoeuvre to evaluate wingtip turbulence and other phenomena. The F-84 installation was slightly inboard from the wingtip, which would eventually be modified to have a variety of electrical and fluid connectors. (Lockheed Martin)

84s was equipped with an articulating jaw that was designed to firmly clamp onto a retractable member on the wingtip of the B-36. Once a solid firm attachment was made, the B-36 would retract the member into a streamlined fairing where fluid, electrical and air connections would be made to allow the F-84 to shut down its engine.

The B-36 system included provisions to launch and retrieve the fighters in flight and to provide fuel, pressurisation, and heating air to the parasites while coupled. In addition, the wing structure of both the B-36 and F-84s were strengthened to tolerate the expected stresses of coupled flight. The Thieblot Engineering Company accomplished the design of the Tom-Tom mechanisms under subcontract to Convair. A fixed mockup of the coupling mechanism was attached to the wing of the JRB-36F, and one RF-84F and seven hours of proximity flight tests were completed on 30 September 1954. Each of the F-84s was equipped with an articulating jaw that was designed to firmly clamp onto a retractable member on the wingtip of the B-36. Once a solid firm attachment was made, the B-36 would retract the member into a streamlined fairing where fluid, electrical and air connections would be made to allow the F-84 to shut down its engine.

After the TIP TOW crash, tests continued for a few months with the RF-84F/JRB-36F/RF-84F array. Only a few hookup attempts were made, and wingtip vortices and turbulence made this operation a very dangerous affair. The first hookup - using only the left-hand fighter - was made on 2 November 1955. In what became the final Tom

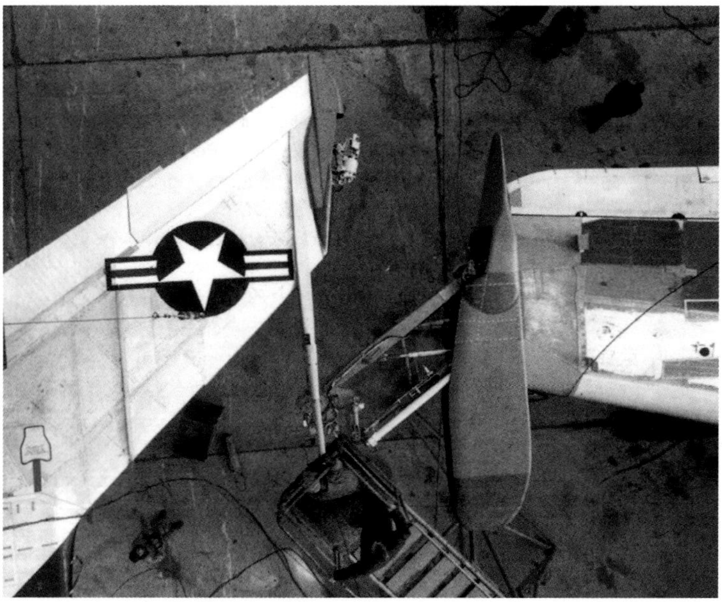

Three views of the flight hardware. The top view shows the claws on the F-84 grabbed a hold of the retractable reciever on the B-36.

The B-36 receiver then retracted until the F-84 mated with a series of electrical, pneumatic and fluid connections inside the B-36 faring. The F-84 would then shut down its engine and be supplied with services from the B-36, including the possibility of being re-fuelled.

Initial trials were conducted on a test rig at Fort Worth, with the F-84 suspended on a rig and slowly moved into position as if in flight - shown here on the right. (Lockheed Martin)

Tom flight, on 26 September 1956, Beryl Erickson found the F-84 he was piloting oscillating violently up and down while attached to the B-36 wingtip. Fortunately, part of the attachment broke and the F-84 fell away from the bomber before any serious damage was done. Since experiments with midair refuelling techniques seemed to offer greater promise for increased fighter ranges with far less risk to the lives of aircrews, the Tom-Tom experiments were cancelled.

There were other parasite concepts that made use of the basic B-36 airframe. In October 1946, the Air Force began the Generalised Bomber (GEBO) study, ultimately studying some 10,000 different bomber configurations. Convair was heavily involved in these studies and released several reports describing aircraft based, at least partially, on the B-36. For example, in a 1950

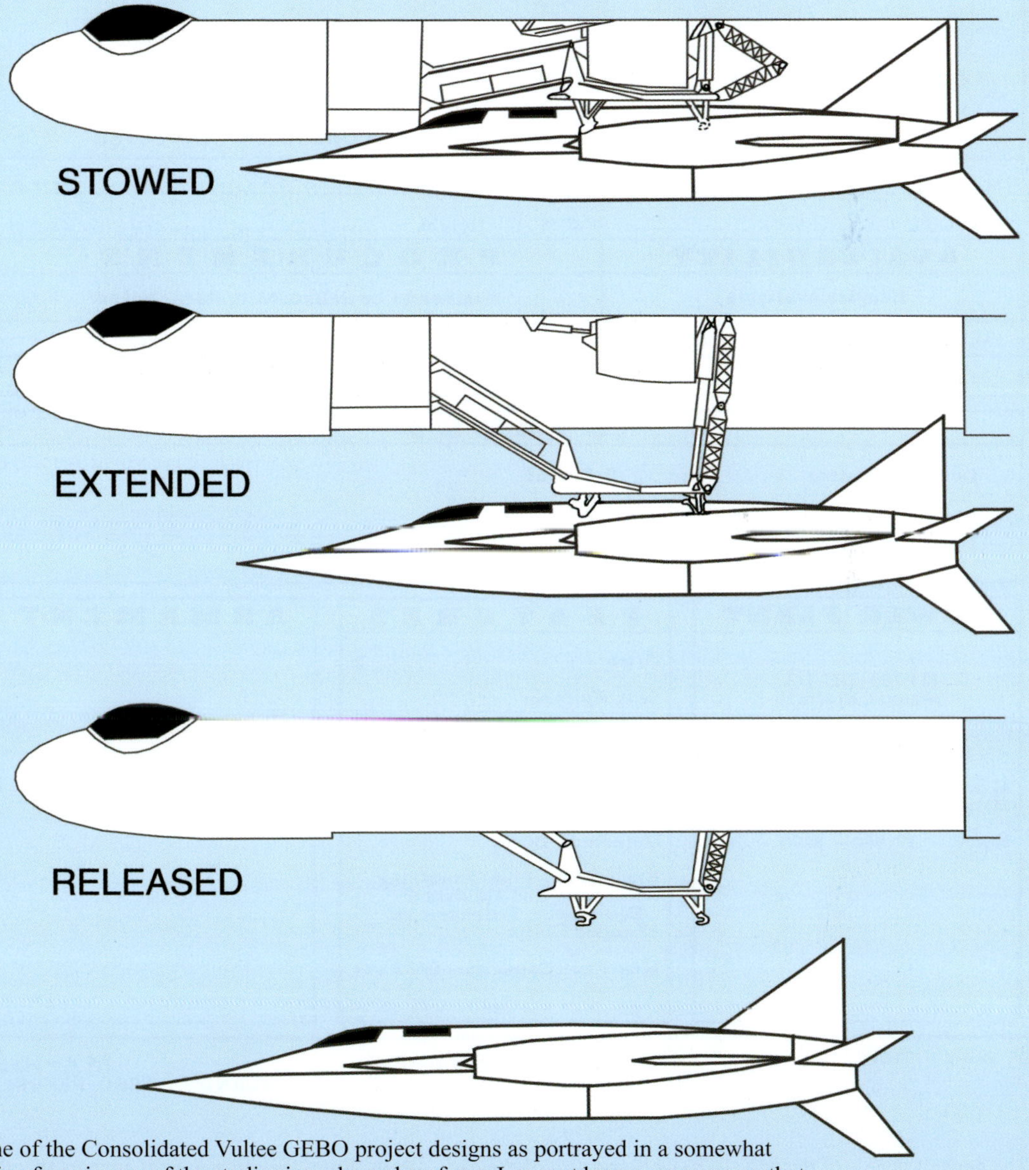

One of the Consolidated Vultee GEBO project designs as portrayed in a somewhat naive form in one of the studies in a cleaned up form. I am not by any means sure that the lower fin of the parasite would have cleared the runway!

(VERSION 1) ~~S-E-C-R-E-T~~ PRELIMINARY

Characteristics Summary

BOMBER. . .LAND BASED REFUEL. . .MX-1626

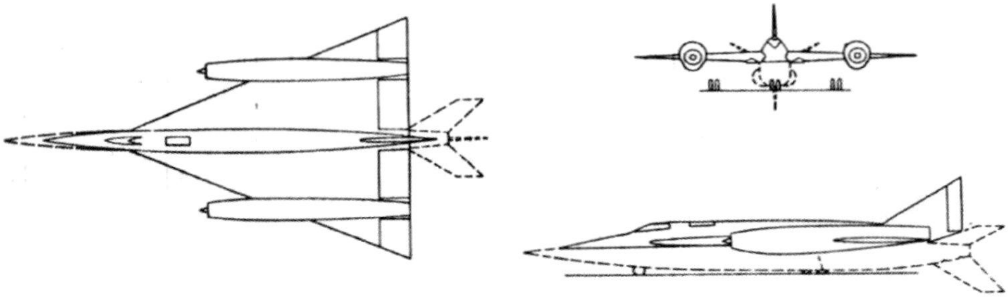

CONSOLIDATED-VULTEE

Wing area	1200 sq ft	Length	81.1 ft
Span	47.3 ft	Height	22.4 ft

AVAILABILITY			PROCUREMENT			
Number available			Number to be delivered in fiscal years			
ACTIVE	RESERVE	TOTAL				

STATUS

1. Design initiated: . . . . 17 Feb 51

POWER PLANT

(3) J53-GE-( )
General Electric

S.L.S.	LB - RPM - MIN
Max: / Mil:	Not available
Nor:	17,560 - 6000 - Cont

FEATURES

Crew: 2

Seat Ejection

Bombing-Navigation Radar

Rendezvous Radar

AFC Equipment

Defensive ECM

Expendable Pod Containing Warhead and Guidance Equipment; Released as Guided Bomb

Max Fuel Capacity: 9532 gal

ARMAMENT

NONE

18 JULY 1951 ~~S-E-C-R-E-T~~ MX-1626 (LAND BASED-REFUELED)

The general details of the MX-1626 GeBo project of the early 1950s. From the three-view it appears that the dorsal fin of the 'weapons pod' was somehow retractable. (Lockheed Martin)

GEBO II report, a small aircraft that looked much like an XP-92 sitting on the top of a B-58 Weapons pod was carried partially submerged inside the bomb bay of a B-36. The two-man 'return component' had a turbojet engine and sufficient resources to return after attacking the target. The jettisonable pod contained three more engines, a 10,000-pound weapons load, and most of the offensive avionics. The parasite had a launch weight of 100,000 pounds and a landing weight of 17,500 pounds. It was to be capable of Mach 1.6 at 48,500 feet. The B-36 would carry the parasite for the first 2,000 miles, then return to base after launch. As with many GEBO concepts, this one quietly faded into oblivion with no hardware development being initiated.

Another of the GEBO studies expanded on the concept that gave birth to TIP TOW and Tom-Tom. Three B-36s would link up in mid-air, wingtip to wingtip. The increase in wing aspect ratio was intended to significantly increase the range of the linked trio, each of which would be equipped with a parasite bomber similar to that described above. There were several other variations on these general themes.

Many ideas came from the GEBO II study. Still, while some military officials were keenly interested in the future use of supersonic bombers, others held doubts about the propulsion systems and materials science required for supersonic operations, as well as the much higher fuel consumption relative to subsonic counterparts.

Despite the scepticism, multiple contractors submitted bids for GEBO II, which was viewed as a significant step towards a development contract. These included Boeing, Convair, Curtiss, Douglas, Martin and North American Aviation. The majority of submissions were relatively straightforward, unambitious, and expensive. Convair, which had built the XF-92A and other delta-wing fighters, evaluated swept and semi-delta configurations, then settled on the delta wing, which offered good internal volume for support systems and fuel. It also provided low wing loading for the airframe size, permitting supersonic flight at 50,000 to 70,000 feet in the mid-stratosphere. Most of the configurations studied mated the delta wing to a relatively slender fuselage housing a crew of two and powered by a pair of jet engines.

The Convair proposal, coded FZP-110, was a radical two-place delta wing bomber powered by three General Electric J53 turbojet engines. The performance estimates included a 1,000 mph speed and a 3,000-mile range. A vital feature of the design was to store consumables, both weaponry and most of the fuel, within a sizeable external pod, which enabled a smaller fuselage. In January 1951, Convair submitted the FZP-110 proposal, which was received later than other competing bids. In December 1951, a revised FZP-016 proposal was presented, which deleted the third engine on the tail, increased the remaining two engines' thrust, and added a third crew member to operate defensive systems.

The Air Force chose Boeing's MX-1712 and Convair MX-1626 design studies for a Phase 1 study. During this period, Convair took advantage of recent developments by General Electric and replaced the two large J53 engines with four smaller J79s optimised for supersonic flight. The recently formulated area rule was also applied to the design, resulting in aerodynamic re-profiling and an even more slender fuselage. Having been refined, Convair redesignated their renewed submission MX-1964.

In August 1952, Convair's design was judged

B-36F 49-2677 is photographed en route from Convair Forth Worth to Wright-Patterson Air Force Base in Ohio on 12 March 1957 with the static test example of the B-58 Hustler slung underneath. The landing gear was kept down for the entire flight. (Lockheed Martin)

superior. Boeing's submission was viewed as being equally good, but their separate contract to produce the Boeing B-52 Stratofortress had undoubtedly influenced this competition. In December 1952, Convair was chosen to meet the new SAB-51 (Supersonic Aircraft Bomber) and SAR-51 (Supersonic Aircraft Reconnaissance) standards, the first General Operational Requirements (GOR) for supersonic bombers. In February 1953, the Air Force issued a contract for

Three views of the B-36F/B-58 static test specimen after its arrival at Wright-Patterson Air Force Base. The 'bumps' on the static example above are the tie-points for the stress cables that will eventually tear the structure apart during the test to destruction. The picture also shows the anti-sway bars strengthening the load by bolting directly to the B-36's main spar.

Left: Visual proof that the inboard propellers were removed to provide clearance for the load.

Below: the arrival at Wright-Patterson drew crowds of interested spectators. (All USAF)

Published every other Wednesday by Convair, a Division of General Dynamics Corporation, for the benefit of Convair people everywhere.

Convairiety

Vol. 10, No. 6 Wednesday, March 20, 1957

Fort Worth and Daingerfield EDITION
Fort Worth news office: ext. 5290; Daingerfield news office: ext. 424

SAN DIEGO, POMONA AND ANTELOPE VALLEY, CALIFORNIA — DAINGERFIELD AND FORT WORTH, TEXAS

WINNER—W. E. Mitchell, center, holds plaque just presented him by Joseph T. McNarney, right, president of Convair. August C. Esenwein, Convair Fort Worth division manager, looks on. Scene was at March 9 Management Club meeting where Mitchell, Dept. 35, won "President's Award" for 1956 cost cutting efforts.

Salk Vaccine Shots Offered To Convair FW

Salk vaccine for protection against polio will be offered to all employees at Convair Fort Worth subject to availability of vaccine supplies, Division Manager August C. Esenwein announced today.

Final plans for the shots—and the dates they will be given—depend upon supplies in the quantities required. Further details will be announced in next issue of Convairiety, April 3. The shots will be given on company time in the plant under supervision of Dr. J. K. Leverett, chief plant physician.

Charge to employees will be $1 per shot for each of the three required for protection. This is to cover cost of buying the vaccine and administering it.

"Without the vaccine, each of us is wide open to contract poliomyelitis—and perhaps to become paralyzed for life," said Esenwein.

"The shots have been proved—throughout the world — as the best protection against that danger.

"For that reason, Convair has decided to make it as easy as possible, and as economical as possible, for every Convair employee to obtain this protection."

Dr. Leverett pointed out that the Salk vaccine is given unqualified endorsement of the medical profession and the National Foundation for Infantile Paralysis.

Vaccine is given by an injection, usually in the arm. For the average person in normal health, there is no after-effect nor reac-

(Continued on Page 8)

Full Division Status Granted Astronautics

Convair this month elevated Astronautics to division status.

It becomes Convair's fifth, the others being San Diego, Pomona, Fort Worth and Daingerfield.

Convair President Joseph T. McNarney announced that J. R. Dempsey, who joined Convair in July, 1953 and became the Atlas program director in June, 1954, will continue to head Astronautics as division manager.

Division status recognizes officially what has been "almost a fact" for some time as Astronautics steadily developed its own autonomy distinct from the San Diego Division. As early as May of last year the organization was well advanced with a full scale executive team already in the saddle.

(Incidentally, much of the credit for the availability of executive level men to take over Astronautics roles has been traced to Convair's executive development program. Twenty-six top management men in a number of fields were transferred without hampering SD operations because replacements trained through the program were available to take over.)

Currently occupying quarters with the San Diego Division, Astronautics will begin moving into its new plant near Montgomery Field during the last days of June. The move will continue, probably until the end of the year when the plant will be fully occupied.

Dept. 35 Foreman Mitchell Earns President Award

Cost saving ideas on fiber glass problems won the 1957 "President's Award" for W. E. Mitchell, Dept. 35 foreman at Convair Fort Worth.

Joseph T. McNarney, president of Convair, presented Mitchell the award at the March 9 "Top Management" meeting of the Convair Fort Worth Management Club.

Mitchell is the second man to win the top award for cost cutting efforts. Luther Parvin, Dept. 7-2, won the award the two years before.

Mitchell was cited for his outstanding CIPs during 1956. He submitted 11. Three were approved and five are still under consideration.

His ideas resulted in savings of $45,513. One was concerned with a method of eliminating voids and rework of fiber glass laminates by sun curing instead of oven curing. Another was a method of triming fiber glass fin tip insulation to tolerance instead of saving them by hand. The other called for machining fiber glass parts while still in the mold has resulted in considerable savings of rejects.

Mitchell's ideas were termed "well beyond normal job expectancy."

The 47-year-old Springtown resident started at Convair nearly 15 years ago as a general helper. He has held the jobs of saw operator, bench sheet metal worker and assistant foreman as well as his current job of foreman.

Mitchell received an engraved plaque and $250 in savings bonds as winner.

Runners-up for the "President's Award" were also recognized for their outstanding efforts. Singled out were: R. C. Rudell, equipment engineer in plant engineering;

(Continued on Page 8)

B-58 Weapon System Big In Business Potential, McNarney Tells Clubmen

"The B-58 weapon system . . . probably encompasses the company's greatest potential for new business over the next 10 years."

Such was the sizing-up given by Joseph T. McNarney, president of Convair, before the Convair Fort Worth Management Club March 9.

About 1,700 Convair people were on hand, making the luncheon meeting in Will Rogers Exhibit Hall one of the biggest club affairs in recent years.

McNarney paid high praise to the Convair Fort Worth people responsible for bringing the B-58 supersonic bomber to its present state of development.

But, he added, there is "too much at stake for us to let ourselves grow fat and happy." He urged a continued "lean and hungry" outlook.

"Ahead of us (in Convair) lie three to five years of turning out the products we've developed up to this point," said McNarney. He named the B-58, the F-102 and F-106, the Terrier missile, the Model 7 Atlas program, the new 880 jet transport and model 440 twin-engine transports for the airlines.

He added that Convair's military business is changing. Twenty per cent of the nation's defense

(Continued on Page 8)

B-58 AT DAYTON—At Wright-Patterson AF Base Friday (March 15), B-58 airframe was hoisted inside hangar after hitching ride from Fort Worth on B-36.

B-58 Airframe Flies to Dayton

(Picture on page 3.)

A Convair B-58 was being readied for the "torture rack" in Dayton this week after it hitched a ride to Wright-Patterson AF Base March 12 slung beneath the belly of a B-36 bomber.

At Wright-Patterson, Convair crews are preparing the airframe of the supersonic bomber for exhausting static tests.

In these, Air Force test specialists working in a special laboratory will use the latest testing techniques to apply stresses and strains which go even beyond the limits of those the B-58 airframe is expected to encounter in flight.

By carefully measuring effects of the stresses and strains, the Air Force will obtain information on how well the B-58 airframe meets specifications.

W. H. Flickinger, static test airframe project coordinator, flew in the B-36 last week as it carried the B-58 to Dayton. He returned Thursday after Convair people at Dayton began their final tasks. Remaining in Dayton as project coordinator is W. B. Long of development department.

Jack Baldridge, pilot, Earl Guthrie, co-pilot, and other members of the crew brought the B-36 back to Fort Worth on Friday.

Applications For FW Scholarships Now 45

Applications for Convair sons scholarship awards were setting an all-time record this year at Convair Fort Worth.

With just 11 days left before deadline, 45 Convair sons had already applied. This is the largest number ever from the program, now in its third year.

Deadline for applications is March 31. Applications and transcripts must be turned in by that time to be eligible for scholarships to be awarded in May.

Tidwell Takes Over New Position As Supt. Of B-58 Pod Assembly

W. H. Tidwell holds the newly created position of superintendent of B-58 pod assembly at Convair Fort Worth this week.

W. H. Tidwell

The move is one of a number which are due to give increased emphasis throughout the division to the pod program. The torpedo-like detachable pod joins with the airframe to make up the complete B-58 weapons system.

For recent photos of the pod, see page 2. It adds "versatility" to the missions the B-58 can perform.

Tidwell formerly was a general foreman. He reports to J. E. Harwell, assistant factory manager.

Tidwell joined Convair in 1942 as a general assembler. He has been with Convair since that time except for a period of duty with the U. S. Marine Corps.

He is a native of Springtown, Texas.

Three F102As Shift To Field Operations, Flight Tests Near

(Picture on page 3)

Three F-102As in Convair Fort Worth's test-to-tactical program were in field operations this month. Flight test work was due to get under way shortly.

Shop engine runs as well as installation of equipment is being done by field operations and electronics department crews on the first three planes.

Actual acceptance test flights are due to get under way about April 1, according to E. E. Finch, modernization manager.

As part of the program, three flight department men have been checked out in the all-weather jet interceptors at Palmdale, B. A. Erickson, manager of flight, A. S. Witchell and Ray Fitzgerald.

Two other pilots are undergoing special training at Perrin AF base, F. J. Voorhies and H. T. Hargis.

Convair Fort Worth employees are modifying an undisclosed number of the jet F-102As to match those being built at Convair San Diego.

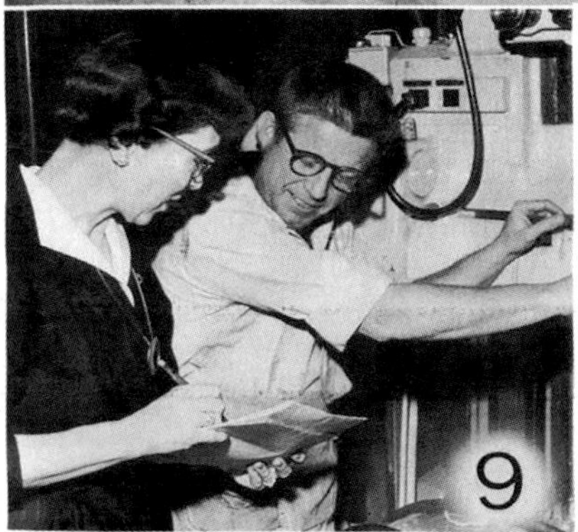

(1), (2), (3) and (4) are scenes at Fort Worth last week before B-36 took off with B-58 fuselage neatly tucked underneath. B-58 airframe was flown to Wright Patterson Air Force Base for testing. (1) includes Convair men T. Morris, B. G. Anders, J. B. Clanton, all Dept. 64, and L. P. McClain of Dept. 74. (4) shows Convair crew that flew B-36. Novel means of transportation—so far as Convairiety knows—is without precedent.

(5) Lt. Col. Frank K. "Pete" Everest, left, AF test pilot known unofficially as world's fastest human being, illustrates a point about flying to Frank Pace Jr., General Dynamics Corporation executive vice president, and Major Gen. Roger Browne, Commander 1st Air Force, during supper party following party premier of movie "The Spirit of St. Louis" in New York City.

(6) Left to right: Major Louis M. Van Der Beek, H. A. Smith, SD chief plant engineer, and Lt. Col. Joseph N. Raymond. Air Force officers are on year's assignment to Convair San Diego as part of AF Air University training program. This is first such team assigned to SD, though others in past have undergone training at Convair Fort Worth.

(7) Inspecting Lindbergh Field from vantage point of Convair SD's radio station are these representatives of Iberia, the national airline of Spain. They are pilots, flight engineers and ground crew members who have attended a two-week training course at SD and are slated to return home next week aboard the first three Iberia 440s.

(8) First F-102A to go through test-to-tactical conversion program at Fort Worth heads for flight test. It is shown on ramp undergoing electronics phase of program.

(9) Mrs. Rebecca Hall Sparling, Convair design specialist, shown here in shops at Pomona plant, last weekend received the 1957 Award of the Society of Women Engineers during the annual convention at Houston, Tex. The award was for "significant contribution to engineering," Mrs. Sparling is in materials research at Pomona and is particularly known for her work in high temperature metallurgy, gas turbine development and nondestructive testing.

Convair's design, designated B-58, on 10 December 1952.

The B-58 programme, unlike those for preceding military aircraft, became recognised as the first weapon system contract. Under this arrangement, Convair acted as the prime contractor responsible for all programme elements, not just the aircraft. As a result, Convair was required to devise or subcontract everything associated with the aircraft's operation, from the engines to training manuals, spare components, and software, over one million items. Early on, the contract was modified to build a pair of XB-58 prototypes, one static test example, eleven YB-58A pre-production aircraft, and thirty-one mission pods, including a free-fall bomb pod, a rocket-propelled controllable bomb pod, a reconnaissance pod, and an electronic reconnaissance pod. The first prototype, serial number 55-660, was rolled out on 31 August 1956, with the maiden flight occurring on 11 November 1956.

Just as with the B-36, there was a need for a static test example, and to get it from Fort Worth to Wright-Patterson Air Force Base, near Dayton, Ohio, Convair used the novel method of ferrying it partially inside the bomb-bay of B-36F, 49-2677 12 March 1957. as shown in two pages of Convairety, the staff news magazine.

The B-36 was quite heavily modified for its taxi work. The inboard fuel tanks were removed from each wing in order to allow sway braces to be bolted to the main wing spars, and certain bulkheads in the bomb bay were modified similar to the FICON carrier aircraft. In addition, the inboard propellers were removed, and the landing gear was left extended for the entire trip.

In Convairety Volume 10, Number 6 dated Wednesday 20 March 1957 it reported: 'A Convair B-58 was being readied for the "torture rack" in Dayton this week after it hitched a ride to Wright-Patterson AF Base March 12 slung beneath the belly of a B-36 bomber.

'At Wright-Patterson, Convair crews are preparing the airframe of the supersonic bomber for exhausting static tests.

'In these, Air Force test specialists working in a special laboratory will use the latest testing techniques to apply stresses and strains which go even beyond the limits of those the B-58 airframe is expected to encounter in flight.

'By carefully measuring the effects of the stresses and strains, the Air Force will obtain information on how well the B-58 airframe meets specifications.

'W. H. Flickinger, a static test airframe project coordinator, flew in the B-36 last week as it carried the B-58 to Dayton. He returned Thursday after Convair people at Dayton began their final tasks. Remaining in Dayton as a project coordinator is W. B. Long of the development department.

'Jack Baldridge, pilot, Earl Guthrie, co-pilot, and other members of the crew brought the B-36 back to Fort Worth on Friday.'

Buck Duck and Rascal - the DB-36H

The B-36 also carried or planned to carry several other winged vehicles, mainly in the form of missiles and decoys. These decoys included the Convair GAM-71 Buck Duck, which never entered production.

On 7 July 1952, the Air Materiel Command issued contract AF33(600)-21997 to Convair to integrate the B-36 with the Bell B-63 (later GAM-

The GAM-71 Buck Duck decoy was originally developed using funding from Convair, but the USAF subsequently funded the development programme. Although Buck Duck was eventually cancelled before going into production, the overall concept was resurrected as the GAM-72 Quail decoy for the B-52. The photographs show the decoy with wings folded, and in the flight position.(Both Lockheed Martin)

63) 'Parasite Pilotless Bomber,' more commonly called Rascal. The name 'Rascal' was an acronym that stood for RAdar SCAnning Link, named for the guidance system used during the missile's dive on the target. The guidance system, developed jointly by Bell Avionics, Radio Corporation of America (RCA), and Texas Instruments, was installed aboard the controlling aircraft. The GAM-63 was powered by a Bell-designed 4,000-pound liquid-fuelled rocket engine with three vertical in-line thrust chambers. The missile was thirty-one feet long with a body diameter of four feet and could carry a 3,000-pound nuclear warhead up to 110 miles at a maximum speed of Mach 2.95. A retractable radio antenna was installed in the aft fuselage of the DB-36H to provide a data link to the missile. The missile itself was carried semi-submerged in the combined bomb bay Nos. 3 and 4, hanging down about eighteen inches while being carried. The 'dished out' area of the bomb bay was equipped with a fibreglass cover that protected the inside of the bomb bay after the missile was released. An electronic guidance package was installed in bomb bay No. 1.

Otherwise, the Rascal carriers were expected to be identical to the standard Featherweight II B-36H configuration, including the use of R-4360-53 engines and J47-GE-19 turbojets. The usual crew of fifteen was expected to be carried, except that the bombardier would be responsible for launching

Right: The only permanent modifications to the DB-36s were the addition of a retractable director antenna and some minor changes to the bombardier's station to allow him to check out, launch, and guide the missile. It was believed that these changes would not adversely impact the standard bomber mission if missions were flown without the Rascal.

Below: A rascal is carried aloft by YDB-36 51-5710. The director antenna towards the tail is in the extended position. (Both Lockheed Martin).

and guiding the missile. Aircraft performance was expected to be unchanged from the standard B-36H.

The contract included thirty hours of wind tunnel tests of the missile and B-36 in the mated configuration and during missile separation. Also included was a mock-up of the forward cabin with the new missile controls and a separate mock-up of the aft Nos. 3 and 4 bomb bays. A single B-36H, 51-5710, was ordered converted into a YDB-36H prototype and the contract included provisions to modify a total of twelve B-36Hs into the 'director-bomber' configuration. The production option was exercised on 26 May 1953, and the original schedule was to deliver all eleven DB-36Hs to the Air Force by the end of 1954. However, delays in the development of the Rascal and its guidance system quickly delayed the programme by about a year. The final schedule called for two deliveries in late 1955 and eight more before 15 November 1956.

The idea behind the Rascal was to improve the kill probability of the B-36 by significantly increasing the target zone performance using the Mach 2 Rascal. This also improved the chances of the B-36 surviving the mission since it no longer had to overfly the target directly and could remain well outside the enemy defence perimeter. The Rascal equipment was designed to be easily removable from the B-36, allowing the aircraft to return to its basic bomber configuration in less than 12 hours. However, certain parts of the DB-36 modification were permanent, although they did not seriously detract from the normal bomber mission. Alterations to the bombardier's position included specialised guidance equipment that would remain with the aircraft, as would the retractable missile guidance antenna in the aft fuselage. Convair demonstrated that a fully-configured DB-36H could be converted back to its basic bomber configuration in three hours twelve minutes - well short of the 12-hour requirement.

The Rascal was loaded into the aft bomb bays and a guidance electronics package was loaded

The only located photograph - albiet poor quality- of the launch of a Rascal missile from a DB-36. (Lockheed Martin)

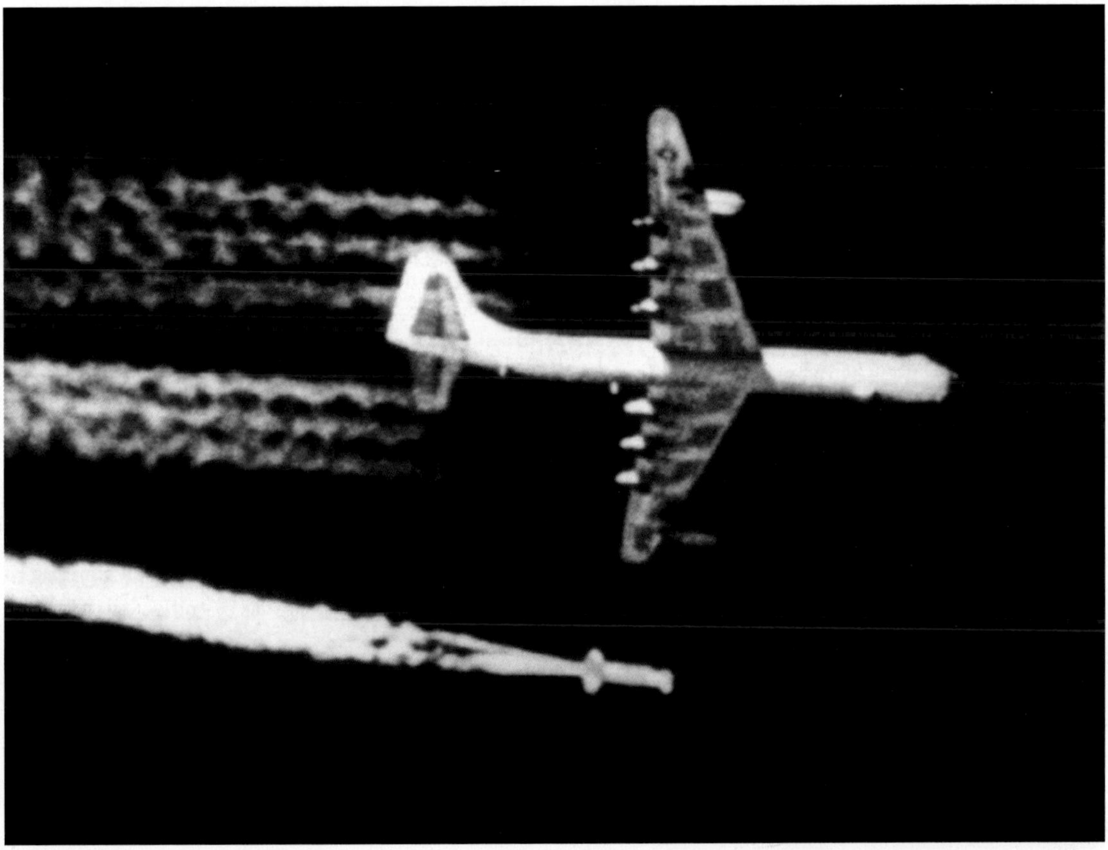

into bomb bay No. 1. In theory, bomb bay No. 2 was available for small bomb loads or perhaps to carry Buck Duck decoys, but this was never explicitly stated. The missile was dropped from the bomber approximately 100 miles from the target, and a lanyard pull ignited the rocket motors after the missile was free of the carrier aircraft. If the lanyard or its associated switch malfunctioned, a timer started the rockets a set time after release. The initial leg of Rascal flight was controlled by a self-contained inertial system that obtained reference information from the B-36 K-3A bomb/nav system prior to launch. This required some modifications to the K-3A, but none of these detracted from the primary functionality of the system. As the missile approached the target area, the bombardier in the B-36 took over the missile's guidance through the data link. The bombardier's station was equipped with a launch panel, terminal guidance equipment, relay antenna controls, and miscellaneous system controls. The guidance package installed in bomb bay No. 1 contained all of the Rascal interface equipment that did not require in-flight access.

Not so much of a little rascal!

Two views of the Rascal missile being loaded into YDB-36 51-5710 at Kirtland AFB in New Mexico. Just visible in the lower picture is the three vertically-stacked rocket nozzles, protected by their canvas covers. (Convair).

A typical mission profile involved loading the missile, taking off, cruising at an optimum altitude - probably around 25,000 feet - climbing to the 42,500-foot launch altitude, launching the missile, guiding the rocket to the target, then returning to base. After takeoff, the missile control operator was responsible for keeping current wind and navigation data loaded into the K-3A system for downloading to the Rascal.

Before the mission reached the point-of-no-return, the missile operator verified that the missile and its guidance system were functional. This included tuning the video relay receiver, altitude phasing, adjusting the terminal guidance tracking indicator, and verifying that the missile control surfaces were all functional. As the mission approached the launch point, the terminal guidance system would be checked again.

The missile was partially preprogrammed for a given flight path, and the carrier needed to approach an aim point along with a heading that connected the aim point and the target. A computer in the guidance package tracked the aircraft heading and azimuth to the target and automatically dropped the missile when the proper position was reached. Immediately after launch, the carrier aircraft initiated a rapid turn to return home while the missile operator and bombardier established a video link with the missile. Although the missile was flying based on its own inertial guidance, the B-36 operator could make minor adjustments via the data link. The missile typically would reach 50,000 feet altitude and a speed of approximately 2.5 Mach during its flight. The terminal guidance portion of the missile's flight was controlled by the operator in the B-36 via the video data link. For air-burst detonations, the missile would still be traveling at approximately 1.3 Mach at the time the warhead exploded.

The fuselage and cabin mock-ups were inspected by the Air Force on 18 November 1952, and the YDB-36H made its first flight on 3 July 1953. The Air Force conducted six flight tests to determine drag changes introduced by carrying the B-63 on the B-36. A total of twenty hours and five minutes were accumulated during the tests that ran from 31 July to 16 August 1953. The basic weight of the DB-36H was 175,917 pounds, with the B-63 adding another 18,200 pounds. During the tests, five hundred gallons of fuel were purposefully left in each inboard wing tank to ensure that centre-of-gravity limits were maintained while carrying the missile. Interestingly, the test series revealed no discernible difference in drag characteristics with or without the missile attached or the aft radome deployed. The test report noted that 'if the pilot did not know he was flying a YDB-36 he would not be able to detect any change in the handling characteristics as compared to a normal B-36F or B-36H under the same weight and c.g. conditions.'

However, the test group did find a few minor items that needed to be corrected. The primary item centred around the retractable lower stabiliser on the missile. When the rocket was installed on the ground, the stabiliser was folded ninety degrees from normal, parallel to the ground instead of perpendicular. Once the aircraft was airborne, the navigator or scanner used a hydraulic hand pump to lower the stabiliser to its flight position. If the B-36 needed to land, the procedure was reversed and the stabiliser folded since attempting to land otherwise would damage both the missile and the DB-36. The test group believed that an electrically-driven hydraulic pump operated from the navigator's station should be provided. The retractable aft radome also proved unsatisfactory, with the retraction mechanism generally refusing to work at high altitudes.

The first Rascal air-launch test occurred on 30 September 1952 from a modified Boeing DB-50D. The first unpowered Rascal drop test from the YDB-36H was on 25 August 1953, and all went well. The aircraft was then grounded while the Bell-designed guidance system was installed. This was completed on 26 February 1954, and the aircraft was redelivered to the Air Force on 22 July. On 6 July 1954, the Air Force released the B-36H 51-5706 that had been used in the Tanbo XIV experiments to the Rascal programme. A week later, this became the first aircraft to enter the Rascal production programme and was redelivered to the Air Force on 21 December. The next day it flew to Holloman AFB to participate in the Rascal test programme.

A total of fourteen F-series Rascals were available for test launches from the DB-36s, and at least two live firings occurred in the first six months of 1955. In addition, six D-series missiles were launched from the DB-50s during the same time. Only two of these launches were considered successful - five of the failures were caused by various power plant malfunctions, and a bad roll rate gyro caused one failure. It could not be determined how many of the remaining missiles were launched before the DB-36/GAM-63 programme was cancelled.

In the meantime, during 1953, the Air Force decided to modify a B-47B, 51-2186, as a Rascal carrier under the designation YDB-47B. A single Rascal was suspended from the starboard side of the fuselage below the wing - the Rascal was a large missile for the medium bomber and could not be carried semi-submerged as it was on the B-36. In addition, two B-47Es, 51-5219 and 51-5220, were earmarked for conversion to YDB-47E Rascal carriers.

SAC felt that equipping the B-47 fleet with the large and bulky externally mounted Rascal would degrade the aircraft's performance to such extent as to make the whole concept of dubious value. SAC also feared that the guidance system would never work well and was reluctant to add even more complex electronic equipment to an already electronically packed B-47. At about a million dollars per aircraft, modification costs were high, and personnel training demands were considerable. Nevertheless, the Air Force decided in June 1955 that the B-47 and not the B-36 would carry the GAM-63. All twelve of the DB-36H modification kits had been manufactured by this time, although they had only been installed on two aircraft.

A total of thirty B-47Bs would be converted to DB-47 configuration as Rascal carriers as part of the new programme. Despite a successful Rascal launch from a DB-47E in July 1955, the entire project seemed to falter. In May 1957, it was announced that only one rather than two DB-47/GAM-63 squadrons would be fielded. That still did not satisfy SAC, which felt that the Rascal programme would be outmoded by the time it achieved operational status.

Nevertheless, by the end of 1957, crews of the 321st Bomb Wing were involved in Rascal training. The Rascal turned out to be a reasonably accurate and effective weapon. Still, the concept rapidly became obsolete in the face of new developments in air-launched missiles. The Rascal programme itself was cancelled on 9 September 1958. On 18 November, AMC was

directed to dispose of the seventy-eight experimental and the fifty-eight production Rascal missiles that had been accepted. By this time, the three DB-36s had already been scrapped.

X-15 mothership?

Another concept that Convair put forward was this artwork showing the proposed carriage of the North American X-15 hypersonic research aircraft by a B-36 sometime in the 1950s. In the end, the X-15 was air-launched from an underwing pylon attached to a Boeing B-152 Stratofortress. The B-36 suggestion did have one slight advantage over the B-52 configuration however. The pilot could board from the mother aircraft and also make a last-minute exit if needed.

There was also a study by NASA for a follow-on to the X-15 that would have reached Mach 10 had it been built. This machine would also used a B-36 as a mothership launch vehicle.

Like the MX-1626, there was a 'decompression chamber' in the B-36, forward the parasite for the crew to board the machine while in fight.

Chapter Eleven

The YB-60

The new decade saw Convair sitting on the cusp of a new era - the jet age. On 25 August 1950, Convair issued a formal proposal for a swept-winged version of the B-36 with all-jet propulsion. The USAF was sufficiently interested that on 15 March 1951, it authorised Convair to convert two B-36Fs - 49-2676 and 49-2684 - as B-36Gs.

Undoubtedly the proposed B-36G was the sleekest of all the B-36 variants - a word not usually associated with describing the B-36 bomber. The swept-wing, all-jet version originated from the formal proposal by Convair to develop the new configuration. Although the aircraft ultimately was equipped with turbojets, turboprops were initially proposed.

Six turboprop engines were the powerplants of choice for the swept-wing B-36F, but it became apparent that eight jet engines of the same J57 type to be used on Boeing's XB-52 were the most promising powerplants. Previously, there had always been a question of poor fuel economy related to turbojets, but the new Pratt & Whitney J57s improved the situation considerably.

Rather than a formal agreement, a letter supplemented the current B-36 production contract. On 15 March 1951, the Air Force authorised Convair to convert two B-36Fs into prototype B-36Gs. Production aircraft numbers 151 and 165 at the Fort Worth plant became YB-36Gs.

They were both equipped with J57 jets but could still be adapted to turboprops if required. The first YB-56G was ready for flight testing in December 1951; the second was two months later. Because of the striking change in the appearance of the YB-36G and the expected greater improvement in performance over a conventional B-36, the Air Force determined that the machine should have a new bomber designation, the B-60.

The YB-60 prototype differed significantly from the B-36 by featuring swept-back wings and swept-back tail surfaces. Wingspan was two hundred and six feet, twenty-four feet less than its predecessor, but it was longer and higher than the B-36F, having a length of one hundred and seventy-one feet and a height of sixty feet five inches to the top of the rudder.

The fuselage from aft of the cabin to near the end of the tail remained the same. The nose was lengthened to accommodate more equipment and tapered to a needle-like instrument probe. With the probe, the actual length of the YB-60 was 1one hundred and seventy five feet two inches. A wider centre chord on the new wing increased the wing area to 5,239 square feet, compared to 4,772 square feet. A wing sweep of thirty-seven degrees was created by inserting a wedge-shaped structure at the extremity of the centre portion of the centre wing. It was necessary to put a cuff on the leading edge of the centre wing to continue the sweep line to the fuselage. The tail cone was modified to house a sixty-seven-foot diameter braking parachute and support a retractable tail wheel. This extra landing gear leg was needed to balance load changes and protect the tail section.

The J47 jet pods being installed on production B-36s'were not used on the YB-60. Instead, Convair had the advantage of utilising nacelles and pods designed by Boeing for its B-52 project. Like the XB-52, the J57-P-3 jet engines were installed in pairs on four pods suspended below and forward of the leading edge of the wings. Each engine produced 8,700 pounds of thrust.

Crew requirements were limited to five; pilot, co-pilot, navigator, bombardier/radar operator, and radio operator/tail gunner. All were located in the forward compartment, pressurised, heated, and ventilated. The three forward turrets were omitted initially; later, the four retractable turrets were deleted, leaving only the twin 20 mm tail guns controlled by AN/APG-32 radar. The K-3A bombing/navigation system, with Y-3A optical and radar bombing sight, allowed a single crew member to act as both radar operator and bombardier. Bomb load capacity was the same as the B-36F, a maximum of 72,000 pounds.

The weight was calculated at 153,016 pounds empty and 410,000 pounds at takeoff. Fuel capacity was 42,106 gallons; oil capacity was 1,010 gallons.

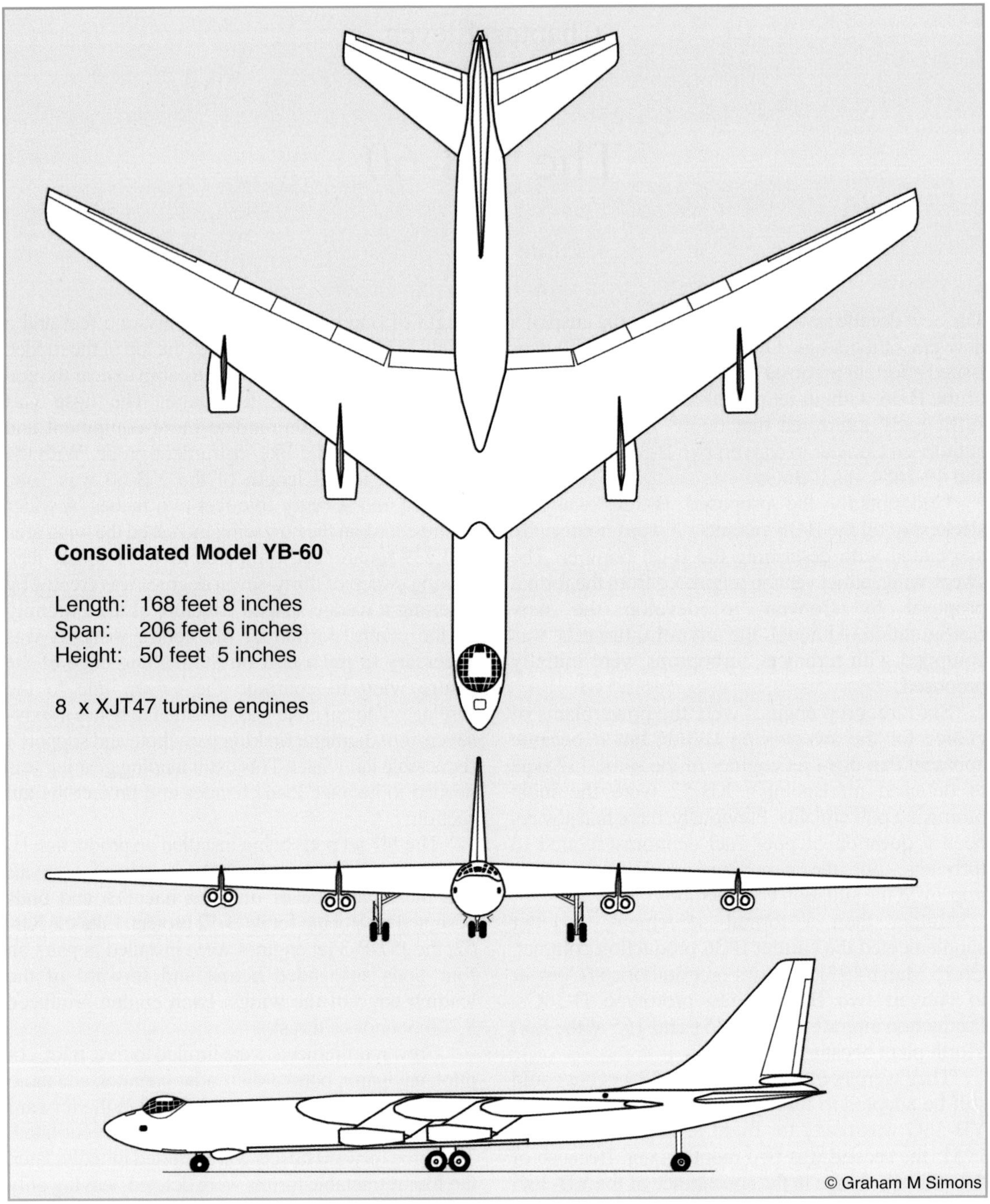

In the spring of 1951, B-36F 49-2676 was moved to the Experimental Building, where the XB-36 was built. Work started on conversion of the airframe to YB-60-1. It was completed in a record time of only eight months, ready for engine installations. The quick fabrication job was that the new jet version of the B-36 had seventy-two per cent parts commonality with the piston engine-powered B-36.

The J57-P-3 engines earmarked for the YB-60 were primarily scheduled for the B-52; consequently, shortages were expected because the J57 engine was a product of intensive effort to develop a high-thrust turbojet with low fuel consumption.

Full-scale testing of the engine prototypes was barely underway in early 1951, and there was limited production in 1952. However, the engines were still

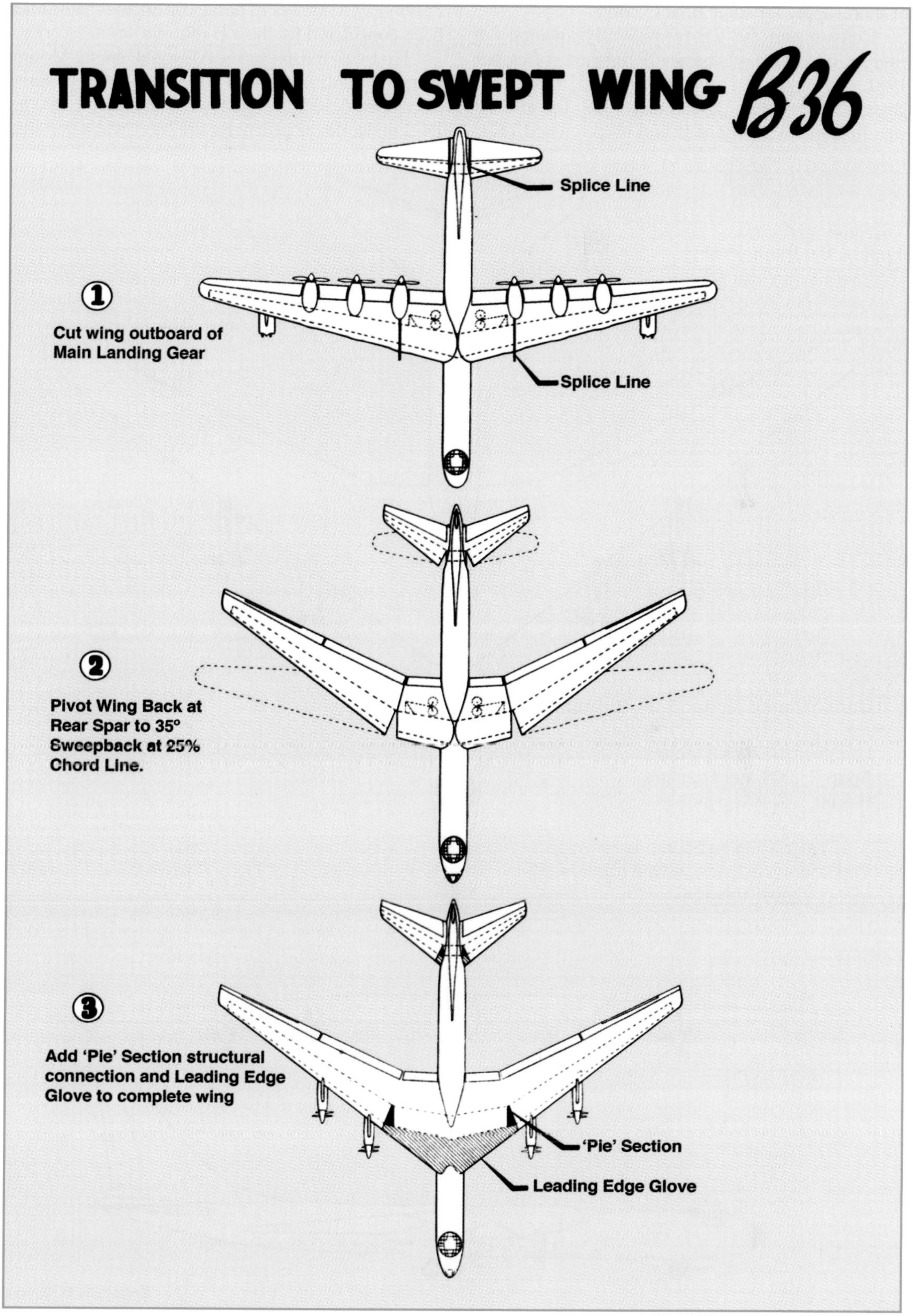
TRANSITION TO SWEPT WING B36
Splice Line
①
Cut wing outboard of
Main Landing Gear
Splice Line
②
Pivot Wing Back at
Rear Spar to 35°
Sweepback at 25%
Chord Line.
③
Add 'Pie' Section structural
connection and Leading Edge
Glove to complete wing
'Pie' Section
Leading Edge Glove

in short supply for some time to come.

Convair and the YB-60 patiently awaited the engines. The plane was basically finished in October 1951. No engines. November passed, December passed. No engines. By January 1952, the aircraft was fully ready to fly, if it had its promised J57s. Previously, a number of turboprop engines had earlier been considered for the YB-60.

First was the use of the Allison (General Motors Corp.) double turbine T40, which was to have developed 6,500 hp. The Pratt & Whitney 6,000 hp PT-2 under development for the Navy was a possible

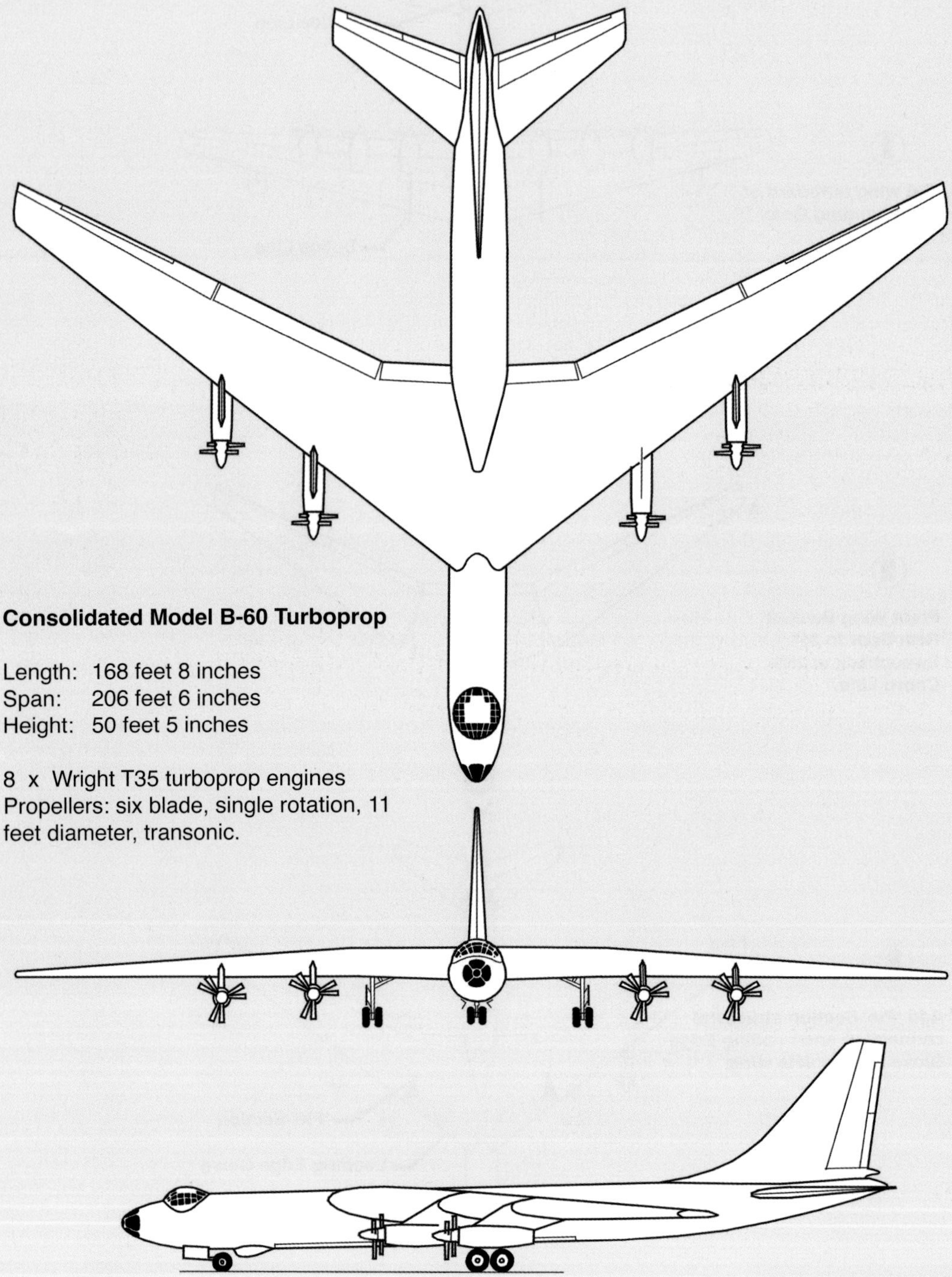

Consolidated Model B-60 Turboprop

Length: 168 feet 8 inches
Span: 206 feet 6 inches
Height: 50 feet 5 inches

8 x Wright T35 turboprop engines
Propellers: six blade, single rotation, 11 feet diameter, transonic.

Above: The first YB-60, 49-2676, is seen under construction in the hangar building at Fort Worth. This little-known photograph shows that originally the aircraft had a production-style nose, not the streamlined test nose with which it was later flown. The nose shown here was different than the 'tactical' nose fitted to the second prototype, being about four feet shorter and not equipped with the AN/APG-32 radar. The shape of the antiglare shield paint makes more sense here than it did after the test nose was fitted just before the aircraft was rolled out. The second aircraft can be seen in the background to the left, confirming that both aircraft were under construction simultaneously, not sequentially as is often reported.

Right: Just before the first YB-60 was completed, a decision was made to fit the aircraft with a more streamlined nose carrying a flight test alpha-beta boom. The demarcation line where the removable nose is attached can be seen just forward of the windscreen, where the pattern on the anti-glare shield changes.

alternative. Whether the YB-60 was to have turbojet or turboprop engines was still a question during most of 1950. Turboprop configurations included provisions for six big engines slung in single pods, three under each swept-back wing. Another plan was for a 12 jet version, placing the engines in paired pods, three under each wing. It would have been some sight on take off.

Convair considered the turboprop version its top priority. Engines under discussion by late 1950 included the Pratt & Whitney T34, developing 5,700 hp, the British Bristol coupled Proteus, generating 6,700 hp, and the Allison T40.

All these engines were in flight test status. Engine manufacturers indicated that one of the chief delays affecting the development of turboprop engines were

The forward fuselage assembly of aircraft 151 carried the name Swept Wing Slugger for a short time before being assembled into the first YB-60 prototype. (Lockheed Martin via author's collection)

difficulties encountered with high-speed propellers and engine controls.

Continued problems with adapting turboprops to the B-36, along with potential overheating eventually led Convair to re-evaluate turbojets as represented by J57s. There never would be a turboprop-powered B-36 or B-52. Some early design concepts of the Boeing machine also called for turboprops. The company's proposed Model 462, featuring six engines, and the four-engine Model 464-17, with contra-rotating propellers, both were to have 5,500 hp Wright T35s installed. It is to be remembered that jet engine technology was still in its infancy. In the post-war World War Two period, turboprops were thought to bridge the gap between the proven piston engine and the then thirsty pure jet engine. Fuel consumption had to be of utmost concern to the Air Force in order to operate any long-range intercontinental heavy bomber over great distances. Of course, refinement of air refuelling techniques would change the situation. But in 1950, only the B-36 had the necessary 10,000 mile range.

Ironically, an intercontinental heavy bomber utilising big turboprop engines was successfully developed by the mid-1950s. It wasn't built by Convair, Boeing, or any other American aircraft company. It was produced by Tupelov for the Soviet Air Force, the famous TU-95 'Bear.'

Although the YB-60 was ready to take to the air in January 1952, the eighth and last 57-P-3 engine did not arrive at Convair's Fort Worth plant until 6 April. The very same day, the YB-60 had its roll-out ceremony. The rakish swept-wing, all-jet B-36 was a reality and was placed on view before hordes of company workers, as well as thousands more military and civilians at nearby Carswell AFB. They all were looking at the largest jet aircraft in the world at that time.

Many must have wondered if this was to be the future in Texas. Construction was immediately started on the second YB-60 after moving to the vacant Experimental Building. It had been decided in August 1951 between the Air Force and Convair that the second prototype would be built as a full tactical model with government-furnished equipment.

On 18 April 1952, only twelve days after roll-out, the YB-60 flew for the first time. At the controls was 35-year-old Convair Chief Test Pilot Beryl A. Erickson. There were an additional six men in the crew, of which two, J D McEachern and W P Easley were aboard six years earlier with Erickson. on the XB36's maiden flight. With thousands of people watching, the sleek. big jet roared into the sky at 4:55 pm and landed 66 minutes afterwards, at 6:01 pm. Later, at a press and TV conference, Erickson characterised the plane as a 'big brother in every sense of the word,' comparing it to the standard B-36 bomber. A S 'Doc' Witchell, the 34-year-old co-pilot, described the flight as 'It's like driving a Cadillac and a Ford.' Erickson added with a grin, 'The B36 is the Ford.' He remarked, 'only the future will tell how high and fast it will go. We went a couple of miles high - Texas miles. And we touched down at fighter speeds.'

During this first flight aloft, the landing gears were left down, a normal procedure on an initial test hop. Although two subsequent flights in the same month were satisfactory, with the YB-60 displaying excellent handling characteristics, trouble was on the horizon.

Beryl Erickson would take the YB-60 up numerous times, but Witchell would fly in it only one more time. A Convair Test Pilot had an interesting job, for Witchell's flight log shows only a few weeks before his first YB-60 flight, he had flown B-47 jets at the Boeing plant in Wichita, Kansas, for transition training, and a Stinson lightplane on a hop to Dallas. Right after his YB-60 flights, he flew brand new B-36F and B-36H shakedown flights, with occasional Stinson hops from Fort Worth to Dallas.

Three days before the YB-60 flew, another aircraft took to the air at another field in the Pacific Northwest. The Boeing YB-52's initial flight was an unqualified success. It flew for 2 hours 51 minutes with enthusiastic reports from pilots, engineers, and

This view of the second YB-60 under construction has seldom been seen outside the Convair photo archives. Note the deployed forward gun turrets on the upper fuselage - confirmation that the 'tactical' configuration included retractable turrets and that they were indeed provided to Convair by the government for inclusion on the aircraft. At this stage, it appears that each turret only has a single cannon installed. The vertical stabiliser was tight for the hangar building and disappeared into the rafters. This would require that the aircraft's nose be jacked up so that the tail would clear both the rafters and the door frame when it was rolled out. An engine container is in the foreground just ahead of the inboard engine pylon, and the removable nose section is in the lower right corner. (Lockheed Martin, via author's collection)

The swept wing of the YB-60 required Convair to develop new trailing-edge flaps. Unlike the complex system used by the Boeing B-52, Convair selected a simple multi-segment, single-slotted configuration. Note that the wing still required small humps to clear the main landing gear and the lack of doors for the upper rear turrets. (Lockheed Martin, via author's collection)

observers (the YB-52 flew before the XB-52 due to mechanical problems). Unfortunately, the fate of the YB-60 and a possible B-60 contract were doomed from the day the first B-52 flight took place.

There wasn't a formal competition between Convair's YB-60 and Boeing's XB-52. But for several years, both vied for the production contract on the next high-performing intercontinental heavy bomber to succeed the B-36. As far back as 1946, when Boeing won a design competition that eventually resulted, after many changes, in the prototype B-52, the goal was to develop a faster, higher flying replacement for the B-36. The timing was critical. The B-36 seemed to be the solution to the strategic bombardment problem as it appeared in 1942. The future B-52 appeared to play the same role in 1949/1950. Under existing state-of-the-art limitations, the vigorous development of the all-jet B-52 afforded the Air Force with its primary hope for carrying out the strategic air mission, precisely, the delivery of the atomic bomb anywhere in the world.

The Joint Chiefs of Staff had decided to hold the B-36 bomber as the 'big stick' of US strategic defence until 1 January 1955, when the B-52 was to start phasing into former B-36 units. Studies conducted by the Joint Weapons Systems Evaluation Board for the JCS showed the inability of current USAF jet fighters to make a significant percentage of successful attacks against the B-36 at combat altitudes. The top speed of the current B-36D model in service was augmented J47 jets was 436 mph, considered sufficient to force enemy interceptors to supersonic speeds if they were to position themselves in time for an attack.

However, as technology progressed at a rapid pace, the B-36s advantage at the time would disappear as newer, higher performance jet fighters were developed.

Air Force thinking in mid-1950 called for equipping at least two Bomb Groups with the turboprop B-36G by June 1954. It was hoped that the projected speed of the B-36s would eventually reach 550 mph at 55,000 feet altitude. Consequently, the Air Force considered ordering one hundred swept-wing B-36Gs out of fiscal 1952 funds.

However, production plans for the B-52, once planned, then delayed except for the two prototypes, might be resumed, depending on the worsening of the international situation. If global conditions worsened, one-half of the one hundred aircraft orders might be switched to Boeing to get the B-52 into production quickly.

The Air Force held back a production go-ahead on the B-52 in favour of an improved B-36 model for the simple reason of economy. A B-36 in 1950 cost $4.1 million per copy. The initial production cost of the B-52 was nearly $8 million each, plus tooling for quantity production.

The international situation did change drastically in June 1950 when the Korean War broke out and eventually involved American armed forces. Tight military budgets were relaxed, and more urgency was given to bomber production contracts.

A final decision needed to be made on the B36s successor. In the fall, the Air Force's Senior Officers Board met in Washington, D.C., to weigh the merits of both machines. Both Convair and Boeing made elaborate proposals before Air Force Under Secretary John A. McCone. Much of the discussion centred on the subject of choice regarding turboprop or turbojet powerplants.

The development status of both types of engines was about the same. McCone and the Senior Officers Board concluded that the answer would likely be apparent within the next eighteen months as to future progress being made on one powerplant type or the other.

A third proposal for the B-36's replacement was submitted to the Air Force, challenging both the swept-wing B-36G and the XB-52. The design proposal, 1211-J, from Douglas Aircraft Company, had been submitted almost a year earlier.

But due to world tension and increased funds now available to the Air Force for research and development, Douglas modified its original strategic bomber proposal and re-submitted for Senior Officers Board consideration once again.

The design of the machine was somewhat similar to Convairs, a swept-wing, turboprop bomber, but with only four engines instead of six. Specifications called for an aircraft with a normal take-off weight of 320,000 pounds, about the same

Although a poor performer, the YB-60 looked sleek and fast when it was in flight. (Lockheed Martin, via author's collection)

The tail wheel was similar to the nose wheel and could be steered during taxi. Based on gross weight and other considerations, the pilots could extend and retract the tail wheel separately from the other landing gear.

The tail wheel had to be retracted before the aircraft could rotate on takeoff, but after sufficient speed had been gained to allow the elevators to become effective. The assembly retracted forward into the pressurised area of the aft fuselage. (Both USAF)

as that of the B-36; the normal absolute range of 11,000 nautical miles; combat altitude of over 55,000 ft; and speed about 450 knots. The normal combat radius was 4,340 nautical miles, with provision to be increased to 5,000.

Special features included a unique, droppable take off gear, droppable wingtip tanks that could carry 50,000 pounds fuel, and an unusually tall tail fln for better longitudinal control and stability.

Crew complement of the Model 1211-J was nine, including relief crew for long-range missions. An escape hatch for the crew was located on the underside of the fuselage between the nose-wheel gear doors and the forward bomb bay. The armament provided was a conventional 20 mm cannon plus provision for firing air-to-air missiles. It was planned that the Douglas design would eventually feature new electronic equipment, not only for locating ground targets but also long-range detection of enemy interceptors and missiles.

More proposals were brought to the Air Force's attention. In addition to the swept-wing B566 and the Douglas 1211-J, there were new proposals from Republic Aircraft, Fairchild Aircraft, which had an unusual fuel carrying wing launched from a railroad flatcar, and Rand Corporation with a turboprop aircraft. There were even two advanced designs of Boeing's B-47 - all proposed substitutes for the B-52. But, in the end, none of these ideas saw the light of day. Only the B-36G proposal became a flying prototype, as the YB-60.

The flight test programme of the YB-60 lasted only nine months. It officially ended with the Air Force cancelling the second phase on 20 January 1953. Convair flew the YB60-1 for sixty-six hours, accumulated in twenty flights; the Air Force, some fifteen hours, in just four flights.

The second machine, the YB-60-5, was never

This is almost certainly a landing photograph by the lack of smoke from the J57s. The tail wheel had to be retracted before aircraft rotation and was not extended until after it had landed and slowed to a taxi. (USAF)

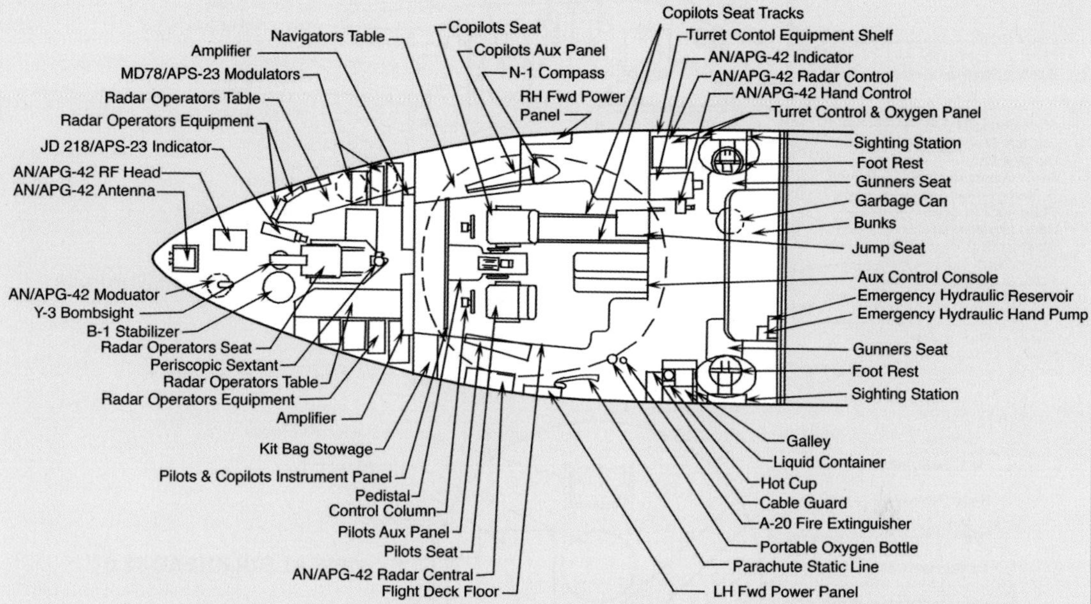

Many published sources describe the B-60 as having only a forward pressurised compartment and a five-man crew. This was true of the first prototype, but was not representative of either the second machine or the planned production model. Here are the production forward and aft crew compartment layouts for the nine-man crew presented at the YB-60 Mock-Up Review, showing the gunners' positions and other tactical and comfort equipment. They have been re-drawn from the originals for clarity.

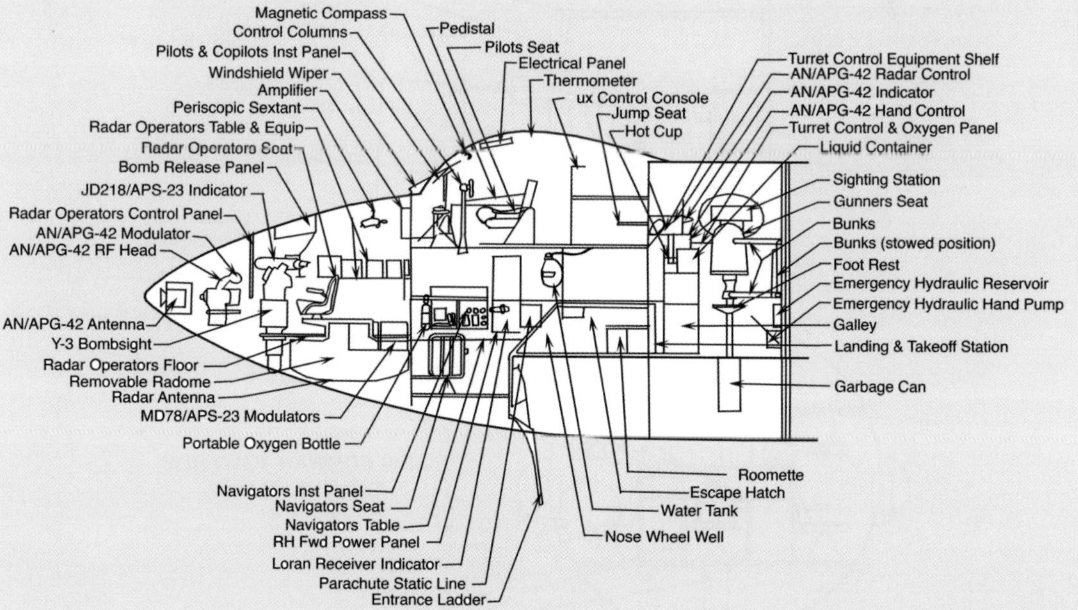

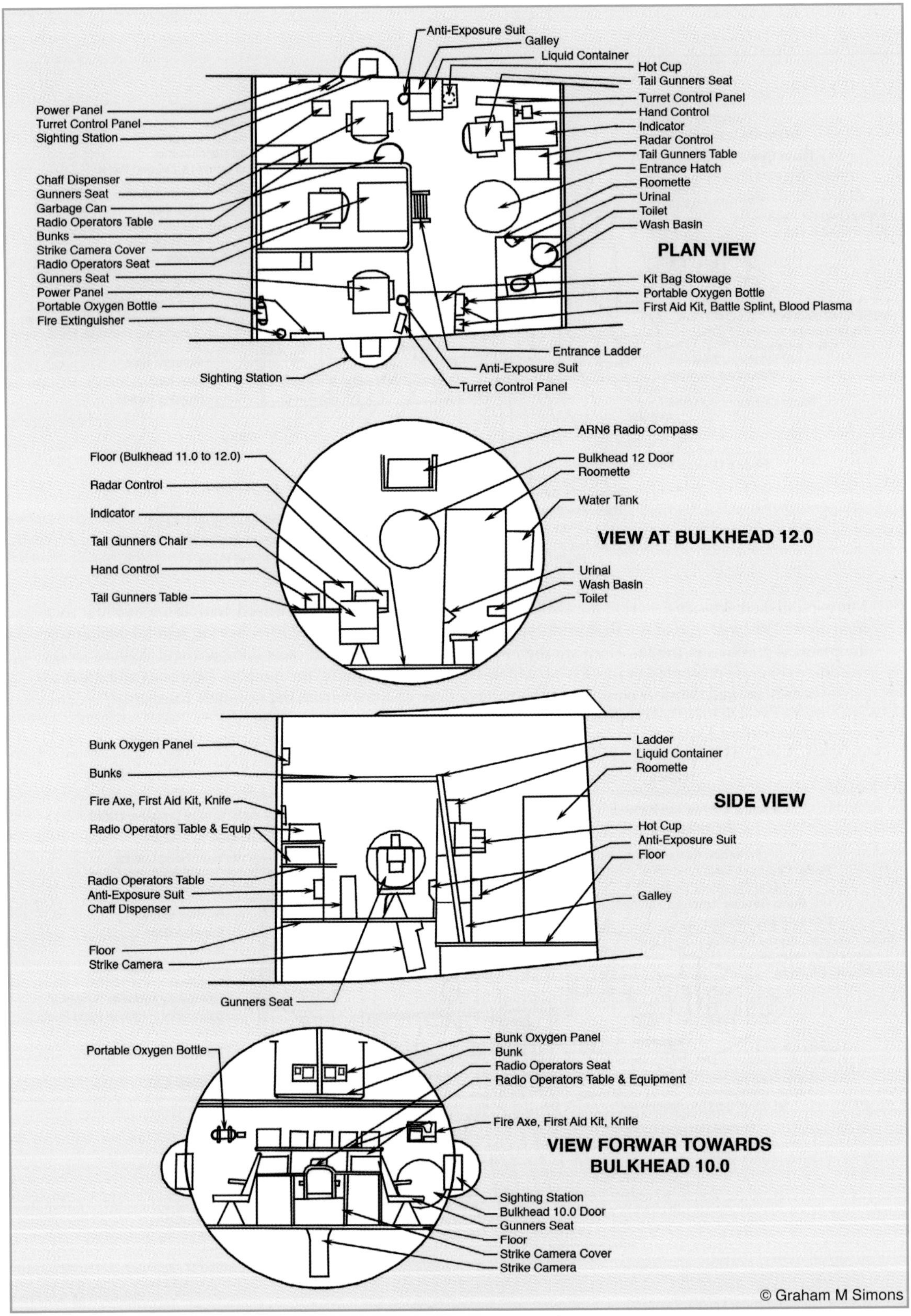
Anti-Exposure Suit
Galley
Liquid Container
Hot Cup
Tail Gunners Seat
Turret Control Panel
Hand Control
Indicator
Radar Control
Tail Gunners Table
Entrance Hatch
Roomette
Urinal
Toilet
Wash Basin
PLAN VIEW
Kit Bag Stowage
Portable Oxygen Bottle
First Aid Kit, Battle Splint, Blood Plasma
Power Panel
Turret Control Panel
Sighting Station
Chaff Dispenser
Gunners Seat
Garbage Can
Radio Operators Table
Bunks
Strike Camera Cover
Radio Operators Seat
Gunners Seat
Power Panel
Portable Oxygen Bottle
Fire Extinguisher
Entrance Ladder
Anti-Exposure Suit
Sighting Station
Turret Control Panel
ARN6 Radio Compass
Floor (Bulkhead 11.0 to 12.0)
Bulkhead 12 Door
Roomette
Radar Control
Water Tank
Indicator
VIEW AT BULKHEAD 12.0
Tail Gunners Chair
Hand Control
Urinal
Wash Basin
Tail Gunners Table
Toilet
Bunk Oxygen Panel
Ladder
Liquid Container
Roomette
Bunks
Fire Axe, First Aid Kit, Knife
SIDE VIEW
Radio Operators Table & Equip
Hot Cup
Anti-Exposure Suit
Floor
Radio Operators Table
Anti-Exposure Suit
Chaff Dispenser
Galley
Floor
Strike Camera
Gunners Seat
Portable Oxygen Bottle
Bunk Oxygen Panel
Bunk
Radio Operators Seat
Radio Operators Table & Equipment
Fire Axe, First Aid Kit, Knife
VIEW FORWAR TOWARDS
BULKHEAD 10.0
Sighting Station
Bulkhead 10.0 Door
Gunners Seat
Floor
Strike Camera Cover
Strike Camera
© Graham M Simons

flown at all. Even though it was ninety-three per cent complete, it did not receive its engines. Moreover, full tactical equipment, such as guns, K-3A system and ECM equipment, was not supplied by the government.

Although the first few flights were relatively successful, and Convair officials were encouraged, this trend did not last long. Test flight results were problematic because the new plane displayed several deficiences. Among them were engine surge, control system buffeting, rudder flutter, and electrical engine control system problems. In addition, speed limitation was imposed by structural considerations at low altitudes and buffering at high altitudes. Also, the YB-60's stability was unsatisfactory because of the high aerodynamic forces acting on the control surfaces and the low aileron effectiveness of the machine.

Perhaps in time, these problems might have been resolved. The Air Force cancelled the B-60 programme on 14 August 1952, before the prototype testing was officially terminated.

The second prototype was never flown, although it was ninety-three per cent complete, basically only missing its engines. The second prototype - which Convair called a B-60, not a YB-60 - was equipped to the expected production standard, including a complete offensive and defensive avionics suite, turrets and guns, etc.

Convair had a few things going for it with the B-60 programme of which the Air Force was aware. The lower cost was one. Final models of the B-36 would drop to less than $4 million a copy. Much of Convair's Fort Worth plant tooling for the B-36 could be readily adapted to the swept-wing configuration. The B-36 was already proven equipment, and significant production could be accomplished in far less time than in the case of the B-52. The B-60 still shared a seventy-two per cent parts commonality. In the area of manufacturing facilities, phase-out of the current B-36 series would place one of the largest aircraft plants in the country in need of new business. On the other hand, Boeing was heavily committed to B-47 production at its Wichita, Kansas, facility, while the Seattle plant built commercial variants and military versions of the KC-135 Stratocruiser.

A beautifully staged photo of the first YB-60 with Billie Whiteside, the son of an Air Force captain dressed as a young cowboy. This was taken during the YB-60's only visit to Edwards AFB, where it was posed in the company of another B-36, thought to be an F-Model. . The Swept Wing Slugger markings had given way to a simple 'Convair YB-60.' Note also the tall ladders to give access to the upper surface of the wings. (USAF)

Due to the poor reliability of the B-36 radar installation, Convair put a lot of thought into the arrangement of the radar and bombing systems for the B-60. Essentially the entire system was mounted in a removable nose section that could easily be changed.

The APS-23 search and attack radar antenna was behind the flush radome. The radome in the extreme nose contained the APG-42 antenna. The K-3A electronics were housed in the larger section and were accessible to the crew in flight. (Both Lockheed Martin)

Convair vainly attempted to convince the Air Force to produce the B-60, even offering to complete the remaining B-36Fs on the production line as B-60s at the same cost. It should be noted, of course, the engines were government-furnished equipment, and they were the expensive part. This proposal was turned down. Convair then tried to convince the Air Force that the YB-60 could be used as an experimental test-bed for turboprop engines, but this too was rejected.

None of these arguments influenced the Air Force. Convair at one point offered to build B-60s on the remaining B-36 production line on an even exchange basis. The Air Force then could have had nearly three operational wings of B-60s, for virtually one with B-36s. The proposal was not accepted.

Poor performance was what killed the YB-60. Speed was a critical factor, and the machine did not have it compared to the newer generation B-52. The YB-60's top speed was 508 mph at 39,250 feet. It

The difference between the prototype nose (left) and the production, or 'tactical' nose, is evident here. Like the B-52, the production B-60 would have used a flush radome to cover the search and attack radar, contributing to the streamlining necessary to achieve the desired high speeds. The production nose was four feet longer than the prototype nose and more pointed overall. By the time the photo at right was taken, the second B-60 had been mothballed, never having flown. (Both Lockheed Martin, via author's collection)

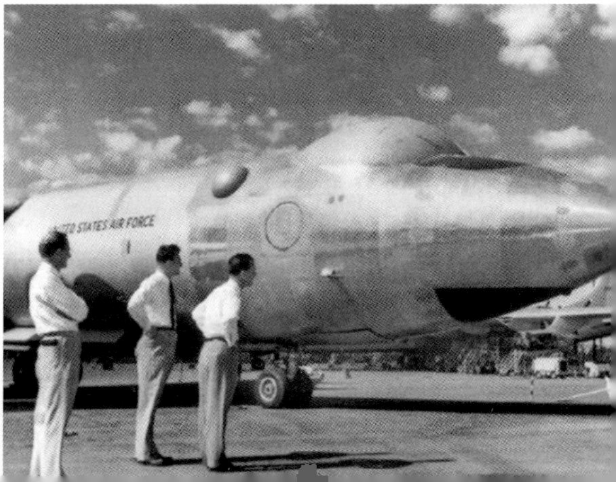

There appears to be few pictures of the two YB-60s together. Here the pair are seen in storage at the north end of the Fort Worth plant. (Lockheed Martin, via author's collection)

supposedly was flown once at 520 mph but was still 100 mph slower than the B-52. At a combat weight of 260,250 lbs, it had a combat ceiling of 44,650 feet. The maximum range was 8,000 miles, with a combat radius of 2,920 miles carrying a 10,000-pound bomb load. The rate of climb at sea level was 1,570 feet per minute, taking 28.3 minutes to reach 30,000 feet. Take off to clear a fifty-foot obstacle was 8,131 feet with a 6,710 foot ground run. Stall speed was 115 knots. Normal cruising altitude was 37,000 feet, with final cruising altitude of 53,300 feet.

Though the YB60's flight test programme ended in January 1953, the Air Force did not accept the two prototypes before 24 June 1954. There were valid reasons for the delay. Convair tried vainly to convince the Air Force that the YB-60s could both be used as experimental test-beds for turboprop engines. Shortage of money and the YB-60's several potentially unsafe characteristics accounted for the Air Force's decision to turn down the tempting proposal. Convair reportedly gave some brief thought about whether the machine could be converted to a commercial jet airliner. Such an aircraft might have flown before Boeing's Model 367-80 jet. But nothing came of the idea. Also, at one time, the YB60 airframe was possibly considered a candidate to become the test vehicle for a proposed nuclear-powered aircraft, the X-6 Project.

The two YB-60s were parked on a corner of the Fort Worth facility, where they sat out in the weather for several months. Finally, on 24 June 1954, the aircraft was officially accepted by the Air Force, but no money was allocated for their continued storage (It was reported that approximately $60 per day was needed.) On 1 July 1954, workmen took axes and blow torches to the aircraft, and by the end of the month, they had both been scrapped, with some of the common components with the B-36F being scavenged for spare parts. It was estimated that $800,000 worth of material was salvaged, including the $29,000 radar computer and two $4,200 landing gear struts from the second aircraft and eight $605 main wheels. The total cost of the YB-60 programme

Right: A S 'Doc' Witchell, pilot and J D McEachern, flight engineer, two members of the YB-60 flight test crew wearing the new David Clark Company T-1 high altitude pressure suits. Lacing along the limbs and torso were tightened after boarding aircraft. The green nylon suits came in twelve sizes and a crew member always wore the same suit. Notice the small oxygen bottles on their left thighs in case of emergency. (USAF)

An overall aerial view of the government-owned plant at Fort Worth run by Convair which occupied over 546 acres across the field from Carswell AFB. The buildings occupied sixty-two acres, with over 4,000,000 square feet of enclosed space and 8,600,000 square feet of paved working areas. Building No. 4 consisted of a 200-foot wide bay used for the main production line for the B-36 and a parallel 120-foot bay used for parts manufacturing. Both bays stretched over 4,000 feet. The adjacent structure, Building 5, was largely uninvolved in B-36 production. Over 31,000 people produced an average of one B-36 per week for most of the run. The plant produced over 68,000 separate parts, in addition to those made by fifty-seven major subcontractors (excluding Convair's San Diego plant) and 1,553 suppliers located in thirty-six states and the District of Columbia. A total of 2,500 machine tools and 126,500 production tools were used for B-36 production. The assembly line integrated 8,500 separate subassemblies and 27 miles of wiring. The pair of YB-60s were parked up on the taxiway on the left of the picture. (Lockheed Martin via author's collection)

was $14,366,022, including the fee paid to Convair.

The following month, on 14 August 1954, the last production B-36 (B-36J, serial 52-2827) rolled off the production line in Fort Worth. Of course, there would be no follow-on continuation with the B-60 programme. Convair, then General Dynamics, would later produce the successful supersonic B-58 Hustler instead.

Convair considered adapting the YB-60 as a commercial jet airliner, again to no avail. A proposal for a 380,000-pound gross weight commercial version powered by eight P&W J57-P-1 engines would cost $7 million, plus an additional $1 million for engines. The airliner would carry 261 passengers, a flight crew of five, and four cabin crew. The aircraft would have a maximum range of 3,450 miles and would be available in December 1956. Interestingly, Convair stated that 'although the aircraft could fly nonstop from New York to London with 261 passengers, it could only carry twenty-two passengers on the return flight because of the prevailing 100 mph east wind encountered at cruising altitude.'

As part of this proposal, Convair surveyed a variety of commercial airports to determine if they could handle an aircraft of this size. None of the three major airports (Los Angles, Chicago Midway, or New York Idlewild) could accommodate the proposed wingspan or gross weight. In addition, none of the airport managers was interested in making significant infrastructure improvements beyond those necessary for the upcoming Boeing 707, which was 50,000 pounds lighter and had a 100-foot less wingspan than the proposed Convair airliner. Convair estimated that operating costs could be covered with an average of 215 passengers per flight. Engineers also noted that the YB-60 derivative only had a projected speed of 432 mph, compared with 600 mph for the Boeing 707 and other competitors. In the end, Convair decided to concentrate on the 880-series of jet transports instead.

Chapter Twelve

The XC-99 and Model 37

The XC-99 was the cargo transport version of the B-36 and was the only one that was ever built. It was, and still is, the largest land-based piston-engined cargo carrier in the world. The XC-99 was the biggest variant of the basic B-36 design and became a one-of-a-kind example.

Consolidated Aircraft hoped that the machine would be the first of a fleet of huge cargo/troop transports for the newly independent US Air Force. It was also envisioned as the first of a new fleet of giant 'Clippers' for Juan Trippe's Pan American World Airways. But it was not to be. However, the XC-99 did prove its worth in Air Force operational service for nearly eight years, from 1949 to 1957.

The design of the XC-99 originated in the early days of the Second World War with a Consolidated Aircraft Corporation commercial landplane study designated Model 36. Model 36 was proposed only six months after the award of the XB-36 prototype contract. The May 1942 design study was based on the XB-36, utilising the bomber's wing, tail, powerplants, and landing gear. Consolidated thought that considerable cost savings could be made in developing the commercial machine by advanced work done on the military XB-36 sister ship, particularly regarding the powerplants and other common parts.

A cargo and troop transport was also proposed, and the USAAF ordered one machine, serial number 43-52436. Contract No. W535-AC-34454 was awarded on 31 December 1942, at an estimated cost of $4.5 million, plus a fixed-fee of $180,000, with delivery to be in twenty-one

The proposed Consolidated Model 36 transport, as planned in May 1942. Notice the twin rudder tail, similar to the XB-36 prototype. (Author's collection)

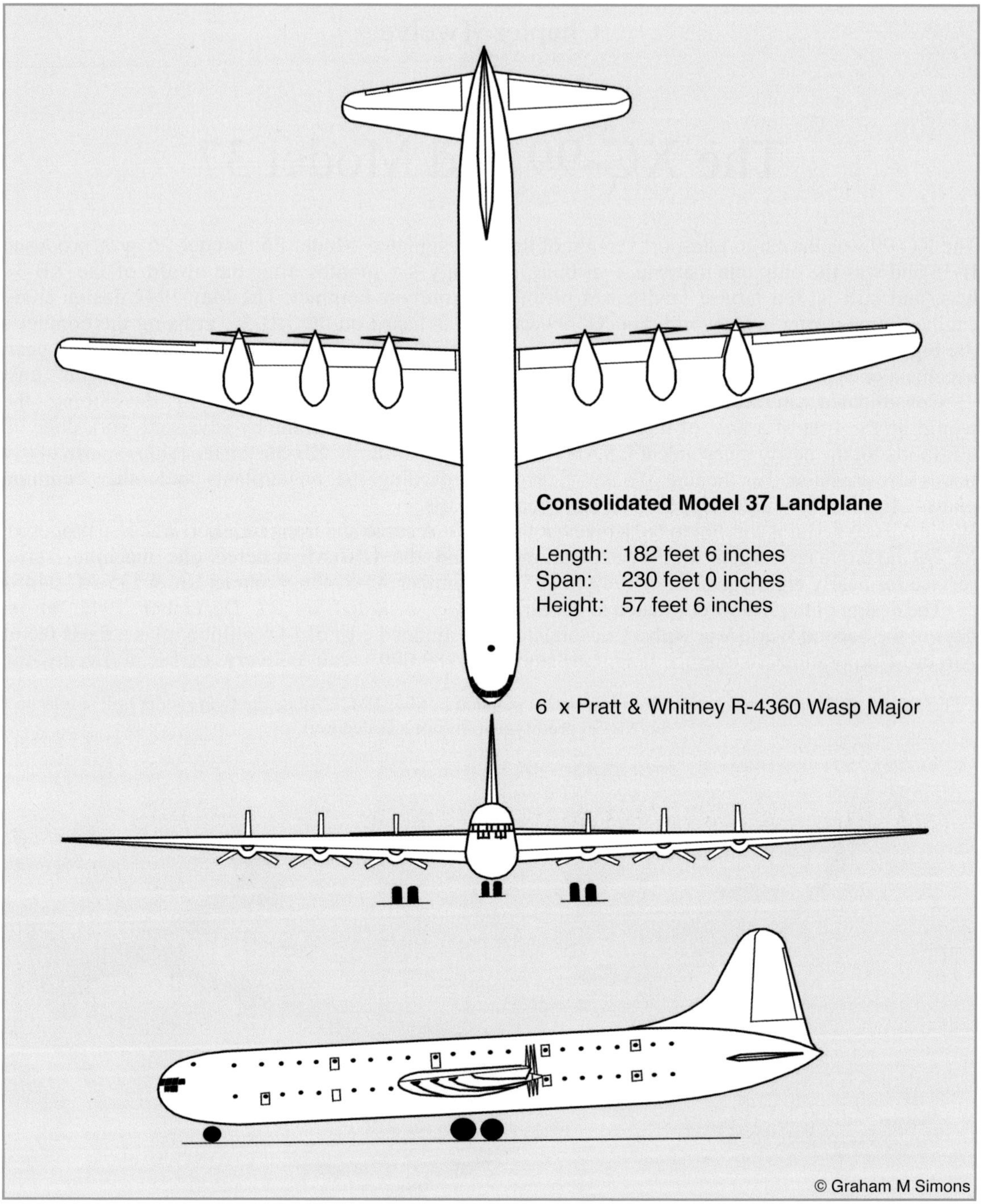

months. The contract specified that the XC-99 project was not to interfere with construction or cause a delay in the delivery of the first XB-36 bomber. Work called for by the contract was to be accomplished at the government-owned plant in Fort Worth, Texas. The aircraft's design and development work proceeded slowly during the war since the project had a low priority.

The Model 36 was slightly smaller in size than the completed XC-99 eventually delivered to the Air Force. The wing was the same dimension, with a 230-foot span, just like its sister ship, the XB-36 bomber. However, the twelve and a half foot diameter of the military fuselage was increased to a thirteen and a half feet by nineteen foot three-inch elliptical fuselage, which was to be formed by two intersecting cylindrical sections.

Fuselage length was 173 feet; fuselage height nineteen feet four inches; horizontal stabiliser fifty-nine feet tall; the height of a twin tail was forty feet, some seventeen and a half feet shorter than the XC-99's single tail. A distinctive design feature of Model 36 was the twin rudder tail also proposed for the XB-36 prototype.

The commercial fuselage was pressurised for high altitude flight, averaging 300 mph cruising speed at 30,000 feet. In addition, the size and capacity of the XB-36 engine turbo superchargers would have been decreased to conform to the commercial version's reduced requirements. Gross weight was to be 265,000 pounds.

The interior layout provided seats for one hundred and forty-four passengers in the day arrangement, which converted to sixty-eight sleeping berths in the night arrangement. Capacity for luggage, mail, and express parcels was approximately 12,000 pounds.

The Model 36 airliner was to have a crew of five, plus a five man relief crew for long-distance flights. Also included on the airliner would be seven stewards and a nurse, presumably female.

By 1944, the Model 36 design had been refined into the Convair Model 37, and as the XC-99 military version reached its definitive form with the same six 3,000 hp Pratt & Whitney Wasp Major engines, wing and landing gear of the XB-36 prototype then under construction at the Fort Worth plant. Work on the XC-99 was also planned for Fort Worth concurrent with work on the XB-36. Around sixty per cent of the parts would be common to both the XB-36 and XC-99. The XC-99's huge fuselage was to be fabricated in two sections in San Diego, and the wing, powerplants, and landing gear were to be shipped from Fort Worth.

Roberts R Hoover, assigned to be XC-99 Project Engineer, had worked previously on the P3Y Catalina project as Assistant Project Engineer and moved from San Diego to Fort Worth with seventeen engineers in August 1942. Detail design work started, and a wooden mock-up was constructed in the plant's paint shop, where the engineering was going on for the XB-36 prototype. In April 1945, Convair asked the Army Air Forces to move the XC-99 project back to San Diego. When signing the contract, the San Diego plant was occupied with the engineering and development of the B-32 heavy bomber and production of B-24 Liberators. Subsequently, conditions had been reversed in 1944, and the Fort Worth plant was conducting all B-32 and B-36 production engineering. This relieved the crowded conditions at San Diego, making space available in the Experimental Shop and engineering. The Army Air Forces let Convair relocate the project back to San Diego under the following conditions: It would not interfere with the development, testing, and delivery of the B-32 bomber; and that the XB-36 would receive at all times higher production priority than the XC-99.

Transfer of the project was completed by May 1944, and Hoover resumed with a nucleus of just seven engineers. He eventually had a staff of around eighty. This was the first time a double load fuselage had ever been built, carrying such high loads. It was a challenge, and a test section of the fuselage was constructed to test various weight limits.

Portions of a wooden mock-up were built once again, mainly the flight deck and a section of the fuselage, including cargo openings. Practice loading was done with vehicles. Jeeps and half-tracks were easily loaded, and it was planned to handle a medium tank eventually. One day, during ramp loading tests in the mock-up, a command car

The fuselage frames of the forward section of the XC-99 comes together in San Diego in March 1945. (Convair via author's collection)

was being loaded, and at one point, slipped back down the ramp, a minor embarrassment to Convair.

The Model 37 would feature an extended fuselage with a length of 182 feet six inches. The fuselage height was twenty feet six inches, a horizontal stabiliser of seventy-seven feet two inches, and a single fifty-seven feet five-inch tail. Gross weight was 265,000 pounds. The cargo/troop transport version could carry fifty tons of cargo, 400 fully-equipped troops, or 300 litter patients with their attendants. The volume of the XC-99's fuselage was the equivalent of ten railroad freight cars. The largest Army Air Forces transport during World War Two carried only fifty soldiers. The range was 1,720 miles with a 100,000-pound load of cargo or 8,100 miles with a smaller load of 10,000 pounds. Cruising speed was 290 mph, and with an estimated top speed of 335 mph at 30,000 feet.

Convair still hoped to sell a commercial airliner version of the Model 37, the basic XC-99 design. Although potential customers were wary about committing to the giant machine, Pan American Airways expressed interest. Discussions were held with PAA in early 1945. Ralph Bayless, Chief Engineer at Convair San Diego, and R R Hoover, Project Engineer, had rooms at the El Cortez Hotel in San Diego and wrote up specifications and performance requirements. Pan American hoped for a high load factor and wanted to get the one-way ticket to Hawaii down to $90.

PAA did order fifteen of the airliners in February 1945. Production on the Convair 'Super Clippers' was to begin as soon as wartime restrictions permitted. Each aircraft was to carry 204 passengers and 15,300 pounds of baggage in a double-deck interior arrangement, with a mix of convertible sleeping berths and coach seating. Spacious lounges would be available to passengers on both levels. In addition, a large galley would offer hot in-flight meals. Located on each end of the long interior cabin, two circular stairways provided access between levels. The scale of the internal arrangement prompted Convair to contract out the airliner's interior design and layout to New York City industrial designer Henry Dreyfuss who had worked on a whole series of aircraft interiors during his long and illustrious career. He created several different seating arrangements, ranging from spacious to high density.

Originally planned to be powered by six 5,000 hp gas turbine engines, the new powerplants never materialised. The fleet of 'Super Clippers' was to use the same 3,000 hp Wasp Majors as the XB-36.

Above: the flight deck of the XC-99, without the crew seats in position. Note the twin sets of throttles for the pilots, a feature not the same as the B-36. The spaciousness is particularly apparent.

Below: Test pilot Russell R Rogers (left) talks with a Convair employee in this posed image. (Both Convair, via author's collection)

Pan American planned that three of the airliners, operating at only fifty per cent capacity, would carry 150,000 passengers between California and Honolulu each year. The other dozen planes would serve the post-war European market, carrying 443,000 passengers yearly. Flying time from New York to London would take just nine hours, not five days by ship. This large passenger load was thought to bring unprecedented low-cost fares to the airline industry. Newspaper articles and magazine stories during 1945 and 1946 touted the exciting future in store regarding post-war air travel in the PAA Super Clippers. Pan American, it was claimed, would be instrumental in ushering in the era of big, wide-body passenger airliners. But this was not to happen for another twenty years, with the advent of the Boeing 747!

Pan American decided to cancel the fifteen machine order but kept an option open on three. However, after re-evaluating traffic on the Califomia-Honolulu route, Pan Am discovered that these three airliners had the capability to carry one hundred and fifty per cent of all traffic generated by all means of transportation on the Hawaii run.

Two views of the interior mockup of the planned Model 37 airliner version of the XC-99.

The main cabin had lounge-style settee seating, while the 'gentleman's restroom' had every facility available. (Both Convair via author's collection)

It simply did not make sense, so PAA dropped the three plane option. With that, it was the end of the Convair 'Super Clippers.' Another factor, stated by Convair, was the failure of availability of the proposed 5,000 hp gas turbine engines, which would have been more economical to operate. Unlike the Army Air Forces, operating Wasp Majors, with each engine requiring 190 gallons of oil alone, it would be too expensive in a for-profit business like PAA.

Cancellation of the PAA option did not dampen Convair's enthusiasm for the Model 57 military cargo/transport version being built during 1946 and 1947. Under Hoover's supervision, as Model 37 Project Engineer, the XC-99 began to take shape in San Diego. After the wings had arrived from Fort Worth, on four railroad flat cars, they were mated with the double-deck fuselage, and the XC-99 was completed.

It was unnecessary to run the R-4360-25 Wasp Majors on test stands as Fort Worth had done for the XB-36. By now, they were proven engines. The engines were, however, run statically on the XC-99 when it was in the experimental yard. There were just a few taxi tests because many of the machine's systems had already been tested on the XB-36. It was important, of course, to check the brakes and other vital systems.

Finally, the XC-99 was ready for flight. The successful first flight was made on 24 November 1947. Piloting the world's largest land aircraft was Russell R Rogers, Chief of Flight Test and Research at Convair San Diego, and Beryl A Erickson, from the Fort Worth plant.

Rogers had soloed when he was just fifteen years old. He had been a Curtiss test pilot for several years until 1932. Later, Rogers joined Convair, bringing over twenty-five years of flying experience to the Flight Test division.

Assisting Rogers was Beryl A Erickson. A veteran of sixteen years flying experience, Erickson was currently test flying B-36 bombers at Fort Worth. Flight engineers on board the XC-99 were Mel Clause and B B Gray. L J Bordelon and Larry Brandvig were stationed in the tail section as powerplant observers. Flight test engineers for the first flight were John T Ready and G W Hofeller, who was seated right behind the two pilots. The radio operator was William C Geopfarth.

On that Sunday morning, crowds gathered atop Point Loma and high ground all over the city to watch the huge machine fly. Traffic around the Lindbergh Field airport area was jammed with sightseers. R R Hoover was on a microphone, making a radio broadcast of the event. He described the take off from a control tower located on the roof of a Convair building. The XC- 99's take-off was slow and steady, slower than its sister machine, the XB-36.

Airborne after a run of approximately 4,000 ft along Lindbergh's mile and a half long runway, the flight was uneventful as the XC-99 cruised leisurely over Southern California for an hour. The second flight was made on 2 December, with Russell Rogers once again at the controls. The two hour, forty-minute test flight went well, as various systems were tested and procedures evaluated.

The co-pilot was Phil Prophett. Hoover was aboard for this second flight. There were no seats on the XC- 99 except for the crew, and he had to sit on the cargo deck floor, a little behind the pilots, strapping himself in with a safety belt to the cargo tie-downs. There was no partition dividing the flight deck and cargo compartment. Hoover recalled in later years how odd it felt to be the sole

Largest Land Plane in World

XC-99 Cargo Carrier, Sister Ship To B-36, Here for Final Testing

BY ROBERT WEAR.

Challenging the airlift load capacity of its sister ship, the B-36 bomber, the XC-99 cargo carrier, largest land plane in the world, has settled down in Fort Worth for final phases of flight testing.

Convair engineers expect to prove within the next 60 days that it will do what it was designed to do—take aloft 100,000 pounds of cargo for the largest load any plane has ever lifted from the earth.

The B-36 only a fortnight ago flew from Fort Worth to Muroc Lake testing ground and dropped two simulated bombs totaling 84,000 pounds, the largest such load any bomber had ever carried.

Ten Freight Car Capacity.

Planned to revolutionize airlift across great distances of the world, the XC-99 has a potential advantage over its bomber counterpart—its double-decked fuselage contains 30,000 cubic feet of cargo carrying space—the equivalent of 10 railroad freight cars.

Roberts R. Hoover, project engineer for the XC-99 since its inception, already has moved his headquarters from the Convair plant in San Diego to the Fort Worth division, to have direct charge of incorporating minor refinements in the plane's equipment found advisable in tests on both the "99" and the B-36.

Maj. Harry A. Blitch, assistant operations and training officer for the 7th Bombardment Wing at Carswell Air Base, reported that the big plane has been earmarked for assignment to the base here, after its acceptance by the Air Force.

The 1,200-mile flight from San Diego to Fort Worth a week ago was the eighth for the massive plane. Fort Worth Convair flight crews are expected to make two additional test flights and the Air Force three, before the ship is accepted.

Its trip from San Diego, accomplished at an average speed of approximately 240 miles an hour, was the second made with the new four-wheel landing gear now standard for the B-36.

Wing, power plant and landing gear assemblies were built in Fort Worth and shipped to San Diego where the fuselage was constructed. Similarity of many components with those of the B-36 made it practical and more economical to bring the ship to Fort Worth for the final touches.

More Orders Expected.

Convair officials have been encouraged in the hope that the Air Force will place a regular order for more of the huge cargo ships, after the success of this first experimental model is shown clearly.

Production facilities in the Fort Worth plant could be adapted to turn out such an order rapidly.

Air Force thinking is reflected in the report by Maj. Gen. Laurence S. Kuter, commanding the Military Air Transport Service which operates the Berlin airlift, published in the February issue of U. S. Air Services magazine. Kuter wrote:

"From Operation Vittles has come a greater appreciation of the meaning for strategic airlift . . Fewer aircraft mean fewer of everything all along the line: trips, flying hours, air crews, maintenance and fuel, fewer terminals, less communications and fewer air traffic problems in all — obviously impressive economies . . . The future of strategic airlift lies in the development and production of the proper transport aircraft, a big plane with the right characteristics."

Wing span of the XC-99 and the B-36 is the same—230 feet. However, the "99" is 182½ feet long and 57½ feet high—20 feet longer and 10 feet higher than the B-36.

By comparison with the Air Force's largest transports in World War II, which carried only 50 soldiers, the XC-99 can haul 400 fully equipped troops or 300 litter patients with their attendants. Its chief wartime use conceivably would be rapid transport of soldiers and materiel in quantities heretofore considered impossible.

Blind Man Dies of Burns

HOUSTON, Feb. 19 (AP).—A blind vegetable dealer died Friday night from burns received in a fire, in an old barn near the Houston Farmer's Market. He was James E. Ricketts, 62, Houston. Hospital attendants said they had been unable to locate relatives.

—Convair Photo Montage.

AIRLIFT REVOLUTIONIZER—Largest land plane in the world, Convair's XC-99, is shown in the center photo standing beside the company's Fort Worth experimental hangar, after its flight from San Diego to undergo final equipment refinements. Its 230-foot wing span, 183-foot fuselage and tail fin towering 58 feet from the pavement are delineated. Upper right, Roberts R. Hoover, XC-99 project engineer here to supervise final work on the ship. Lower left diagram shows the double-deck arrangement of the fuselage.

Opposite page and above: a pair of articles from the Fort Worth-Star Telegram newspaper of 20 February 1949. It shows both the thinking and data of the machine, along with a picture of the project engineer Roberts R Hoover.

passenger in the cavernous upper deck. He thought it was like, 'sitting in a bowling alley, two or three lanes wide.'

The next eighteen months were spent conducting the company's extensive flight testing programme, and the XC-99 became a familiar sight over San Diego, and of course, so did the distinctive heavy-throated sound of its engines. Convair wanted to maintain good public relations, so when the San Diego Council of Churches complained about the noise of the XC-99 disturbing Sunday church services, pilot Russell Rogers promptly changed the machine's take-off time from 11 am to 1 pm, after services had concluded.

The XC-99's huge single-wheel landing gear it shared with the XB-36 was replaced with the standard four-wheel gear of the early production B-36. Installation of the four-wheel gear in San Diego had been accelerated by a structural failure of the single-wheel landing gear installed on the YB-36, the second B-36 prototype. The XC-99 first flew with its new four-wheel landing gear on 24 January 1949.

The XC-99 was flown to Forth Worth on 11 February for completion of the Phase I flight test programme, and to ready the machine for acceptance by the Air Force. Phase II testing was conducted by Air Materiel Command Flight Test Division at the Convair Fort Worth plant from 23 April to 7 May. This testing disclosed that the aircraft exceeded the guaranteed performance figures of the Model Specifications.

A 100,000 pound payload had been lifted for the first time by a Convair crew on 15 April, setting an unofficial world record. The previous record had been established by a Convair B-36B, operated by the Eighth Air Force, with a 84,000 pound load consisting of two 42,000 pound dummy 'Grand Slam' conventional bombs.

The XC-99 was officially delivered to the Air Force on 26 May 1949. Accepting for the Air Force was Captain Robert Walling on behalf of Air Materiel Command. On one of the acceptance flights before delivery, Walling put the XC-99 through its paces, including a hair-raising dive. It was required to perform a steep dive and pullout before Air Force acceptance. The AF officer aboard for this test was terrified during this manoeuvre. Shortly after the XC-99 nosed over and started a screaming dive towards the earth downhill, the pale-looking officer declared the test 'passed' as soon as he could!

Assigned to the 7th Bomb Wing at Carswell

AFB, Texas, it was to undergo extensive inspections before later reassignment to another Texas airfield, Kelly AFB. The Air Force's flight test programme for the XC-99 was conducted by the 456th Bomb Squadron, which made a complete overall inspection the following month.

R R Hoover was in Fort Worth when the first flight was made by an Air Force crew, piloted by Captain Dean G. Curry of the 492nd Bomb Squadron, 7th Bomb Wing. He specifically remembers this first flight. He knew the planned flight was for about an hour and twenty minutes. The weather was just a little windy, so Hoover called the Convair tower and asked what the weather prediction was for the day. The man in the tower was a pretty good forecaster and told him that if the XC-99 didn't get back in fifty minutes, it would have to stay up at least an hour and a half to avoid a storm coming through the area with eighty miles an hour winds. Captain Curry circled the runway and started to bring the XC-99 in for a landing with forty miles an hour crosswinds and gusts up to sixty miles an hour. He crabbed the aircraft sideways into the wind and managed to straighten the aircraft out over the runway just as he neared the pavement. Hoover thought it quite a feat of flying and was surprised the pilot handled the difficult landing as well as he did. The big slab-sided fuselage of the XC-99 acted like a giant sail, catching the wind easily.

Captain Curry accomplished a total of six landings at Carswell in the newly inspected XC-99. During the remainder of June, he logged five more flights, of which one was a night mission and one was an emergency landing at Kelly AFB, the plane's future home.

An eventful Operation Elephant.

The XC-99 made a noteworthy 1,150 mile round trip flight from Kelly AFB to San Diego in June 1950. The purpose was to test the modifications and repairs done to the aircraft at Kelly AFB during the past year. It would also ferry ten B-36 engines and sixteen propellers, a record payload, and foreshadow a series of flights shattering nearly every international weight-lifting record.

Details of the flight were as follows: on 27 June 1949, the XC-99 arrived from Carswell AFB to undergo modifications, including the installation of R-436041 engines. Upon completing the work, the aircraft suffered an explosion in the Number 3 fuel tank, which was declared accidental and caused the aircraft to be grounded for extensive repairs.

All repair work was completed by 25 June 1950. The XC-99 was airborne on 5 July from Kelly with Colonel Fred Bell as pilot and Captain M W Neyland as co-pilot. The initial flight was of three hours duration, and the only difficulty experienced was damage to the nose wheel doors. A week later, on 10 July, the XC-99 made another shakedown flight lasting two hours. The flight was routine and uneventful. As the nose wheel doors repair was not finished, the nose doors were left off the aircraft.

After the completion of this flight, it was decided that the XC-99 would need a flight test of greater duration than two or three hours to fully test all the installations that had been made at Kelly AFB under the modification programme.

Therefore, Major-General Clements McMullen authorised a flight to San Diego for the dual purpose of a thorough shakedown test of the aircraft and airlifting of B-36 engines and propellers, equipment that was in critical short supply. It seemed the most expeditious method to accomplish an overhaul of the equipment and return to service.

The main cargo for the return flight from San Diego would be R-4360-41 Wasp Major engines and Curtiss-Wright C63SP-A21 propellers. During preparations for the flight, it was discovered that the San Diego division did not have empty wooden crates to properly store the big nineteen-foot diameter propellers for the return flight.

It was thought prudent to lift an R-4360-41 aboard the XC-99 with its cargo lifting mechanism to test this operation. Some difficulties were encountered, such as an engine attached to its stand could not be effectively lifted to the upper deck; computations that the floor area of the upper deck was not sufficient to ensure a safe floor loading, and power of the upper deck hoist was inadequate for continuous usage.

The XC-99 was ready to fly on 12 July. It took off from Kelly AFB at 06:10 hours with a gross weight of 245,396 pounds. Shortly after take-off, the Number 6 engine began backfiring, and water injection was used to clean out the powerplant. After several more injections, the engine performed normally for the rest of the flight.

At 08:15 hours, it became necessary to use fuel from the Number 5 gas tank. When this tank valve was placed in the 'on' position with the Number 6 valve off, all engines on the right side lost power. The electrician made an in-flight check of the valve in the wing, and the motor assembly was found lying near the valve. The hinge pin had vibrated out. The valve was positioned back, and the motor assembly was replaced. Electric control of the fuel transfer system was again possible. At 09:41 hours, the Number 6 propeller became inoperative in the automatic position. Manual control of this propeller was used for the remainder of the flight.

The XC-99 arrived in San Diego at approximately 11:00 hours. After coming down to 700 ft, the aircraft entered the Lindbergh Field traffic pattern. The landing gear was extended, and the left scanner in the rear of the aircraft reported that the fixed fairing on the left main gear was mangled and hanging loose. The fairing was visually checked, and it was noted that two steel cables were securing it in place. A normal landing was made at 11:12 hours, San Diego Pacific

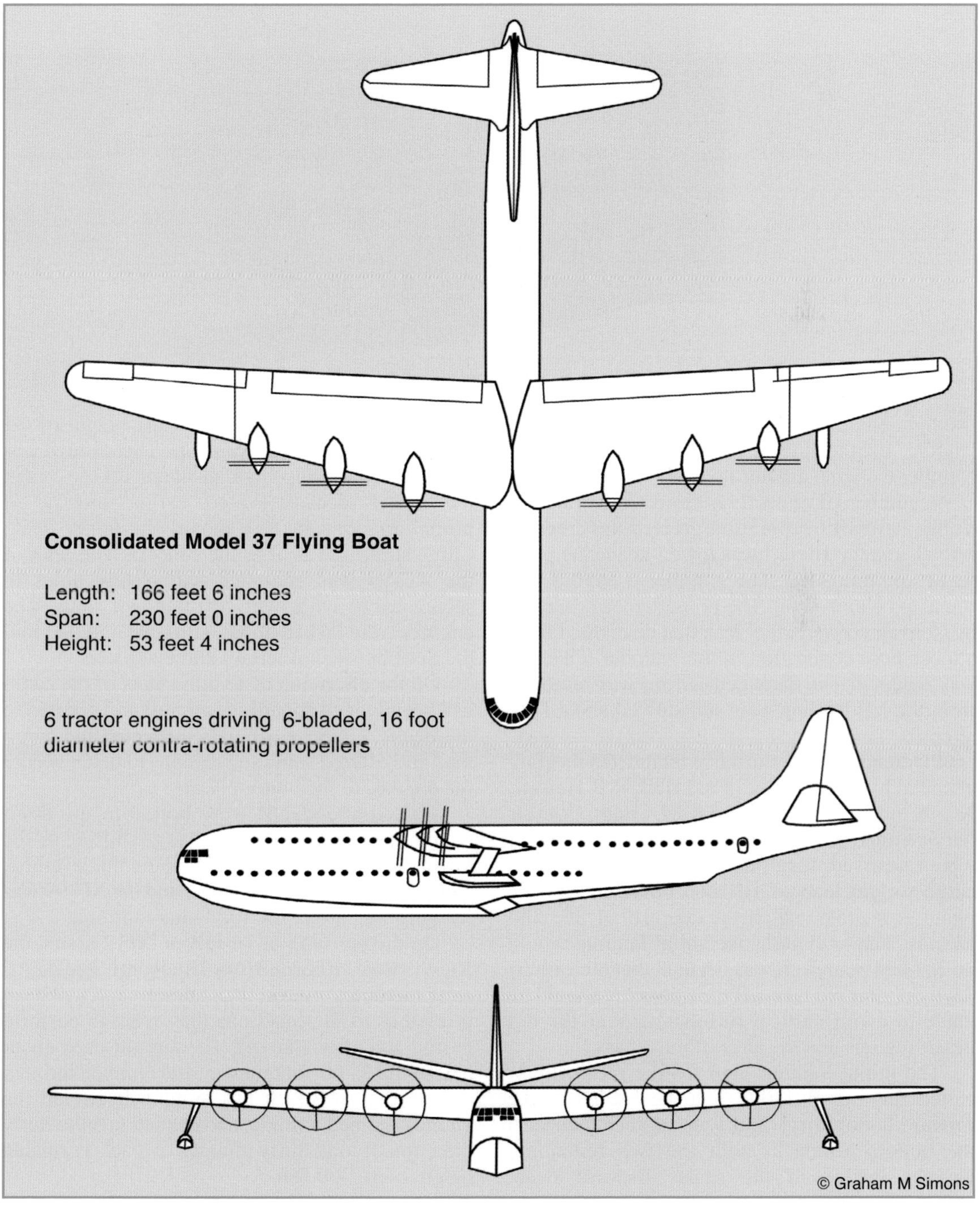

The nose of the XC-99 before the aircraft was fitted with the thimble radome. This picture also shows the almost slab-sided fuselage. The size of the flight deck windows is also very noticable. (USAF)

Daylight Saving Time. Reverse pitch was used on landing, and the aircraft yawed to the left because Number 6 engine did not reverse.

A number of executives from Consolidated-Vultee Aircraft Corporation greeted the crew on arrival, and the aircraft was towed inside the plant fence and unloaded. The Number 6 engine was found to be low on oil. The propeller was changed by Convair crews. A fuel leak that developed from a loose hose connection in the Number 6 nacelle was repaired. The damaged fairing was removed from the left landing gear and stowed aboard the aircraft.

Planning for the return trip included a meeting attended by pilot Colonel Fred Bell; R R Hoover, XC-99 Project Engineer, and K.M. Smith, Convair Service Representative. All particulars of the flight were discussed, resulting in approving the total cargo weight load of 101,266 pounds, with the plane at a gross weight at take-off of 303,334 pounds. The total gross weight at landing would be 261,034 pounds. It was decided that the earliest daylight morning take-off time possible should be made to avoid vertical turbulence over the hot desert regions that the aircraft must pass.

The initial loading plan for the return flight called for four R-4360415 to be loaded in the forward bottom deck and four engines loaded in the bottom aft deck, with the two remaining engines loaded in the upper forward deck. However, due to the limited lifting height of the upper hoist, this was not possible. Therefore, it was decided in San Diego to load all ten R4360-41s in the lower decks. Boxed cargo, mostly of propellers, was loaded aboard the upper deck. Cargo shifting was of prime concern. The floor of the XC-99 was equipped with screw holes to secure cargo with over 700 tiedown rings. The engines were lashed down with rope and tied into the floor by special screws and eye-plates.

On the afternoon of 13 July, most of the cargo had been loaded aboard the aircraft and secured to the decks. Convair officials inspected the cargo load and offered some suggestions to better secure the engines to the bottom decks.

The engine stands were bolted to the floor, eliminating any possibility of cargo shifting on the lower decks. Finally, at 21:00 hours that evening, all preparations were complete, and the XC-99 was ready for departure the following morning.

On the morning of 14 July at 06:12 hours, the XC-99 was airborne from Lindbergh Field. All crew members were at their stations and had been briefed as to the functions they were to perform during and after take off. The aircraft used about half of the 8,700-foot runway and climbed through an overcast at 300 ft per minute. It circled the vicinity, gained altitude, and headed in an easterly direction. It took thirty minutes to reach a cruising height of 11,000 feet.

Forty minutes after take-off, the Number 6 engine started backflring again. The engine was cleaned by water injection as before, but to no avail. Opposite Gila Bend, Arizona, the engine was feathered and remained so until in the traffic pattern at Kelly AFB.

Indicated airspeed, at 10,000 feet altitude, with the five operating engines was 150 mph. The operation of the aircraft for the remainder of the flight was uneventful.

Weather conditions en route proved satisfactory until the XC-99 passed over the Fort Stockton, Texas, area. Concentrated cumulus clouds were encountered, and deviations from the flight course were made to avoid passing through turbulence. The aircraft's altitude was altered to 4,000 feet, which permitted good visibility and less turbulence. During the entire flight, a maximum of 1.4 positive Gs was encountered.

At 14:15 hours, Central Standard Time, the plane passed over Kelly. The Number 6 engine was restarted for landing and deceleration purposes. At 14:25 hours, the XC-99 landed and taxied into a parking position. Maj. General McMullen, commanding officer, greeted the crewmembers after their successful flight.

On Monday, 17 July, unloading operations began. The first cargo to be unloaded was the five engines on the lower deck, followed by all cargo from the upper deck. The five engines from the lower forward deck were removed from the aircraft last. This prevented the machine from assuming a tail-heavy attitude.

Several suggestions for design improvement to the XC-99 were made after this record weight-lifting flight. They included: installation of four traversing hoists; protection of all hydraulic lines, electrical lines, and other operating mechanisms in the vicinity of the cargo hoisting areas; a fuel transfer system that permitted transfer of fuel across the fuselage; a more convenient location of some engine instruments; and cabin and cockpit cooling capability on both ground and in the air.

Despite technical and mechanical problems with the aircraft, Operation Elephant was considered a success, and many more record-breaking flights would follow in years to come. In September 1950, the XC-99 got its orders and proceeded to Kelly AFB with a team of Convair and Air Force engineers. It was assigned to the San Antonio Air Materiel Area (SAAMA) as a project aircraft.

Colonel Theodore W. Tucker, Deputy of Operations at SAAMA, was named project officer and chief pilot due to his experience as a B-36 pilot. The following month, an operational test programme was begun to determine its capacity for moving heavy loads long distances at a reasonable cost. Largely on the XC-99s performance in operation would rest the Air Force's decision to move ahead into an era of huge "super-freighters" or remain with present operational cargo aircraft produced in greater numbers.

Loading of the XC-99 in 1950 would be considered somewhat primitive by today's standards of nose and/or tail ramps. The double-deck fuselage, with each level containing two cargo sections, was equipped with power hoists. Access to the lower cargo floors was through an opening in the bottom of the fuselage forward of the wing and another forward of the tail. Hatches for loading the upper deck were located over the lower deck openings.

Mobile cargo, such as trucks, jeeps, and similar equipment, was driven up the ramps at the lower forward and lower rear cargo openings. For weight-saving reasons, these narrow ramps were built in pairs for each opening and permitted adjustment sideways for the various treads of vehicles. Trial loading of such equipment into a full-scale mockup was made before the XC-99 design was finalised.

It was anticipated that various other types of cargo, including packaged, crated, and barrelled items, would be carried in the XC-99. Other possible cargo loads would include some non-powered wheeled equipment, requiring a winch to pull them up and down the cargo loading ramp.

These needs led to the development of specialised cargo hoists. As a result, four hoists were installed in the XC-99, one in each cargo compartment. A number of safety features were built into the hoists to prevent their inadvertent operation during gusty flying conditions, prevent damage to the structure, and set the traverse brakes automatically in the event the aircraft manoeuvred unexpectedly.

To improve and simplify loading procedures on the XC-99, Convair proposed a new production version of the aircraft to the Air Force, called C-99. With this proposal, Convair entered the competition in the strategic transport field, along with the Douglas C-124A and Boeing C-97. Both of which had already been purchased by the Air Force.

Redesign of the C-99 was done by a Convair Fort Worth division engineering team headed by J

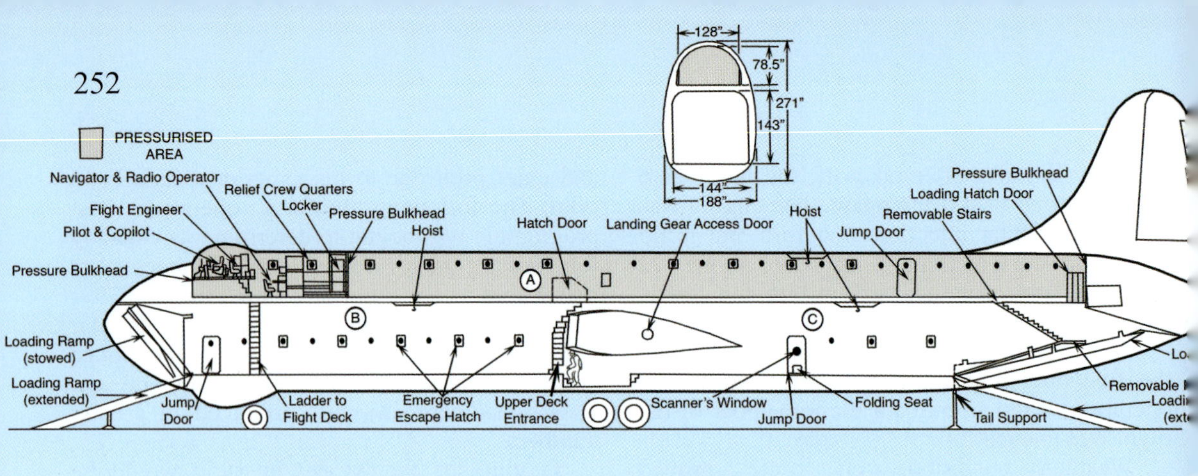

A cutaway of the proposed C-99 showing the internal differences when compared to the XC-99.

W Larson, the chief engineer at Fort Worth.

The C-99 would have major changes. The newly installed six R-436041 3,500 hp engines would be replaced by a new model of the Pratt & Whitney Wasp Major, rated at more than 4,000 hp with a Variable Discharge Turbocharger (VDT). In addition to the increased horsepower, this VDT version offered greater fuel economy, increasing the range of the C-99 (as once proposed for the B-36 bomber, this VDT engine later failed to go into actual production).

The fuselage would be redesigned to permit pressurisation of the upper deck for the transport of troops and hospital cases. The lower deck would be used exclusively for cargo, and would be unpressurised. Pressurisation would also enable the C-99 to operate - on return hauls - as a hospital aircraft, carrying 343 litters and 33 medical attendants. With cargo in the lower compartment, the C-99 could carry 183 troops in the upper compartment. Total troop capacity in both compartments would be 401 combat-ready troops with field equipment.

The nose wheel installation would be lowered, so it did not protrude into the lower cargo compartment and a lengthened nose wheel would make the cargo floors level, whereas the XC-99 had a slight forward slope. The most obvious visual changes would have been the incorporation of the bubble-type canopy of the production B-36s with a three-level flight deck and the modification of the XC-99s nose and tail to be equipped with integral loading ramps and clamshell doors. The new doors would provide a twelve foot by thirteen foot entrance opening at each end of the XC-99. This would permit vehicles, including the largest Army tanks and USAF trailers, to be driven under their own power into the lower cargo department.

On a trans-Atlantic mission, a fleet of forty-four C-99s could transport an entire US Army airborne division of 17,500 troops. It was estimated by Convair that about seventy per cent of B-36 parts and tooling could be used in a mass-production version of the C-99. Preliminary cost estimates, on this basis, would cost the Air Force about $1.5 million a copy and be competitive with the Douglas and Boeing entries on the price factor. The Air Force did not take Convair up on the C-99 proposal.

However, the C-99 proposal did catch the attention of another government agency, the US Post Office. Officials at the Post Office had been watching, with increased interest, the long-distance weight-lifting tests of the XC-99 as the railroads pressed Congress for doubling rates in pay for handling the nation's mail. Faced with a railroad proposal to increase pay for mail hauling by 95%, the Post Office Department was re-examining the feasibility of shifting the major portion of the US mail to the airlines.

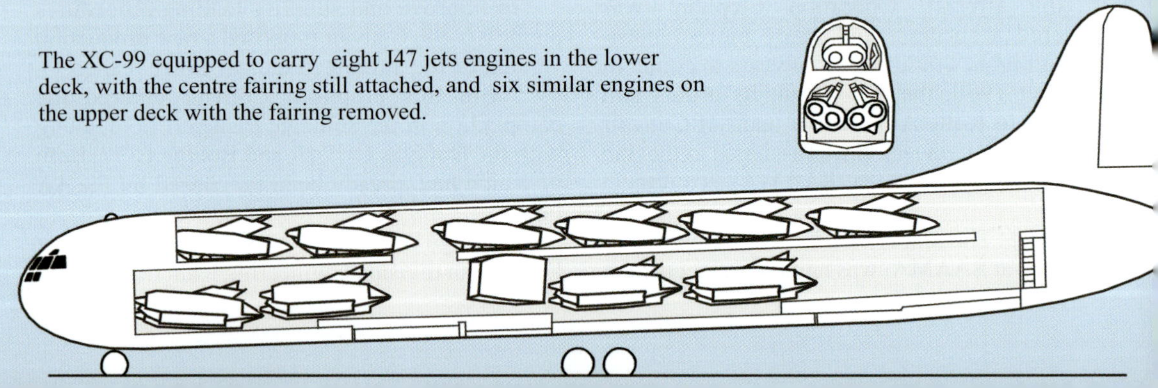

The XC-99 equipped to carry eight J47 jets engines in the lower deck, with the centre fairing still attached, and six similar engines on the upper deck with the fairing removed.

Convair estimated that the XC-99's interior capacity was equivalent to four standard railroad mail cars, and the ability to transport a 100,000 pounds payload would result in a direct flying cost of 34.7 cents per ton-mile between New York and Chicago, and a direct flying cost of 4.6 cents per ton-mile between Chicago and New Orleans, or between Chicago and Los Angeles, with a payload of 95,000 pounds.

The C-99 transport configuration for postal service would not have differed much from the existing XC-99. Provisions for postal use could readily be installed and would use present cargo tie-down fittings. The upper deck of this 'flying Post Office' would be 130 feet long, with a central location for en route sorting of parcel post. The mail would be stowed adjacent to loading hatches forward and aft of the sorting station.

The forward lower deck would have stowage for pre-sorted parcel post. The lower aft deck in the C-99 postal version would be equipped with complete en route sorting stations for 1st, 2nd, 3rd, and 4th class mail.

Loading of the mail could be accomplished with present standard Post Office platforms. The use of pre-loaded lightweight pallets, which could be loaded rapidly and secured for flight, would result in an added time-saving. The four interior hoists could be used simultaneously to load mail.

On the central upper deck, the parcel post sorting station would have sorting tables and bag racks similar to standard Post Office facilities. This would enable mail clerks to sort mail en route between terminals for distribution at the destination.

In 1949, surface carriers were paid $253 million for mail hauling. The airlines were paid $54 million for hauling a fraction of the surface mail figure. The railroads were paid 8.085 cents a ton-mile, and the proposed hike in pay would boost railroad pay to 16 cents per ton-mile.

The big four airlines in 1950 were being paid 3.50 to 3.60 cents per ton mile, and payments to all air carriers for domestic air transport averaged $1.32 per ton-mile. Convair's C-99' flying Post Office' seemed attractive. Assistant Postmaster General John Redding said that the gap between air and surface mail transportation, though still wide, was closing. Initiative on the part of the airlines, he said, could bridge the gap. One airline had already offered to carry the mails at 3.15 cents per ton-mile.

Post Office officials even considered asking the Air Force for the loan of the XC-99 to test the feasibility of mail transportation by the aircraft to key distribution centres, such as Washington DC, New York, Chicago, Los Angeles, San Francisco, and New Orleans.

The Air Force stated that utilising the XC-99 to test its airmail capabilities would not impair the aircraft's long-range weight-lifting test schedule. In addition, the security of information in connection with the XC-99 was not a factor since the aircraft was not on the classified list.

Like the PAA Super Clippers, the flying Post Office never progressed beyond the proposal stage. However, Convair showed creativity and inventiveness in trying to find new markets for the Model 37 design.

In its first seven weeks of operation as a freight carrier, the XC-99 hauled 1,114,654 lbs of high priority cargo. This total was accomplished in five roundtrip missions out of its home base, Kelly. Missions included three flights to various military bases in the West, one to Macon, Georgia, and a record-making non-stop flight across the continent with 85,000 pounds of air materiel.

In all, the XC-99 flew 17,182 miles on its introduction as an air freighter, ferrying military supplies a total of 602,000 ton-miles. On the transcontinental run, the XC-99 carried about twice as much freight as its nearest rival, the C-124, which required two hops for the 2,200-mile flight. Twenty-three international records for cargo flown various distances at different altitudes were shattered by the XC-99, including two broken on its transcontinental trip. Every flight took a lot of planning; even the temperature had to be considered. Cool air gives more lift, and more than once, a trip had to be postponed during the hot Texas summer.

As the XC-99's long-distance, weight-lifting capability evaluation programme continued, the Korean Conflict came into the picture on 25 June 1950. The new war made an enormous logistic demand for the movement of supplies to West Coast ports, and within days the XC-99 began its contribution. On 10 October, it amazed airfreight airmen by hauling forty-two badly needed C-54 engines to McChord AFB, Washington, in one non-stop flight from Kelly. It carried twenty-seven of them on the lower deck and fifteen on the upper. On arrival at McChord, the aircraft taxied down a perimeter track with only one foot clearance on each side and then backed into the loading area by reversing propellers. Mc Chord airmen had never seen an aircraft back up before!

Most XC-99 flights were routine events with

The single US Air Force Convair XC-99, 43-52436, in flight with a Convair B-36B-10-CF Peacemaker 44-92062. The date is 1949. I do not doubt the authenticity of the image, but it does seem very strange to see two such huge aircraft flying in close proximity to each other! (USAF)

no significant problems. But on one flight, almost everything that could go wrong did go wrong. On this particular Air Force test evaluation flight, the XC-99 was the cause of much apprehension and used up a lot of crewmembers' adrenaline. Through a series of personnel errors and equipment problems, the XC-99 experienced a burnt-out auxiliary power unit, wheel well doors being blown off, a gaping hole in the rudder, hydraulic lines rupturing oil, windows breaking out, flight instruments failing to work correctly, and a red warning light as an indication of an unsafe landing gear lock.

After a crewman made a visual check to assure the gear was locked for landing, the pilot discovered that the XC-99 had no brakes or propeller reverse! He set the plane gently down, and it rolled a long way to a stop off the runway. The test pilot's skill was thoroughly tested that day on the XC-99.

In the first six months of 1951, the XC-99 underwent more modifications at Kelly AFB, sealing up fuel tanks, beefing up the main landing gear, adding another cargo door, and installation of a cargo elevator. The plane returned to service in July under the direction of Captain James M. Pittard, Jr., Project Officer. Captain Pittard was eventually to fly more hours than any other Air Force pilot in the XC-99.

In April 1952, pre-loaded cargo bins made at Kelly were added to the XC- 99 for small, high-density, high-priority items to be packed on the upper deck. This new bin arrangement allowed the top deck to be loaded in less than thirty minutes and loading a single bin took less than four minutes. Each of the thirteen bins loaded aboard had a cargo capacity of two tons, and the total loading time for the XC-99 took a little over three hours. The gross take-off weight of the XC-99, fully loaded, was now 322,000 pounds. With a 21,116-gallon fuel capacity, the aircraft had a range of 8,100 miles and an operational top speed of just over 300 mph.

The nominal Air Force flight crew for the XC-99 included pilot, co-pilot, two flight engineers, navigator, radioman, and two rear scanners. No aircrew ever had such room. There were eleven bunks, two hot plates, an electric oven, an icebox, a dining table with chairs, a food storage compartment, and a roomette-size compartment just for the aircraft commander's relaxation.

The XC-99 was in continuous operation from July 1951 to May 1952. It was put on a schedule and flown to the West Coast twice a week, usually to McClellan AFB, near Sacramento, California. It flew 600 hours during this period and airlifted seven million pounds of equipment, nearly half of which supported the Korean effort. Captain Pittard noted that the XC-99 reached the 1,000-hour flying mark in July 1952.

In June 1955, the XC-99 made a round trip from Kelly AFB to the Convair plant in Fort Worth. The Air Force claimed a new passenger-carrying record for land-based aircraft of 212 persons, including the crew. This was the only time the XC-99 was ever used to carry a load of passengers.

An unusual cargo load was carried by the XC-99 from Florida to California once. MGM Studios contracted the machine to fly a number of antique aircraft for use in filming the aviation epic, Wings of Eagles. Arriving in Los Angeles, the XC-99 was greeted by a noisy crowd, mostly of women. The happy crew's ego was shattered, however, when the ladies demanded to see movie actor John Wayne, whom they believed was aboard. It was one of the few times the XC-99 was upstaged.

The XC-99 flew more hours than any other Air Force experimental aircraft. It could fly more cargo further and cheaper than any other aeroplane in history. But its very capacity frustrated all efforts to give the go-ahead for production models. It could haul cargo for 3.16 cents per ton-mile, compared to 3.26 cents for other smaller military cargo-carrying aircraft already in the inventory. The problem was that for a trip to be a financial success, the XC-99 had to carry nearly a full cargo load from Kelly AFB to its destination and then find at least a 60,000-pound load waiting for the return trip. At that time, there simply was no cargo route that could provide that much tonnage.

An impressive total of 7,400 flying hours on its frame had taken its toll. It had been flown 1,486,000 miles by aircrews at Kelly. XC-99 flights were cancelled in March 1957, and the evaluation programme came to a quiet end. SAAMA maintenance at Kelly estimated that nearly 145,000 man-hours and one million dollars would be needed to replace structural sections that had reached limitation by the patch and reinforcement method, undergo essential modifications, and other general repairs for its return to service.

The XC-99 was grounded. There was the possibility it would wind up on the scrapheap. Former crew members, Air Force historians, and San Antonians all protested the scrapping. While proposals for preservation were made, the XC-99 languished in a quiet corner of Kelly. Serious consideration was given to flying it to Dayton, Ohio, and placing it in the Air Force Museum collection. The idea was abandoned because of the expense of putting it in flyable condition for just one flight. Also, Dayton had no building, at that time, able to house the XC-99.

Another idea was to place it in a downtown parking lot next to a department store, which the store eagerly offered, and establish the city Chamber of Commerce within the fuselage. This plan caused quite a stir until a city counsellor suggested that having to dismantle a portion of the city just to move the XC-99 downtown would be prohibitively expensive. The mayor of San Antonio then proposed that the city raise funds to repair it sufficiently for a ten-mile flight across town to the International Airport, where it would become a tourist attraction. The city council liked the idea until it was found to be illegal for the Air Force to donate anything to a city or an individual. San Antonio still wanted the XC-99, and found a way to get it.

On 6 November, 1957, the Disabled American Veterans received title to the machine. After some difficulties, the XC-99 was moved to a spot just off the main runway at Kelly AFB, where it had flown from so many times before. Put on public display for over thirty years, the plane eventually fell into disrepair. In 1993, the Kelly Field Heritage Foundation purchased the XC-99 from the last group having custodianship of the aircraft for $65,000. On 13 May the old piston-engined cargo machine was moved from a field adjacent to

XC-99 at Kelly AFB, Texas, while attached to the Military Air Transport Service 1700th Air Transport Group, 1954. Note the San Antonio Air Materiel Area (SAAMA) tail marking, indicating the aircraft was assigned to the Air Materiel Command. (USAF)

The by now sectionalised XC-99 in open storage outside the Annexe of the National Museum of the USAF at Dayton, Ohio. The extremes of temperature and the humidity variations of Ohio meant that this was a far-from-ideal environment for outside storage. The remains of the XC-99 were transferred to the storage compound at Davies-Monthan AFB in Arizona, where it is stored to this day.
(National Museum of the Uinted States Air Force)

the base back onto Kelly AFB for planned restoration. However, fundraising was difficult, and a new museum that would have featured the XC-99 failed to become a reality. Since then, the plane has been donated to the Air Force Museum, which now had taken responsibility for it.

The XC-99 sat on a ramp area, bordering Upson Park, on the base's west side near the Texas Air National Guard flightline. It was not open to the public, nor was it visible from nearby Military Drive.

However, deterioration of the airframe due to the high magnesium content was beyond local abilities to address. The aircraft was later moved to a grassy field near the base, and in 1993, the USAF moved it back to Kelly AFB. In 1995, Kelly AFB was identified for closure via the Base Realignment and Closure scheme (BRAC). Although some portions would remain under USAF control as the Kelly Field Annex to adjacent Lackland AFB, a new location was deemed to be identified for the XC-99.

Disassembly of the aircraft began at Kelly Field in April 2004. and the airframe was moved in pieces from Kelly to the National Museum of the United States Air Force (NMUSAF) at Wright-Patterson Air Force Base. By the summer of 2008, the transfer was complete, and the parts were lying outside the museum. The aircraft had continued to suffer additional corrosion during its years in Texas and was found to be in worse condition than expected, with the restoration task being beyond the resources of the museum in a realistic time scale. In addition, some major components, such as the wing spar, would need to be replaced entirely.

In an effort to preserve the aircraft for future restoration, the XC-99 was later moved incrementally to the 309th Aerospace Maintenance and Regeneration Group (309 AMARG) storage facility at Davis–Monthan Air Force Base in Tucson, Arizona, where it will remain in an area containing other aircraft belonging to the NMUSAF until the museum can restore it. However, in 2014, Lieutenant General John L. Hudson, USAF (Retd), director of the NMUSAF said that there would be insufficient resources for restoration for the foreseeable future.

Chapter Thirteen

The NB-36H and X-6

Public interest in atomic energy became almost an obsession following World War Two. The scientists who had developed the nuclear bomb had also hypothesised many other uses for the atom. Ideas ranged from power generation to atomic excavation to nuclear propulsion for land, sea or air vehicles. There were proposals for atomic-powered ships, submarines, locomotives, automobiles, and aircraft. By today's standards, most were farfetched, but in the 1950s, all were considered worth pursuing, often at considerable expense.

In 1942, Enrico Fermi, an Italian-American physicist and the creator of the world's first nuclear reactor and his associates involved with the Manhattan Engineer District discussed atomic power to propel aircraft. A study during 1946 by the Johns Hopkins Applied Physics Laboratory defined the potential benefits and challenges associated with using nuclear energy for aircraft propulsion. High on the list of problems was a lack of data on the effects of radiation on materials used in any design. Other concerns were:

- The possible release of radioactive products during normal operation or an accident.
- Shielding the crew and persons on the ground.
- Selecting test sites.

Although the effects of radiation were not fully understood, the requirements for an operational nuclear aircraft were not materially to increase the general background radiation levels, and that all harmful radiation would be restricted to within the aircraft or a predesignated exclusion area.

Given the apparent benefits, in May 1946, the Air Force initiated the Nuclear Energy for the Propulsion of Aircraft (NEPA) project to develop long-range strategic bombers and other high-performance aircraft. The NEPA contract was awarded to the Fairchild Engine & Airframe Co., and the work was conducted at Oak Ridge, Tennessee. By 1948, the Air Force had invested approximately $10 million, and studies continued until 1951.

When the Atomic Energy Commission (AEC) was created in January 1947, the fate of the military-only NEPA effort became uncertain. The programme was continued mainly to allow time for the AEC to devise its own strategy. In May 1951, the NEPA project was effectively replaced by the Aircraft Nuclear Propulsion (ANP) programme, a joint effort between the AEC and the Air Force to develop a full-scale aircraft reactor and engine system. Another factor that led to the ANP programme was a 1948 MIT study group operating under the title 'The lexington Project' who concluded that 'nuclear aircraft (manned) were likely less difficult than nuclear ramjets, which, in turn, would be less difficult than nuclear rockets to develop.' Ironically, this turned out to be the opposite of how events turned out. Although nuclear ramjets (Project Pluto) and nuclear rockets (Project Rover) were successfully tested at the levels needed for operational use, an operational-level atomic aircraft powerplant was never developed.

Italian-American Enrico Fermi b: 29 September 1901, d: 28 November 1954) He was a physicist, and received the 1938 Nobel Prize in physics for identifying new elements and discovering nuclear reactions by his method of nuclear irradiation and bombardment.

However, during early 1951 the Joint Chiefs of Staff had endorsed the military necessity of an atomic-powered aircraft, clearing the way to continue the programme at a higher priority.

As part of the ANP programme, contracts were issued to General

Above: The field adjacent to the north yard at Convair Fort Worth with the no longer needed XB-36 prototype, minus engines, in a fenced-off area. Some aircraft in the yard here had been damaged in the 1 September 1952 tornado but were later repaired. Three B-36s have no tails, and other aircraft parts are stowed nearby. The small, low building in front of the XB-36 is the new nuclear development building constructed for the ANP Programme.

Below: Further north of the nuclear development building was this small complex under construction, where nuclear materials would be kept and the airborne test reactor would be loaded in a special pit. The site was surrounded by Lake Worth on three sides. (Both National Atomic Museum)

Electric to develop the P-1 (later P-3) direct-cycle turbojet and to Pratt & Whitney to develop an indirect cycle turbojet. Development work was primarily accomplished in government-funded laboratories adjacent to the GE plant in Evandale, Ohio. Work was also begun on the new Connecticut Aircraft Nuclear Engine Laboratory (CANEL) located in Middleton, Connecticut, to provide research and test facilities.

In the direct-cycle engine, air from the compressor stage of a turbojet was directed through a reactor core to be heated instead of burning jet fuel like a regular engine. The air, also acting as the reactor coolant, would be rapidly heated, then directed into the turbine section to be discharged through the tailpipe. The hot air spinning the turbine provides the power to run the compressor, and the cycle continues indefinitely.

An indirect system is very similar, except that the air passes through a heat exchanger instead of passing through the reactor itself. A working fluid carries the heat generated by the reactor - either liquid sodium or pressurised water - to the heat exchanger, theoretically allowing more heat energy to be transferred, increasing the system's efficiency. In addition, there would be no need for a continual flow of chemical fuel - such as kerosene - to the engines in both systems, although almost all designs allowed the engines to burn conventional fuel to spool them up and down as needed.

General Electric ran a series of successful experiments using the direct-cycle concept. The Heat Transfer Reactor Experiment (HTRE) series used three reactors, HTRE-1 through HTRE-3. The water-moderated HTRE-1 successfully ran a single modified J47 engine - designated X39 by GE - solely under nuclear power. HTRE-1 was principally a proof-of-concept reactor but achieved several full-power runs that demonstrated the feasibility of operating a jet engine on nuclear power. HTRE-2 was HTRE-1 modified to test advanced reactor sections in a central hexagonal chamber. The experience gained from both reactors was used in the construction of HTRE-3, which was the final test item designed to prove the feasibility of producing an actual aircraft powerplant. HTRE-3 was the closest flight article the programme came from - a solid moderated reactor that powered two X39s at higher power levels. The proposed P-1 powerplant was based on the HTRE-3 configuration and used four modified 17,500 pounds thrust General Electric J53 engines, designated X40, instead of the J47/X39s, but the J53 was a paper engine that never materialised.

The modifications to a standard turbojet engine - be it a J47 or J53 - to enable it to be atomic-powered were relatively straightforward. The entire combustion section was replaced with a ducted compressor outlet and an inlet scroll. Air entered the compressor in the normal fashion and was compressed. But instead of flowing into the combustor, the air was ducted into the reactor core, where it was heated as it made its way through the reactor. On the other side, it was ducted into the engine's turbine section, which then turned the compressor section through the normal shaft connecting the two. In many ways, it was not unlike some of the compounding techniques investigated that used an R-4360 as a heat source for a turbine engine.

Most of the proposed X39 and X40 configurations included a chemical combustor just upstream from the turbine. This combustor allowed the turbojets to be started on chemical power (i.e. kerosene) and then be switched over to atomic heat as the reactor was brought up to operating temperatures. The operational system could also utilise the chemical combustor during takeoff and landing and possibly during target penetration when the relatively slow response time of the reactor could be a disadvantage.

Concerns about crew shielding

Initially, the Lexington Report concluded that nuclear-powered flight could probably be achieved with sufficient effort, but, because of the prohibitive state of the art of shielding at that time, doubted whether a manned nuclear plant was feasible.

The shielding problem was eased with the application of the concept of a split shield. In this configuration, only the neutron shield and part of the gamma shield surround the reactor, while the rest of the heavy gamma shield was wrapped around the rear and sides of the crew compartment. This produced a significant saving in shield weight in the case of the necessarily bulky air cycle shield. It also rendered radioactivity in heat exchangers more tolerable, which permitted the use of coolants such as sodium which became radioactive. In addition, optimisation of light and heavy materials distribution within the shield and suppression of secondary gamma-ray production lead to further decreases.

Although considerable progress was made in

Two views of B-36H 51-5712 following the tornado at Carswell on 1 September 1952. The nose was removed and the severely damaged aircraft was converted into the NTA. (Both National Atomic Museum)

reducing the estimated shield weight, it was still the heaviest single component of a nuclear-powered aircraft. The power, the separation distance between reactor and crew, and the biological tolerance determined the shielding required.

The separation distance between the reactor and crew was clearly a specific design problem. In a subsonic aircraft, this distance was about fifty feet, whereas in a subsonic machine, this increased to around one hundred feet due to higher power and, therefore, greater radiation.

Oak Ridge National Laboratory made major contributions to the ANP Programme through its research on radiation shielding, especially in developing the theory and design of 'divided shields', a two-part shielding system consisting of a thick shield around the reactor to protect the crew and equipment against direct radiation, plus a relatively thin shield surrounding the crew quarters to protect against air scattering effects. This system served to distribute the weight of shielding material, as well as to reduce weight requirements. It was eventually installed on the Convair NB-36H.

In mid-1951, the Defense Department informed the Joint Committee that the joint Chiefs of Staff had established a military requirement for the construction of a nuclear powerplant suitable for aircraft propulsion.

So it was that General Electric were awarded Air Force contract No AF 33(038)-21102, effective 21 March 1951, to develop a nuclear turbo-jet engine, and AEC contract No AT(11-1)-171, effective 29 June 1951, to develop a nuclear reactor to be used in conjunction with the engine, to meet Air Force requirements for aircraft propulsion. After studying the requirement for several months, General Electric chose the direct air cycle concept, using an air-cooled reactor with metallic fuel elements and water as the moderator and structural coolant. The resulting powerplant, designated P-1 (and later, P-3), was planned to be test flown at the earliest possible date in a suitable test-bed aircraft

Under the auspices of Project 1589, during February of 1951, the Air Force awarded Convair contract No AF 33(038)- 21117 to modify two standard B-36Hs to carry the P-1 powerplant. These aircraft were redesignated X-6. Initial ground testing was scheduled for 1954, and the first flights were projected to take place in early 1957. All ground and flight testing involving the P-1 was to take place at the AEC's National Reactor Testing Station (NRTS) near Idaho Falls, Idaho.

In addition to the two X-6s, Convair's contract called for the modification of a third B-36H for shield testing. It would remain conventionally powered but would be extensively modified to carry a small nuclear reactor and associated test instrumentation.

Air Force requirements were redefined at several stages during the ANP Programme. The preliminary design of an airframe for a development aircraft, the NX-2, was completed. In its work, Convair conducted extensive environmental studies, including both shielding and radiation effects. This work was done at company facilities in Fort Worth, Texas. Two test reactors were employed, one a pool-type installation, known as the Ground Test Reactor (GTR) and the other, a tank-type structure, known as the Aircraft Shield Test Reactor (ASTR). Additional measurements were made with ASTR installed in the NB-36H, serving as a radiation source during actual flight operations.

In spring 1952, General Electric began work

on an experimental nuclear powerplant to be tested in a modified B-36, with a first flight date projected for 1956. The GE aircraft propulsion project became a separate department and began working on a six-day week schedule. Later in the year, the ANPO was established to coordinate Defense Department and ABC participation in the programme. 1953 saw Pratt & Whitney receive an AEC backup contract on the ANP Programme for indirect-cycle work.

But with the change of the Administration in Washington DC, the first of major cutbacks occurred. The new Secretary of Defense, Charles E Wilson, decided to cancel the Convair-GE aircraft nuclear propulsion programme. However, the GE engine programme was retained by USAF Secretary Harold Talbott's diversion of unallocated funds to the project. But only a year later, the Air Force wanted to cancel the entire B-36 airborne nuclear reactor test project as a budget-cutting measure.

The Joint Committee submitted a report in 1954 to President Eisenhower, Secretary of Defense Wilson and the Atomic Energy Commission Chairman, calling for a sharply stepped-up effort to achieve nuclear flight. A high-performance test programme was initiated a year later, aimed at testing a prototype propulsion plant about 1959.

Meanwhile, back at Fort Worth, aircraft shielding for an airborne test reactor, built and designed by Convair, was successfully ground tested. The Air Force decided in 1954, under the WS-125A nuclear bomber programme, to develop a high altitude, subsonic bomber with supersonic cruise capability.

In 1954, Raymond Clare Briant, who was then the director of the ANP Project, stated that 'manned nuclear aircraft pose the most difficult engineering development job yet attempted within this century.'

'In the spring of 1948, when the Lexington Project was organised, there were very justifiable doubts as to whether a nuclear aircraft was feasible at all or could justify the expense and effort it would require. While these doubts cannot be completely resolved until a nuclear airplane has actually flown, they have been sufficiently allayed by the Lexington Report and by subsequent progress.'

Unfortunately the ANP programme was not very well organised. Instead of trying to develop one aspect of the technology to a working stage the effort was spread out over a number of areas. Part of the problem was that, under the conventional guidelines, the AEC was responsible for reactor development while the Air Force was responsible for the development of the remainder of the system. Therefore the project was divided

Above: A sample of the six-inch thick plexiglass windshield for the NB-36H. showing its optical clarity.

Right: Convair build a forward fuselage mock-up. Note that the crew access door was seperate from the nosewheel doors. (Both National Atomic Museum)

into two parts that needed to work closely together, but these two parts were managed by totally separate entities.

Pratt & Whitney and General Electric were to be engine contractors, and Convair and Lockheed airframe contractors. The following year, the USAF announced engine-airframe company teams for the WS-125A project, selecting GE and Convair as one team, Pratt & Whitney and Lockheed as the other. Also, in 1955, the Navy began nuclear-powered seaplane studies. Finally, on 17 September 1955, the NB-36H was flown in Fort Worth for the first time, with the reactor operating in flight. The future looked promising, indeed, for nuclear propulsion flight programmes at the time. And the B-36 would play a role in the effort to advance to nuclear-powered flight.

The NB-36H, at Convair Fort Worth, was B-36H 51-5712 that had been assigned to the programme on 11 May 1953. This particular machine had been considerably damaged in the tornado that struck Carswell AFB on 1 September 1952. Nearly half of SAC's B-36 fleet was hit. Rather than repair the nose section of this B-36H, it was kept by Convair and reassigned to ANP Programme. It made sense to use the damaged aircraft rather than pull a completed B-36 off the production line.

Modifications were made to the selected B-36H at the Convair Fort Worth plant. They included: a redesigned nose section, quite different from the standard bubble canopy of production B-36s, that more closely resembled the nose outline of conventional commercial transports of the day, such as the DC-6 or Constellation; bomb bay modifications to house the airborne nuclear reactor; large air scoops on each side of the rear fuselage to duct air to the reactor; closed-circuit television system to monitor the reactor controls; and colourful blue accent streaks along the fuselage and on the nose, with red flashes on the jet engine pods. A three-vaned orange radiation symbol marked the vertical tail, and a circular atom symbol graced the nose section close to normally where a

Above: By 27 December 1954 the new nose area is almost complete. It was skinned in aluminium, even though it was not subjected to pressure cycles. The large rectangular area is where the seperate crew module would be installed.

Right: the lead and rubber-lined crew 'capsule' is loaded aboard the XB-36H. Seemingly, this was a trial fit as the aircraft is not yet painted. (Both Convair)

There is evidence of a 'dating sequence' as to when pictures were taken of the 'nuclear' B-36. In the colour picture above, the aircraft bears the word 'Convair' on the nose, and the type-name 'NB-36H' below it. It has not yet had the additonal word 'Crusader' applied aft of the atomic logo.

This contrasts with the earlier picture, right, that shows the flight crew posing before the aircraft and the name 'XB-36H. (both Convair)

military unit emblem might be placed. It was given a name and christened Convair Crusader.

A unique aspect of the NB-36H was installing a windshield made of transparent shielding that varied from nine to eleven inches thick. In addition, the crew compartment was a special shielded capsule that protected the crew and instruments from radiation effects. It also made the flight deck so quiet that the pilots commented that they frequently felt as though they were flying a glider - a very big glider.

The NB-36H crew on its first flight included A S Witchell, pilot; L C Brandvig, copilot; J D Mc Eachem, flight engineer; S M Andrich, flight test engineer; and J C Nance, nuclear test engineer. Only pilots, flight engineers, and reactor crew were aboard during flight tests. The rear scanners, normally on a B-36 crew, were replaced by the closed-circuit television system in the aft compartment, which also monitored the aircraft's six piston and four jet engines, in addition to reactor controls.

The airborne reactor, designated ASTR, was a low-power unit, rated at one megawatt, about equivalent to one hundred and fifty pounds of thrust if it were part of a propulsion system. In operating condition, the reactor and its shielding weighed 35,000 pounds. Carrying the reactor was no problem since the B-36 was built with bomb bay sections capable of carrying 40,000 pounds.

The NB-36H took off under the power of its conventional engines. The nuclear reactor was not operated during take-off and was not turned on until the aircraft was at a safe altitude, over an unpopulated area, where testing with a 'hot' reactor began.

These tests provided a variety of data on airborne reactor operation. The major purpose of these tests was to reaffirm ground data; gain experience in airborne reactor handling and equipment functioning, and evaluate the effectiveness of crew shielding and any effects on flight instruments and the airframe itself. New types of nuclear instrumentation were also checked out on the NB-36H.

Other technical personnel necessary for tests aboard the NB-36H were stationed aboard a B-50 bomber flying in formation at a discreet distance. Among the B-50 crew were ten engineers trained as parachutists. They were part of the safety precautions surrounding these tests. If there was a disaster involving the NB-36H, it was their job to jump near the disaster area and cordon it off, working with local law enforcement groups. All flying with the reactor operating was done over isolated areas to cut to a minimum the risk of endangering the public.

There is some confusion over exactly what type of aircraft was used to escort the B-36. I have used the designation B-50, for certain, the type

The Aircraft Shield Test Reactor (ASTR) was a water-cooled, water-moderated, enriched-uranium thermal reactor installed in the NB-36H. The ASTR provided a high flux of radiation for airborne and ground shielding experiments but did not provide any power for the aircraft. The NB-36H would eventually make a total of forty-seven flights, but the ASTR was only carried on twenty of them. The last flight lasted nine hours and five minutes, most of it spent at low altitude over the Gulf of Mexico.

Above left: the holding pit carrage set to hold the ASTR in storage..

Above: The ASTR was a 1,000 kilowatt, air -cooled unit weighing 35,000 pounds. Visible here is the rear and right side of the unit with a myriad of pipes, conections, inlet and outlet lines, ion chambers and gamma monitors.

Left: the loading pit for the ASTR reactor. (All Convair)

shown in a number of films made jointly by the Department of the Air Force and Convair to record the progress of the tests. Some sources say it was a B-29, an older machine, but very similar in appearance.

Furthermore, there are stories - possibly urban myths, but one that is certainly backed up by an entry in the NB-36H flight log - that a Fairchild C-119 Flying Boxcar was also used as an escort. According to the legend, on board were a platoon of US Marines tasked similarly to the technicians on the B-50. With typical Marine 'dark humour', they supposedly wore shoulder patches depicting a growing mushroom cloud and the legend 'Glow in the Dark Platoon.'

In the fall of 1956, the original designation XB-36H was redesignated NB-36H, and testing continued of the nuclear reactor operating in flight. Also, around that time, the Air Force cancelled the W5-125A programme, a nuclear-powered bomber, a bad omen for the NB-36H. In all, forty-seven flights were flown by Convair crews in the world's first aircraft to carry an operating nuclear reactor. The Convair Crusader flew its last test flight on 28 March 1957.

Concerned over the on and off again

The XB-36H by the still covered reactor pit at Forth Worth on 13 July 1955. The strange tapered, stepped item on top of the fuselage behind the cockpit windows is the open upper hatch into the shielded crew capsule. (Convair)

development status of projects related to the aircraft nuclear propulsion programme, Major General Donald J Keirn, Air Force Deputy Chief of Staff for the development of nuclear weapons, blamed 'financial timidity and nearly continuous review by various scientific groups or committees' for delays in the programme to develop a nuclear-powered aircraft.

In a speech to the American Ordnance Association meeting in Washington, DC, General Keirn said that much of the advice and information received from scientific groups called in by the Air Force, ABC, and the Department of Defense had been helpful. But he charged that some of the scientific advice received was based on insufficient fact and outlined two examples. First, General Keirn indicated that the ANP programme would have been much further along if it had not been for the scientific conservatism of some of its advisers. He went on to say that technical advancement of the programme required a 'healthy concurrent hardware testing program' to take full advantage of existing knowledge. But, he added, 'This fact does not seem to be fully appreciated by some scientists, who continually advise less effort on hardware development, pending further achievements in improved materials.'

General Keirn said a programme to flight test a nuclear propulsion system in a modified B-36 was cancelled in early 1953, '...because the military potential of the airplane/powerplant system was extremely limited, and the cost was not considered justifiable on the benefits of

Maj. Gen Donald John Keirn
(b. 24 Feb 1905, d, 11 May 1980)

By now christened the Convair Crusader, but still wearing the designation XB-36H the aircraft was one of the more colourful B-36s, seen in flight here with its B-50 escort. Or at least, that is the common understanding of this image - but I have my doubts. I think it's a representation - a painting, or even a digital image. My reasons for thinking this are twofold. Firstly, other images show that the 'Crusader' name was added after the designation was changed to NB-36H. Secondly, every image I have seen of the two aircraft in flight together show the B-50 flying behind and very slightly below the B-36, as it had sampling equipment on board to constantly monitor any 'leakage' from the nuclear reaction on board the larger aircraft . Who knows what the image is? (Convair)

I have not been able to locate one complete view of the NB-36H cockpit, but these three images show the commander's (left) and copilot's (right) stations with the central console in the middle. The pictures were taken from the central entrance way on 15 May 1956. (All Convair)

Not the sharpest of images, but one that does show what was probably the most elegant of B-36 colour schemes with the blue and red cheat line down the fuselage and yellow-and-orange radiation warning on the fin. The jet nacelled and reactor air intake markings were trimmed in red. (Convair)

technical development alone.' More recently, in late 1956, he said work on a nuclear-powered bomber for the WS-125A project was '...re-oriented because the technical risk of success was considered too severe to justify the high cost.'

He went on to say that the United States will, '...soon be ready to embark on an experimental flight development phase, looking forward to a prototype aircraft as the next logical step in the program.'

WS-125A was accordingly cancelled in early 1957. However, there remained occasional flickers of renewed interest in nuclear-powered aircraft into the early 1960s. The Continuously Airborne Missile Air Launcher (CAMAL) concept called for a nuclear-powered strike aircraft able to stay aloft on airborne alert for 2-5 days.

This led to Dromedary, a turboprop design capable of an airborne alert for seventy to one hundred hours and able to stand off outside hostile territory and launch the 600-1000 nautical mile range Skybolt ballistic missile. These ideas meant research into aircraft nuclear propulsion continued, although in only a fairly desultory fashion.

In the autumn of 1957, General Electric proposed anaccelerated programme to get a flying testbed with a nuclear powerplant into the air as soon as possible. Proposals were made in the Department of Defense to the Deputy Secretary of Defense for an early flight programme utilising a modified conventional military aircraft as a flying testbed. The Joint Committee gave strong support to this proposal. In a letter to President Eisenhower, they urged a vigorous programme looking toward early nuclear flight, both as a military requirement and to bolster American scientific prestige following the launching of the Soviet Sputnik.

The US Navy had also occasionally expressed interest in nuclear-powered turboprop flying boats. In April 1955, Operational Requirement CA-01503 sought a nuclear-powered seaplane capable of high subsonic speeds primarily to attack ports and warships using conventional and nuclear weapons with the secondary roles of mining and reconnaissance. The USN desired to have a prototype available for its evaluation no later than 1961. By mid-1956, the Navy had decided a solely-USN power plant was unjustifiable and that the Navy's aircraft would use the USAF's WS-125A power plant. The cancellation of the WS-125A thus terminated the USN's plans as well. At one stage, it looked very likely that the UK would sell three mothballed SARO Princess flying boats to the US Navy for nuclear-power trials, but funding oscillated and eventually was not forthcoming.

After some indications of a favourable reception to these proposals, the President's Adviser on Science and Technology appointed a special panel early in 1958 to review the programme. This was the eighth in a series of committees in the executive branch that had been asked to review the ANP programme since its inception in 1946. This panel, which was later reconstituted as an advisory group to the Defense

Another view of the XB-36H, showing the huge air intake on the rear fuselage to aid cooling of the on-board nuclear reactor. (Lockheed Martin,via author's collection)

Department, recommended against proceeding with a flight programme.

In March 1958, President Eisenhower informed Congress there was no urgency in the nuclear aircraft propulsion programme, and rejected an accelerated programme, instead authorising a continued low-budget development programme.

Further afield, the USSR was also busy. In the late 1950s, Tupolev designed but did not build two nuclear-powered bombers: the subsonic Tu-119 and supersonic Tu-120. The Soviet leadership thought the projected payloads and speed were inadequate for the costs involved. Tupolev was though authorised to continue research on nuclear aircraft. Accordingly, a Tu-95 turboprop bomber was modified at a nuclear complex near Semipalatinsk in Kazakhstan to allow flying a nuclear reactor, becoming the Tu-95LAL (Letayushchaya atomnaya laboratorya – flying atomic laboratory). Mirroring the NB-36H trails, some 34 Tu-95LAL flights were undertaken in 1961 with the reactor on board but without providing propulsion. The tests similarly revealed that a nuclear-powered aircraft was impractical with the technology of the time. The heavy reactor and shields consumed the gain in performance from not carrying chemical fuel, and so Soviet interest in nuclear-powered aircraft declined.

General Keirn was appointed to head ANPO, the joint Air Force and ABC organisation charged with developing a nuclear-powered aircraft. He appeared to be the right man since he had a reputation for getting things done. Early in World War Two he went to Great Britain to study British jet development, and for his success in putting the first American jet into the air, he received a special recognition award in 1944. He did not think that

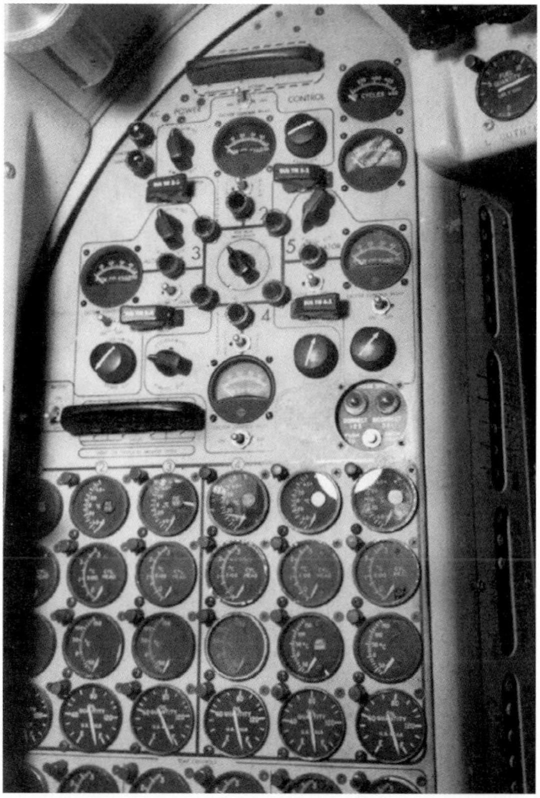

his new task was comparable to that of Admiral Hyman G Rickover, the pioneer of the nuclear US Navy. He commented, 'Putting a nuclear-powered plane into the air is a much more difficult job technically than putting nuclear power in a submarine." The major difficulty was one of weight, while the submarine task was primarily one of engineering since weight was not the prime consideration.

Moving to Washington, DC, in April 1946, General Keirn became liaison officer for the Manhattan Engineering District. While serving in that capacity, he participated in the atomic bomb tests at Bikini in July and August 1946. The following May, he was appointed special assistant to the director of the Division of Military Application, Atomic Energy Commission. He entered the National War College in October 1949 and graduated the following June.

The ANP programme was always torn between buying an effective military combat machine and just getting an aircraft into the air. Both the USAF and the Navy wanted an aircraft that would contribute to their strategic missions. General Keirn said that he did not believe the nuclear aircraft would necessarily be inferior to existing aircraft. It might not have the speed and altitude of the present jet aircraft, but it would have other important characteristics, such as improved endurance, lasting days, not hours. He envisioned using the nuclear-powered machine for long-

The flight engineer's station was totally different to that of other B-36s and was decidedly cramped. He sat at the very back of the crew capsule (opposite page, bottom) with panels on either side.

The left hand panel is the two pictures above, while the right hand one is on the right here. The throttles were below the right hand panel and are just visible in the picture on the opposite page. (Convair)

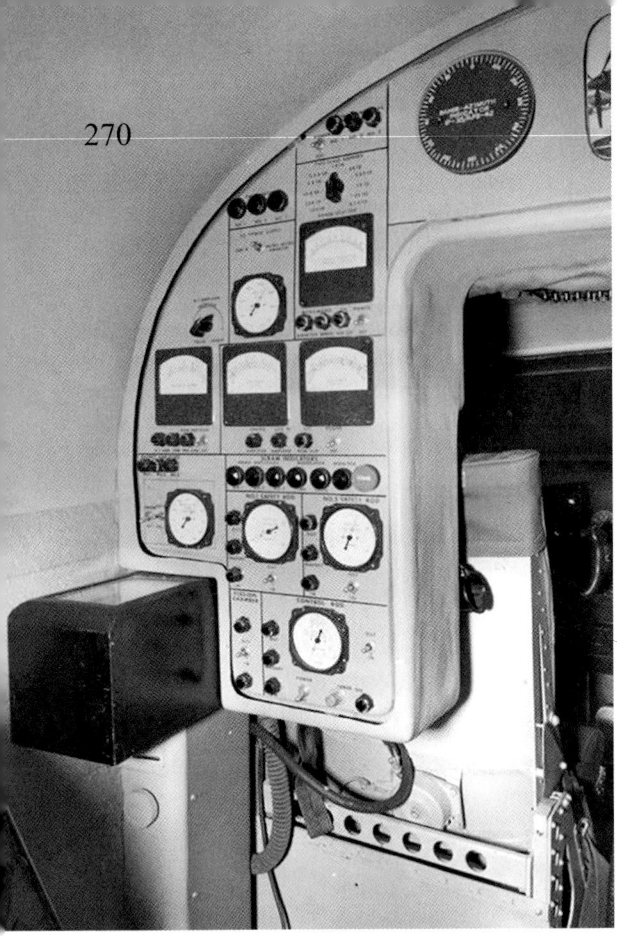

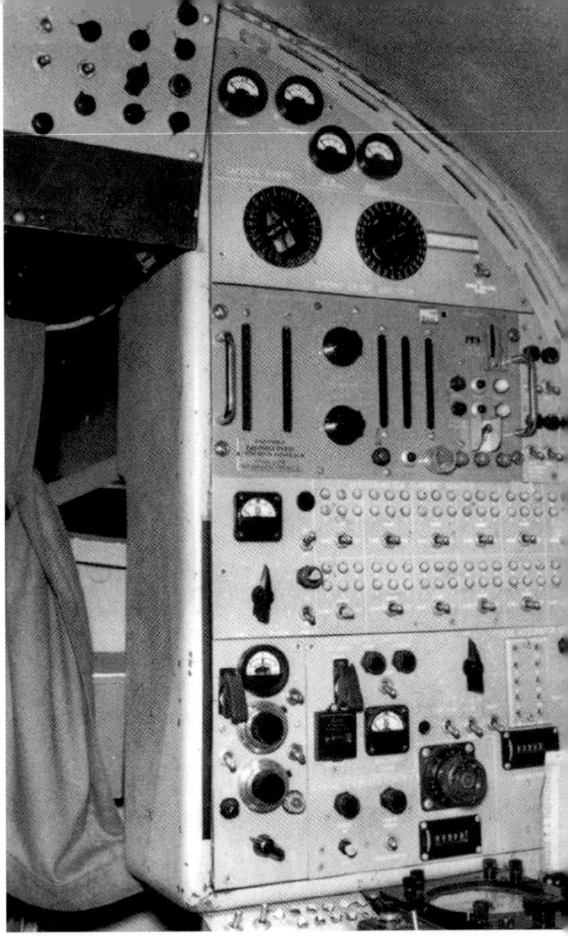

The nuclear engineer's station (left) was responsible for operating the reactor in flight. The flight test engineer's station (right) allowed recording of data while the aircraft was airborne. (Convair via authors collection)

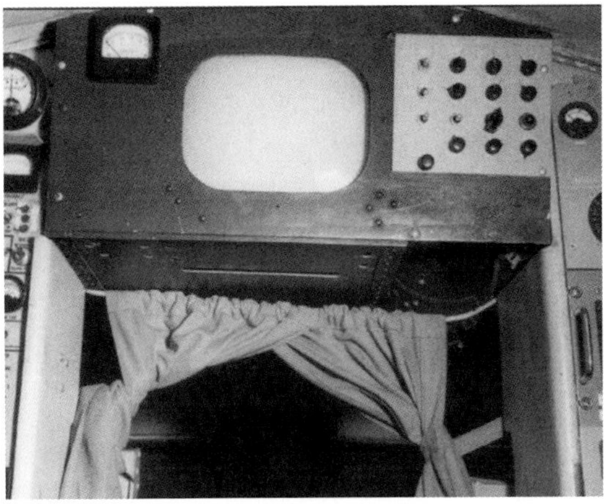

The flight engineer was also tasked with monitoring the closed-circuit television system that replaced the observer's looking forward and monitoring the propellers etc. The TV system was located above the doorway to the flight deck between the nucerlar engineer and flight test engineer.

The lower hatch, right, was the normal way of boarding and disembarking the aircraft. The thickness of the hatch shows the level of shielding applied to the crew capsule. (Both Convair)

XB/NB-36H Flight Log

Date	Programme Flt No	ASTR Flt No	Flt. Time (hh:mm)	Comments
20/07/1955	1	-	1:15	Dummy ASTR; vibration survey; empty water system.
13/08/1955	2	-	5:50	Dummy ASTR; vibration survey; full water system.
01/09/1955	3	-	0:30	No ASTR; shakedown flight; empty water system.
02/09/1955	4	0	3:55	ASTR checkout; non-critical; vibration survey.
16/09/1955	5	—	0:15	Upper hatch opened on takeoff. Flight aborted.
17/09/1955	6	1	5:50	ASTRcheckout; 1st critical; five and ten KW.
23/12/1955	7	—	5:05	Shakedown flight; empty water system.
07/01/1956	8	—	2:15	No data.
07/02/1956	9	-	0:25	No data; engine No. 6 fire warning. Flight aborted.
13/02/1956	10	2	8:55	First experiment data flight.
21/02/1956	11	-	0.25	No information available.
26/02/1956	12	3	8:15	Data flight.
16/03/1956	13	—	3:40	Dummy ASTR; instrumentation checkout.
29/03/1956	14	4	4:50	Data flight; cut short due to stuck valves.
04/03/1956	15	—	2:05	No data; gasket leak.
07/04/1956	16	—	3:45	No data; electrical control problems.
12/04/1956	17	—	0:20	No data; shakedown flight for #3 and #4 propellers.
13/04/1956	18	5	8:40	Data flight.
25/04/1956	19	—	0:20	No data; landing gear did not retract. Flight aborted.
27/04/1956	20	6	10:10	Data flight
10/05/1956	21	—	1:15	No data; C-119 chase broke down.
12/05/1956	22	7	9:30	Data flight.
23/05/1956	23	8	10:55	Data flight
13/06/1956	24	9	9:40	Data flight
22/06/1956	25	10	9:10	Data flight
29/06/1956	26	11	7:30	Data flight
31/07/1956	27	-	2:10	No data; autopilot test and shakedown flight
09/08/1956	28	—	1:40	No data; autopilot problem
17/08/1956	29	—	2:00	No data
28/08/1956	30	—	1:20	No data; autopilotproblem
30/08/1956	31	12	5:20	Data flight
07/09/1956	32	13	8:35	Data flight
13/09/1956	33	-	1:10	
26/09/1956	34	14	8:10	Data flight
11/10/1956	35	15	6:25	Data flight
26/10/1956	36	16	7:30	Data flight
27/10/1956	37	17	6:35	Data flight
22/11/1956	38	—	2:45	
28/11/1956	39	18	8:40	Data flight
28-12/1956	40	19	6:15	Data flight
171/01/1957	41	-	1:45	
27/02/1957	42	20	9:05	Data flight; low altitude (400 feet) over Gulf of Mexico
08/03/1957	43	—	0:25	
09/03/1957	44	—	0:50	
12/03/1957	45	—	0:55	
14/03/1957	46	-	0:30	
28/03/1957	47	—	8:10	Data flight; last flight of programme

215:75 hours total NB-36H flight time over 47 flights.
167.0 hours nuclear flight test time in 17 flights.
89.0 hours ASTR flight operating 'critical' time in 21 flights.

A large model of the X-6 was built to demonstrate how the P-1 powerplant and R- 1 reactor would be remotely manipulated while the system was on the ground. This model - and the images of it - explain the concept far easier than thousands of words can. A large reactor pit would serve to store the assembly. The latter would be moved via a permanent railroad system and a dedicated transportation dolly. (Lockheed Martin, via author's collection)

range surveillance missions or early warning of bombers coming over the Arctic pole. As a cargo/troop transport, the nuclear-powered plane would have the advantage of flying great distances without relying on large stocks of fuel put down in advance for ground refuelling.

Appointed deputy chief of staff for research of the newly organized Air Research and Development Command, General Keirn moved to Wright-Patterson Air Force Base, Ohio, in December 1950, and to Baltimore, Md., the following June, in that capacity. He assumed command of the 1009th Special Weapons Squadron at Bolling Air Force Base, Washington, D.C., in September 1951.

In August 1952 General Keirn was named chief of the Aircraft Reactor Branch, Reactor Development Division, of the Air Research and Development Command, in Washington, D.C., and in February 1953 was appointed chief of the Office of Aircraft Nuclear Propulsion there. On 4 June 1957 he became assistant deputy chief of staff for development for Nuclear Systems, Headquarters US Air Force, with duty station at Baltimore, Md.

With General Keirn now heading the Aircraft Nuclear Propulsion Office, the United States probably had the best chance it ever had to produce a nuclear-powered aircraft ultimately. The American nuclear aircraft propulsion programme continued on a limited basis until the next Administration finally terminated it in 1961. President Kennedy's budget message, given on 28 March 1961, stated, '...the possibility of achieving a militarily useful aircraft in the foreseeable future is still very remote...we believe the time has come to reach a clean-cut decision in this matter.'

Although the ANP programme was dead, work

The front view of X-6. Ground clearance of P-1 was reasonably tight. Note how the X-6 fuselage flattened as it faired into the powerplant/reactor bay. The flat siding continued through to the empennage. In effect, except for the wing, the X-6 would have amounted to a new derivative of the circular cross-sectioned B-36 fuselage. (Lockheed Martin, via author's collection)

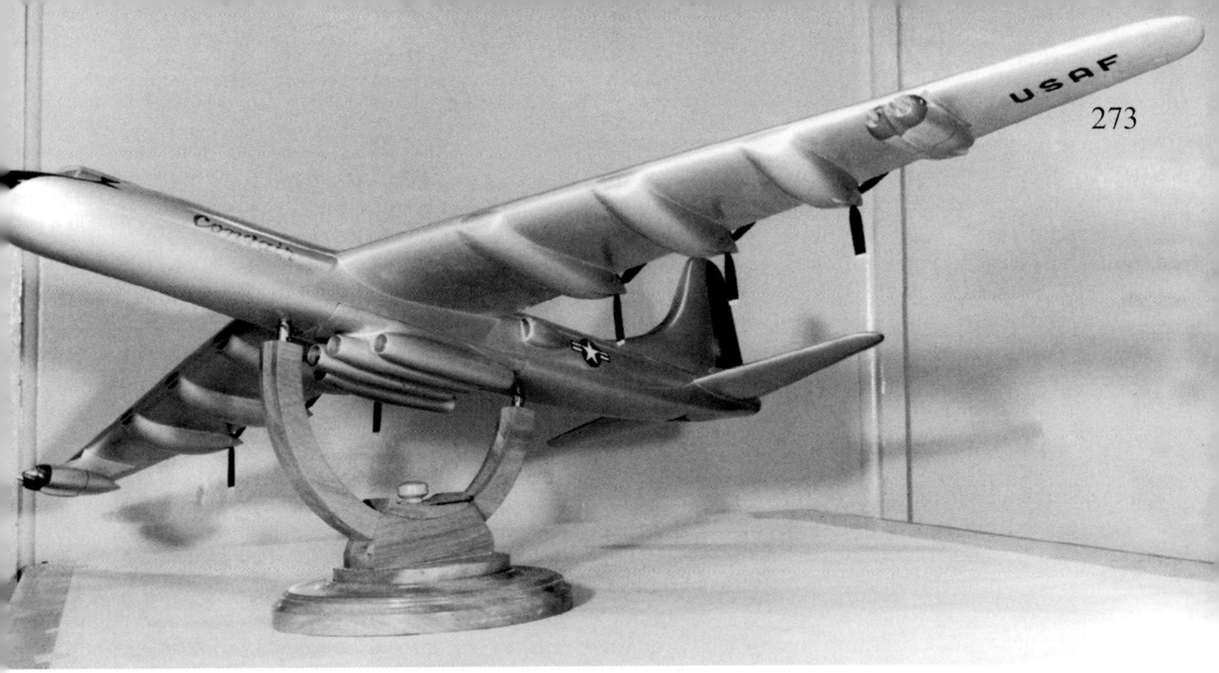

The Convair X -6 configuration as proposed for construction and flight test. Nuclear J57s were clustered under the wing centre section with the P- 1 powerplant in the aircraft's aft bomb bay. The X-6 had a flat-sided rear fuselage and large reactor bay cooling intake - it would have taken an incredible fourteen engines of three different types into the air! (Lockheed Martin, via author's collection)

was allowed to continue on scientific research in the fields of high-temperature materials and high-performance reactors.

The NB-36H had been scrapped by this time, but not before it had played its role in trying to develop a nuclear-powered aircraft for the United States.

The Convair X-6

The second flight vehicle planned by the ANP project team would actually use a nuclear reactor for flight. The Convair X-6 was a proposed experimental aircraft project to develop and evaluate a nuclear-powered jet aircraft. The project was to use a Convair B-36 bomber as a testbed aircraft, and though one NB-36H was modified during the early stages of the project, the programme was cancelled before the actual X-6 and its nuclear reactor engines were completed. The X-6 was part of a larger series of programmes that ran from 1946 through 1961. Because such an aircraft's range would not have been limited by liquid jet fuel, it was theorized that nuclear-powered strategic bombers would be able to stay airborne for weeks at a time.

At the time, it was expected that the J53 turbojet would form the basis of the X40 direct-cycle atomic-powered engine. The J53 was a high-performance design, and it was felt that conversion to nuclear power would present no more difficulty than any other design then in use. The propulsion system would weigh 165,000 pounds, consisting of a 10,000-pound reactor, 60,000 pounds of reactor shielding, 37,000 pounds of crew shielding, and a total engine weight of 18,000 pounds plus an additional 40,000 pounds for ducts and accessories.

The complete X-6 was expected to have a gross takeoff weight of 360,000 pounds. The reactor shield was sixty feet long, and twelve feet in diameter, extending the entire length of the normal B-36 bomb bays and a four-inch-thick lead gamma shield was installed directly in front of the reactor. Additional side shielding around the reactor was provided by a two and a half-inch thick layer of polyethene sandwiched between two sheets of aluminium, one of which was the exterior skin.

An additional shield was located on the back of the crew compartment, about sixty-five feet forward of the reactor. This shield was designed to allow exposure of 0.25 Roentgen per hour - considerably less than the 1 Roentgen estimated in 1951. The crew compartment was identical to the one designed for the NTA, with the exception of modified controls and displays to accommodate the new P-1 powerplant.

The four J53/X40 engines were arranged in a horizontal bank under the fuselage slightly forward of the reactor itself. Each engine was positioned so that air from its compressor stage could be ducted straight into the reactor and discharged through the engine turbine section. The R-1 reactor was air-cooled and water-moderated, but the water could also serve as an additional core coolant if necessary. The core was 5.25 feet in diameter, 3 feet long, contained 143 pounds of enriched uranium, and weighed a total of 4,000 pounds.

In operations, the X-6 would take off and climb to test altitude using the six R-4360 piston and four J47 turbojet engines (or eight J57s in the case of the YB-60 design). The four X40 engines would be idling using kerosene with the reactor shut down for safety reasons. Once the test altitude was reached, the reactor would be made critical, and the four atomic engines would be spooled up using the chemical fuel. Once the X40s were up to speed, they would be switched to reactor power, and the ten conventional engines would be shut down or idle. When it was time to land, the procedure would be reversed.

As the programme progressed, there began to be concerns over the proposed J53 engine. As a result, the Air Force, AEC, and General Electric examined the J47, a proposed GE-X-5-0, the Pratt & Whitney J57-P-5, and the Wright YJ67-W-1. All had drawbacks. The J47 was rejected as not being powerful enough to allow a meaningful test. The GE-X-5-O was a true paper engine that would require at least forty-eight months of development. The J57-P-5 was also considered underpowered, but two banks of three engines would probably provide sufficient thrust for the flight-test series. The YJ67 suffered a similar problem, but it was believed that a single bank of five engines would be adequate.

By this time the flightworthy propulsion package had been designated P-3, but retained the same basic components as the original P-1 installation. The most significant change was that the airflow through the reactor was now back-to-front (compressor air would enter the rear of the reactor), allowing a better centre-of-gravity location in the X-6 airframe. The entire R-3 engine package, including the necessary shielding, weighed 140,000 pounds. Assuming the J53/X40 engines could be brought to maturity, a total of 26,000 pounds of force would propel the X-6 at 300 mph at 15,000 feet.

Project Cancelled

During early 1953 the Eisenhower Administration determined that a nuclear-powered aircraft had no military value, and Secretary of Defense Charles Wilson omitted the ANP in the FY54 budget. After several weeks of negotiation and compromise, the ANP project avoided complete cancellation, but the X-6 experiment was history. The NB-36H flight tests, however, continued.

Throughout most of its life, the ANP programme was plagued by a lack of direction. Neither the Air Force, the Department of Defense (DoD), nor the AEC maintained a concise set of goals. The Air Force favoured the development of an atomic-powered bomber because they wanted to keep manned aircraft an integral part of the deterrent force. Missiles were not showing a great deal of promise, and the Air Force set the priority for the ANP much higher than that for strategic missiles.

The programme was waning when a new

The P-1 powerplant consisted of the R-1 reactor and four heavily modified Pratt & Whitney J47 turbojet engines. This aft view of P- 1 shows the engine's staggered arrangement with two in the centre positioned slightly forward of two outboard engines. The size of the reactor is also apparent when viewed in the X-6 bomb bay. (Lockheed Martin, via author's collection)

It was planned that all activities surrounding the P-1 and R-1would be handled remotely through then-state-of-the-art robotic devices, as the radiation hazard was considered significant. (Lockheed Martin via author's collection)

motivation rocketed onto the scene, quite literally - the Soviets launched Sputnik I. The launch of Sputnik started not only the space race, but also a technological race. President Eisenhower was urged to speed up the ANP programme in order to produce an operational atomic-powered aircraft in answer to the USSR's space endeavours.

In October 1954, the SAC issued a mission requirement for an advanced jet heavy bomber to replace the upcoming B-52 and B-58 beginning in 1965. General LeMay wanted a bomber that had the range and payload capability of the B-52, combined with the supersonic speed of the B-58. The ARDC responded by issuing Weapon System requirements WS-110A and WS-125A during February 1955. These called for advanced bombers that would have a Mach 0.9 cruise speed to an area some 1,150 miles from their target, then 'dash' at Mach 2-plus to the target at high altitude, slowing again to Mach 0.9 for the trip home. The WS-110A was to use conventional jet fuel, while the WS-125A was to be nuclear powered. SAC wanted one, or both, of these advanced bombers to be operational by 1963.

Contracts were awarded to Convair/General Electric and Lockheed/Pratt & Whitney teams in March 1955. The Convair/GE partnership proposed the NX-2, which used two atomic-powered 55,000-pound thrust X211 (XJ87) engines and two conventional turbojets. The companies also studied the possibility of installing chemical (kerosene)-fuelled afterburners on the atomic engines, but the exhaust plume was considered too radioactive for this to work well.

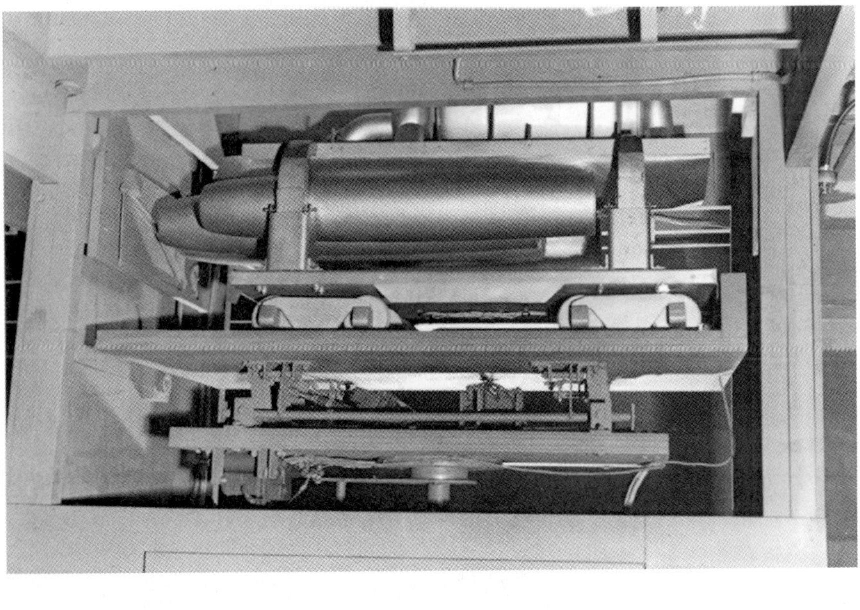

The large X-6 model included a detailed sub-model of the P- 1/R-1 storage pit and its special elevator for removing the P-1 from the X-6 bomb bay. The P- 1, excluding shielding, would have weighed about 14 tons. (Lockheed Martin ,via author's collection)

When correctly positioned over the reactor pit, the X-6 sat on movable pads which allowed the aircraft to be moved in fine increments forward/ or backwards, left or right to allow correct reactor aligment/ (Lockheed Martin, via author's collection)

The proposed X-6 reactor pit was equipped with a massive lead-lined cover that would roll into position on a set of steel tracks. This contained the P-1 powerplant after it was removed via bomb bay-mounted suspension chains that operated like a remotely-controlled crane. (Lockheed Martin, via author's collection)

The aircraft had a large swept-wing mounted on the aft fuselage, and a delta canard mounted far forward. This concept continued in direct competition with the North American XB-70A Valkyrie but was cancelled in 1956 due to technical problems and cost overruns. The idea was revived for a short time as the Continuous Airborne Missile Air Launcher (CAMAL), but this too fell by the wayside during 1958.

Many involved in the ANP programme favoured an early flight date to support the WS-125 requirements. Additional impetus came from a spreading rumour that the Soviets had already flown an atomic-powered aircraft. With typical American hypocrisy of the time, Senator Richard B Russell from Georgia issued a statement saying: 'The report the Russians have test-flown an atomic-powered aircraft is an ominous new threat to world peace and yet another blow to the prestige and security of our nation and the free world. It follows in tragic sequence the Russian success of last fall in launching the first earth satellite.' It seems that anything the USSR did would end the world, while if the Americans tried the same thing, they were world saviours!

On 1 December 1958, Aviation Week ran an editorial in which it announced that the Soviets had flown an atomic-powered bomber prototype. This was accompanied by sketches, complete with large red stars and speculative data. Time has shown this information to be false. There were, however, other rumours. A flying boat, proposed in 1950, would have had a flying weight of 2,000,000 pounds and used four atomic turbo-prop engines. The wingspan was more than 420 feet, and the total power of the engines exceeded 500,000 hp. This aircraft was supposed to carry 1,000 passengers and 200,000 pounds of cargo at a speed of 450 mph. In fact, the Soviets did modify a Tupolev Tu.95 to carry a small reactor for airborne tests, much like the NB-36H. A later version was to have been flown using nuclear-powered Kuznetsov turbo-prop engines, but this never took place.

Ultimately the dwindling federal budget made the USAF choose between the far-fetched WS-125 and the more conventional WS-110. The Air Force chose the WS-110, which eventually resulted in the North American XB-70 Valkyrie. In the end, the ANP programme had simply been around for too long while producing too few results. On 28 March 1961, President Kennedy issued a statement cancelling it. In it he wrote, 'Nearly 15 years and about $1 billion have been devoted to the attempted development of a nuclear-powered aircraft, but the possibility of achieving a militarily useful aircraft in the foreseeable future is still very remote.'

At the time of cancellation, the total amount spent on atomic aircraft development was $1,040 million, broken down as $839 million for research and development and $201 million for facilities and equipment. Funding was provided by the Air Force, AEC, and Navy, supplying $518 million, $508 million, and $14 million, respectively.

In the event, neither X-6 was built. The sole NB-36H eventually was decommissioned at Convair's Ft Worth, TX facility during late 1957 and, after languishing as a hulk at the plant for many months, was eventually scrapped on site.

The X-6/P-1/P-3 airframe/powerplant project was the first US attempt to build and test-fly a nuclear-powered aircraft. The availability of research funding following the contract award to

When the ASTR programme came to an end during 1957, the crew capsule was removed from the NB-36H for disposal. The NB-36H sat at Convair for many months before being scrapped on site. It seems the disposal crew were not to concerned about residual radiation! (Lockheed Martin via author's collection)

Convair stimulated nuclear propulsion research in the US. It led to the design, development, and static testing of nuclear-powered aircraft engines for the first time in history. The technology base generated by this effort remains the largest and most comprehensive information resource on nuclear aircraft propulsion in the world.

Though considered ancillary to the primary X-6 programme objectives, the relatively trouble-free NB-36H project proved productive in terms of actual flightworthy hardware and fundamental data. Experiments with shielding and studies of the numerous hazards associated with using and supporting an airborne reactor were completed successfully using this exotic aircraft. More than anything, it underscored the difficulties in working with nuclear fuel.

In the end, a better technological solution won out. For both the US and the USSR, the ICBM fitted with lightweight thermonuclear warheads offered a much better answer to the problem of a long-range, highly survivable nuclear strike. The considerable effort and funds expended in investigating nuclear-powered human-crewed aircraft yielded much technical information and engineering expertise but ultimately little else.

Chapter Forteen

Demise

The end of the B-36 was much like the beginning - protracted and confusing - something it should not have been. By 1953 the USAF had decided to phase out the B-36 in favour of the Boeing B-52 Stratofortress. The B-52 promised a quantum leap in performance over the B-36, but it would come at a tremendous cost on time and money, and its development dragged in for several years behind schedule. The B-36 was outmoded by mid-1955, but it served well as SAC's primary strategic bomber and perhaps the major deterrent to Soviet aggression. In February 1956, the B-36 began to be replaced by B-52s. However, defence cutbacks in Fiscal Year 57 and 58 slowed the B-52 procurement process and caused the final phase-out date for the B-36 to be changed from the end of FY57 to the end of FY59.

Nevertheless, the first early model B-36s began arriving at Davis-Monthan AFB, outside Tucson, Arizona, in February 1956. The San Antonio Air Materiel Area (SAAMA) of the Air Materiel Command was responsible for disposing the retired B-36s, just as it had been responsible for supporting operational B-36s. Over the next thirty-nine months, a two-step process would strip useable parts off the retired machines, cut them into manageable pieces. The first step involved the Mar-Pak Corporation and USAF personnel removing a controlled list of parts from each aircraft that would eventually find use on still-operational B-36s and other aircraft types. The second step used a large guillotine to chop the airframes into small pieces and portable ovens to smelt them into metal ingots.

However, it was not just a matter of scrapping the aircraft during that time. The delay in B-52 procurement meant that the B-36 would need to serve longer than initially planned. It was complicated because the procurement of spare parts had been halted in anticipation of the aircraft's retirement, leaving the remaining B-36 squadrons short of critical components. The need to keep the B-36s operational occurred so abruptly that the contracts with Mar-Pak had to be modified.

Initially, a total of 135 B-36s had been authorised for disposal during FY58 on contract AF33(600)-33903. In August 1957, this number was reduced to ninety-five, at a rate of ten per month. This was a tiny amount compared to the quantities of other aircraft being retired - partially due to the defence cutbacks and partially due to an overall modernisation of the Air Force in the post-Korea period.

In FY58 alone, 3,945 aircraft were scheduled to be disposed of; FY59 showed 1,529, and FY60 had 1,148. It presented a problem for the Air Force, particularly the Air Materiel Command, responsible for procuring, storing, and transporting spare parts for the operational units. If the economic times had been good, it is likely that retired aircraft would have been stripped of major serviceable items, engines, mainly, and cut up for scrap. However, the fiscal crunch forced the Air Force to salvage many more parts from the retired aircraft to keep similar operational aircraft flyable.

Yet, at the same time, it was not desirable to salvage too many parts, since counting and storing them would have put unacceptable burdens on other parts of the logistics system.

It required a careful juggling act by the Air Force and the personnel on-site at Davis-Monthan. In the case of the B-36, parts could be used not only on other B-36s but also on many other contemporary aircraft. Since they still represented a significant portion of the strategic deterrent, the operational part of the B-36 fleet needed to be maintained until its eventual retirement. Interestingly, most B-36s arrived at Davis-Monthan straight from their last operational sortie.

Various configurations of the basic R-4360 engine used by the B-36 were also used on the B-50, C-97, C-119, and C-124. As a result of the phase-out of the B-36, 1,218 R-4360-41/41A engines were declared surplus, the last in December 1959. A further 2,830 R-4360-53 engines became available as later model B-36s were retired, including engines held as spares and war reserves. As the engines became available, personnel from SAAMA began to reclaim

B-36s in the boneyard at Davis-Monthan. Note the wall of propellers removed from the aircraft in the foreground. (USAF)

crankshafts, cylinders, and other items common to all R-4360 configurations. A total of $22,000 worth of parts were removed from each R-4360 engine. These parts were then refurbished as needed and utilised by other users, particularly the C-97 and C-124 units. This recycling of parts saved several million dollars during FY58/59.

There were some unexpected requirements for reclaimed B-36 parts. In April 1958, the commander of the 19th Air Division requested SAAMA save one hundred crash axes with insulated handles from B-36s being reclaimed. It turned out that the crash axes being procured with the new B-52s were deemed unsatisfactory by the flight crews. Although new axes only cost $7 each, there were no funds available to procure them. Salvaging axes from the retired B-36s proved to be the answer, and these axes likely flew with the early model B-52s until they were retired.

Mar-Pak (and the AASB in some instances) had been responsible for reclaiming all valuable and hazardous equipment from the B-36 airframes.

Among the dangerous materials to be removed were twenty separate assemblies that contained minor amounts of radioactive material. It was common practice at the time to use elements such as Radium-226 as a light source for instruments and to include Thorium-232 in some optical glass. Other Thorium isotopes were also used to impart strength to the magnesium alloys on the B-36, but this was such a trace amount as to be considered inconsequential. Today it is still used for the same purpose.The radioactive items were:

ITEM	ISOTOPE	LOCATION
Eight-Day Clock	Ra-226	Flight Engineer Sta.
Bomb Bay		
Setting Gauge	Ra-226	Bombardier Sta.
Bombsight Azimuth	Ra-226	Bombardier Sta.
Bombsight Housing	Ra-226	Bombardier Sta.
Bombsight Lens	Th-232	Bombardier Sta.
Bombsight Sight Angle	Ra-226	Bombardier Sta.
Circuit Breaker	Ra-226	Copilot Station.
Circuit Breaker	Ra-226	Flight Engineer Sta.
Long Range Switch	Ra-226	Tail Gunner Sta.
Oxy Mask	Ra-226	Nav Position (L/H).
Oxy Pressure Gage	Ra-226	Radio Operator Compt.
Oxy Regulator	Ra-226	Throughout Aircraft.
Range Switch	Ra-226	Aft Left Gunner Sta.
Range Switch	Ra-226	Aft Right Gunner Sta.
Switch	Ra-226	Pilot Overhead (R/H).
Switch	Ra-226	Pilot Console.
Tachometer	Ra-226	Pilot Panel (left side).
Target Switch	Ra-226	Tail Gunner Sta.
Tune For Max	Ra-226	Navigator Sta.

In April 1958, Convair was authorised to dispose of all the special tooling required to build and support the B-36 production line at Fort Worth. The value was estimated at $500,000, but the USAF did not want to incur the estimated $20,000 expense to store the tooling until the final B-36 phase-out. It was also decided to dispose of thirteen all-weather maintenance docks, seven empennage work stands, and 446 miscellaneous work stands and platforms in Fort Worth. Experience had shown that the cost of dismantling such structures by contractor personnel generally exceeded the return generated from selling the scrap - in this case, estimated at $38,000 for Convair to perform the work. Instead, the Air Force decided to solicit bids on a per-pound as-is/where-is basis, with all necessary dismantling, loading, and hauling at the bidder's risk and expense. A bidder was selected in early June, and by the end of July 1958, all of the material had been removed from the Fort Worth facility. The Air Force realised a profit of $28,051 from the transaction.

Reclamation reached past disposing of the aircraft. In 1953 a series of ten permanent maintenance docks had been installed at Kelly AFB to support the B-36. These docks had originally cost $352,000, and later modifications added another $137,900. By the end of 1958, the docks had been declared excess, and SAAMA began a search for any Air Force unit that had potential uses for them. Eventually, the San Bernardino Air Materiel Area (SBAMA) enquired if the docks could be modified for use with C-133s. SAAMA engineers determined that they could be used for the new transport aircraft and sent an engineering package to SBAMA for approval. After no reply, SAAMA proceeded with

Another view of the B-36s in the boneyard at Davis-Monthan along with a detailled look at the 'fence' of propellers removed from the aircraft. Two machines that can be identified on the left: '2710' is 49-2710, and was sent to MASDC 1 July 1958. '3723' on the right is 51-13723. (Both USAF)

CONVAIR

Published every other Wednesday by Convair, a Division of General Dynamics Corporation, for the benefit of Convair people everywhere.

Convairiety

Vol. 11, No. 11

Wednesday, May 28, 1958

Fort Worth and Daingerfield EDITION

Fort Worth news office: ext. 8245; Daingerfield news office: ext. 424

SAN DIEGO, POMONA AND ANTELOPE VALLEY, CALIFORNIA

DAINGERFIELD AND FORT WORTH, TEXAS

LAMPLIGHTER—Putting new light bulb atop flagpole at Convair Fort Worth is R. K. Bowlin of plant engineering.

Flag Pole Scaled By 'Lamplighter'

R. K. Bowlin of plant engineering at FW has made his semi-annual climb up Convair's 100-ft. flag pole in role of lamplighter.

It is a spectacular operation and involves running a stout cable through the flag pulleys. Riding in a boatswain's chair, Bowlin was pulled to the top by a truck attached to the other end of the cable.

B. T. Frost of plant engineering reported that two warning lights are located on top of the pole, but only one burns at any single time. When it burns out, the spare is used until conditions are favorable for an ascension. New bulbs are required about twice a year.

The trip up and down is completed in a matter of a few minutes, probably to the relief of the lamplighter.

Standards Engineer Wins NASC Election

P. A. Little, Convair Fort Worth standards engineer, is new vice chairman, western division, National Aircraft Standards Committee. He was elected in May at a national meeting of the group in New York City.

Little, a Convair employee 15 years, is in the materials process group.

Pace Tells Club B-58 Is 'Greatest Vehicle of Peace'

Frank Pace Jr., president of General Dynamics Corporation, told a capacity Convair Fort Worth Management Club audience Friday night that "the kind of thinking in Fort Worth is as good as any I have seen anywhere."

"You have built one of the greatest vehicles of peace in our time," he told the audience of 1,200. "With the B-58, you have added something to the free world arsenal of which we all can be proud."

Describing General Dynamics' defense business, Pace noted that the United States once was protected by two oceans.

"Now, for the first time in history," he said, "another nation has the capacity to destroy us.

"I believe we will be living with a cold—or hot—war for as long as you and I shall live. It puts a new focus on what we must do."

General Dynamics, Pace said, can offer a real service to the nation if it provides the country with the best possible defense at the lowest possible price.

He said Convair forms an essential ingredient of the corporation, and said, "I will be a disappointed man" if Convair is not the leader in the industry for the next decade.

Pace described the corporation as a "series of successive successes" conceived and generated by the late John Jay Hopkins, but emphasized that the corporation is "not tied to a single man or a single idea."

"The men who head the various divisions are extremely competent," he explained. "Any one of them could take my place."

He said efficiency of various divisions enables a general office force of only 110 people to oversee the activities of 93,000 employees in the General Dynamics family.

In a review of each of the divisions, Pace said the most outstanding group of scientists in the country—and possibly the world—is with General Atomics.

"I believe we will someday see an atomic revolution that will equal or surpass the industrial revolution. When that day comes, we will be ready.

"Nowhere in industry can our long-range planning be equalled."

Pace, who spoke without notes, received a standing ovation. He was introduced by August C. Esenwein, Convair Fort Worth manager.

FOR A GOLFER—Frank Pace Jr. shows new golf bag to, left to right, Dick Curry, Management Club president; August C. Esenwein, division manager; and I. M. Laddon, a General Dynamics Corporation director. Bag was gift of club to Pace, who also is president of International Golf Association.

Convair to Observe Memorial Day Friday

Convair personnel everywhere will enjoy a holiday Friday (May 30) in observance of Memorial Day.

Only those employees notified in advance will be required to work. Normal work schedules will resume June 2 except for those working Saturdays, who will report May 31.

Fort Worth employees will find Memorial Day ceremonies at Carswell AFB of special interest.

Carswell to Bid 'Farewell to B-36' On Memorial Day

Carswell AFB's last Convair Fort Worth-built B-36 will be honored in a special Memorial Day ceremony and Open House at the base Friday (May 30).

All Convair Fort Worth people who helped build B-36s are especially invited to the holiday program, which will include an extensive display of modern aircraft and missiles.

During the program, B-36 number S/N 51-5704—Carswell's last—will take off and make her last flight—into retirement. It will end a ten-year reign of the B-36 at the Fort Worth base.

And, according to Maj. T. N. Mallard, general projects officer for the special ceremony, the program may be the last opportunity for people of Fort Worth to see the huge ten-engine airplane.

Appropriately, Convair's supersonic B-58 Hustler will play a big part in the show. The delta-wing bomber is slated to be on display on the ground, and is tentatively scheduled to join the B-36 and a B-52 in a flyby.

The entire program, called "Operation Milestone," will be a tribute to the men who built the B-36, who flew it, and who maintained it at Carswell AFB.

"We especially invite all Convair people who helped build the B-36 to attend the program," said Major Mallard. The show will be open to the public.

Open House will be from 9 a.m. until 3 p.m., with a ramp ceremony scheduled at 9 a.m. The ramp program will be a reenactment of the delivery of the first B-36 which came across the runway to Carswell in June, 1948.

Col. John Roberts, who was present on that occasion, also will be at the ceremony Friday.

At 11 a.m. there will be a parade by the 19th Air Division. The last B-36 will take off and fly over, and is scheduled to be joined by the B-58 and a B-52.

"The B-36 holds an honored spot in the hearts of many pilots," Mallard said. "When the chips were down, she always did the job."

August C. Esenwein, division manager, and G. S. Green, assistant manager of customer service, will represent Convair on the reviewing stand. Green was in charge of transition flying which gave familiarization flights to crews when Carswell got its first planes.

LAST CHANCE—Friday, May 30, a holiday at Convair Fort Worth, is last chance for Convair employees and families to take close look at one of B-36s they built. Going over arrangements for Open House at Carswell were Col. John Roberts, acting commander of the 19th Air Division at Carswell, and G. S. Green, who was co-pilot with B. A. Erickson on first flight of first B-36.

FW Pay Boost Involves Vast Tabulating Task

Pay increases affecting approximately 46,500 individuals in Pomona, San Diego, Astronautics and Fort Worth Divisions of Convair went into effect this month, dating from May 12.

In round numbers, 2,500 at Pomona, 20,000 at SD Division, 7,000 in Astro, and 17,000 at Fort Worth get raises.

The decision to make more than 17,000 wage and salary increases—and to make them effective as of May 12—started a chain reaction at Convair Fort Worth this month which built up to a monumental task for the three departments most directly involved.

Pencils started flying, typewriters clacking and electronic calculators whirring and flashing. Personnel, general accounting and industrial accounting departments all went into all-out effort to bring records up to date and to get the increased wages and salaries into hands of employees as quickly as possible.

Increases announced on May 14 and May 15 for most hourly employees and all salaried employees will amount to an estimated $8½ million in the first 12-month period, according to F. E. Chambers, manager of industrial relations and security.

Hourly employees in three groups benefit by the first pay increases announced. The groups are employees represented by the Federated Independent Texas Unions; employees non-represented; and employees represented by the International Association of Machinists (except Dept. 81 employees whose collective bargaining representation is pending action of the National Labor Relations Board).

The new higher rates for those employees will show up for the first time on paychecks they receive on May 29. (Employees will be paid on Thursday, since Friday is Memorial Day and a holiday.) Higher rates for salaried employees will appear for the first time on checks they receive June 13.

When the pay increase decision was made, it was already too late to change the figures on which May 23 paychecks were computed for hourly employees affected. It also was too late to change the figures on paychecks which salaried employees will receive May 29.

As a result, some 17,000-plus special checks will be written and issued. These checks, to give each employee the benefit of the increase back to the May 12 effective date, will be distributed about June 11.

Similar increases will go into effect for employees represented

(Continued on Page 6)

ONE A SECOND—Checks reflecting new increases are clacked out at more than 75 a minute by check-writing machine as Frank Furr monitors.

disposing of the docks, partially through donations to local schools and some through sales to contractors for $700 each. When SBAMA finally requested the docks, they were no longer available, although SAAMA found suitable replacements. As a result, all of the docks at Kelly had been disposed of by September 1959.

A total of 385 B-36-type aircraft had been manufactured, including the two original prototypes. Of these, forty-one had been destroyed or otherwise disposed of during the service life of the type, including the original XB-36 and the YB-36A. It left 344 aircraft to be reclaimed as the B-36 was phased out of service. SAAMA awarded four separate contracts to Mar-Pak Corporation for the reclamation of these aircraft. The first contract - AF33(600)-33547 - was signed on 30 June 1956 and covered the reclamation of twenty-six early-model aircraft. The second contract, AF33(600)-33903, was signed on 3 December 1956 and originally covered 135 aircraft. However, the Air Force removed eleven aircraft from this contract and allowed ten of them to be reclaimed by government personnel to determine if that method was more cost-effective. The eleventh aircraft, 44-92024, was selected by the Arizona Aircraft Storage Branch (AASB) for extended storage at Davis-Monthan AFB to display it at the Air Force Museum eventually. After a later B-36J, 52-2220 was pulled from the last Mar-Pak contract for display at the Museum, the original aircraft was reclaimed, and the carcass was transferred to the Davis-Monthan fire department and used as a fire trainer.

The experiment to determine if it was more economical for personnel from the AASB to reclaim aircraft had some unexpected repercussions. In early 1957 the AASB, eager to increase its usefulness, requested and received permission to reclaim 10 B-36s, subsequently removed from the second Mar-Pak contract. The reclamation of the ten aircraft began on 3 June 1957 and was completed on 28 June 1957. The unit cost for reclamation was calculated as $5,193.23 per aircraft. The price for Mar-Pak to accomplish the same work was $6,000 per aircraft. However, the AASB pointed out that when Mar-Pak did the job, the AASB incurred $1,214 in expenses during the receiving and processing of the aircraft prior to transferring them to Mar-Pak, this made the contractor cost $7,214, almost fifty per cent higher than the AASB cost. If this saving was spread over the remaining 184 B-36s, the total savings to the government was $372,026.12, a considerable amount of money at the time.

After studying the service test results and analysing the cost figures, SAAMA recommended to headquarters that AASB be allowed to reclaim the remaining B-36s. Headquarters AMC concurred with the recommendation and on 13

Opposite page: How Carswell bade farewell to the B-36 - the date of Convairiety was 28 May 1958.

Below: Around the same time these eight B-36 Peacemakers met with the scrapmen - a sad end. (USAF)

A Mar-Pak advert from the US press offering B-36 partsfor sale.

August 1957, advised SAAMA that AASB should conduct further reclamation work at a rate of ten aircraft per month. However, eighteen days later, the authorisation was rescinded, and the AASB was informed that additional contracts should be negotiated with Mar-Pak to do the work. As a result, the AASB was restricted to receiving the aircraft and processing them into storage prior to transferring them to Mar-Pak. The mystery behind this sudden reversal was cleared up when it was learned that Congressional pressure had been applied to award Mar-Pak contracts.

In support of the Mar-Pak request for reinstatement, cost figures had been compiled by the contractor alleging to prove that the work could be accomplished more economically by Mar-Pak. These figures were in direct contradiction to the figures previously collected by the AASB; which set of figures was correct was never cleared up.

Informal reports indicated that Mar-Pak used cameras with telephoto lenses that showed up to fifty people working on or standing near one B-36 aircraft during the AASB reclamation. This photo was used to allege poor work methods and excessive personnel used by the AASB for the task. If the photos existed, the AASB explained they were probably taken during a shift change when people were simply transiting the area and were not directly involved in the ongoing work. It really did not matter - the Ohio congressional delegation had made sure that all future work would go to Mar-Pak. To ensure the AASB could not again try to wrest the work away from Mar-Pak, Headquarters AMC immediately cut the AASB staff by one hundred and thirty people.

In fairness to Mar-Pak Corporation, it should be noted that the experience gained during the learning curve on the earlier contract did allow the company to increase the efficiency of the operation and lower costs. It might well be that it was in the best interests of the US Government for the reclamation programme to be continued by contract. In any case, it was a moot point.

The signing of the third contract, AF33(600)-35907, had been delayed while the Air Force determined the relative merits of contractor versus Air Force reclamation. When it was finally signed on 16 October 1957, the contract covered the reclamation of ninety-five aircraft.

Subsequently, two supplemental agreements added eight additional machines. One of the 103 aircraft on this contract was given to the New

Mexico Institute of Mining and Technology at Socorro, New Mexico. The aircraft, 51-5720, was slowly dismantled, and portions of it used in live weapons effects testing conducted under Navy auspices. As late as 1990, significant parts of the centre wing structure remained in the aircraft scrapyard at New Mexico Tech, as the school was later renamed. The restoration team restoring the B-36J at Fort Worth have removed portions of skin from the remains in Socorro for use on their aircraft.

The fourth and final Mar-Pak contract, AF33(600)-37911, was signed on 31 July 1958 and originally covered eighty-one aircraft, mostly late-model B/RB-36Hs and B-36Js. Four aircraft - 51-13730, 52-2217, 52-2220, and 52-2827 - were withdrawn from the contract and given to various museums around the country. The last B-36 was flown to Davis-Monthan on 11 February 1959 from Biggs AFB, and on 24 April 1959, Mar-Pak completed the last reclamation contract. All that remained now was another contractor's final smelting of the skeletonised airframes.

The carcasses of the B-36s needed to be smelted into ingots to recycle the metals. The smelting was accomplished on-site at Davis-Monthan by various contractors. As of 1 July 1957, the value of all assets reclaimed from B-36s totalled $53,541,682.22; $36.5 million of this represented material which had direct application to other aircraft in the Air Force inventory. Expenses incurred by the Air Force and Mar-Pak totalled $1,125,927.34, as well as an additional $209,271.50 in transportation costs.

A year later, the total value of reclaimed assets had climbed to $108,243,731.28, and another year later amounted to $159,030,324.17, exclusive of reclamation and transportation costs. Additional savings of $39,580,155.75 were realised using reclaimed parts for various aircraft types. The total cost to reclaim the B-36 assets were placed at $2,812,434.87, with $4,125,347.01 being spent repairing the pieces and putting them into a serviceable condition. Transportation added $450,645.96 to this total. It represented an actual return to the Government of $151,641,896.33 - almost ten per cent of the roughly $1,532 million costs of the B-36 procurement.

And Finally - the Black Beetle

No book on the B-36 would be complete without at least a passing mention to the M-497 railcar, nicknamed Black Beetle by the press. This was an experimental jet-powered railcar testbed of the New York Central Railroad, developed and tested in 1966. A pair of second-hand General Electric J47-19 jet engines and part of their mounting pylon, originally used for the Convair B-36 Peacemaker, was mounted upside down on the roof, above the cab of a model RDC-3 Budd Rail

M 497, the Budd railcar with the pair of J47-19 jet engines from a B-36 over the driver's cab. (Allan Keyes Collection)

Diesel Car configured as a of coach and baggage railcar, which had received a streamlined front cowling. This unit had originally been purchased new in January of 1953 to provide light passenger service along its former Michigan Central lines between Detroit and Mackinaw City, Michigan.

The idea began humbly enough as merely a concept over coffee a year earlier in 1965 when engineers Don Wetzel and Hank Morris began tossing around using a jet engine to power a locomotive to offer high-speed passenger service.

Wetzel was not only the railroad's Assistant Director of Technical Research at NYC's Technical Research Laboratory in Cleveland but also a pilot and licensed engineer.

After pitching the thought to then-president Alfred Perlman, the project was given the go-ahead. Perlman was a foreword thinking railroad man who knew how to manage a company and had brought the New York Central back from the brink.

At Cleveland's Collinwood Technical Center, maintenance crews tore down the M-497 to be fitted with jet engines and more than fifty different instruments to measure a wide range of characteristics from speed to stress and ride quality.

The jet engines were mounted to the top of the car directly above the cab, which truly gave it a look from a science fiction movie. Their bright red paint scheme around the intakes only added to the sci-fi look. To reduce wind speed, designers added a custom slant nose to the front of the car, which was purely a cosmetic feature that fitted over the existing cab shape. In all, the railroad officially stated the project had cost around $30,000, although it is said the actual price tag was likely higher.

I have only been able to locate one picture of 'The Black Beetle' in full flight as it were. This image was taken duing one of the record-breaking runs during 1966. (Allan Keyes Collection)

By July, the car was ready for service and the location to make the initial run was chosen by Charles T Popma, NYC's Assistant Vice President of Engineering.

Popma decided that the best stretch of right-of-way would be along the mainline between Butler, Indiana and Air Line Junction, near Toledo, Ohio, which offered more than sixty-eight miles of nearly tangent double-track.

Performing the run required the railroad to update the trackage to NYC's first-class specifications, given the speeds the Black Beetle was likely to reach.

The tests, two on each day, were performed on Saturday 23 July and Sunday 24 July and Mr. Perlman himself was present for both. The M-497 reached a top speed of 183.68 mph, a record for a light-rail vehicle at the time and still stands today in the United States.

Even with this spectacular performance, and even though it had been built relatively cheaply, using existing parts, the project was not considered viable commercially. The railroad gathered valuable test data regarding the stresses of high-speed rail travel on conventional equipment and tracks then existing in America. Unfortunately, the data was largely ignored. The New York Central Railroad was headed for a merger with its arch-rival Pennsylvania Railroad that was already heavily involved in the Metroliner project, funded by the US Department of Transportation.

M-497 continued to serve for Penn Central after the jet engines were removed until retirement by Conrail in 1977. The engines were re-used as X29493, an experimental snowblower. Like most similar jet engine blowers, it was effective at clearing snow and ice but also tended to dislodge the ballast.

Chapter Fifteen

Strategic Air Command - the movie

It is impossible to write about the B-36 without mentioning Strategic Air Command - a 1955 American military aviation film starring James Stewart and June Allyson, directed by Anthony Mann, and released by Paramount Pictures. It was the first of four Hollywood films that depicted the role of SAC in the Cold War era.

The movie was something special right from the beginning. One of several that could loosely be called 'propaganda flicks' during the height of the Cold War, Strategic Air Command touched the hearts and souls of many people. It was also a good aeroplane movie.

Strategic Air Command was the second film released in Paramount's then-new widescreen format called, VistaVision. It had colour by Technicolor and Perspecta pseudo-stereo sound. It would also be Stewart and Mann's eighth and final collaboration and the last of three films that paired Jimmy Stewart and June Allyson, the others being The Stratton Story and The Glenn Miller Story.

A film poster from the movie, heaily featuring the B-36. (authors collection)

The Plot

In 1951, Robert 'Dutch' Holland, played by James Stewart, was a professional baseball player with the St. Louis Cardinals. A B-29 bomber pilot during World War Two, he retains a commission as a lieutenant colonel in the United States Air Force Reserve but is on inactive, non-drilling status. During spring training at Al Lang Field in St. Petersburg, Florida, he is recalled to active duty for twenty-one months. He reports to his posting at Carswell Air Force Base, a bomber base in Fort Worth, Texas, to qualify on the Convair B-36. He arrives in civilian clothing for which he is rebuked by General Hawkes, played by Frank Lovejoy, the commander of SAC, and replies that his uniforms are 'the wrong color'. The comment suggests that he had been inactive at least since the Air Force discontinued the brown United States Army Air Forces uniform in favour of a blue service dress uniform three years earlier, in 1949. The General's character is obviously patterned after the real SAC commander of the time, 'Old Iron Balls' himself, General Curtis LeMay.

Dutch is given a staff job with the Bombardment Wing at Carswell that involves a lot of flying. He soon has a B-36 crew of his own, selecting a former World War Two colleague as his flight engineer, and becomes

Two images taken during filming by the front gate of Carswell AFB. Note the Eighth Air Force emblem over the gatehouse.
(Lockheed Martin, via author's collection)

enamoured with both flying and the role of SAC in deterring war. He is joined by his wife, Sally, played by June Allyson, who had not bargained on being an Air Force wife, and who struggles with his repeated absences and the dangers of flying. On any given night, Dutch might find his aircraft on airborne alert far from the continental United States, in secret, only telling his wife when he returns days later. Even so, Sally tells Dutch that she is happy as long as they can be together, no matter what he decides to do with his life.

The plot attempts - and succeeds - to show that when introduced, the B-36 is a complex aircraft, but improvements are being worked on all the time. One challenge was leakage from the fuel tanks, but a new fix is introduced to address this once and for all. On their next flight, Dutch's crew have to fly their B-36 from Carswell AFB to Thule Air Base, Greenland. The fix does not work, and one of the engines bursts into flame, causing the entire left wing to catch fire. The crew is forced to abandon the aircraft and bail out over the ice and snow of Greenland before arriving at Thule. Dutch and his radar navigator stay on board for a forced landing, which causes Dutch to injure his right shoulder.

Dutch becomes a favourite of General Hawkes, and he is rewarded with a revised assignment flying the new Boeing B-47 Stratojet at MacDill Air Force Base, Tampa, Florida, across the bay from St. Petersburg where his old baseball team continues to conduct its spring training. Promoted to 'full bird' colonel and made deputy Wing commander of his B-47 Wing at MacDill AFB, Dutch decides, to Sally's displeasure, to remain in the Air Force rather than return to baseball at the end of his active duty obligation.

They encounter severe wind and storms on a full B-47 wing deployment exercise that involves flying nonstop from MacDill to Yokota Air Base,

Japan. Low on fuel, they divert to Kadena Air Base, Okinawa. As they prepare to land, Dutch realizes that his shoulder injury from the B-36 crash was worse than he thought, and his arm is almost immobile. He cannot operate the engine power levers during the final landing phase, and he has to rely on his co-pilot to do so, while Dutch works the flight controls with his left arm and two feet.

This injury not only bars him from further flying and causes the Air Force to medically discharge him, but it also appears to threaten his baseball career. General Hawkes suggests that he would make an excellent team manager.

Production

In real life, during World War Two, Stewart had been a B-17 instructor pilot, a B-24 squadron commander, and a Bomb Group operations officer, completing twenty combat missions. At the time of filming, Stewart, much like the character he portrays, was also a colonel in the Air Force Reserve, serving with the Strategic Air Command when on duty and at the time was qualified as a pilot on the B-47. However, much of the B-47 flying was performed by his friend and fellow Air Force pilot, Maj. (later Col.) A.W. Blizzard, Jr. Stewart's military service and lifelong interest in aviation greatly influenced the making of the film. He pushed for an authentic but sympathetic portrayal of the Strategic Air Command, which led Paramount to put together a strong cast of Hollywood veterans and production people, including June Allyson, Frank Lovejoy, director Anthony Mann, and the top stunt pilot of the day, Paul Mantz. The film accurately portrays from the perspective of the 1951 starting point of the script the duties and responsibilities of an Air Force strategic bomber pilot, and the demands such service places on family life.

The film includes dramatic aerial photography, for which it was awarded a special citation by the American National Board of Review. It is also the only motion picture to highlight the Convair B-36. The propeller-driven B-36 was then near the end of its service life and was about to be replaced by the jet-powered B-47 Stratojet, followed by the Boeing B-52 Stratofortress. The aerial footage was accompanied by a dramatic and soaring musical score composed by Victor Young.

One of a series of cinema lobby-cards for Strategic Air Command. The B-36 was very much in evidence. (Author's collection)

Another film poster for the movie - but this time in French! (author's collection)

Obviously, the film was made with the full cooperation of the US Air Force, and it was filmed partly on location at MacDill Air Force Base, Tampa, Florida; Lowry Air Force Base, Colorado, and Carswell Air Force Base, Texas.

The baseball shots were filmed with the cooperation of the St. Louis Cardinals at their spring training home of Al Lang Field in St. Petersburg, Florida, just across Tampa Bay from MacDill AFB.

Stewart's character is based on the real-life military career and an actual mission flown by Brigadier General Clifford Schoeffler, who had crashed during an Arctic B-36 mission and survived. Brigadier General Schoeffler was on site at Carswell Air Force Base during the filming of Strategic Air Command as a consultant.

Some commentators have speculated that the plot was inspired by Boston Red Sox legend Ted Williams, a World War Two veteran recalled for Korean War service as a US Marine Corps aviator at the height of his baseball career.

In Omaha, Nebraska, the Storz Mansion was the scene of opulent parties celebrating the film. Its premiere was held in Omaha, the home of Offutt AFB and SAC Headquarters, with guests that included Stewart and Allyson and the Strategic Air Command commander, General Curtis LeMay.

Shot in the new VistaVision process, it had an impressive soundtrack that accurately captured the thunder of the B-36. The film was the sixth highest-grossing film of 1955. Critics were lukewarm about the performances of all except for Stewart, who was called 'capable', 'charming', and 'competent.' Public reaction centred on the spectacular aerial footage, so much so that the B-36 and B-47 aircraft were arguably the film's real stars. Its release led to a twenty-five per cent increase in USAF enlistments.

Strategic Air Command was followed by two more military aviation films that were also supportive of SAC's mission, Bombers B-52 (1957), and A Gathering of Eagles (1963).

Incidentally, I last saw the B-47 cockpit used in the film on display at the March Field Air Museum at March Air Reserve Base (former March AFB) in Riverside, California.

From a technical viewpoint, the movie featured some of the most accurate sets ever built. In order to construct the full-scale mock-up of a B-36 interior, Paramount sent a crew to measure every inch of both the interior and exterior of a real B-36B. As part of the assignment, all of the interior spaces were photographed, most with various rulers or measuring tapes placed in full view to aid the construction team back at the studio.

Unfortunately, Paramount did not document what aircraft they photographed, and no other records could be found that shed any light on the subject. Over the passing years enthusiasts and historians have found it is easy to rule out a B-36A since there was operational equipment on the aircraft, meaning it was either a B-36B or B-36D - all that had been built at the time. Through endless reviews of the photographs many have come to the conclusion that it was a B-36B, most likely between serial number 44-92063 and 44-92087. No-one seems able to be any more accurate than that!

Bibliography

Baker, David. Convair B-36 Peacemaker 1941-1959 Owners Workshop Manual, J D Haynes & Co, Somerset UK 2020.
Barlow, Jeffrey G. Revolt of the Admirals: The Fight for Naval Aviation, 1945-1950. Washington, D.C.: Naval Historical Center, 1994.
Convair B-36 Peacemaker Pilot's Flight Operating Instructions. USAF.
Convairiety – Vol.01, No. 01: 1 September 1948.
Convairiety – Vol.01, No. 02: 15 September 1948.
Convairiety – Vol.01, No. 03: 29 September 1948.
Convairiety – Vol.01, No. 04: 13 October 1948.
Convairiety – Vol.01, No. 05: 27 October 1948.
Convairiety – Vol.01, No. 06: 10 November 1948.
Convairiety – Vol.01, No. 07: 24 November 1948.
Convairiety – Vol.01, No. 08: 8 December 1948.
Convairiety – Vol.01, No. 09: 22 December 1948.
Convairiety – Vol.02, No. 01: 5 January 1949.
Convairiety – Vol.02, No. 02: 19 January 1949.
Convairiety – Vol.02, No. 03: 2 February 1949.
Convairiety – Vol.02, No. 04: 16 February 1949.
Convairiety – Vol.02, No. 05: 2 March 1949.
Convairiety – Vol.02, No. 06: 16 March 1949.
Convairiety – Vol.02, No. 07: 30 March 1949.
Convairiety – Vol.02, No. 08: 13 April 1949.
Convairiety – Vol.02, No. 09: 27 April 1949.
Convairiety – Vol.02, No. 10: 11 May 1949.
Convairiety – Vol.02, No. 11: 25 May 1949.
Convairiety – Vol.02, No. 12: 8 June 1949.
Convairiety – Vol.02, No. 13: 22 June 1949.
Convairiety – Vol.02, No. 14: 6 July 1949.
Convairiety – Vol.02, No. 15: 20 July 1949.
Convairiety – Vol.02, No. 16: 3 August 1949.
Convairiety – Vol.02, No. 17: 17 August 1949.
Convairiety – Vol.02, No. 18: 31 August 1949.
Convairiety – Vol.02, No. 19: 14 September 1949.
Convairiety – Vol.02, No. 20: 28 September 1949.
Convairiety – Vol.02, No. 21: 12 October 1949.
Convairiety – Vol.02, No. 22: 26 October 1949.
Convairiety – Vol.02, No. 23: 9 November 1949.
Convairiety – Vol.02, No. 24: 23 November 1949.
Convairiety – Vol.02, No. 25: 7 December 1949.
Convairiety – Vol.02, No. 26: 21 December 1949.
Convairiety – Vol.03, No. 01: 4 January 1950.
Convairiety – Vol.03, No. 02: 18 January1950.
Convairiety – Vol.03, No. 03: 1 February 1950.
Convairiety – Vol.03, No. 04: 15 February 1950.
Convairiety – Vol.03, No. 05: 1 March 1950.
Convairiety – Vol.03, No. 06: 15 March 1950.
Convairiety – Vol.03, No. 07: 29 March 1950.
Convairiety – Vol.03, No. 08: 12 April 1950.
Convairiety – Vol.03, No. 09: 26 April 1950.
Convairiety – Vol.03, No. 10: 10 May 1950.
Convairiety – Vol.03, No. 11: 24 May 1950.
Convairiety – Vol.03, No. 12: 7 June 1950.
Convairiety – Vol.03, No. 13: 21 June 1950.
Convairiety – Vol.03, No. 14: 5 July 1950.
Convairiety – Vol.03, No. 15: 19 July 1950.
Convairiety – Vol.03, No. 16: 2 August 1950.
Convairiety – Vol.03, No. 17: 16 August 1950.
Convairiety – Vol.03, No. 18: 30 August 1950.
Convairiety – Vol.03, No. 19: 13 September 1950.
Convairiety – Vol.03, No. 20: 27 September 1950.
Convairiety – Vol.03, No. 21: 11 October 1950.
Convairiety – Vol.03, No. 22: 25 October 1950.
Convairiety – Vol.03, No. 23: 8 November 1950.
Convairiety – Vol.03, No. 24: 22 November 1950.
Convairiety – Vol.03, No. 25: 6 December 1950.
Convairiety – Vol.03, No. 26: 20 December 1950.
Convairiety – Vol.04, No. 01: 3 January 1951.
Convairiety – Vol.04, No. 02: 17 January 1951.
Convairiety – Vol.04, No. 03: 31 January 1951.
Convairiety – Vol.04, No. 04: 14 February 1951.
Convairiety – Vol.04, No. 05: 28 February 1951.
Convairiety – Vol.04, No. 06: 14 March 1951.
Convairiety – Vol.04, No. 07: 28 March 1951.
Convairiety – Vol.04, No. 08: 11 April 1951.
Convairiety – Vol.04, No. 09: 25 April 1951.
Convairiety – Vol.04, No. 10: 9 May 1951.
Convairiety – Vol.04, No. 11: 23 May 1951.
Convairiety – Vol.04, No. 12: 6 June 1951.
Convairiety – Vol.04, No. 13: 20 June 1951.
Convairiety – Vol.04, No. 14: 4 July 1951.
Convairiety – Vol.04, No. 15: 18 July 1951.
Convairiety – Vol.04, No. 16: 1 August 1951.
Convairiety – Vol.04, No. 17: 15 August 1951.
Convairiety – Vol.04, No. 18: 29 August 1951.
Convairiety – Vol.04, No. 19: 12 September 1951.
Convairiety – Vol.04, No. 20: 26 September 1951.
Convairiety – Vol.04, No. 21: 10 October 1951.
Convairiety – Vol.04, No. 22: 24 October 1951.
Convairiety – Vol.04, No. 23: 7 November 1951.
Convairiety – Vol.04, No. 24: 21 November 1951.
Convairiety – Vol.04, No. 25: 5 December 1951.
Convairiety – Vol.04, No. 26: 19 December 1951.
Convairiety – Vol.05, No. 01: 2 January 1952.
Convairiety – Vol.05, No. 02: 16 January 1952.
Convairiety – Vol.05, No. 03: 30 January 1952.
Convairiety – Vol.05, No. 04: 13 February 1952.
Convairiety – Vol.05, No. 05: 27 February 1952.
Convairiety – Vol.05, No. 06: 12 March 1952.
Convairiety – Vol.05, No. 07: 26 March 1952.
Convairiety – Vol.05, No. 08: 9 April 1952.
Convairiety – Vol.05, No. 09: 23 April 1952.
Convairiety – Vol.05, No. 10: 7 May 1952.
Convairiety – Vol.05, No. 11: 21 May 1952.

Convairiety – Vol.05, No. 12: June 4 1952.
Convairiety – Vol.05, No. 13: June 18 1952.
Convairiety – Vol.05, No. 14: 2 July 1952.
Convairiety – Vol.05, No. 15: 16 July 1952.
Convairiety – Vol.05, No. 16: 30 July 1952.
Convairiety – Vol.05, No. 17: 13 August 1952.
Convairiety – Vol.05, No. 18: 27 August 1952.
Convairiety – Vol.05, No. 19: 10 September 1952.
Convairiety – Vol.05, No. 20: 24 September 1952.
Convairiety – Vol.05, No. 21: 8 October 1952.
Convairiety – Vol.05, No. 22: 22 October 1952.
Convairiety – Vol.05, No. 23: 5 November 1952.
Convairiety – Vol.05, No. 24: 19 November 1952.
Convairiety – Vol.05, No. 25: 3 December 1952.
Convairiety – Vol.05, No. 26: 17 December 1952.
Convairiety – Vol.05, No. 27: 31 December 1952.
Convairiety – Vol.06, No.01: 14 January 1953.
Convairiety – Vol.06, No.02: 28 January 1953.
Convairiety – Vol.06, No.03: 11 February 1953.
Convairiety – Vol.06, No.04: 25 February 1953.
Convairiety – Vol.06, No.05: 11 March 1953.
Convairiety – Vol.06, No.06: 25 March 1953.
Convairiety – Vol.06, No.07: 8 April 1953.
Convairiety – Vol.06, No.08: 22 April 1953.
Convairiety – Vol.06, No.09: 6 May 1953.
Convairiety – Vol.06, No.10: 20 May 1953.
Convairiety – Vol.06, No.11: 3 June 1953.
Convairiety – Vol.06, No.12: 17 June 1953.
Convairiety– Vol.06, No.13: 1 July 1953.
Convairiety – Vol.06, No.14: 15 July 1953.
Convairiety – Vol.06, No.15: 29 July 1953.
Convairiety – Vol.06, No.16: 12 August 1953.
Convairiety – Vol.06, No.17: 26 August 1953.
Convairiety – Vol.06, No.18: 9 September 1953.
Convairiety – Vol.06, No.19: 23 September 1953
Convairiety – Vol.06, No.20: 7 October 1953.
Convairiety – Vol.06, No.21: 21 October 1953.
Convairiety – Vol.06, No.22: 4 November 1953.
Convairiety – Vol.06, No.23: 18 November 1953.
Convairiety – Vol.06, No.24: 2 December 1953.
Convairiety – Vol.06, No.25: 16 December 1953.
Convairiety – Vol.06, No.26: 30 December 1953.
Convairiety – Vol.07, No. 01: 13 January 1954.
Convairiety – Vol.07, No. 02: 27 January 1954.
Convairiety – Vol.07, No. 03: 10 February 1954.
Convairiety – Vol.07, No. 04: 24 February 1954.
Convairiety – Vol.07, No. 05: 10 March 1954.
Convairiety – Vol.07, No. 06: 24 March 1954.
Convairiety – Vol.07, No. 07: 7 April 1954.
Convairiety – Vol.07, No. 08: 21 April 1954.
Convairiety – Vol.07, No. 09: 5 May 1954.
Convairiety – Vol.07, No. 10: 19 May 1954.
Convairiety – Vol.07, No. 11: 2 June 1954.
Convairiety – Vol.07, No. 12: 16 June 1954.
Convairiety – Vol.07, No. 13: 30 June 1954.
Convairiety – Vol.07, No. 14: 14 July 1954.
Convairiety – Vol.07, No. 15: 28 July 1954.
Convairiety – Vol.07, No. 16: 11 August 1954.
Convairiety – Vol.07, No. 17: 25 August 1954.
Convairiety – Vol.07, No. 18: 8 September 1954.
Convairiety – Vol.07, No. 19: 22 September 1954.
Convairiety – Vol.07, No. 20: 6 October 1954.
Convairiety – Vol.07, No. 21: 20 October 1954.
Convairiety – Vol.07, No. 22: 3 November 1954.
Convairiety – Vol.07, No. 23: 17 November 1954.
Convairiety – Vol.07, No. 24: 1 December 1954.
Convairiety – Vol.07, No. 25: 15 December 1954.
Convairiety – Vol.07, No. 26 29 December 1954.
Convairiety – Vol.08, No. 01: 12 January 1955.
Convairiety – Vol.08, No. 02: 26 January 1955.
Convairiety – Vol.08, No. 03: 9 February 1955.
Convairiety – Vol.08, No. 04: 23 February 1955.
Convairiety – Vol.08, No. 05: 9 March 1955.
Convairiety – Vol.08, No. 06: 23 March 1955.
Convairiety – Vol.08, No. 07: 6 April 1955.
Convairiety – Vol.08, No. 08: 20 April 1955.
Convairiety – Vol.08, No. 09: 4 May 1955.
Convairiety – Vol.08, No. 10: 18 May 1955.
Convairiety – Vol.08, No. 11: 1 June 1955.
Convairiety – Vol.08, No. 12: 15 June 1955.
Convairiety – Vol.08, No. 13: 25 June 1955.
Convairiety – Vol.08, No. 14: 13 July 1955.
Convairiety – Vol.08, No. 15: 27 July 1955
Convairiety – Vol.08, No. 16: 10 August 1955.
Convairiety – Vol.08, No. 17: 24 August 1955.
Convairiety – Vol.08, No. 18: 7 September 1955.
Convairiety – Vol.08, No. 19: 21 September 1955.
Convairiety – Vol.08, No. 19: 28 September 1955.
Convairiety – Vol.08, No. 20: 5 October 1955.
Convairiety – Vol.08, No. 21: 19 October 1955.
Convairiety – Vol.08, No. 22: 2 November 1955.
Convairiety – Vol.09, No. 01: 11 January 1956.
Convairiety – Vol.09, No. 02: 25 January 1956.
Convairiety – Vol.09, No. 03: 8 February 1956.
Convairiety – Vol.09, No. 04: 22 February 1956.
Convairiety – Vol.09, No. 05: 7 March 1956.
Convairiety – Vol.09, No. 06: 21 March 1956.
Convairiety – Vol.09, No. 07: 4 April 1956.
Convairiety – Vol.09, No. 08: 18 April 1956.
Convairiety – Vol.09, No. 09: 2 May 1956.
Convairiety – Vol.09, No. 10: 16 May 1956.
Convairiety – Vol.09, No. 11: 31 May 1956.
Convairiety – Vol.09, No. 12: 13 June 1956.
Convairiety – Vol.09, No. 13: 27 June 1956.
Convairiety – Vol.09, No. 14: 11 July 1956.
Convairiety – Vol.09, No. 15: 25 July 1956.
Convairiety – Vol.09, No. 16: 8 August 1956.
Convairiety – Vol.09, No. 17: 22 August 1956.
Convairiety – Vol.09, No. 18: 5 September 1956.
Convairiety – Vol.09, No. 19: 19 September 1956.
Convairiety – Vol.09, No. 20: 3 October 1956.
Convairiety – Vol.09, No. 21: 17 October 1956.
Convairiety – Vol.09, No. 22: 31 October 1956.
Convairiety – Vol.09, No. 23: 14 November 1956.
Convairiety – Vol.09, No. 23: 16 November 1955.
Convairiety – Vol.09, No. 24: 28 November 1956.
Convairiety – Vol.09, No. 24: 30 November 1955.
Convairiety – Vol.09, No. 25: 12 December 1956.
Convairiety – Vol.09, No. 25: 14 December 1955.
Convairiety – Vol.09, No. 26: 26 December 1956.

Convairiety – Vol.09, No. 26: 28 December 1955.
Convairiety – Vol.10, No. 01: 9 January 1957.
Convairiety – Vol.10, No. 02: 23 January 1957.
Convairiety – Vol.10, No. 03: 6 February 1957.
Convairiety – Vol.10, No. 04: 20 February 1957.
Convairiety – Vol.10, No. 05: 6 March 1957.
Convairiety – Vol.10, No. 06: 20 March 1957.
Convairiety – Vol.10, No. 07: 3 April 1957.
Convairiety – Vol.10, No. 08: 17 April 1957.
Convairiety – Vol.10, No. 09: 1 May 1957.
Convairiety – Vol.10, No. 10: 15 May 1957
Convairiety – Vol.10, No. 11: 29 May 1957.
Convairiety – Vol.10, No. 12: 12 June 1957.
Convairiety – Vol.10, No. 13: 26 June 1957.
Convairiety – Vol.10, No. 14: 10 July 1957.
Convairiety – Vol.10, No. 15: 24 July 1957.
Convairiety – Vol.10, No. 16: 7 August 1957.
Convairiety – Vol.10, No. 17: 21 August 1957.
Convairiety – Vol.10, No. 18: 4 September 1957.
Convairiety – Vol.10, No. 19: 18 September 1957.
Convairiety – Vol.10, No. 20: 2 October 1957.
Convairiety – Vol.10, No. 21: 16 October 1957.
Convairiety – Vol.10, No. 22: 30 October1957.
Convairiety – Vol.10, No. 23: 13 November 1957.
Convairiety – Vol.10, No. 24: 27 November 1957.
Convairiety – Vol.10, No. 25: 11 December 1957.
Convairiety – Vol.10, No. 26: 26 December 1957.
Convairiety – Vol.11, No. 01: 8 January 1958.
Convairiety – Vol.11, No. 02: 22 January 1958.
Convairiety – Vol.11, No. 03: 5 February 1958.
Convairiety – Vol.11, No. 04: 19 February 1958.
Convairiety – Vol.11, No. 05: 5 March 1958.
Convairiety – Vol.11, No. 06: 19 March 1958.
Convairiety – Vol.11, No. 07: 2 April 1958.
Convairiety – Vol.11, No. 08: 16 April 1958.
Convairiety – Vol.11, No. 09: 30 April 1958.
Convairiety – Vol.11, No. 10: 14 May 1958.
Convairiety – Vol.11, No. 11: 28 May 1958.
Convairiety – Vol.11, No. 12: 11 June 1958.
Convairiety – Vol.11, No. 13: 25 June 1958.
Convairiety – Vol.11, No. 14: 9 July 1958.
Ford, Daniel. B-36: Bomber at the Crossroads. Air and Space/Smithsonian, April 1996.
Freeman, Roger. The US Strategic Bomber Mcdonalds Illustrated War Studies 1975.
Grant, R.G. and John R. Dailey. Flight: 100 Years of Aviation. Harlow, Essex, UK: DK Adult, 2007.
Jacobsen, Meyers K. Peacemaker. Airpower, Vol. 4, No. 6, November 1974.
Jacobsen, Meyers K. and Ray Wagner. B-36 in Action (Aircraft in Action Number 42). Carrollton, Texas: Squadron/Signal Publications Inc., 1980.
Jacobsen, Meyers K. Convair B-36: A Comprehensive History of America's 'Big Stick'. Atglen, Pennsylvania: Schiffer Military History, 1997.
Jacobsen, Meyers K. Convair B-36: A Photo Chronicle. Atglen, Pennsylvania: Schiffer Military History, 1999.
Jenkins, Dennis R. B-36 Photo Scrapbook. St. Paul, Minnesota: Specialty Press Publishers and Wholesalers, 2003.
Jenkins, Dennis R. Convair B-36 Peacemaker. St. Paul, Minnesota: Specialty Press Publishers and Wholesalers, 1999.
Jenkins, Dennis R. Magnesium Overcast: The Story of the Convair B-36. North Branch, Minnesota: Specialty Press, 2002.,
Johnsen, Frederick A. Thundering Peacemaker, the B-36 Story in Words and Pictures. Tacoma, Washington: Bomber Books, 1978.
Knaack, Marcelle Size. Encyclopedia of U.S. Air Force aircraft and missile systems Volume II: Post-World War II Bombers, 1945–1973. Washington, DC: Office of Air Force History, 1988.
Leach, Norman S. Broken Arrow: America's First Lost Nuclear Weapon. Calgary, Alberta: Red Deer Press, 2008.
Miller, Jay and Roger Cripliver. B-36: The Ponderous Peacemaker. Aviation Quarterly, Vol. 4, No. 4, 1978.
Miller, Jay. Tip Tow & Tom-Tom. Air Enthusiast, No. 9, February–May 1979,
Morris, Lt. Col. (ret.) and Ted Allan. "Flying the Aluminum and Magnesium Overcast". The collected articles and photographs of Ted A. Morris, 2000.
Orman, Edward W. One Thousand on Top: A Gunner's View of Flight from the Scanning Blister of a B-36. Airpower, Vol. 17, No. 2, March 1987.
Puryear, Edgar. Stars in Flight. Novato, California: Presidio Press, 1981.
Pyeatt, Don. B 36: Saving the Last Peacemaker (Third Edition). Fort Worth, Texas. ProWeb Publishing, 2006.
Shiel, Walter P. The B-36 Peacemaker: 'There Aren't Programs Like This Anymore'. cessnawarbirds.com.
Taylor, John W.R. Convair B-36. Combat Aircraft of the World from 1909 to the present. New York: G.P. Putnam's Sons, 1969.
Thomas, Tony. A Wonderful Life: The Films and Career of James Stewart. Secaucus, New Jersey: Citadel Press, 1988.
Wagner, Ray. American Combat Planes. New York: Doubleday & Company, Inc., 1968.
Wilson, Stewart. Combat Aircraft since 1945. London: Aerospace Publications, 2000.
Winchester, Jim. Convair B-36. Military Aircraft of the Cold War (The Aviation Factfile). Rochester, Kent, UK: The Grange plc., 2006.
Wolk, Herman S. Fulcrum of Power: Essays on the United States Air Force and National Security. Darby, Pennsylvania: Diane Publishing, 2003.
Yenne, Bill. Convair B-36 Peacemaker. International Air Power Review, Vol. 13, Summer 2004. London: AirTime Publishing Inc., 2004.

CONVAIRIETY
SAN DIEGO, CALIF. DAINGERFIELD, TEX. FT. WORTH, TEX.
Vol. II, No. 3 52 Published Every Other Wednesday Wednesday, February 2, 1949

B-36's PARADE AT CAPITAL AND AT HOME

New Badge System For SD Planned

A new badge system which will more closely parallel that in effect in FW was in store this week for Convair SD.

Under the proposed system, approximately 1,000 persons who now carry yellow first shift badges will receive red and white striped badges which will better denote their positions.

The striped badges will be given to professional administrative personnel, flat salaried but non-supervisory. Badges, in addition to department and clock numbers, will carry names and job titles. Primarily affected are large groups in Engineering.

Supervisors on all shifts will continue to carry red badges. However, changing second shift badges from dark to light green is being considered to give greater distinction. White will remain the color for third shift badges. The new system is expected to go into effect about Mar. 1.

Rain, Snow, Sleet Plague Convair FW

Rain, snow and sleet all at the same time was just one variety of ever-variable weather visited upon the Convair FW division last week.

As CONVAIRIETY'S deadline passed, Ft. Worth and most of Tarrant county was covered with a film of solid ice.

Work on B-36's parked outside on the ramp was slowed, but inside work continued as usual. There were comparatively few late arrivals and absentees reported, considering the weather.

Turn in Your Name For B-36

Have you turned in your name for the B-36?

Time is running out. In less than four weeks the contest will close and the judges will start sifting through the entries to determine the winners of the $50 first prize. Deadline is Feb. 28.

Turn in your suggestion to Industrial Relations at SD or FW. Just write your suggestion on a slip of paper, sign your name and department number. Only one suggestion per customer.

THE CAPITOL—As seen from a Ft. Worth B-36, one of five that led a sky parade for President Truman's inauguration.

Cutlass Strafes Convair FW Like 'Berserk Mallard'

A jet job of breath-taking speed strafed the runway near Convair FW a few days ago and spectators aren't over the shock yet.

It was the new Chance-Vought XF7U-1 Cutlass Navy fighter which is making use of the long Carswell Air Force Base runways for an exhaustive flight test program.

A CONVAIRIETY news report from the scene brought forth some vivid figures of speech: Sighted at a distance of several miles the plane was described as "barrelling like a mallard gone beserk with a blowtorch in its tail feathers." With swept-back wings and with two vertical stabilizers and rudders located in the trailing edge of the wing, the plane looks like anything but a conventional aircraft. It is powered by two Westinghouse turbo-jets in the tail.

The Cutlass, after buzzing the field, landed and halted near the Convair FW hangar. Joel R. Baker, Chance-Vought test pilot, climbed out as unconcerned as if he had just brought down an elevator from the second floor.

"What were you making when you buzzed the field?" he was asked.

"I can't say in so many words," he replied, "because of Navy regulations. But it was something over 600 m.p.h."

B-36 NEWS DIRECT—News leaves B-36 by radio as Tech. Sgt. Elwood W. McLemore taps out a dispatch while Cpl. Armando Villareal looks on.

FW Man's Car Hits Concrete Abutment

John Wilson, Convair FW Mating and Wing (46), suffered critical injuries Jan. 24 when his car struck a concrete abutment in the drive approaching the Convair plant. Wilson was blinded by a torrential early morning rain. He suffered a broken nose and internal injuries.

XC-99 Flies Seventh Test at San Diego

Convair's XC-99 resumed its test flight program Jan. 24 with a one hour, 36 minute hop, its seventh flight and the first since last spring. Originally scheduled for a longer trip, the world's largest land plane returned to Convair SD to adjust a malfunctioning landing gear door which prevented complete retraction of the right landing gear.

FW THANKED FOR TOYS

A letter of thanks to all Convair employees came last week from the All Church Federation which operates a children's home in which scores of new toys donated by Convair employees were distributed at Christmas time. The collection was sponsored by the Convair FW Foremen's Club.

TESTS AT CONVAIR FW—This wicked looking U. S. Navy fighter landed at Convair FW last month to initiate an extensive flight testing program at Convair FW. It is Chance-Vought made F7U-1 Cutlass. Craft buzzed field at "upwards of 600 miles per hour" before landing.

Ships Lead Salute To Air Force

Convair B-36's which led the sky parade at President Truman's inauguration, paraded again last week in a thundering salute over Ft. Worth and Carswell Air Base on the seventh anniversary of the Eighth Air Force.

Last Friday's air show coincided with the annual Southwestern Exposition and Stock Show.

A total of 11 B-36's—six more than flew over Washington — took part in the review despite freezing weather.

This was the second mass flight within a few weeks which drew the nation's attention to the B-36. The other, viewed by packed thousands in the nation's capital, is described in the accompanying first person story:

'30 Seconds Over Capital' Offers Thrill of Lifetime

By BOB VOLLMER
(Convairiety Ft. Worth Editor)

How does it feel to fly to Washington in a Convair-built Air Force B-36 for the inauguration and return to Ft. Worth in time for dinner? To the Air Force crew that flew our B-36, it was just a "routine mission." But to a groundlubber it was the biggest bang in a lifetime.

First, there's the thrill when Capt. William Waltman at Carswell Air Force base puts you on the passenger list. The little matter of getting up at 1 a.m. doesn't pose much of a problem; you were too excited to sleep anyhow.

Since you're not a flyer or a crewman, you don't have the proper clothes. And you've heard stories about it being colder than Siberia when a 36 is forced to high altitudes to find good weather.

So you start looking for warm clothes. You don't have any. You decide to try the layer system. First comes wool pajamas, then underclothes, two shirts, two sox, two of everything except neckties.

With aviation-writer Robert Wear (Ft. Worth Star-Telegram) and photographer Johnny Mazziota (formerly at Convair FW) you arrive at base operations at 3 a.m.

By 4 a.m., you're on the ramp. In the 15-degree temperature you're shivering like a rivet gun. Your ship is "010" and you meet the men who'll fly it. They belong to the 26th Bomb Squadron, 11th Bomb Group of the 8th Air Force. First pilot is Capt. Edward L. Warner, big, tall and slow-talking. Second pilot is Maj. Charles T. Moreland, commanding officer of the 11th Bomb Group, and co-pilot is Capt. George J. Benedict. They look as if they had stepped from an Air Force recruiting poster.

Ducks must have learned to waddle from watching a man wearing a seat-type parachute! With the 'chute banging behind you, you clamber ungracefully aboard. The engines are idling comfortably. The pilot releases the brakes. The huge craft moves slowly to the taxi strip. Another B-36 is ahead, just taking off.

To make certain you don't miss anything, you keep looking over the shoulder of Staff Sgt. George A. Taggs, scanner at lower right blister. You see only gray pavement in the dim pre-dawn light. The engines change to a throaty roar. The floor trembles. You're moving down the runway. Before you realize it, the pilot has pulled her off. You're on your way to Washington!

Once in the air, crew and passengers settle down for a 2,500 mile trip. Scanners at the four blisters in the aft compartment watch the six engines on the trailing edge of the wing to spot trouble.

Passing over Dallas, 30 miles

(Continued on Page 8)

POW-WOW — While crewman stands watch on B-36 intercommunication system and at a blister, these airmen are interviewed by Convairiety newsman during flight. Airmen are St. Sgt. Floyd O. Johnson, St. Sgt. George A. Taggs and Sgt. Eugene Harris.

Index

CONVAIRIETY

SAN DIEGO, CALIF. DAINGERFIELD, TEX. FT. WORTH, TEX.

Vol. II, No. 8 · Published Every Other Wednesday · Wednesday, April 13, 1949

AIR FORCE UPS BOMBER ORDERS BY 36

B-36 Flies With Added Power From Jet Engines

Newest version of the Convair B-36, in which four jet power plants supplement the six conventional engines, made its first flight at 5:50 p.m. Saturday, March 26.

At the controls were B. A. Erickson and A. S. Witchell. The former, Convair FW's chief of Flight Test (6-8), also was one of the men to first fly the XB-36 and the XC-99. Other crew members were: W. P. Easley and J. D. McEachern, flight engineers, Master Sgt. G. S. Fish and R. O. Garlington, scanners, and Robert Moller, flight test analyist.

Although the first flight occurred on a non-work day, several thousand Convair FW workers parked cars adjacent to the air field and waited for hours to view the take-off. The plane took off with thousands of feet of runway to spare and in a few minutes climbed over Lake Worth and circled westward out of sight. It returned three hours and 15 minutes later, landing at 9:05 p.m.

The four jet engines are hung under the wings, two on each side. They give added power, when needed in takeoff or over target, for the plane's six 28-cylinder, 3500 horsepower reciprocating engines.

Convair Annual Report Sent Out At Both Plants

Copies of the Convair 1948 annual report were scheduled last week to go out to employees at both SD and FW divisions. Pictured on the cover of the 12-page report was a natural color photograph of the FW-built B-36.

"The annual report . . . holds definite promise that our period of serious losses has been halted and that we are in a position to enter an era of profitable operations," LaMotte T. Cohu, Convair president, stated in a letter to all Convair employees accompanying the report.

"Additional orders, both military and commercial, must be realized before we can expect a level and a stability of operations justified by both our facilities and our production team. That is our immediate problem and we are working constantly for its solution," he continued.

"Our recent record of producing excellent military aircraft and meeting delivery schedules has placed us in the front ranks of suppliers of the United States Air Force and the Naval air arm.

"We have some corners yet to turn but we are headed in a forward direction."

SUPPLEMENT TO TELL STORY OF B-36

The Houston Chronicle will tell the story of the FW-built B-36 in a magazine supplement of the April 24 edition. Space given the B-36 will be the greatest given any story thus far in the magazine section. The cover will feature a color photograph of the big bomber. Inside pages will be both in color and black and white.

XC-99 Makes First Test Hop at FW

First of several test flights scheduled at Convair FW for the XC-99 before delivery to the Air Force was completed successfully April 6 when the giant transport chalked up five hours and 30 minutes in the air.

It was the first flight since the double-decked cargo and passenger version of the B-36 bomber was flown here from San Diego.

BRITISH VISITORS

Cleanliness of Convair SD as well as production methods pursued at the plant were described as "impressive" by two British visitors last week. They were F. V. Smith, general works manager for A. V. Roe & Co. Ltd. of Manchester and S. W. D. Lockwood of Armstrong Whitworth Ltd., Coventry. They are on tour of American airplane factories.

"PEACEMAKER"

'Peacemaker' Unanimous Choice For B-36 Name

B-36 Peacemaker—

That's the winning name out of more than 600 submitted in the contest for the most appropriate designation for the world's largest bomber.

And that will be the official name of the aircraft if the Air Force and Munitions Board Aircraft Committee agrees with the unanimous decision of the three contest judges and the 60 Convair folks who all nominated Peacemaker for the name.

Eleven such nominations were made in San Diego, 49 in Ft. Worth.

Who will win the $50 first prize will be determined by a drawing within the next few days, and the winner announced in the April 27 edition of CONVAIRIETY.

Peacemaker was at the top of the lists submitted by all three judges: Amon Carter, publisher of the Ft. Worth Star-Telegram; Maj. Gen. Roger M. Ramey, commanding the Eighth Air Force, and LaMotte T. Cohu, Convair president.

Each of the 60 persons who submitted the winning name will receive an official certificate.

According to Evatts Haley, of Canyon, Tex., historian and authority on early-day Texas, the word Peacemaker most frequently was applied to the Colt .45 revolver so often used to settle disputes.

Entrants explained that in 1949 the B-36 occupies somewhat the same position as the famous gun and could become the world's greatest peacemaker.

One contestant proposed that the famous Colt .45 with its ham-

(Continued on page 8)

Production In Quantity Wins Favor

Orders for 36 more B-36 airplanes, in addition to all previous orders, awaited fulfillment this week at Convair FW.

Announcement that the Air Force wants the additional planes came last week in a bulletin from LaMotte T. Cohu, president and general manager. Cohu issued the following statement:

"We have received notice that, because of the steadily improved performance of the Convair B-36 and the Boeing B-47 bombardment airplanes, the Air Force has cancelled its orders for the Boeing B-54 and will purchase, in place of the B-54, a substantial number of additional B-36s and a few more B-47s.

"This increased order of B-36s materially improves the position of your company in the industry and should improve the prospects of all of us."

In answer to a CONVAIRIETY query, an Air Force spokesman explained that the latest order is in addition to the original 95 B-36s ordered as well as additional to the "substantial number more" which was called for early in January.

Snyder Will Speak For FW Foremen

Wives of Convair FW foremen's club members on Saturday night, April 23, will have a chance to see what goes on in a foremen's club meeting and at the same time be royally entertained, according to Sam E. Keith, Jr., club president.

The dinner meeting will start at 6:30 p.m. in the Convair cafeteria, and will include entertainment prior to the principal address. Speaker will be nationally famous Colyer Snyder, writer, traveler and commentator, who will discuss "What's Ahead for the Foreman."

Ryan Praises FW's March Safety Mark

Convair FW during March achieved the best record in safety and housekeeping of any month in the last 12, according to Ray O. Ryan, division manager.

"I wish to express my appreciation to all employees for your efforts, and urge each individual of our organization to help, where possible, to improve upon these accomplishments."

Ryan asked special attention be given to maintaining orderly work areas, and to observing division and departmental safety regulations.

SD MAN INJURED

Kenneth Rinker (27 SD) was reported recovering this week at La Mesa hospital after suffering serious injuries in an automobile accident April 2 while en route to Warner's Hot Springs. The car in which he was riding overturned and Rinker suffered head injuries. He is not expected to return to work for a month.

LEAPS INTO AIR—The new B-36 with two jet engines slung under each wing virtually leaped into air on its first take-off using all ten engines—four jets and six 3,500-horsepower reciprocating engines. Jets leave almost indistinguishable trail of dark smoke.